IDEAS IN CONTEXT

Edited by Quentin Skinner (General Editor) Lorraine Daston,
Dorothy Ross and James Tully

The books in this series will discuss the emergence of the intellectual
traditions and of related new disciplines. The procedures, aims and
vocabularies that were generated will be set in the context of the
alternatives available within the contemporary frameworks of ideas and
institutions. Through detailed studies of the evolution of such traditions,
and their modification by different audiences, it is hoped that a new picture
will form of the development of ideas in their concrete contexts. By this
means, artificial distinctions between the history of philosophy, of the
various sciences, of society and politics, and of literature may be seen to
dissolve.

The series is published with the support of the Exxon Foundation.

A list of books in the series will be found at the end of the volume.

THE DEVELOPMENT OF DURKHEIM'S SOCIAL REALISM

ROBERT ALUN JONES

CAMBRIDGE
UNIVERSITY PRESS

CAMBRIDGE UNIVERSITY PRESS
Cambridge, New York, Melbourne, Madrid, Cape Town, Singapore, São Paulo

Cambridge University Press
The Edinburgh Building, Cambridge CB2 2RU, UK

Published in the United States of America by Cambridge University Press, New York

www.cambridge.org
Information on this title: www.cambridge.org/9780521650458

© Robert Alun Jones 1999

First published 1999
This digitally printed first paperback version 2005

A catalogue record for this publication is available from the British Library

Library of Congress Cataloguing in Publication data
Jones, Robert Alun.
The development of Durkheim's social realism/Robert Alun Jones.
p. cm. (Ideas in context: 55)
Includes bibliographical references and index.
ISBN 0 521 65045 3 (hardback)
1. Durkheim, Emile, 1858–1917. 2. Sociology – History.
3. Sociology – Methodology. 4. Realism. I. Title. II. Series.
HM19.J67   1999
301´.09 – DC21 99–11995 CIP

ISBN-13 978-0-521-65045-8 hardback
ISBN-10 0-521-65045-3 hardback

ISBN-13 978-0-521-02210-1 paperback
ISBN-10 0-521-02210-X paperback

To the memory of my father

In sum, Montesquieu does not sufficiently appreciate how much, in Bacon's words, the subtlety of things surpasses the subtlety of the human mind.

Quid Secondatus Politicae Scientiae Instituendae Contulerit
(Montesquieu's Contribution to the Rise of Social Science)

We can see now the link which binds Rabelais and his age to the Middle Ages and Scholasticism. In spite of everything the book remains the object of a superstitious cult, albeit one of quite a different kind; the text remains something sacrosanct. But as against this, what a transformation, what a revolution has taken place! Something quite different is being sought for in the book: beyond the book, behind it, one can just see emerging, however timidly and uncertainly, the Thing.

L'Evolution pédagogique en France

Contents

Acknowledgments

The ideas contained in this book have evolved over a number of years, and been presented in varying forms and stages of completion at numerous conferences, as contributions to edited volumes, as journal articles, and even on the World Wide Web. Among the many people who have commented on these arguments, and saved me from numerous, egregious errors, I am especially grateful to Daniela Barberis, Philippe Besnard, Geof Bowker, John Brooks, Charles Camic, Lew Coser, Norm Denzin, Terry Godlove, Neil Gross, Doug Kibbee, Riki Kuklick, Rick Layton, Harry Liebersohn, Robert McKim, Willie Watts Miller, Andy Pickering, Bill Pickering, Warren Schmaus, Ivan Strenski, Leigh Star, Olivier Tschannen, and Ed Tiryakian. Julia Grossman transcribed the Sens lectures (chapter 3) from microfiche to readable French, and Henrietta Boudros corrected the resulting typescript. Catherine Max and Elizabeth Howard, my editors at Cambridge University Press, have been a constant source of support and encouragement. Finally, thanks must go to my colleagues in the Program for the Study of Religion at the university of Illinois, for providing an extraordinarily congenial and intellectually stimulating environment during the months the manuscript was being completed.

Note on texts and references

In some cases, I have made use of existing translations of Durkheim's works, while in others I have relied on my own translations. To avoid confusion, my practice has been as follows. Where referring to Durkheim's works in the body of the text, I have consistently used the original title, together with the date on which that work first appeared – e.g., "La Science positive de la morale en Allemagne" (1887), *De la division du travail social* (1893), and so on. Where I have cited a specific passage, I have provided the date of the text used (whether the original or the translation), a letter (if necessary to indicate which text published during that year), and the page(s) cited. A citation from my translation of "La Science positive de la morale en Allemagne," for example, appears as (1887b: 141–2), while a citation from W. D. Hall's translation of *De la division du travail social* appears as (1984: 291–341). Where I have cited André Lalande's recently discovered notes from Durkheim's philosophy lectures at the Lyçée de Sens (1883–4), I have used the date 1884, followed by the page numbers of the original manuscript at the Bibliothèque de la Sorbonne (MS no. 2351).

Introduction: sociology and its history

This book has two main goals. The first is to explore the meaning and significance of the constellation of ideas in Durkheim's work that is often characterized as his "social realism" – i.e., the view, epitomized in *Les Règles de la méthode sociologique* (1895), that social phenomena should be studied *comme des choses*, as real, concrete things, subject to the laws of nature and discoverable by scientific reason. The second, subsidiary goal is to exemplify a particular way of thinking and speaking about the history of sociological theory, one that might best be described as "historicist," "nominalist," and/or "pragmatist." For me, the first goal has always been the most important. But since so much of what I have to say about Durkheim presupposes some grasp of my views on sociology and its history, this introduction will begin with a brief explanation of the second.

In a famous essay published in 1984, Richard Rorty suggested that we think of the history of ideas as comprising different kinds of "conversations" that we imagine and reconstruct, sometimes between ourselves and classic writers of the past, and sometimes among the classic writers themselves. In "rational reconstructions," for example, we imagine and then converse with an "ideally reasonable and educable Durkheim" – e.g., the Durkheim who speaks *our* language, who might be brought to describe himself as having overstated the "objectivity" of social facts, the "normality" of crime, or the "pathology" of the forced division of labor. Once our concepts and language are thus imposed on Durkheim, and he has been brought to accept such a new description of what he meant or did, he becomes one of us, our contemporary, a fellow-citizen, a colleague in our disciplinary matrix (1984: 51–2). The goal of such "rational reconstructions," Rorty tells us, is *reassurance* or *self-justification* – i.e., our quite natural and reasonable desire to see the history of sociological theory as "a long conversational interchange" in a fairly stable idiom, and thus to assure ourselves that "there has been rational progress in the course of recorded history – that we differ from our ancestors on grounds which our ancestors could be led to accept" (1984: 51). I take this to be the kind of reconstruction in which most sociologists are engaged when they write or speak about Marx, Durkheim, and/or Weber.

As an historian, of course, I sometimes find such reconstructions hopelessly anachronistic (Jones 1977: 282–9). More recently, however, I've come to agree with Rorty that this kind of *self-conscious* anachronism has a kind of justification. When theorists say (anachronistically) that Durkheim anticipated or adumbrated ideas of which he cannot have been aware, they (presumably) mean that, in an imagined conversation with present-day theorists about whether or not he should have held certain other views, Durkheim would have been driven back on a premise that he never formulated, dealing with a topic he never considered – a premise that might have to be suggested to him by a friendly rational reconstructor (Rorty 1984: 53). For all their anachronism, therefore, rational reconstructions at least serve to expand the circle of what Rorty has called "edifying conversational partners," embracing the mighty dead as well as those still living; and as long as sociologists *are aware* that Durkheim is thus being described as holding beliefs he never held, and performing actions he never performed, such imaginary conversations seem unobjectionable, and might be extremely useful.

But there is also a second, more genuinely "historical" type of reconstruction. Here we are less interested in the Durkheim who might be led to converse with us than with imagined conversations between Durkheim and his contemporaries, in *their own* language rather than ours – in short, to embrace the historicist commitment to understand the past, in so far as it is possible, "in its own terms." As Rorty has observed, the value of *these* reconstructions lies, not in reassurance or self-justification, but in *self-knowledge* or *self-awareness* – i.e., "in the fact that, instead of supplying us with our usual and carefully contrived pleasures of recognition, [the classic writers] enable us to stand back from our own beliefs and the concepts we use to express them, perhaps forcing us to reconsider, to recast or even . . . to abandon some of our current beliefs in the light of these wider perspectives" (Skinner 1984: 202, 197–8; Jones and Kibbee 1993: 156). To read these more *historical* reconstructions, to imagine these conversations that take place in an entirely different idiom, is quite literally to encounter other vocabularies – many of them impressive enough to induce doubt and reflection about our own.

Among the most distinguished examples of such genuinely historical reconstructions are the works of Quentin Skinner, who has followed the lead of philosophers like J. L. Austin (1975) and R. G. Collingwood (1939) by encouraging us to ask what the classic writer "was doing" in saying what he said, and reconstructing the questions to which the classic text was a putative answer. Consider the effort of Descartes, both in the *Discourse* and in the *Meditations*, to vindicate the idea of certain, indubitable knowledge. Why, Skinner asks, was this an issue for him at all? Since Descartes was an epistemologist, and since certainty is one of the central problems of epistemology, more traditional historians of ideas have scarcely acknowledged the question, concentrating instead on what Descartes actually said about how we can achieve such certainty. But this, Skinner objects, is an instance of "insufficient puzzlement" – i.e., by leaving us without any sense of the specific question to which Descartes may have intended his doctrine of certainty as a solution, this traditional approach also leaves us without any understanding of what he may have been *doing* in presenting his doctrine in the precise form in which he chose to present it (1988: 282–3). In fact, it now seems clear that Descartes was responding to the Pyrrhonian skepticism of writers like Montaigne, an action that helps to explain both the character of his anti-skeptical arguments and the strategies he used to advance them. Yet until scholars like Richard Popkin (1969) and E. M. Curley (1978) became "sufficiently puzzled" about the problem to which Descartes was responding, both the arguments and the strategies remained opaque because the question itself had never been raised.

Similarly, there has been no lack of discussion of Durkheim's social realism in the secondary literature. Since Durkheim was a sociologist, and since a commitment to the "reality" of social phenomena seems almost an unquestioned article of faith among sociologists, there has been little discussion of *why* this was a commitment for Durkheim in the first place. The conversation has focused instead on the primarily methodological issue of *how* social facts might be studied *comme des choses*. Though hardly silent on Durkheim's social realism, therefore, sociologists have in this sense been "insufficiently puzzled" about the question to which social realism was presumably an answer – the problem for which it was offered as a solution. In short, we have lacked an account of what the early Durkheim was *doing* in developing his realist social theory between the early 1880s and the publication of *Le Suicide* in 1897.

What was Durkheim doing? What was the question for which social realism was Durkheim's answer? Briefly, I will suggest that the question was not unlike that to which Plato replied in the early Socratic dialogues. There Socrates interrogates various Athenians concerning the nature of some virtue, repeatedly entrapping them in contradictions and inconsistencies. The reasonable first impression here is that Plato's intention was to contrast the rigor and precision of Socrates' arguments with the sloppiness and stupidity of those of the Athenians. But so frequently does this pattern recur (and so determinedly confused are some of Socrates' interlocutors) that the way to an alternative interpretation seems open. One such alternative argument is that Plato was pointing to a state of incoherence in the moral language of Athenian culture – i.e., that the conceptual apparatus which the Athenians had inherited from the societies represented in the Homeric epics (societies based primarily on kinship) was simply inadequate in the quite different context of the Greek *polis*. It was this linguistic incoherence and its resulting tensions, so the argument goes, which were explored artistically in the tragedies of Sophocles; and at least one purpose of the early Platonic dialogues would thus have been to purge the Greek language of these Homeric survivals, and to replace them with Plato's own, more coherent and well-ordered normative vocabulary (MacIntyre 1981: 131–45).

In the argument that follows, I will suggest that something similar was at stake in Durkheim's effort to contrive the language of social realism. It is impossible to read the lectures that posthumously became *L'Education morale* (1925) and *L'Evolution pédagogique en France* (1938), for example, without becoming aware of Durkheim's searing contempt for the vocabulary of Cartesian metaphysics. This is not to say that Durkheim considered himself anything but a rationalist; on the contrary, he regarded Cartesianism as "deeply rooted in our national thinking," and "one of the characteristic traits of the French mind" (1961: 253). But Durkheim also considered the conceptual apparatus of Cartesian rationalism – in which complexity was consistently reduced to simplicity, the concrete to the abstract, observation and experience to logic and reasoning, things to ideas – as deeply problematic, admirably suited, as he said, to the mechanical, mathematical certainties of the 17th century, but completely inadequate when applied to the social and ethical demands of advanced industrial societies. In particular, Durkheim regarded modern societies as enormously complex wholes which, subjected to the principles of an "oversimplified rationalism," would be reduced to their constituent elements, and thus deprived of any objective moral foundation whatsoever. In an age of individualism, egoism, and anomie, it was essential that the institutions of the Third Republic become the primary focus of a citizen's duties and obligations; and no "mental construct," no Cartesian *idée claire et simple*, could ever become the object of such unqualified allegiance. "It would be absurd," Durkheim insisted, "to sacrifice the real, concrete, and living being that we are to a purely verbal artifact. We can only dedicate ourselves to society if we see in it a moral power more elevated than ourselves" (1961: 257).

For Durkheim, this was why social phenomena should be understood *comme des choses*, as real, concrete things, subject to the laws of nature, resistant to human will, and discoverable by scientific reason through their properties of externality and constraint. Sociologists, of course, describe this as a *methodological* injunction, one that has become a standard part of most introductory sociology textbooks. The point of my argument, however, will be that Durkheim's interests and purposes were at least as much *moral* and *political* – i.e., to construct a normative vocabulary, a new way of speaking about duties, obligations, and ideals that would take the place of the Cartesian idiom. Like Plato, therefore, Durkheim was pointing to a general state of crisis in the moral language of his culture, and attempting to replace it with metaphors more adequate to the needs of his time.

If we think of Durkheim in this way – i.e., as someone cobbling together a language rather than discovering something about Nature – his social realism appears less as a coherent doctrine or theory than as an assortment of rhetorical strategies. On the one hand, it described society as not only "similar to" nature, but as itself a *real, natural thing, a part of nature*, and subject to its laws. On the other hand, this same vocabulary insisted that society is a *particular, distinctive* part of nature, a reality *sui generis*, irreducible to the laws discovered by psychologists or biologists. There was always a precarious tension, if not conflict, between these two metaphors – the former vulnerable to the criticism that it explained social phenomena by referring to non-social (e.g., psychological and bio-logical) causes, and the latter to the charge that sociology is not a "science" at all. Durkheim's description of society as an external, regulative force, epitomized in his treatment of anomic suicide, thus had to be balanced with his depiction of society as the source of positive, collective ideals, exemplified in his treatment of aboriginal religion. If Durkheim often spoke like an empiricist when attacking Descartes in *L'Education morale*, he could also sound like a rationalist when criticizing Mill in *Les Règles* (indeed, by 1897, he would embrace the "rationalist empiricism" of Hippolyte Taine). Finally, if this ingenious manipulation of these multiple rhetorical strategies is one measure of the extent of Durkheim's achievement, it has also contributed to the linguistic incoherence of subsequent sociological debate – including disagreement over the meaning and significance of Durkheim's works.

This essay is an effort to reconstruct Durkheim's shaping of this vocabulary. In chapter 1, for example, I describe the social, political, and religious context of the Third Republic, with special emphasis on the years 1879–85, during which the republican project of laicizing French education was effected. In one sense, this "reform that contained all other reforms" became the vehicle whereby sociology was institutionalized in French primary and secondary education; but in a larger sense, this final collapse of the Church as a source of authority created the moral vacuum that social realism was supposed to fill. In this sense, I shall argue, sociology was less an end in itself than a means to the achievement of moral and political goals. In chapter 2, I discuss Durkheim's views on the history and theory of moral education, particularly as reflected in the lectures posthumously published as *L'Evolution pédagogique en France* (1938) and *L'Education morale* (1925). These lectures represent a relatively late stage in the development of Durkheim's thought, and they are introduced early in my book for two reasons. First, they provide us with Durkheim's most self-conscious reflections on the policies of educational reform described in the chapter that immediately precedes them. Second, if – as I have suggested – Durkheim's social realism constitutes a vocabulary constructed to serve quite concrete interests and purposes, these lectures afford the clearest sense of what these interests and purposes were. In effect, they provide the context within which the development of that vocabulary – the subject of the subsequent chapters – makes the most sense. By my describing these commitments up front, in considerable detail, the reader will be better prepared to understand the significance of arguments made in Durkheim's earlier works.

In chapter 3, I return to a more conventional, chronological approach to the development of Durkheim's thought, discussing André Lalande's recently discovered lecture notes from Durkheim's philosophy course taught at the Lycée de Sens in 1883–4. These notes make it clear that, as late as 1884, Durkheim had not yet embraced anything resembling his later social realism. On the contrary, his views on morality and society seem to approximate the neo-critical individualism of Charles Renouvier's *Science de la morale* (1869). The Sens lectures also provide a context within which to discuss the influence of Durkheim's teachers at the Ecole Normale Supérieure – the historian Numa Denis Fustel de Coulanges (1830–89) and the philosopher Emile Boutroux (1845–1921) – as well as Charles Renouvier (1815–1903). The same lectures set the stage for chapter 4, where I discuss Durkheim's important visit to Berlin, Marburg, and Leipzig in 1885 and 1886, which brought him into contact with German political economy, jurisprudence, and most importantly, the experimental psychology and ethics of Wilhelm Wundt (1832–1920). By the time Durkheim returned, he seemed to have lost much of his interest in Renouvier's ethics (although not in Renouvier), and had begun to construct the vocabulary that would inform *L'Evolution pédagogique en France* and *L'Education morale*. These views are already evident in Durkheim's two doctoral theses – i.e., the Latin thesis on Montesquieu (1892) and *De la division du travail social* (1893), as well as *Les Règles de la méthode sociologique* (1895). It was the latter work that embroiled Durkheim in the famous controversy with Jean-Gabriel Tarde (1843–1904), his most formidable critic; and it was in the context of his response to Tarde and the early stages of his involvement in *L'Affaire Dreyfus* that Durkheim revisited the works of Rousseau, offering a lecture course on *Le Contrat social* that was clearly instrumental in developing the powerful social realism of *Le Suicide* (1897) and later works. The discussion of the Latin thesis, the quarrel with Tarde, and the lectures on Rousseau thus complete chapter 5 – Durkheim's fragmentary notes on *Emile* completing the circle, recalling Durkheim's lectures on the history and theory of moral education and their role within the laicizing reforms of the Third Republic.

As this brief summary suggests, I've avoided (except where

particularly pertinent) any detailed discussion of the events of Durkheim's life, as well as thematic summaries of his most familiar works (of which many excellent examples already exist in the secondary literature). Instead, I've focused on texts that are perhaps less familiar to sociologists (e.g., the Sens lectures, book reviews, the "German" essays of 1887, the Latin thesis, the lectures on *Le Contrat social* and *Emile*, etc.) and those intellectual influences (e.g., Fustel, Boutroux, Renouvier, Wundt, Montesquieu, Tarde, Rousseau, etc.) that encourage us to see Durkheim's project as the metaphorical construction of a new moral vocabulary for the Third Republic. In short, I've tried to reconstruct an imagined conversation between Durkheim, his contemporaries, and his antecedents. In Skinner's formulation, it is the context of the things that he himself might, at least in principle, have accepted as a description of what he was doing. (It is also, I should add, what he rather clearly *did* say he was doing in *L'Evolution pédagogique en France* and *L'Education morale*.) Most importantly, because this is a self-consciously "historical" – by contrast with "rational" – reconstruction, the Durkheim who emerges from this re-description is not necessarily "one of us," not a "fellow citizen" or "participant in the same disciplinary matrix." On the contrary, he is concerned with the quite specific and contingent problems of the Third Republic, and social realism is described as an answer to *his* questions, not to *ours*. Why, then, one might ask, should we continue to read Durkheim's works? And why in particular should we re-describe them in this historicist manner? How is the promise of "self-knowledge" or "self-awareness" to be realized in more concrete terms? Recalling that to read Durkheim in this way is to encounter vocabularies other than one's own, I suggest in my conclusion that intellectual history might afford a catalyst for what Rorty has called an "ironist" perspective on our current intellectual commitments, one that would encourage some salutary doubt about our "final vocabularies." I can think of few things that would be more useful.

CHAPTER I

The reform that contained all other reforms

"When a people has achieved a state of equilibrium and maturity," Durkheim observed in his seventh lecture on moral education, "when the various social functions, at least temporarily, are articulated in an ordered fashion, when the collective sentiments in their essentials are incontestable for the great majority of people, then the preference for rule and order is naturally preponderant." It was this moral situation, for example, that had characterized Rome under Augustus, and France under Louis XIV. By contrast, "in times of flux and change, the spirit of discipline cannot preserve its moral vigor since the prevailing system of rules is shaken, at least in some of its parts. At such times, it is inevitable that we feel less keenly the authority of a discipline that is, in fact, attenuated" (1961: 100–1).

Durkheim had no illusions about the type of society or historical period in which he was living: "Now," he emphasized, "we are going through precisely one of these critical phases. Indeed, history records no crisis as serious as that in which European societies have been involved for more than a century. Collective discipline in its traditional form has lost its authority, as the divergent tendencies troubling the public conscience and the resulting general anxiety demonstrate. Consequently, the spirit of discipline itself has lost its ascendancy" (1961: 101). As we shall see, this was the problem for which Durkheim's solution was social realism. But in order to understand this solution – and why it *seemed* such a plausible solution to Durkheim – we must first have some grasp of the problem itself.

THE COALITION OF THE THIRD ESTATE

In 1872 the population of France was 36,103,000. By 1886, it had risen to 38,517,000, an annual increase of only 89,700. The birth rate had begun a steady fall, while the death rate would scarcely vary

9

until the end of the century. By the early 1890s there would be more deaths than births, an event so unprecedented that alarmed onlookers dubbed it the "stagnation." The traditional, fertile, Catholic family had confronted its modern, Malthusian counterpart. "Parents," Mayeur and Rebérioux have observed, "calculated and looked ahead, concerned to rise socially and to provide a good future for their children. This 'bourgeois' conception of the family spread progressively to all layers of society, reflecting the aspirations of individualism and egalitarianism" – a movement which particularly affected the lower middle class (1984: 43).

The ideological response to this stagnation was mixed. Local authorities and the French Parliament remained utterly indifferent, oblivious to the notion that the state should assist the family in a liberal social order. The disciples of Frédéric Le Play, in *La Réforme social*, combined the defense of the family with "counter-revolutionary" demands, blaming the Civil Code, compulsory sharing, and revolutionary individualism while simultaneously extolling the virtues of the male-dominated family. These Le Playists exerted considerable influence on the conservative right and "social" Catholicism, but otherwise remained an isolated intellectual current. Elisée Reclus' *Nouvelle Géographie universelle* (1877) reflected the more widespread sentiment that population decline indicated a "complete lack of confidence in the future," a social malaise or even national decadence (Lukes 1972: 195). By 1896, Jacques Bertillon had founded the Alliance pour L'Accroissement de la Population Française, and in his classic study of suicide just one year later, Durkheim insisted that both the decrease in births and the increase in suicides were the consequence of a decline in domestic feelings, an increase in migration from the country to the towns, the break-up of the traditional family, and the "cold wind of egoism" that had ensued (1888: 463; 1897: 198–202; Lukes 1972: 194–5).

In fact, from 1871 on, 100,000 people left the countryside each year for the towns, a consequence of the difficulties of agriculture, the increase in agricultural yields (which deprived some peasants of their jobs), the decline of rural industries, better transportation, military service, and higher, more regular urban wages (Mayeur and Rebérioux 1984: 44). But despite the fact that any agglomeration of more than 2,000 inhabitants was called a "town," the urban population remained relatively small, forming 31.1 percent of the population in 1872 and only 40.9 percent by 1901 – a growth rate slower than that of any neighboring industrial country. The working population thus remained largely agricultural, constituting 67.5 percent of the total in 1876, and 61 percent as late as 1896. France was also a country of low demographic pressure, and thus one from which few people emigrated. Conversely, before and after 1876, the number of foreign immigrants in France rose from 800,000 to 1 million, and the relative stability of the latter figure thereafter must be understood in light of the naturalizations produced by the law of 1889. Italians, Belgians, Spaniards, and Germans settled either just inside the French border or in the urban, industrial regions, competing with French workers and, as the economic depression of the 1880s deepened, provoking xenophobic reactions in Lyons and Marseilles.

Economic growth, which had been rapid before 1860 and steady if unspectacular for the twenty years thereafter, slowed dramatically after 1880, a consequence of the decreasing per capita productivity of the labor force and the declining rate of urbanization. With an annual growth of exports of 0.86 percent from 1875 to 1895 and her balance of payments in deficit, France, once the second largest industrial power in the world, quickly slipped to fourth (Mayeur and Rebérioux 1984: 46). Under these circumstances, the French aristocracy retained an undeniable prestige, but retained power only through those matrimonial alliances and corporate directorships which produced effective relations with the upper middle class. The power of the latter was derived from banking and industry, the liberal professions and service to the State. Heirs to the jurists and civil servants of the monarchy, the upper middle class was ideologically divided, some maintaining the Enlightenment belief in progress and loyalty to the Republic, while others were more attached to social "order" than to individual freedom, resigning themselves to a more pessimistic view of history consistent with both experience and the teachings of the Catholic Church.

The more "ordinary" middle class included bankers in small towns, industrialists with moderate-sized enterprises, unemployed landlords, members of the liberal professions, salaried magistrates, officers, engineers, and teachers like Durkheim. Enjoying a stable currency and no income tax, the urban bourgeois with an annual income of 20,000 francs paid as little as 2 percent in taxes. A doctor, lawyer, or engineer who had been prudent under the prosperity of the Second Empire could retire in his fifties with no decline in his standard of living, a prospect which gave rise to the unregulated aspirations symptomatic of Durkheim's "economic anomie" (1897: 254–8). "Conservatives of the time," Mayeur and Rebérioux warn us, "like to assert that the individualism bred by the Revolution had undermined the family, but in fact family feeling had changed rather than weakened. The bourgeois family looked inward, concentrating on the child and his future. It was a family of limited births, anxious to rise in the world through birth control and saving" (1984: 71).

The lower middle class comprised those small building contractors, small employers, independent craftsmen, and retail shopkeepers who lacked the education and/or income of the ordinary middle class, yet avoided manual labor and retained an economic independence which distinguished them from the rural or industrial worker. Less independent, though still removed from manual labor, were the wage-earning clerks, accountants, civil servants, primary school teachers and tax-collectors who were paid little but enjoyed stable employment and a pension. Most important, it was this group – growing in size as the depression decimated the independent lower middle class – which, together with the small town and the provincial school, provided a largely republican road from peasantry to bourgeoisie: "The peasant's son," Mayeur and Rebérioux observe, "was a school-teacher or a clerk; his grandson could become a doctor or a graduate of a technical college and thus join the bourgeoisie proper. The lower middle classes were a half-way stage between the rural population and the elites." "It was the good fortune of the Republic," they add, "and one of the reasons why it took root, to have thus offered numerous jobs to a social stratum anxious to rise in the world" (1984: 70).

The industrial working class was very small, numbering less than 5 million in the 1870s, and only 6 million by 1900. Except for Paris and the industrial south-east, there were no real spatial concentrations of workers, and the majority were employed by extremely small industrial establishments. To speak of "the conditions of the working class" is thus quite difficult, for these conditions varied widely depending upon geographical location, skills, education, and ethnic and historical traditions. But a few conditions – the absence of savings and security, the difficulty of access to education and culture, and, above all, the spectre of unemployment during the years of the great depression – were experienced by all. The working class was thus primarily agricultural, and remained so until the end of the century. But the living conditions, manners, and mentality of the peasants changed. Railways, especially the little cross-country lines, and improvements in local roads, went far to break down provincial isolation. The town was easier to reach, and its culture was felt through the schools, compulsory military service, mail-order catalogues, and cheap newspapers. If not for themselves, the agricultural working class could at least anticipate an easier, less trying life for their children and their children's children (Mayeur and Rebérioux 1984: 50, 53–4, 45).

In sum, from the early days of the Third Republic until the end of the century, French society was to change very little, and least of all in its traditional social and economic inequalities. Durkheim's consistently uniformitarian view that revolutions are as rare as unicorns thus reflected not only his deeply conservative nature but also a keen perception of the realities of his own society. In fact, those who made the republican victory possible – the peasantry and the rising middle class – expected no profound transformation of social relations. What they did expect was the end of the political influence of the traditional upper class as well as the Catholic Church, for this in turn would provide them with at least the opportunity to rise socially.

These expectations were intimately bound to the precarious future of the Third Republic. On July 19, 1870, the government of Napoleon III had declared war on Prussia. By September 2, after the battle of Sedan, the technically backward French army had surrendered, and Napoleon himself was taken prisoner. Two days later, the Second Empire destroyed, Paris insurrectionaries led by Leon Gambetta and Jules Simon established a "Government of National Defense," and, following the precedents of 1792 and 1848, declared the Republic. Prussian forces laid siege to Paris and, by September 23, had severed its contact with the outside world. Paris held out for another four months, as Gambetta formed a provincial "Army of the Loire" in support; but on January 28, Paris capitulated, and a furious Gambetta resigned rather than stage a provincial coup.

Since France now possessed no government with which Bismarck could negotiate, he insisted on the election of a Constituent Assembly by universal male suffrage. The election, held on February 8, 1871, showed that again, as in 1797 and 1848, France – and especially the peasantry – distrusted republicanism. Of 645 persons elected in the various departments, 400 were monarchists, and nearly half of these were landowners. Suspected of bellicosity abroad and instability at home, of opposition to the Church, and of egalitarian and even socialist tendencies, republicans won only 200 seats. "So now we have a republic?" observed Zola's peasant-hero Jean Macquart, in *La Débâcle* (1892). "Oh well, all to the good if it helps us beat the Prussians"; but then Macquart shook his head, "for he had always been led to fear a republic when he worked on the land. And besides, in the face of the enemy he didn't think it was a good thing not to be all of one mind" (1972: 403).

The prospects for a restoration, however, were complicated by the fragmentation of the Right. The Bonapartists, the biggest losers at Sedan, returned only 20 supporters from Corsica and the two Charente departments. On the extreme Right, approximately 80 members of the Assembly supported the restoration of the Bourbon comte de Chambord; but these extremists, whose support came from rural France and the Catholic Workers' Circles founded in 1871 by Albert de Mun, were ultramontane on religious matters, defended the Syllabus and papal infallibility, and hoped to see Pius IX (then imprisoned in the Vatican) restored to his temporal powers. "Men of principle to whom politics were alien," Mayeur and Rebérioux observe, "they were to be awkward elements in coalitions of the right. Accustomed to read events as decrees of providence, they would not hesitate on occasion to follow the worst possible policy, being convinced that the renewal of Catholic France would only come about through catastrophe" (1984: 11). Distinguished from the extreme Right by its acceptance of parliamentary government, political and even economic liberalism, was a "center Right" of moderate legitimists. Religiously, this group had given up its Voltairean tone of the 1830s, and many had become liberal Catholics; but, while this separated them from the extreme Right (they had been disappointed with Pius IX's proclamation of the Syllabus and papal infallibility), they insisted that the State maintain respect for the Catholic Church. This in turn distinguished them from a group with which they otherwise had much in common – i.e., a "center Left" of Orléanists, suspicious of the Church, and led by Adolphe Thiers, for whom the elections of 1871 proved a personal triumph.

An elder statesman of 73, Thiers had been a leader of the Opposition and a sharp critic of Napoleon III's foreign policies since 1863. Although he refused to join the Government of National Defense (it contained far too many republicans), he had demonstrated his patriotism by serving on several diplomatic missions on its behalf. As the only political figure whose reputation emerged unscathed from the disasters of 1870–1, he was elected in 26 different departments. In the Pact of Bordeaux of February 17, 1871, Thiers was appointed "head of the executive authority of the French Republic" and "under the control of the Assembly," a deliberately ambiguous title and description designed to avoid prejudice with respect to the eventual form of government France might decide to adopt. The National Assembly was but temporarily a "repository of the sovereign authority," and was to act only "provisionally" until "a decision was taken on the institutions of France." In sum, the government was only very precariously a "republic" at all.

The French government thus established, Bismarck insisted on the harshest of terms: an indemnity of 5 billion gold francs (to be paid within three years), an army of occupation in twenty departments, and the annexation of Alsace and most of Lorraine.[1] When the newly elected National Assembly accepted these terms on March 1, 1871, the result was the outbreak of revolutionary violence known as the Paris Commune. Thiers transferred his government to Versailles, Paris was left in the hands of the Communards, and civil war ensued. When the Commune was at last suppressed and order restored on May 28, 1871, the National Assembly dealt ruthlessly with the revolutionaries: 20,000 were executed, 38,000 taken prisoner, 13,450 sentenced to various prison terms and 7,500 deported to New Caledonia. But for the Paris Commune and its ruthless suppression, however, the birth of the Third Republic might have been still more difficult than it was. On the one hand, the proscription and exile of so many "extremists" provided the nascent and extremely precarious Republic an opportunity to evolve in a more peaceful, orderly fashion, and even to attain a degree of constitutional legitimacy. On the other hand, the absence (or at least quiescence) of these same elements helped to remove the long-held association of republicanism with violence, instability, and disorder – something essential if the Republic were to win the allegiance of its hard-working, law-abiding, and largely provincial citizenry.

[1] Alsace and Lorraine contained great iron ore deposits, important textile works, rich forests, excellent soil, and a population of 1,600,000. Moreover, while the Alsatians spoke German, most of them were self-consciously French, having shared in its culture and history since the 17th century. The loss of Alsace and Lorraine was thus a particularly devastating condition of the peace, and one to which the French never reconciled themselves.

In May, 1871, however, the position of France within the larger European community was hardly encouraging, particularly by contrast with its apparent fortunes just fifteen years earlier. At the conclusion of the Crimean War (1854–6), J. P. T. Bury has observed, Great Britain was an ally, Russia had been firmly defeated, Italy and Germany were simply "geographical expressions," and France was incontestably the foremost power in Europe. By the spring of 1871, Britain was no longer an ally (indeed, France had no allies); Russia had gained a modification of the Black Sea clauses of the Treaty of Paris; without any *quid pro quo*, France had been forced to withdraw her troops from Italy, allowing the Italian government to occupy Rome, complete the unification of Italy, imprison Pius IX in the Vatican, and end the temporal power of the papacy; and, worst of all, Germany, whose population already outnumbered France by more than 4 million people, had achieved national unity, declared itself an Empire, and would soon become the greatest industrial power on the Continent. "The hegemony of Europe," Bury concludes, "had passed from France to Germany, and Bismarck, not Thiers, was now the chief arbiter of continental disputes" (1985: 135).

For the French, the natural consequences of this situation included a revulsion for war, a powerful desire for peace and order, the constant affirmation and re-affirmation of patriotism, the elevation of the "sacred" French army to a status beyond political argument altogether, and an utter indifference to the restoration of the temporal power of the Pope. Henceforth, public opinion would favor those like Durkheim, whose republican zeal was tempered by opposition to insurrection and revolution. In the by-elections of July 2, 1871, such republicans, including 35 radicals, captured 100 seats while the royalists gained only 12. For the most part, this was a vote for the conservative republic of Thiers, or the "moderate Left" led by Jules Simon, Jules Grévy, Jules Ferry, and Jules Favre – successful bourgeois who desired peace and rejected the Republican Union radicals led by Gambetta. But Gambetta himself was re-elected in Paris, indicating that conservatives had failed to identify the radical left with the Commune, and also that their success in February had been more the result of a desire for peace than a desire for monarchy.

The "very type of the prudent bourgeois," Thiers approached the problems of reconstruction in a conservative, business-like manner.

The prosperous years of the Second Empire providing a substantial degree of economic resilience, the two loans raised to meet Bismarck's "crushing" war indemnity were easily and quickly covered and, by December 1873, the entire country was cleared of German soldiers. A proposal to introduce an income tax was dismissed and, under the stress of competition from the New World, Thiers initiated the first steps toward a return to the protectionism characteristic of France before 1860. "The Republic will be conservative," Thiers explained, "or it will not be at all" – an attitude no doubt reassuring to the rising middle class and its ever-swelling ranks of investors (Bury 1985: 137).

Similarly, any illusions that the demise of the Empire would result in the dismantling of the highly centralized Napoleonic administrative structure were quickly dispelled, as the traditionalist Thiers refused to allow free election of mayors in any but towns of under 20,000 inhabitants, and neither he nor his successors made any attempt to limit the powers of the Prefecture of Police. While efforts to reform the French army on the model of its demonstrably superior Prussian counterpart were always subservient to the interests of the economy, the latter were sufficiently auspicious by 1875 to permit passage of a bill providing for an increase of 150,000 men, and serious discussion of more modernized equipment and the development of a reserve. When the increasingly voluble *revanchiste* sentiments which accompanied these measures led Bismarck to rattle his sword in the German press, the Foreign Minister Decazes successfully aroused the diplomatic intercession of both Britain and Russia on France's behalf, demonstrating that for all its success in 1870–1, Germany had no *carte blanche* on the Continent.

This conservative, provisional Republic was one that moderate legitimists could at least temporarily swallow. What was less palatable was Gambetta's republican radicals, whose resurgence was increasingly evident in repeated by-election victories, the founding of the newspaper *La Républic française* (1871), and Gambetta's own charismatic presence at numerous political banquets throughout the country. But in fact, Gambetta, who in 1869 had subscribed to the famous Belleville electoral program, was rapidly becoming more moderate. In particular, he acknowledged the imminent rise of what he called "a new social stratum" – petits bourgeois, shopkeepers, clerks, and artisans – the class which had profited from the prosperity of the Second Empire, swelled the ranks of investors in the provisional Republic, and thus accelerated the work of post-war reconstruction; and now, given the appropriate education and opportunity, this class would surely support the Republic and strengthen its institutions (Thomson 1968: 79, 82–4; Bury 1985: 150).

In short, Gambetta ceased to be a Radical and became what he himself described as an "Opportunist" – a name which would characterize the moderate Left to the end of the century. Doctrinaire tenets were shelved in the interest of practical ends, and the electorate was increasingly reassured that, if Gambetta remained a republican and an anticlerical, he was no revolutionary. In fact, those who insist on reading *De la division du travail social* as a "dialogue" with Marx's ghost should be reminded that revolutionary socialism was virtually non-existent at the parliamentary level of French politics during the period in which that work was conceived.[2] The first series of Jules Guesde's *L'Egalité* appeared only in November 1877, and the second in January 1880. Between the two, the Socialist Workers' Congress of France was held at Marseilles (October 1879), denouncing Gambetta's followers and adopting a Marxist program. But the actual texts of Marx and Engels were almost unknown, and only in 1885 did Guesde's Parti ouvrier publish a complete translation of the *Communist Manifesto*.

The reasons for this quiescence, in sharp contrast to the powerful Social Democratic Party in Germany, are not far to seek. France, as we have seen, was still a country of peasants rather than urban-industrial workers, and those Paris revolutionaries who had survived the suppression of the Commune were either in prison or in exile, not to be pardoned until 1879. Even after the republican victory of 1879, when most of Gambetta's erstwhile radicals joined the opposition in their hatred for Ferry and the Opportunists, the extreme Left remained irretrievably split. A group led by Charles Floquet and Henri Allain-Targé, which (paradoxically) called itself "the parliamentary group of the radical Left," demanded revision of the

---

[2] In his review of Antonio Labriola's *Essais sur la conception matérialiste de l'histoire* (1897), Durkheim acknowledged that "Either the collective consciousness floats in a vacuum, a sort of unrepresentable absolute, or it is related to the rest of the world through the intermediary of a substratum on which it consequently depends . . . [And] of what can this substratum be composed if not of the members of society as they are socially combined?" But Durkheim immediately added that there was no reason to associate this principle with the socialist movement, "of which it is totally independent. As for ourselves, we arrived at this proposition before we became acquainted with Marx, to whose influence we have in no way been subjected" (1978c: 127).

constitution, abolition of the Senate and the Presidency of the Republic, administrative decentralization, election of judges, and separation of Church and State; but their reforms remained primarily political rather than social in nature. The socialists themselves split over party organization (unitary or federal?) and tactics (revolutionary or reformist?) at St. Etienne in 1882. The Marxist followers of Guesde joined the Parti ouvrier, while the "possibilists" – those who wished to practice "the politics of the possible," and for whom the Republic took precedence over the class struggle – formed the Fédérations des travailleurs socialistes. And in the rural south-east, the disciples of Louis-Auguste Blanqui and Edouard Vaillant formed the Comité révolutionnaire central (1881), a closed group of anarchist "companions" who rejected politics altogether. In short, apart from the conquest of a few town halls, "the various brands of socialism scarcely counted on the political level" (Mayeur and Rebérioux 1984: 75).

As Mayeur and Rebérioux have emphasized, the problem of explaining the republican victory is largely one of asking the right question. If we ask why the efforts at restoration failed, for example, the answer is both obvious and unhelpful. They failed because both the peasantry and the Orléanist legitimists feared the comte de Chambord more than they feared the Republic. If we ask why the constitutional laws were passed, the answer is equally obvious and equally unhelpful. They were passed because they were a temporary expedient, providing a conservative, parliamentary form of government while the Orléanists awaited their opportunity to establish a liberal monarchy. The much better question, therefore, is why this provisional, centrist government was gradually undermined by a widening rift between republicans and conservatives, and eventually gave way to a new "coalition of the Third Estate" (1984: 36–7).

What, then, gave rise to this rift and, eventually, this coalition? The effort to depict the conflict between republicans and conservatives as one of social class is doomed to failure; for in fact, the breadth of republican appeal largely transcended such divisions. A substantial number of upper middle-class bankers, businessmen, and industrialists, for example, had long been enamored of the ideas of Saint-Simon and Comte, embraced the faith in social progress, and firmly believed that a society open to talent and ability was the best means to ensure it. No less supportive of the Republic was Gambetta's "new social stratum" – the group produced by the economic prosperity of the Second Empire – which now sought secular enlightenment and social advancement for their children. The support of the peasantry – more fearful of both revolution and reaction – might not be taken for granted; but republican propaganda, which succeeded in raising fears of clerical reaction and/or the restoration of monarchy, combined with republican promises of free, secular education and universal military service, proved increasingly seductive. Finally, the industrial working class – never a decisive element in the coalition in any case – voted for the Republic if it voted at all (Mayeur and Rebérioux 1984: 37–40).

This breadth of appeal helps to explain at least two noteworthy features of the policies of the republicans once in power. The first, as both their Roman Catholic and (later) their radical socialist opponents pointed out, was that the Opportunists had no social policy whatsoever – i.e., no intention of significantly altering the traditional class structure of French society. On the contrary, aside from some early public works programs for the construction of ports, canals, and railways, the characteristic republican posture was one of resistance to State intervention in the economy, support for agriculture and protectionist industry, and aggressive colonialism (Bury 1985: 152; Mayeur and Rebérioux 1984: 94). When Ferry revealed his plan for a society "without God or King," therefore, Jaurès was wont to observe that this did not exclude the factory owner (McManners 1972: 46). The reasons for this exclusively political nature of the republican reforms are obvious. France was still a land of peasants – 65 percent of the population were still country dwellers – who had little direct interest in the social problems of workers. Those who were interested (and had survived the suppression of the Commune) were either in prison or in exile, while the remaining republicans were, like Ferry and Auguste Scheurer-Kestner, themselves bourgeois who distrusted social change. Finally, the republican ascendancy itself was palpably the consequence of coalition politics, depending heavily on the gradual seduction of the peasantry and the conversion of important Orléanists like Thiers. Had serious social and economic change played a part in the republican agenda, this seduction and conversion would clearly have been undermined (Bury, 1985: 152–3). These were caveats to which Durkheim was not oblivious. Although a friend of Jaurès and sympathetic to socialism, his response to revolutionary proposals, simply and repeatedly, was "I fear a reaction" (Lukes 1972: 323).

THE NEW ANTICLERICALISM

The second noteworthy feature was the central place of laicization within these political reforms. One has to read Gambetta's speech of May 4, 1877, Langlois observes, in order to understand "what remains, after one hundred years, astonishing: that it was indeed the denunciation of clericalism that held the republican camp together" (1996: 117). In fact, the conflict between republicans and conservatives was largely an ideological one over the place of the Church in French society. In particular, the Church was held responsible for denying both the middle classes and the peasantry that "enlightenment" which had been the promise of the French Revolution. In a sense, therefore, the defeat of the conservatives and the republican ascendancy marked the culmination of the great movement which had been begun in 1789 (Mayeur and Rebérioux 1984: 37). The historic alliance of Church and State in France was based upon the Concordat of 1801, a settlement signed by a Bonaparte wary of a Catholic reaction against a "godless" Republic and a Pius VII eager to heal the schism between "refractory" and "constitutional" clergy. Both parties gained. On his side, the pope received the right to depose French bishops and discipline pro-revolutionary clergy, thus ending the autonomy of the pre-revolutionary Gallican church. Henceforth, the head of State would nominate bishops, to whom the pope would then grant canonical institution. The publicity of Catholic worship, in such forms as processions in the streets, was again permitted; and Church seminaries were allowed to re-open.

Bonaparte gained still more. By signing the Concordat, the pope virtually recognized the Republic. The Vatican agreed to raise no questions over former tithes and former church lands, the new owners of former church properties thus gaining clear titles. Religious toleration was preserved through Bonaparte's minimal, factual, and thus harmless admission that Roman Catholicism was the religion of "the great majority of French citizens"; and while the clergy were to be compensated for loss of tithes and properties by receiving a salary from the State, Bonaparte simultaneously dispelled the notion of an established church by placing Protestant ministers of all denominations on the payroll as well. To these provisos, Bonaparte unilaterally appended his "Organic Articles" – a code of ecclesiastical law whose Gallican objectives were to increase the authority of the bishop over the parish priest, that of the State over the bishop, and to limit the power of the pope over the French clergy (McManners 1972: 4; Dansette 1961, 129–37).

During the First Empire and the regimes that followed, McManners observes, either side could have made the Concordat unworkable. The Vatican might have looked askance at changes of government, while French rulers might have asked in what sense the majority of citizens were Roman Catholics. But the Church believed in an alliance with the State on principle, and anticlericals were happy to see ecclesiastics bridled by specific agreements. Both sides thus had an interest in making the settlement work, and by 1870, "custom and compromise under successive regimes had filled the interstices of the original Concordat until the structure had acquired a venerable air, hallowed by time and seemingly irreplaceable" (McManners 1972: 5). To those who would eventually fill the ranks of the Opportunists, however, the Church seemed a growing and increasingly threatening presence. In the syllabus of 1864 which accompanied the encyclical *Quanta Cura*, Pius IX startled the modern world by condemning propositions which seemed self-evident to reasonable persons, including the suggestion that the Roman pontiff should reconcile himself to "progress, liberalism and modern civilization." "In this enigmatical form," commented the duc de Broglie, the pope seemed "to embrace in the same condemnation the press, railways, telegraphs, the discoveries of science" (McManners 1972: 19). And on July 18, 1870, the bishops assembled in St. Peter's voted the constitution *Pater aeternus*, declaring the pope preserved from error when he speaks *ex cathedra* in matters of faith and morals. However ambiguous the Syllabus, and however limited the definition in *Pater aeternus*, McManners observes, in the eyes of other Christians as well as unbelievers, the Church "was irretrievably set on the path of absolutism in ecclesiastical government and, by analogy and from the experience of the present pontificate, of reaction in matters social and political" (1972: 1).

Despite this reactionary posture, the Church enjoyed at least an ephemeral rise in popularity as a consequence of the Franco-Prussian War. The clergy had distinguished themselves as chaplains and orderlies, and some of the Catholic gentry as military officers. Bishops had defied the victorious Germans and denounced their demands for hostages, the Archbishop of Rheims demanding to be the first of the sureties they put on trains against the possibility of derailment. As the Commune decreed the separation of Church and

State, confiscated ecclesiastical property, occupied church buildings and storehouses, and "executed" more than fifty priests as well as the Archbishop of Paris, the Church gained further respect and sympathy from respectable society. As the Empire collapsed and Paris made war on Versailles, all who had anything to lose embraced an institution long regarded as the last bastion of conservatism (McManners 1972: 32–3).

Was Catholicism still the religion of "the great majority of French citizens"? Official statistics of the 1870s suggest that it was, listing 35,000,000 people as Catholics, in contrast to 600,000 Protestants, 50,000 Jews, and only 80,000 "free-thinkers" (McManners 1972: 5). There was a diocese corresponding to almost every department, and 36,000 parishes, an average of one to every thousand inhabitants. Each had its *curé* or *desservant* (priest in charge), and some had *vicaires* or other assistant clergy – a total of 51,000 priests engaged in the parochial ministry. These were supported by 4,000 other secular priests who were canons, directors of seminaries, or schoolmasters. The supervision of religion was, in terms of the numbers of people dependent upon it, one of the principal civil ministries. The annual budget for religion exceeded 50 million francs (McManners 1972: 20, 78). Although the Concordat had not provided for the return of the religious congregations, they had in fact returned in force, including traditional orders like the Trappists, Benedictines, and Dominicans, and a variety of new organizations reflecting the idiosyncrasies of local environments. Male congregations – only 5 of which enjoyed state authorization – had increased from 59 (in 1856) to 116 (embracing 30,000 members) by 1877. Among them were the 60 houses and 2,000 members of the Society of Jesus, active again as schoolmasters despite a Restoration decree prohibiting them from teaching. In their 29 colleges, the Jesuits taught 11,000 pupils, approximately one-fourth of all pupils in colleges run by religious orders. Congregations of women, enjoying authorization under a law of 1825, multiplied even earlier and more rapidly. By 1875 there were more than 127,000 nuns, or one to every 280 members of the population – 3 times more than on the eve of the Revolution (McManners 1972: 20–1; Bury 1985: 157; Mayeur and Rebérioux 1984: 78). In addition to the sheer numbers of Catholics and the strength of their clergy, a variety of social services seem to have been almost entirely in Church hands. In 1880, for example, the hospitals and hospices run by the religious orders dealt with 114,199 persons in need of assistance. More than

60,000 children were received in Catholic orphanages and work-rooms; and to these must be added the Catholic apprenticeship schools, Church clubs, rest homes, and lunatic asylums (Mayeur and Rebérioux 1984: 79). But it was in education that the power of the Roman Catholic Church in France seemed to be at its height.

In spite of the anticlericalism which survived the First Empire and continued into the 1830s and 1840s, the Church had repeatedly tried to improve its position by undermining the university monopoly of higher and secondary education. Its struggle, eloquently served by the new school of Liberal Catholics led by the Comte de Montalembert, was rewarded in 1850 by the Loi Falloux – a gesture of domestic politics by Louis Napoleon to French Catholics which would secure the position of Catholics in education for the next thirty years. The State monopoly was broken. Henceforth, there were be two categories of school: the public schools founded and maintained by communes, departments, or the State; and the already flourishing free schools founded by private individuals or associations. In effect, this meant that any authorized or tolerated religious association could open a school, and be subject only to the most nominal State inspection. Until the Second Empire stopped the practice, local authorities could hand over their own schools to the charge of religious orders; and since monks and nuns required no salaries, frugality repeatedly overwhelmed anticlericalism in the deliberations of rural councillors. The religious orders – and particularly the Jesuits – came to play an increasingly important part in education (Bury 1985: 81–2; McManners 1972: 21). By 1870, almost 40 percent of the nation's children were educated in Church schools.[3] The sons of the aristocracy, magistrates, and army officers were consistently sent to the *collèges* of the orders – particularly those of the Jesuits, who specialized in training young men for the Polytechnique and the naval and military academies. The education of women came even further under the influence of the Church. Three-fifths of all girls were taught by the sisters of the congregations, and even in anti-

---

[3] McManners estimates that in more than 300 *collèges* and in 80 or more "Little Seminaries," there were 70,000 pupils, by contrast with 116,000 in the lay establishments of secondary education. In primary schools of the orders, approximately 1,500,000 of the country's 4,000,000 children received their education. Even the State schools, with exclusively lay personnel, were much under the influence of the Church. Their day began with prayers, there were crucifixes on the walls, the bishop sat in the Conseil Académique of the Department, and there were representatives of the episcopate on the Conseil Supérieur de l'Instruction Publique (1972: 21–2).

clerical areas, there was a widespread belief that nuns should be in charge of feminine education. When an attempt was made under the Second Empire to establish State secondary schools for girls, Mgr. Dupanloup protested that many of the teachers would be men, some irreligious, and some even youthful. The project collapsed when clerical journals published the names of the girls attending (McManners 1972: 21–2). As late as 1930, André Siegfried could still observe that there was no type of Frenchman more typical than the anticlerical deputy whose wife was a devout Catholic and whose daughters were educated in a convent (Bury 1985: 159).

In higher education, a law of July 12, 1875 was to increase the Church's influence still more. It allowed the opening of "free institutes of higher education" – in short, Catholic universities – and allotted the award of degrees to mixed boards of examiners consisting of professors from State faculties and from their Catholic counterparts. Instantly such universities appeared at Paris, Lille, Lyon, Angers, and Toulouse, and with substantial means at their disposal, they soon attracted first-rate faculties and competed effectively with the State universities. Bishops continued to sit on the Conseil Supérieur, while priests sat on the academic boards. Religious instruction, given by chaplains, formed part of the timetables of *lycées* (Mayeur and Rebérioux 1984: 79). "Au point de vue sociologique," Durkheim would say in 1905, "l'Eglise est un monstre" (1905: 369). If so, in 1870 it was a very large *monstre* indeed, and one that threatened to grow still larger.

Not surprisingly, the 1870s and 1880s became a period of renascent Catholic spirituality[4] and mass pilgrimages, the latter inspired in part by the desire to offer reparation for sins reputed to have brought on the Prussian defeat and the horrors of the Commune. The chief resort for such journeys was the shrine of Paray-le-Monial, where the faithful made "the consecration of a penitent France to the Sacred Heart of Jesus." The Augustins de L'Assomption, a brotherhood founded in mid-century, set the pattern by negotiating cheap railway fares, printing song sheets, and publishing a newspaper, *Le Pèlerin* (McManners 1972: 22). Revelations, prophecies, and miracles multiplied. Yet despite its popularity after the War and the

---

[4] Even the youthful Durkheim did not escape. Davy tells us that, while a student at the Collège d'Epinal in the early 1870s, he experienced a brief crisis of mysticism under the influence of an old Catholic schoolmistress – something he rapidly surmounted (Lukes 1972: 41).

Commune, its 35,000,000 followers, the strength of its clergy, its control of social services, its power over French education, and its renascent spirituality, the Catholic Church in France was a deeply troubled institution.

Some of these troubles were internal, others derived from the social and economic changes of late 19th-century France, and still others could be attributed to the increasingly zealous activities of non-Catholic or anti-Catholic groups. But whatever the causes, they were sufficient to render the Church extremely vulnerable to the attacks of anticlericals like Durkheim after 1879. Not least among the Church's internal difficulties, for example, was its lack of a central organization or a distinctive French voice. Nothing had replaced the Assembly General of the Clergy of the *ancien régime*, the Concordat had been negotiated by the Pope alone, and after 1811, there had been no more plenary meetings of the French episcopate. If the Church of France was to speak as a unity, therefore, the lead would have to come from the Vatican, where Pius IX, having lost the protection of French troops to the Franco-Prussian disaster, had declared himself a "prisoner" of the new kingdom of Italy. The history of the French Church in the 1870s and 1880s, therefore, was one punctuated with ultramontanist calls – most of which fell upon deaf republican ears – for the "liberation" of the Pope. A second difficulty was that French clergy themselves were divided in their degree of ultramontanist zeal. McManners notes that, by 1870, the social gulf between the lower clergy and the French episcopate had largely evaporated, but that a cultural and intellectual gulf had endured. The parish clergy came consistently from the less-educated classes, while the bishops typically possessed literary and classical educations, and were utter strangers to the parochial ministry.[5] Enjoying a salary 20 times that of a *curé*, a bishop inevitably appeared to those below as an aloof, superior figure. By contrast, only one secular priest in ten enjoyed security of tenure; the others could be moved by the bishop at will and, if accused of offences, disciplined without due process (1972: 25).

Under these circumstances, one can see why that "ghostly

---

[5] Of 167 holders of episcopal office between 1870 and 1883, McManners observes, only 21 were of noble birth, 56 were from bourgeois or rich peasant families, and 90 were of "the people." Only 18 had spent significant time in the parochial ministry before their elevation, 23 had risen through diocesan administration, and more than 90 had been teachers in seminaries or holders of academic chairs (1972: 25).

Gallicanism which lingered on in the episcopal palaces after 1870" had largely disappeared from the presbyteries. In fact, under Pius IX the Roman *Curia* consistently lent a sympathetic ear to the complaints of French parish priests, who were further encouraged by Louis Veuillot's *L'Univers*, the principal Catholic newspaper. Widely read in rural districts, *L'Univers* denounced Gallicanism and Liberal Catholicism alike, while simultaneously demanding allegiance to the Chair of Peter, and rendered compromise with even a moderate republicanism unthinkable (McManners 1972: 23). While it is difficult to imagine that a country with a priest for every 639 inhabitants might lack an effective parochial ministry, this was the principal thesis of the abbé Bougaud's *Le grand péril de l'Eglise de France* (1878), which noted the decline in annual ordinations from 1,753 (in 1868) to 1,582 (in 1877). The aristocracy and bourgeoisie were still interested in the religious orders for their daughters; but 9 out of 10 candidates for the ministry came from the families of peasants and artisans. With his 850 francs, McManners observes, a *desservant* earned the wage of a *gendarme*; a *vicaire* received less than half as much; and even a *curé*, of whom there were only 5,600, could rise only to 1,500 (1972: 27). Respect for apostolic poverty notwithstanding, the ministry was a low-status occupation.

As the intellectual foundations of Christian belief came under increasing attack from Biblical criticism, natural science, and the comparative study of religion, it is understandable that a ministry thus recruited would be found wanting; and to compound the problem, the educational program of the seminaries was limited to meditation, pious exercises, and the rehearsal of antiquated dogma: "In ancient manuals written in dog latin," McManners observes, "seminarists studied theological courses consisting of fragments of the Scriptures, the Fathers, and the Councils tacked together. The chronological difficulties of Genesis were still explained by the theory of 'jour-époques,' the millennial 'days' of creation, and the implausibility of the Flood story was overcome by confining it to a segment of the earth's surface" (1972: 27–8). McManners finds only two diocesan prelates who, in the 1870s and 1880s, had any first-hand knowledge of the new German biblical criticism that had already inspired Robertson Smith and, largely through Smith, would influence Durkheim; and McManners adds that even Mgr. Dupanloup, the great Liberal Catholic, was helpless in the face of Renan's *Vie de Jésus* (1863).

Even the figure of 35,000,000 French Catholics seems dubious. Many of these, McManners insists, "accepted no obligation beyond making their Easter communion, many merely attended mass occasionally, or came to church to be married or were brought there to be buried, many were nominal Catholics whose allegiance did not extend beyond the census forms" (1972: 5). A more certain guide, he adds, are the statistics of voting in national elections. In every instance, when the country had a chance to pronounce on the anticlerical policies of the 1870s and 1880s, it endorsed them. "True," he admits, "the issue was never clear-cut; even so, the voting could not have consistently gone this way unless there had been large numbers of 'Catholics' of various kinds who refused to put institutional loyalty before what they regarded as the best overall decision for the political administration of the country." Catholicism, it seems, was not unmixed with an anticlericalism of its own. Clemenceau could thus refer to a France "qui a des habitudes cultuelles, mais qui a en horreur le gouvernement des curés" (McManners 1972: 11).

Quite aside from its internal difficulties, the Church faced serious problems adapting to the social and economic transformation of France in the late 19th century. The population of the diocese of Paris, for example, rose from 1,953,000 (in 1861) to 2,411,000 (in 1877) to 3,849,000 (in 1906); and as the conditions of the Concordat made it difficult to endow new parishes, and the government made no provision for moving priests from old ones, the traditional parochial system foundered.[6] Similar problems afflicted Marseilles, Lille, Saint-Etienne, and Lyon. In *Le Présent et l'avenir du Catholicisme* (1892), the duc de Broglie thus argued that the Church was being defeated not so much by skepticism as by administrative breakdown under the sheer weight of numbers. To this, one must add the indifferent knowledge of an urban, working-class world possessed by a clergy of rural origins, whose language, values, and morals were largely those of an earlier age. The traditional palliative of alms-giving, widely endorsed and practiced, was ill-fitted to cope with urban discontent and misery. In Lille where, under the Second Empire, 30 percent of the deaths were from consumption and diseases of the lungs, rickets and syphilitic debility, the Catholic "Society for Good Books"

[6] In 1861, McManners observes, there were 134 parishes and 661 priests; in 1877, 159 "parishes" (including new chapels) and 723 priests; and in 1906, 185 "parishes" and 866 priests. In the XIIe and XXe *arrondissements*, parishes of 50,000 souls were common (1972: 7).

distributed Mme de Gaulle's *Georges: ou le bon usage des richesses*. The presence of the Church at ceremonial functions was undermined, a sharp fall in the number of baptisms and a rise in the number of civil marriages and burials occurring after 1875. The city, Mayeur and Rebérioux emphasize, "a modern Babylon which the Church distrusted, was the citadel of religious indifference" (1984: 104), and comparisons of the new districts in Paris with "heathen lands afar" were not uncommon (McManners 1972: 30, 7).

The Church was no more able to appeal to the middle classes. The old, "Voltairean" bourgeoisie of the provinces had largely been reconciled to a vague kind of faith; but Gambetta's "new strata" was utterly indifferent if not hostile. The growth of ultramontanism among French Catholics, their loyalty to a Pope who had promulgated the Syllabus and the Decree of Infallibility, their campaigns for the defense of the Temporal power before 1870 and its restoration thereafter, and their unconcealed support for Royalists and opposition to the Republic led this new bourgeoisie, whose rise was intimately bound to the values of science, education, and progress, to see in the Church a force of reaction and obscurantism (Bury 1985: 157). Even the religious faith of the aristocracy, reputedly rediscovered in the Revolution, might be questioned: "Catholicism," as Anatole France dryly observed, was "still the most acceptable form of religious indifference" (McManners 1972: 10).

To these difficulties of the Church must be added the much wider breadth of opinion to which the French population would be exposed. Thanks to the invention of the rotary press, post-free railway distribution, and the mass appeal of advertising, the penny newspaper, which accounted for almost half the papers printed in 1870 and three-quarters by 1880, easily reached the countryside (Mayeur and Rebérioux 1984: 116). To this were added the local weekly or bi-weekly newspapers, and the illustrated magazines and catalogues from major Parisian stores. Quite aside from manifestly anticlerical publications like Guérolt's *L'Opinion nationale*, these carriers of a new, popular, Parisian culture, together with military service and improvements in transportation, broadened the horizons of the French people and undermined local, traditional values (Bury 1985: 157; McManners 1972: 14; Mayeur and Rebérioux 1984: 117). Similarly, to the middle-class resentment of priestly intervention in the life of the family, the popular writer added "a *frisson* of sensibility" (McManners 1972: 15). From George Sand's *Lélia* (1833) and Marguerite Gautier's *La Morte amoureuse* (1836–7) to Anatole France's *Thaïs* (1890), the theme of the futility of asceticism and its betrayal of the most valued human emotions was repeatedly explored. The positivism of Gambetta's "new strata" was satisfied by the determinism of the Goncourts, de Maupassant, and especially Zola, whose *Histoire naturelle et sociale d'une famille sous le second Empire* began to appear in 1871. Led by the "Parnassians" C.-M.-R. Leconte de Lisle, R.-F.-A. Sully-Prudhomme, and Françoise Coppée, poetry conformed just as easily to the ideology of faith in science and progress (Mayeur and Rebérioux 1984: 120–1).

Recognizing these difficulties afflicting the Church, it is worth recalling that the Roman Catholic was not the only religious confession in late 19th-century France. There were 580,000 Protestants in France in 1872, and their economic standing and intellectual significance far transcended their numbers (Bury 1985: 156). After the synod of 1872, a division in the Reformed Church produced a liberal Protestant minority which practiced ecclesiastical democracy, rejected theological dogma, reduced religion to a rational morality, encouraged freedom of inquiry, and thus became another component of the secular, republican idea. Protestants like Ferdinand Buisson (whom Durkheim replaced at the Sorbonne in 1902), Félix Pécaut, J. Steeg, and Elie Rabier played important roles in Ferry's educational reforms, and the neo-Kantian philosopher Charles Renouvier (1815–1903), whom Durkheim called "mon educateur," called on republicans to become Protestants (Mayeur and Rebérioux 1984: 107–8).

The Jewish minority comprised 50,000 by 1870, most of them living in Paris (McManners 1972: 5). While those who had recently immigrated from Eastern Europe remained isolated by their language (Yiddish) and retained their religious traditions, Alsatian Jews like Durkheim were largely assimilated. Granted citizenship and the right to vote in the Civil Constitution of the Clergy (1790), these assimilated Jews remained attached to the tradition of the Revolution, and consistently supported the progressive, secular Republic. The "tens of thousands" of freemasons (Mayeur and Rebérioux 1984: 109), whose numbers doubled between 1862 and 1889, were also ardently republican (Bury 1985: 157). The largely middle-class lodges became centers of anticlerical feeling where republican politicians could discuss the strategies of "laicization" more conveniently than in cafes or at private dinner parties (McManners 1972:

18). Finally, Bury insists that the majority of the brilliant young men trained at the Ecole Normale Supérieure after 1848, as well as the majority of those republican leaders who were not Protestants, were simply agnostics, for whom "the cult of the Great Revolution had become almost a religion, and, in so far as it affected their political thinking, intensified the political offensive of the Left against the Church" (1985: 156). McManners estimates that there were 80,000 "free-thinkers" in France in the 1870s (1972: 5).

Both internal and external difficulties of the Church, therefore, conspired to make anticlericalism an established feature of French life by 1870. Anticlericalism, of course, may be traced back to the literate sensibilities of the Enlightenment, the jest books of the Renaissance, and even the sullen resentments of the Middle Ages. McManners goes so far as to suggest that it might be an instinctive reaction to the presence of any organized, authoritative priesthood. The priest is there to be loved or hated, not to seek that quiet social acceptance which is the goal of most ordinary citizens. The confessional and its place in the lives of women had always aroused resentment and, quite aside from the occasional incidents of clerical immorality seized upon by Guérolt's *L'Opinion nationale*, there was a widely held view that celibacy and especially monasticism represented defiance of the fundamental virtues of the bourgeois family. "Parents" McManners observes, "were entitled to enjoy their children's company: when his daughter entered a convent, the baron de Ponnet wrote to his friends on black-edged notepaper. Men without children of their own, without a stake in the country and uncommitted to society ought not to direct the consciences of women and the minds of schoolboys" (1972: 14–15).

But the 19th century brought new fuel to this slowly burning fire. After his conversion to anticlericalism, for example, the works of the great romantic historian Jules Michelet increasingly emphasized the abuses of the confessional, the political maneuvers of the Jesuits, the Gallican tradition of opposition to Roman encroachments, the sufferings of French Protestants, and the glory of the Declaration of the Rights of Man and the Citizen. To those for whom the Revolution meant ancestral lands freed from the tithe and the acquisition of ecclesiastical properties, Michelet's writings – incongruously related to memories of the Napoleonic domination of Europe – became "a patriotic Bible whose contents resembled a bloodstained and triumphant Old Testament story . . . Against the

Catholic myth of a Christian France," McManners observes, "had arisen the counter-myth of a revolutionary France, the standard-bearer of liberty" (1972: 15–16).

"Scientific" historical scholarship was still more devastating when applied to the sacred texts themselves. Between 1858 and 1865 the *Revue germanique* published the latest results of German biblical scholarship, introducing doubts about Christology and chronology, miracles, prophecies, the sequence of particular documents, and the very authenticity of certain texts. Much of this could be dismissed as obscure, recondite, and therefore trivial; but in 1862, Ernest Renan – who had attended Catholic seminaries and even taken minor orders before abandoning the faith – used his inaugural lecture as professor of Hebrew at the Collège de France to deny the divinity of Jesus Christ. One year later Renan published his *Vie de Jésus*, which combined erudition and literary skill to an unprecedented effect, explaining the Resurrection as a mere rumor propagated by Christ's followers and eliminating supernatural elements from the Gospels altogether. More than 60,000 copies of *La Vie de Jésus* were sold within the first year of publication (Renan 1991: vii; McManners 1972: 16). The discoveries of natural science were no less important. In 1862, for example, a French translation of Darwin's *Origin of Species* was published with a preface denying the Christian doctrine of creation; and after the Franco-Prussian War, the widely recognized superiority of German science and secular education was cited by Renan as a cause of the disasters at Sedan. Henceforth, promising young *agrégés* like Durkheim would be sent to Germany to study, and they would return, also like Durkheim, committed to the overthrow of the elitist, humanist, and largely Catholic-supported system of French education. Anticlericalism was thus bound up, not just with positivism and empiricism, but with both domestic and international politics as well.

For those wishing to understand Durkheim, however, the most interesting aspect of anticlericalism was its similarity to Catholicism. In each case, a determined core of "true believers" was outnumbered by a wider circle of occasional conformists and nominal adherents. Moreover, the spheres of nominal Catholicism and ambiguous anticlericalism overlapped, as those Catholics who resented clerical domination and right-wing politics mingled with anticlericals – like Durkheim – whose hatred for priests was not unmixed with a respect and even nostalgia for the moral uniformity of the medieval community. It was in this context that the possibility of a purely lay morality, based on a "science of ethics," was first conceived; and it was the belief in this possibility, as well as the quasi-religious belief in science and progress generally, which distinguished this anticlericalism from that of earlier ages: "Many of the opponents of the Church," McManners reminds us, "had a reluctant admiration for the system of moral influence they were proposing to destroy, and a vision of a faith to replace it. It was not *écrasez l'Infâme*, but a different sort of bitterness, compounded of attraction and repulsion, a love–hate relationship" (1972: 17). As we shall see in chapter 2 (see esp. pp. 48–9), even Durkheim's attitude toward the Church was not unmixed: "there were aspects of Catholicism," Pickering reminds us, that Durkheim "greatly respected and continued to do so to the end of his life" (1984: 427)

The Opportunists who came to power in 1879 thus confronted a Church afflicted with serious internal and external difficulties, whose values were largely if not unambiguously discordant with the middle-class, quasi-religious belief in positivism and social progress, and whose political candidates they had repeatedly (and now decisively) defeated at the polls; but it was also a Church which had the respect and even affection of the majority of the population, one whose moral authority the Opportunists envied and longed to replace with their own, equally fervent brand of secular ethics.[7] More pragmatically, while radicals like Paul Bert might attack the State-supported religion and seek to overthrow the Concordat, Opportunists like Ferry saw the Concordat as an instrument for controlling the Church, particularly through the opportunities for clerical appointments and the suspension or abolition of ecclesiastical salaries it provided. And Leo XIII, who had replaced Pius IX in 1878, was considerably less hostile to a France which protected overseas missions and seemed benign by comparison with the newly unified Italy or Bismarckian Germany. Through his *nuncio* in Paris, the pope urged French Catholics to practice moderation in response to the new republican policies (McManners 1972: 45; Mayeur and Rebérioux 1984: 85).

Republican administrators thus turned quite naturally to the

---

[7] Ferry told Jean Jaurès that he wished "to establish humanity without a God and without a King," but added to his wife that he was "the elected representative of a people that makes wayside altars, that is fond of the Republic but is just as fond of its processions" (Mayeur and Rebérioux 1984: 84).

Church's educational establishments – "the surest guarantee of its continued influence" – as the focal point for their reforms. In such establishments, McManners emphasizes, "so many young minds were imprinted with a permanent allegiance to religion, or a subconscious residual respect for its practices" (1972: 45). Such establishments also bore the weight of accumulated resentments – they were patronized by the upper classes, administered corporal punishment, taught children to admire unrevolutionary mendicant saints, and emphasized impractical subjects to the children of a class with rising social aspirations. "A frontal attack on religion," McManners emphasizes, "on the ceremonies by which wives set so much store, the consolations available in the hour of death, the *curé* and all his supporters," would surely have failed (1972: 46). But a "flank attack" on clerical education, which left the Church undisturbed in the private sphere of the family, would surely receive political support. This support was eagerly sought. "The most urgent of all reforms," Gambetta had declared upon signing the Belleville program of 1869, "must be the liberation of universal suffrage from every sort of tutelage, obstacle, pressure and corruption" (Bury, 1985: 156). Indeed, "universal suffrage" had voted Royalist or Bonapartist in 1849, 1851, and 1852, and would do so again in 1870 and 1871. The way to ensure that it would vote republican, or so thought the republicans, was to provide free, compulsory, and above all secular primary education.

Laicization, however, was more than a means to winning over new generations to the Opportunist regime. After the disasters of 1870–1, it became a commonplace to compare pupils of the Jesuits with the more efficient German officer corps, "trained in academies which honoured Protestantism and science." Laicization was thus viewed as a means to repair the negative consequences of an elitist, humanist, and increasingly impractical form of education, to eradicate differences of geographic region and social class, and to unite the French people and restore their sense of national pride. Secularism, in short, became synonymous with patriotism. Ferry ordered 20,000 copies of Déroulède's *Chants du soldat* (1872) – a collection of popular, patriotic hymns – to be distributed to the primary schools, extolled military training for children, and advocated the creation of cadet battalions in Paris. The motto of the Ligue de l'Enseignement became "for the fatherland, by book and sword," and Ferdinand Buisson, Director of Primary Education at the Ministry of Public

Instruction from 1879 to 1896, sat on the managing committee of the Ligue des patriotes as well (Mayeur and Rebérioux 1984: 86; McManners 1972: 47). The morality of the state, Claude Langlois agrees, "would replace that of the Church; the government's truth would replace the Vatican's. Rather than smash old idols, the Republic merely substituted new ones" (1996: 109–10).

In sum, laicization – the removal of clerical control over French education – was less a neutral political posture than a "civil religion" of its own, deeply inspired by neo-Kantian morality and Liberal Protestantism. Buisson founded the newspaper *Le Christianisme libéral* at Neuchâtel in 1866, and in 1869 published *La Foi laïque*, calling for a Christianity freed from obligatory dogma, the belief in miracles, infallible books, and priestly authority, and while Director of Primary Education was heard to speak of hymns and ceremonies for a new "mystique civile religieuse." Félix Pécaut, a former pastor and Director of Studies at the Ecole Normale Supérieure of Fontenay-aux-Roses, gave future heads and mistresses of teachers' training colleges a lecture on morality each morning, followed by a secular hymn. Other Republicans were less given to such enthusiasms, but all believed in science, progress, and patriotism (Mayeur and Rebérioux 1984: 86–7; McManners 1972: 47–8). As Claude Nicolet observed, the republicans were thus made aware of "the fundamental and ineluctable link between the political and the spiritual," for "the anticlerical battle was the prerequisite of all political action," and thus quite literally "the *motor* of history" (Langlois 1996: 120).

In spite of its non-revolutionary goals – or rather because of them – the movement toward laicization grew rapidly. The Ligue de l'enseignement, founded in 1866 by Jean Macé, served as an umbrella for a variety of disparate groups unified in defining free, compulsory, secular education as the overriding national necessity. From 1870 to 1877, it grew from 18,000 to 60,000 members (Mayeur and Rebérioux 1984: 86). "The organizers of the league," Auspitz observes, "deliberately set out to establish a secular voice and organization in French politics, a presence in every commune and department that would urge the existing government in a 'modern' direction and provide an alternative to a society based on the Catholic Church" (Auspitz 1982: 6–7). Similarly, the Société pour l'étude des questions d'enseignement supérieur, founded in 1879, sought to influence sympathetic ministers like W. H. Waddington and Ferry to reform higher education on the model of Protestant Germany; and the *Revue internationale de l'enseignement,* which began to appear in 1881, presented a series of studies of both German and French education – including the important products of Durkheim's 1885–6 visit to Berlin, Marburg, and Leipzig – which created the theoretical foundations for the policies of laicization.

On February 4, 1879, the Waddington ministry was formed with Jules Ferry as Minister of Education. On March 30, 1885, the second Ferry cabinet would be overthrown by news of the Lang Son disaster, a minor reversal in the Third Republic's aggressive colonial policies seized upon by Ferry's opponents. During the period of remarkable political stability which intervened, Ferry would be Minister of Education for five years and Prime Minister for three; and it was during this period, undisturbed by opposition from both Left and Right, that the governing republicans constructed their system of free, compulsory, secular education. Born near St. Dié in the Vosges, Ferry embodied a variety of conflicting religious impulses. His father and the males of his family were Voltairean free-thinkers; by marriage he would enter the milieu of rich Protestantism; and his sister Adèle, who raised him, was a fervent Catholic who constantly prayed for his salvation. Like Gambetta, Ferry was trained at the bar and won his political reputation in the opposition struggle near the end of the Second Empire; but in 1870, while Gambetta became the hero of the French provinces, Ferry held the thankless tasks of rationing food supplies and suppressing the January insurrection in Paris, for which he won the successive titles of "Ferry-Famine" and "Ferry-Massacre." But, despite his understandable unpopularity with a section of the Parisians, Ferry won increasing respect during the 1870s, until he became the acknowledged leader of the Gauche Républicaine, one of two main opposition groups in parliament (Bury 1985: 155).

Not surprisingly, Ferry's primary intellectual inspiration came from Condorcet and Comte, whose beliefs in science, progress, and the power of education he embraced without reservation. But, much like Durkheim, Ferry also held a deep respect for the medieval Church, whose schools unified society, mitigated inequalities, taught morality, and thus provided the ethical foundations for an entire social order. "So too," McManners explains Ferry's thinking, "the new lay education would unite Frenchmen in a common patriotism, fitting them for the day when they would challenge the Germans and recover Ferry's homeland of Lorraine; it would help the poor to rise, give women equality with men, and in the factories, where hierarchy was inevitable, it would make inferiority tolerable by creating an equality of dignity. As for morality, at last it could be separated from those 'high metaphysical questions about which theologians and philosophers have disputed for 6,000 years' " (1972: 49).

The republican ascendancy of 1879–85 is recalled primarily for its anticlerical legislation; but in fact, laicization as a general policy was directly or indirectly related to a variety of other reforms. The Opportunists began, for example, by eliminating those legal measures from which they had suffered in the days of "moral order." A drinking shop law made it possible to open or move a tavern – the Republican "church" – without administrative authorization. A law of June 30, 1881 made it possible to hold public meetings without similar authorization, requiring only a simple declaration and the formation of a committee. A law of July 29, 1881 granted an extraordinary degree of freedom to the press, resulting in an unprecedented expansion of journals for the expression of opinion. A law of March 4, 1882 granted municipal councils the right to elect their mayors; and a law of April 5, 1884 confirmed the election of mayors and their deputies, as well as the public nature of council meetings: "The town halls," Mayeur and Rebérioux explain, "were centres of life and political education, especially in the country. The activities of the municipal councils, especially in religious affairs (subsidies for buildings, payment of curates, vetoes on processions) and educational matters (creation of schools, laicization of the staff) were the occasions of important debates" (Mayeur and Rebérioux, 1984: 82). Administrative and constitutional reforms were limited. Once in power, the Opportunists abandoned the rhetoric of decentralization, preserving the administrative structure established by Napoleon. The "republican form of government" was made immune to revision, a measure which made royalist propaganda into an act against the constitution. A constitutional revision of 1884 abandoned the creation of further life-senators, and recruitment by competitive examination was introduced into the Diplomatic Service, the Conseil d'Etat, the Cours des comptes, and the Inspection des finances. But the electoral laws maintained the dominance of rural France, and the extreme Left failed to achieve its goals of universal suffrage and the abolition of the upper chamber (Bury 1985: 153–5; Mayeur and Rebérioux 1984: 82–3).

The intimate connection between laicization and the revival of French political fortunes was reflected in colonial policies as well. Explaining to the Chamber why he sent Admiral Courbet's squadron into the Gulf of Tonkin in 1885 – an act which eventually brought about his fall – Ferry presented arguments which were simultaneously economic, humanitarian, and political. France was committed irretrievably to industrialization, and the colonies would provide markets for her products in the face of mounting international protectionism; the "superior races" had a duty "to civilize the inferior races," by exporting enlightenment and social progress; and an expansionist policy was the mark of national greatness, while one of contemplation or abstention was simply a further step on the road to decline and decadence. So there was no apparent contradiction between laicization and colonial expansion; on the contrary, the first seemed to justify the second: "After all," Mayeur and Rebérioux observe, "laicization taught the end of traditional beliefs and civilizations and the victory of a progress based on science and reason. The Alliance Française, founded in 1884, aimed at disseminating this ideal beyond the seas. Once again we can see that there is unity in the opportunist republicans' conception of the world and their political philosophy" (1984: 99–100).

Laicization, in short, was the reform that contained all other reforms: "when the whole of French youth has . . . grown up under this triple aegis of free, compulsory, secular education" Ferry predicted in the *Revue pédagogique* in 1882, "we shall have nothing more to fear from returns to the past, for we shall have the means of defending ourselves. [This means consists of] the spirit of all these new generations, of these countless young reserves of republican democracy, trained in the school of science and reason, who will block retrograde attitudes with the insurmountable obstacle of free minds and liberated consciences" (Mayeur and Rebérioux 1984: 85). Quite outside the sphere of education, the Ferry reforms included a number of measures designed to destroy the traditional, almost subliminal presence of the Church in the everyday lives of French citizens. In 1880, for example, the law which forbade work on Sundays was annulled. A law of July 28, 1881 abolished the denominational character of cemeteries; and another law of November 15, 1887 encouraged citizens to make preliminary arrangements for civil funerals. Mayors of communes were given control of religious processions; hospitals were laicized through the gradual expulsion of the Sisters of Mercy; crucifixes were removed from courtrooms; clergy were eliminated from the administration of charitable organizations; army and military hospital chaplains were abolished; prayers at the opening of each parliamentary session were abolished; and on July 27, 1884, divorce was restored to the Civil Code, from where it had been absent since 1816.[8]

On July 14, 1880, the anniversary of the Fall of the Bastille was observed as a national festival for the first time since the Revolution. Schoolchildren were required to participate, in order to "rescue the younger generations from superstitious practices," and replace the "old dogmas" with the new, civil religion. "It would be very wrong," Mayeur and Rebérioux insist, "to underestimate the popular fervor and enthusiasm on the occasion of the first festivals of the 14 July and to fail to recognize the emotional power of the myth of the Republic . . . The popular festival with its balls in the squares and fireworks was a sort of political liturgy" (1984: 118). Durkheim himself spent the entire day celebrating in the streets (Lukes 1972: 48). In the sphere of education *per se*, a law of February, 1880 excluded from the Conseil Supérieur de l'Instruction Publique those "not involved in education and in particular ministers of religion," thus ending the system created by the Loi Falloux and reinstating the university as an autonomous body. Henceforth, the Conseil Supérieur would play an essential part in producing the reform legislation of the Third Republic, through its permanent committee as well as specialized associations like the Society for the Study of Questions of Secondary Education and the Society of Higher Education. Another law of March 18, 1880 ended the practice, established in July, 1875, of conferring university degrees by mixed boards of examiners: "The examinations and practical tests which determine the award of degrees," the new law stated, "can only be taken before State faculties." The same law denied the title of "university" to the Catholic "institutes of higher education" given life by the 1875 legislation (Mayeur and Rebérioux, 1984: 87–8).

Ferry's most controversial act, however, was his introduction of the infamous "Article 7," which forbade members of unauthorized congregations to direct or teach in any educational establishment whatsoever. This revival of the question of State recognition for

---

[8] McManners 1972: 59. Divorce by mutual consent, however, was not reintroduced. An interesting defense of such self-restraint on the part of republican administrators can be found in Durkheim's "Le Divorce par consentement mutuel" (1906).

congregations was palpably a device to deprive certain citizens, and particularly the Jesuits, of their right to teach. It was thus as unpalatable for some on the Left as for those on the Right and, after a violent debate, the article was rejected by the Senate. Undeterred, Ferry and Freycinet simply decided to enforce the already-existing, long-unobserved statutes against unauthorized congregations. In the decrees of March 29, 1880, therefore, Ferry ordered the dissolution and disbandment of the Jesuits within three months. All other congregations which failed to obtain permission to reside and operate in France within a prescribed time period were also to be dissolved. Conservatives and Catholics were passionately indignant. A number of communities refused to obey the decrees, and approximately 400 magistrates resigned rather then enforce them. In the case of refusal, however, troops were called in to secure the expulsion, and the resignation of conservatively disposed magistrates simply provided Ferry with the opportunity to replace them with magistrates whose Republican sentiments were unqualified. It is a clear measure of the government's popular support that, in all but a few departments, the Catholic right failed miserably in its efforts to mobilize crowds against this, perhaps the most heavy-handed act of laicization (Bury 1985: 158; Mayeur and Rebérioux 1984: 77).

If the religious congregations were thus to be ousted, however, it was the obligation of the State to provide for the education of every child in France. The essential stipulation here was that such education be free, compulsory, and secular. "Making it free," Mayeur and Rebérioux explain, "made it possible to make it compulsory and this, in a country divided in its beliefs, involved making it secular" (1984: 89). The decisive measure here was the law of March 28, 1882, which made education compulsory from six to thirteen years, and eliminated religious instruction from the timetable. The teacher, insisted Buisson, "confines himself to inculcating in his pupils the fundamental ideas which recur in all religious denominations and even outside them" (1984: 90). The phrase "every child in France" was meant to include females. As early as 1878, Camille Sée, a young Jewish deputy in Ferry's party, had proposed a bill which sought to end the influence of the Church over middle-class girls by providing them with State-supported, secondary education; and on December 21, 1880, this bill became a law. The education provided by the Camille Sée law was innovative in two ways. First, it was to be provided by female schoolmistresses, a condition which required the creation of teachers' training colleges for women. Indeed, a decree of August, 1879 had already ordered each department to establish an Ecole Normale for this purpose, and in July, 1880, an Ecole Normale Supérieure was established at Fontenay-aux-Roses, under the leadership of the Protestant Pécaut, to train lecturers for these *collèges*. Second, this education was to be secular – i.e., the teaching of morality was compulsory but that of religion was optional. By ending "intellectual and moral divorce" in marriage, the law sought to provide "republican companions for republican men." Ferry, in particular, was delighted with a measure which carried women "towards the light, towards knowledge, towards secular science" (1984: 89).

The complete laicization of the teaching staffs came more slowly, as Ferry wished to avoid any disruptive opposition and, in any case, needed the time to train the appropriate teachers. By the appearance of the "Goblet law" of October 30, 1886, however, members of the religious orders were explicitly denied further recruitment into the State's primary schools, and their replacement with exclusively lay personnel was required within the next five years. In secondary education, the timetable was reformed in 1880 to reduce the role, so prominent in Jesuit pedagogical method, of memorization, composition, and Latin recitation. The classical humanistic subjects retained their primacy, but science and modern languages were given a larger place, and an underlying philosophy of educational realism became perceptible: "The observation of things," Ferry emphasized, "is the basis of everything."[9] Ferry and his successors also worked to restore the rapidly stagnating French system of higher education. Chairs and lectureships were created, new faculties were built, the reconstruction of the Sorbonne was started in 1889, and a plan was prepared (to be fully implemented in the law of July 10, 1896) for the creation of autonomous universities uniting the faculties and schools of individual towns. The magnitude of the change was reflected in the national budget. From 1875 to 1879, more money was allocated to religious functions than to public education (55

[9] The significance of this reform should not be exaggerated. Ancient languages still occupied a third of the timetable in secondary classes, and reforms of 1884 and 1890 would reduce the relative importance of science, modern languages, and history. Students pursuing this largely literary *baccalauréat ès lettres* could also take "preparatory" courses for the *baccalauréat ès sciences* after their second or third form; but the distinction between the two *baccalauréats* was not eliminated until 1890 (Mayeur and Rebérioux 1984: 88, 110).

million francs versus 46 million), while from 1885 to 1889, spending on the former had declined to 48 million versus 120 million on the latter (Langlois 1996: 121).

In retrospect, the laicization of French education seems to have been completed even as, for a variety of reasons, its popular mandate evaporated. By 1886, for example, the Republic could no longer ignore Rome, where Leo XIII had largely restored the international prestige of the *curia* and was cultivating improved relations with Germany. French diplomatic isolation could be avoided only through an alliance with the Tsar, who was unlikely to cast his lot with radical anticlericals. In the Near East and China, moreover, French influence depended in part upon the protectorate over missions conferred by Rome. Inseparable in the minds of Ferry and the other Opportunists, laicization and colonialism proved ill fitted to one another in practice. Anticlericalism, Gambetta stated succinctly, "is not for export" (McManners 1972: 61). Domestic political considerations were still more decisive. In the elections of 1885, conservative groups increased their seats from 100 to 201, while the republicans fell from 457 to 383, leaving the Chamber divided between three political blocks of roughly equal size. In the center were the "Opportunist" followers of Ferry and Gambetta; to their left was a somewhat larger group divided between radicals and the more extreme socialists; and on the right was a growing conservative opposition of either Bonapartist or Royalist persuasions. The political confidence which had inspired the forceful expulsion of religious orders from the universities was now thoroughly shaken (McManners 1972: 61, 62).

Finally, the elimination of the possibility of presidential dissolution after the constitutional crisis of 1877 had been followed by a spirit of "proud irresponsibility" among the deputies in the Chamber: "Secure in their seats for a tenure of four years," McManners observes, "incurably suspicious of intelligent leadership, and with local rather than national interests in the forefront of their minds, they made politics a game of intrigue and tried to keep the workings of a modern State under the day-to-day supervision of parliamentary debates" (1972: 61–2). It was the disillusionment with such politicians, exacerbated by the revelations of corruption which forced the resignation of President Grévy, which fed the Boulangist fires of 1887 and 1888. In the effort to persuade Catholics to withhold their support from General Boulanger, moderate republicans quite naturally tried to suppress their reputation for anticlericalism. By December, 1888, facing 200 supporters of the Church in the Chamber, Ferry publicly acknowledged that his anticlerical policies could not be pressed farther. But by then, of course, laicization was a *fait accompli.*

The France that emerged from the Franco-Prussian War and the Paris Commune thus comprised a variety of socio-economic strata – e.g., an upper middle class long attracted to the belief in positivism and social progress; a "new social stratum" that sought enlightenment and upward mobility for its children; a peasantry increasingly exposed to improvements in transportation and communications, and as fearful of restoration as it was of revolution; a small industrial working class indifferent to revolutionary socialism, etc. – whose shared ambitions were to avoid revolution and/or reaction, improve education and, above all, rise economically and socially. Loosely aligned, these strata constituted the infrastructure for the "Opportunists," who found a stable, reliable source of political support in the reform that contained all other reforms – laicization.

A number of developments – e.g., *Quanta Cura* and *Pater aeternus,* the ephemeral efflorescence of the Church following the Franco-Prussian War, a staggering Catholic majority in the general population, the resurgence of the religious congregations, virtually complete control of social services, its powerful role in education, etc. – spawned fears that the strength of the Church was growing, and might prove an obstacle to the otherwise upwardly mobile *bourgeois.* But other factors – lack of a central organization or distinctive French voice, internal division over ultramontanist policies, the poverty and low status of the clergy, attacks from Biblical critics, evolutionists, and social scientists, rural clergy ignorant of an increasingly urban world – suggested that the Church was vulnerable to attack. This could not be a frontal attack, for the Church enjoyed the respect and affection of the majority of French citizens, and the Opportunists themselves were less interested in destroying its moral authority than replacing it with their own secular ethics. Instead, the Opportunists focused on the Church's educational establishments, which bore the weight of numerous resentments, including its tradition of teaching impractical subjects to the children of a class with rising social aspirations. By associating the palpably superior German military with "academies which honoured Protestantism and science," the Opportunists effected a parallel association between secularism and patriotism.

Theoretically, Langlois observes, this effort to find a secular substitute for a discredited Catholicism was inspired by Rousseau's insistence, in *Le Contrat social*, that every society requires a common religious foundation as the basis of its morality; and operationally, it began with an appreciation of the immense success of the Church in mobilizing and indoctrinating the faithful, offering comfort even as it provoked feelings of guilt. When it came to training today's patriot or tomorrow's republican, therefore, it made sense to adapt Catholicism's sources of energy in order to generate revolutionary enthusiasm. "National education," Langlois thus cites the pastor Rabaut Saint-Etienne, "consists in seizing the child still in the cradle, and even earlier, for the unborn child already belongs to the nation. The nation takes hold of the whole person and never lets go" (1996: 135).

CHAPTER 2

The subtlety of things

In 1902, after a lengthy parliamentary inquiry into secondary education led by Louis Liard, a course in educational theory was created and immediately required of all candidates for the *agrégation* at the university of Paris. Not without difficulty, Liard persuaded Durkheim to take on the responsibility, and the course – later published as *L'Evolution pédagogique en France* (1938) – was taught at the Ecole Normale Supérieure each year from 1904 to 1913 (Lukes 1972: 379). But there can be little doubt of Durkheim's commitment to the project, which reflected his opinion of the reforms we have just described: "Everybody feels that [secondary education] cannot remain as it is," he observed, "without having any clear idea about what it needs to become." So here we see Durkheim's skeptical, even cynical assessment of merely political reforms, in so far as they lacked a moral infrastructure. For Durkheim, the regulations and decrees of the previous twenty years "cannot have any real authority unless they have been proposed, planned, publicized, and in some way pleaded for by informed opinion, unless they express it in a thoughtful, clear, and co-ordinated way, instead of trying to create and control it through the medium of officialdom." Moreover, it was essential that the "great task of reconstruction and reorganization" be the work of those people to be reorganized and reconstructed: "Ideals cannot be legislated into existence," Durkheim echoed Rousseau's discussion of civil religion, "they must be understood, loved and striven for by those whose duty is to realize them" (1977: 7–8).

To this end, Durkheim prepared a course that was both theoretical and historical. The *theory* was important because it was insufficient simply to tell teachers what to do; in addition, they had to be made to understand *why* they were doing it – i.e., they "must be familiar with the problems for which these prescriptions provide

45

provisional solutions" (1977: 4). The *history* was important for reasons that Durkheim had given in *Les Règles de la méthode sociologique* (1895), in his defense of the "genetic" method: "In order to fully understand the development of any living phenomenon," Durkheim again argued, "we should need to begin by discovering the composition of the initial germ which stands at the origin of its entire evolution . . . Thus, in order to understand the way in which the educational system which we are to study has developed, in order to understand what it has become, we must not shrink from tracing it to its most remote origins."[1]

THE PREEMINENCE OF BOOKS

These "most remote origins" were both Roman and Christian, a contradictory bequest that had fateful consequences for French education.[2] The Roman origins of Christianity meant that its language, culture, and social organization were irremediably pagan; and where pagan religion was a system of ritual practices without obligatory authority, Christianity was a system of ideas and a body of doctrines. "To be a Christian," Durkheim observed, "was not a matter of carrying out certain material operations according to the traditional prescriptions, it was rather a question of adhering to certain articles of faith, of showing certain beliefs, of accepting certain ideas." Moreover, unlike the handing down of traditional practices, the communication of Christian ideas and feelings required a distinctively Christian education, and hence the cathedral and monastery schools; but education, in turn, required a culture, and the only culture was pagan (1977: 21-2).

These remarks had a contemporary reference, for an argument of the laicizing movement had been that the Church had "seized" the schools in order to prevent any culture from "embarrassing the faith." But the real truth, Durkheim insisted, was that the schools

---

[1] Durkheim 1977: 18-19; 1982: 156-8. Though not a professional historian, Durkheim had been a pupil of Fustel de Coulanges, and thus knew how to read primary sources. Indeed, he read Alcuin in the original, and the great medievalist Christian Pfister found no complaint with the chapters on the Carolingian renaissance: "His documentation," Halbwachs reports, "was as substantial as possible: the majority of his lectures included bibliographies which bore witness to massive reading" (1977: xiii).

[2] Durkheim 1977: 32-4. Here again, and more specifically, Durkheim may have been indebted to Fustel. His account of the Frankish invasions, for example, appears at least implicitly as "anti-Germanist" as Fustel's. Cf. Fustel's *Histoire des institutions politiques de l'ancienne France* (1875-89).

began by being the work of the Church, so that from their conception, they "were stamped with an ecclesiastical character which they subsequently had so much difficulty in erasing" (1977: 25). Moreover, only the Church, with its pagan (materialist) past and future (idealist) orientation, could thus have served as a bridge between the Roman and Germanic societies. But if the schools thus began by being essentially religious, the pagan origins of Christianity also assured that they would contain an uneliminable element of secularity; and however feeble and rudimentary it was to begin with, Durkheim observed, this secular spirit would grow and develop. Like the aboriginal institutions described in *Les Formes élémentaires de la vie religieuse*, "from their origins, the schools carried within themselves the germ of that great struggle between the sacred and the profane, the secular and the religious" (1977: 25–6).

To this problematic, dichotomous legacy, Christianity added an element unknown to antiquity – the idea of *conversion*. In antiquity, the goal of education had been to transmit a number of specific talents, which might be learned from a variety of different teachers. The Greeks, for example, sought to inculcate skills that would increase the "aesthetic value" of the individual, while the Romans stressed the "tools" people needed to perform their roles in society. Christianity, by contrast, was "a certain *habitus* of our moral being" epitomized in the Christian belief in that "profound movement" whereby "the soul in its entirety, by turning in a quite different direction, changes its position, its stance, and as a result modifies its whole outlook on the world." Imbued with this idea, Christianity "developed an awareness that underlying the particular condition of our intelligence and sensibility there is in each one of us a more profound condition which determines the others and gives them their unity" (1977: 29). Rather than decorating a man's mind with ideas or developing certain habits, Christian education became construed as a kind of gradual conversion, an attempt to act "powerfully on the deepest recesses of the soul," to effect the transformation of "the whole man" (see Durkheim 1961: 109–10). This could be achieved, Durkheim observed, "only by making children live in one and the same moral environment, which is constantly present to them, which enshrouds them completely, and from whose influence they are unable, as it were, to escape" (1977: 29). Durkheim called this "academic organicism" – i.e., the idea that teaching must not be too diffuse, that the disparate branches of learning should be grouped together, that all should be infused by the same spirit and taught from the same point of view – and he considered it intrinsic to Christianity itself (1977: 93).

These passages illuminate two elements of Durkheim's sociology that have frequently been ignored. The first is that, for all his advocacy of secular education, Durkheim's thought, like that of Hegel (whom he occasionally, startlingly, resembles), was deeply rooted in the Judaeo-Christian tradition. For the passages, as their unconscious lapse into the present tense implies, were hardly dispassionate descriptions of a Christian "contribution" to the historical development of French education; rather, they express one of Durkheim's most fundamental convictions concerning what French education ought to be: ". . . the principal aim [of education] is not to give the child a more or less large number of pieces of knowledge," he insisted, "but to imbue in him some deep and internal state of mind, a kind of orientation of the soul which points it in a definite direction, not only during childhood but throughout life." If the production of Christians was no longer the goal of French education, therefore, the goal of producing "whole men" remained the same: "Our conception of the aim has become secularized," Durkheim acknowledged, and "consequently the means employed must also change; but the abstract outline of the educational process is not changed. It is still a question of getting down to these deep recesses in the soul about which antiquity knew nothing." Like their cathedral and monastery counterparts, therefore, modern schools must provide a "morally cohesive environment," which "closely envelops the child and which acts on his nature as a whole" (1977: 30).

The second element, which disappears almost entirely from stories of "Durkheim-as-child-of-the-Enlightenment," is his palpable fascination (shared by Burke and later romantics) with the medieval period in European history. The very phrase, "the Middle Ages," itself a product of the eighteenth century, was one of which Durkheim disapproved,[3] for it evinced the Enlightenment's contemptuous and mistaken notion that the medieval period was "a mere hyphen" between classical antiquity and modern civilization, between "the moment when ancient civilization burned itself out and the moment when it was reborn in order to embark again upon

---

[3] In *De la division du travail social*, for example, Durkheim frequently refers to "Christian societies" rather than "the Middle Ages." But the latter phrase appears quite frequently in *L'Evolution pédagogique en France*.

a new career." On the contrary, Durkheim argued, if the content of medieval education was taken from paganism, it was expounded in an entirely new way, according to an entirely new conception of the human soul; and in this sense, the medieval period "sowed the seeds of an entirely new civilization" (1977: 31).

But of course these seeds required the proper soil in which to take root, and Durkheim's account was consistently one in which social and intellectual history went hand in hand. As European society became more organized and centralized under Charlemagne, for example, its educational needs required an organized, centralized institution, the Ecole du Palais. Led by Alcuin (c. 730–804), the greatest scholar of the Carolingian Renaissance, the Ecole attracted scholars from throughout western Europe, and introduced the *septem artes liberales*, with its distinction between the *trivium* (grammar, rhetoric, and dialectic) and *quadrivium* (geometry, arithmetic, astronomy, and music). The first was a purely formal curriculum designed to instruct the mind about the mind itself – i.e., "with general forms of reasoning, with abstractions made from their application to things, or perhaps with what is even more formal than thought, namely language." By contrast, the second curriculum was comprised of "branches of learning related to things," whose purpose was "to generate understanding of external realities and the laws which govern them, the laws of number, the laws of space, the laws concerning the stars, and those which govern sounds" (1977: 47–8).

Again, the distinction held a contemporary resonance for Durkheim, not simply because it adumbrated the later distinction between the humanities and the sciences, but also because it reflected Durkheim's sharp contrast between the Cartesian emphasis on *idées claires et simples* and the study of social facts *comme des choses*. For the centrality of the *trivium* (the "normal course of studies") by contrast with the supererogatory *quadrivium* (reserved for "a small elite of specialists") lent the *septem artes liberales* an unmistakably formal and abstract character. The goal of these studies was to train the mind in large generalities and fundamental principles, Durkheim observed, regardless of how these generalities or principles might be applied; and however "vacuous, sterile, and purely mechanical" it might appear to us, Carolingian grammar thus laid the foundations for the vast, ensuing edifice of medieval logic, the distinctive contribution of Christianity to Western thought (1977: 62).

The University of Paris, far from being the achievement of Abelard (1079–1142), enjoyed a similarly sociological explanation (Durkheim 1977: 76–7). The Crusades called for by Pope Urban II (c. 1042–99) unified European society and stimulated geographic mobility, and the early 12th-century consolidation of the Capetian monarchy made the cathedral and monastery schools of Paris increasingly attractive to mendicant scholars. By the end of the century, the demand for education far outstripped anything the Church could provide, and individual teachers were necessarily authorized to open schools in their own homes, outside of the cathedrals and monasteries. There was soon a large population of both teachers and pupils operating outside of any ecclesiastical atmosphere, subject to only indirect and remote regulation by the Church. The reader familiar with book 2 of *De la division du travail social* will recognize Durkheim's prototypical explanation (drawn from Darwin) for evolutionary social change – an increase of population volume and density leading to conflict, competition, differentiation and, ultimately, the emergence of new forms of social organization (Durkheim 1984: 208–17; 1977: 78–9).

The reader familiar with the Preface to the second edition of the same work, not to mention the conclusion of *Le Suicide*, will also recognize Durkheim's focus on corporate groups (Durkheim 1933: 411–35; 1951: 78–92). The medieval corporations had emerged when workers in the same occupation formed associations to secure their legal rights. These associations then became monopolies, as workers tried to restrict the rights thus secured to their own group; but each association also imposed duties and obligations on its members and, if these were not met, removed their rights and privileges. The teachers operating outside of the French ecclesiastical structure organized themselves as such a corporation – i.e., the university of Paris – and their unity was increased further when the Pope, acknowledging the university's international character, placed it under the protection of the Holy See (1977: 85).

This observation was important, for Durkheim was arguing, not simply that the European universities were international in their origins, but also that they could become "narrowly nationalistic" in the present only by betraying their "essential nature." The "renaissance" of the French universities in the late 19th century, he added, had been precisely an attempt to open them to "foreign students and teachers," to "multiply the opportunities for looking at the world from a different conceptual point of view," and to become "centers of international civilization" (1977: 86). As we shall see in chapter 4 (especially pp. 185–207), it is difficult to read this passage without thinking that German experimental science was at the top of Durkheim's list of "different conceptual point[s] of view." French nationalism as well as the "old" rationalism of Descartes were twin obstacles, mutually and repeatedly indicted in Durkheim's program for social and educational reform.

Durkheim recognized that the medieval corporations, once established and recognized, almost immediately developed a resistance to change, an unresponsiveness to the new needs of their environments; and the university was no exception. The evolution of education, Durkheim explained to his students, "always lags very substantially behind the general evolution of society as a whole. We shall encounter new ideas spreading throughout the whole of society without palpably affecting the university corporation, without modifying either its course of study or its methods of teaching" (1977: 163–4). As we shall see, the particular "new ideas" with which Durkheim was concerned were those of experimental science, introduced by Galileo and Bacon in the early 17th century, but penetrating the walls of the university only two centuries later. But it would be a mistake to think that Durkheim's assessment of the corporatist structure of the medieval universities was wholly negative. On the contrary, he regarded this form of social organization, with its combination of unity and diversity, as the single greatest contribution of the Middle Ages to French education (1977: 161–2).

Durkheim's interpenetration of social and intellectual history is nowhere more evident than in his account of Scholastic philosophy. Given its peculiar origins, the medieval university of the Scholastic period was both an ecclesiastical and a secular body, composed of laymen who retained their clerical appearance, and clerics who had become secularized. As a consequence, religion and philosophy, faith and reason were scarcely differentiated. "It was not a question of juxtaposing reason and doctrine," Durkheim explained, "but rather of introducing reason into doctrine, of rendering faith rational" (1977: 96). The 17th century's liberation of secular from spiritual studies had thus been purchased at an exorbitant price – i.e., a wholly artificial dissociation of sacred from profane, a "thoroughly mediocre kind of eclecticism," and a "lamentable restriction" on the university's field of operations. "How much more interesting," Durkheim challenged his audience,

was the age which we are presently studying, when no one was yet trying to separate these inseparable aspects of human life, when no one had yet attempted to channel and to build a dam between these two great intellectual and moral streams as if it were possible to prevent them from running into one another! How much more vital was this general, tumultuous *mêlée* of beliefs and feelings of every kind than the state of calm, which was artificial and only apparent, which was characteristic of succeeding centuries! (1977: 96–7)

Durkheim's "man of the future" thus bore an uncanny resemblance to a man of the past – neither the *bourgeois* of the Enlightenment nor the aristocrat of the *ancien régime*, but the lay-cleric of medieval Scholasticism. His intentions were thus reconstructive, an attempt to reproduce that medieval unity of "religion and philosophy, faith and reason" which preceded the 17th century. The significant qualification was that the religion, like Rousseau's, had to be civil, and the faith, like Kant's, quintessentially moral.

An equally favorable judgment (and one equally ill fitted to the notion of Durkheim as heir of the Enlightenment) is rendered on the specific content of the Scholastic teachings. In the 13th and 14th centuries, Durkheim observed, education was less a question of learning certain truths than one of learning what certain authorities said about them. Study thus dealt, not with lists of *problems*, but with lists of *works*, the latter being subjected to the exegetic method, including both *expositio* (i.e., the dialectical analysis of the text in the effort to reveal the necessary connections between its propositions) and *quaestiones* (i.e., the extraction of all the controversial propositions from the text, which then provided the pretext for debate). The purpose of such exercises, Durkheim pointed out, was to train students in dialectic, which meant that the role of logic in medieval education was extremely important. Moreover, it was logic of a special kind: "It was far less a question of teaching people how to reason," Durkheim explained, "than of teaching them how to debate. What was taught above all was the art of arguing against another person, the art of refutation even more than the art of proof" (1977: 141).

It was precisely this emphasis on exegesis, dialectic, and debate which left Scholasticism vulnerable to the derisive criticisms of the Renaissance and Enlightenment. But here again Durkheim ap-

peared as a defender of Scholastic thought and practice rather than
as an Enlightenment critic: "the way in which a principle may thus
be abused," he argued, "in no wise proves that the principle is
unsound, for the principle may be a very good one, capable of
producing a beneficial effect even if some people operate it clumsily
or to excess." But *did* this emphasis on debate serve any purpose?
Durkheim had a typically Burkean argument for suspecting that it
did: " . . . the very fact that [the Scholastic practice of debate]
played so important a role in European education for nearly three
centuries scarcely justifies the historian in supposing that it was
simply the monumental educational aberration which the pundits of
the Renaissance believed it to be."[4]

To identify this distinctive function of debate, Durkheim turned to
his favorite classical author, and virtually the only philosopher before
Comenius and Montesquieu whom he truly admired. Aristotle,
Durkheim observed, had constructed a theory about the art of
debate "to which the Middle Ages added nothing of essential
importance" (1977: 143; see also Challenger 1994). Indeed, its
contribution to the social organization of the university notwithstanding, the medieval period had contributed nothing to the
creation of new knowledge, simply borrowing what had already been
achieved by the Greeks and especially Aristotle (Durkheim 1977: 164).
According to Aristotle, therefore, true learning takes place only when
one can demonstrate the existence of necessary connections (i.e.,
connections of such irresistible cogency that no intelligent being can
deny them without self-contradiction). Such demonstrations are
made by showing that the terms of a proposition include some
"property" or "constituent part" which necessarily implies some
other term, and thus forms a unity with it; and the supreme example
of such propositions are those of mathematics, which Aristotle thus
regarded as the model for all scientific demonstration.

Durkheim fully agreed with Aristotle on the exemplary role of
mathematics with regard to the demonstration of necessary connections, for mathematical concepts are simple, possess few properties,

---

[4] Durkheim 1977: 143. Lukes 1972: 77–8, has pointed to another "strikingly Burkean" passage
in Durkheim's 1887 essay on "La Science positive de la morale en Allemagne," even
comparing it with a passage in the *Reflections*. While Lukes ascribes such conservative views
to Durkheim's "early period," as the passage from *L'Evolution pédagogique* testifies, this was a
standard argument that Durkheim produced regularly throughout his life. See, for example,
Les Formes élémentaires (1915: 87).

comprise a limited number of constituent elements and are, in any case, human constructs (1977: 144). But in *ethics*, Durkheim argued, not even entertaining the older rationalism of Kant, connections can be established only through *observation* and *induction*, neither capable of yielding necessary connections. But, fortunately, there remained an alternative form of demonstrative argument – in place of the particular concept we wish to analyze, we substitute other concepts related to the original. We then verify propositions respecting these concepts, and retrospectively apply these propositions to the original. This extension of more general propositions to particular cases, Durkheim admitted, could yield only "plausible," and never "absolutely compelling," propositions of its own. But at least these propositions have a good chance of being true, and thus there are *good* – if not decisive – reasons for believing them. Inevitably, of course, this procedure yields a variety of propositions which are both equally plausible and logically incompatible. Confronted with this situation, Durkheim argued that we must never accept any argument on the basis of the reasons adduced in its support alone; rather, we must compare each proposition (and its associated arguments) with every other – in short, we must debate.

This was Durkheim's account of what Aristotle had done in the *Nicomachean Ethics*, a work which Durkheim had taught regularly at Bordeaux after 1888:

> whenever Aristotle confronts a problem he imposes upon himself as a strict methodological rule to assemble and examine the different solutions which his predecessors had given to this problem, so that he could set them beside his own, so that he could examine them simultaneously, in other words so that he could debate them. Indeed he often thinks up his own objections to his thesis. And he debates with imaginary adversaries.[5]

This is a passable account of Durkheim's own dialectical method, used wherever the evidence ran short, and particularly in his characteristic "argument by elimination" (Lukes 1972: 31–3). But most importantly, it is Durkheim's answer to the question of the real value of debate to scholars of the Middle Ages. Far from being the way to knowledge, Durkheim insisted that dialectic and debate were

---

[5] Durkheim 1977: 146. According to Lukes 1972: 106, Durkheim, the philosopher Octave Hamelin, and the specialist on Aristotle, Georges Rodier, offered "special tuition" on selected texts, in the effort to combat what they perceived as the "anti-scientific doctrines" then attracting many would-be schoolteachers. See also Durkheim 1982: 129–33, and Mauss 1925: 15.

introduced at precisely the point where knowledge, in any strict sense, was seen to be impossible: "There was no question of making debate a substitute for proof," Durkheim argued, "but rather of setting debate beside proof in that area where strict proof had not as yet penetrated" (1977: 147). And in the Middle Ages, the range of impenetrability was immeasurably large, for the idea of experimental science did not yet exist.

This was the most important point of Durkheim's entire discussion of the Scholastic period, for it revealed what was, to him, the critical, decisive difference between his age and theirs – the Scholastic focus on *books* in sharp contrast to the modern focus on *things*. The Scholastics knew what observation was, Durkheim acknowledged, but they did not know that observation could be organized and transformed in such a way as to furnish the elements of a rule-governed demonstrative proof. The idea of experimental reasoning – that well-conducted, systematic observations might be combined to prove scientific laws – was to be the distinctive contribution of Galileo; and the idea that this form of reasoning was a *sui generis* logical operation, a new method of proof, would emerge only with Bacon. In its absence, scientific proof was quite naturally regarded as synonymous with mathematical proof, and the enormous realm of experience, about which only "plausible" propositions were assumed possible, was left subject to the dialectical method. During the medieval period, therefore, knowing how to think consisted in knowing how to debate (1977: 152).

To be able to debate, of course, one had to be familiar with the full variety of arguments, and thus with the texts within which these arguments were contained. The almost superstitious respect which the Scholastics showed toward books was thus the consequence not of their believing that these books contained demonstrable truths, but rather of the view that they contained resources which might be useful in the dialectical pursuit of "merely plausible" propositions. In short, Durkheim concluded that the cult of the book was the product of specific historical conditions, "the necessary consequence of a certain view of science which was forced upon the age" (1977: 153). Here again, Durkheim's treatment of past ideas scarcely concealed his present purposes. His whole point was to show that the Scholastic emphasis on dialectic was the natural consequence of specific historical causes; and since, by the late 19th century, these causes no longer existed – i.e., we are aware of the nature and value of experimental reasoning – the argument that the study of *books* should be preeminent loses, and should lose, all credibility, to be replaced by the study of *things*: "Today we know that there is an alternative method of proof, a different mode of argument," Durkheim observed, "and it is now no less essential that we inculcate this mode of argument in our children than it was necessary to teach the scholars of the Middle Ages the art of dialectic."[6]

Durkheim's notion that the study of experimental reasoning should thus replace dialectic in the public schools was not entirely unqualified, for he understood that even the natural sciences "still do not cover and will never cover some more or less substantial portions of reality, for the simple reason that they are incapable of exhausting it." Where experimental science provides no clear answers, we must still be capable of action, and thus of some sort of reasoned reflection; and here, Durkheim insisted, "we must proceed as best we can by means of analogies, comparisons, generalizations, suppositions: in a word, by using dialectic" (1977: 154–5). Since the propositions we reach by this kind of reasoning could never be more than plausible, it necessarily gives rise to controversy, and this was nowhere more true than in that particular realm of nature dealt with by the social sciences, where the application of experimental reasoning had barely begun, and where the study of books as well as things was still justified (1977: 155). But there can be no doubt that Durkheim's vision of the future of social science was one in which the former was steadfastly and increasingly replaced by the latter.

THE PREEMINENCE OF STYLE

The term "Renaissance" is ordinarily used to designate that cultural movement that began in Italy with the rise of Petrarch (1304–74), spread throughout the rest of Europe, and concluded sometime near the end of the 16th century. Its essential features are often described as a renewed concentration on the world of nature and of man, in sharp contrast with the "darkness" of the Middle Ages; and its principle cause, according to this view, was the rediscovery of the literary masterpieces of antiquity. Like the word itself, this concep-

---

[6] Durkheim 1977: 154. This replacement of dialectic by experimental reasoning is quite natural, Durkheim added, for the latter is itself a kind of dialectic: "Just as dialectic consists in a systematic confrontation of opinions, so experimental reasoning consists in a systematic confrontation of facts."

tion of the Renaissance was a product of the French Enlightenment. And just as he had quarreled with the Enlightenment's understanding of medieval Scholasticism, Durkheim found its interpretation of the nature and causes of the Renaissance sociologically incoherent.

Durkheim's initial objection, for example, simply rephrased his argument against the Enlightenment notion of the Middle Ages as "a mere hyphen" between ancient and modern societies. The notion that humanity "strayed from its natural path for fifteen centuries," he observed, "is historically incredible" (1977: 167). Durkheim's second objection was drawn directly from the opening pages of *La Cité antique* (1864), where Fustel de Coulanges had argued against the French revolutionary's tendency to find their models in Roman civilization (1977: 168; Fustel 1956: 11). Like Fustel, Durkheim considered the Enlightenment resurrection of Rome as the model for its political and social reforms historically anachronistic. And third, Durkheim insisted that it was simply not true that classical literature was "unknown" during the Middle Ages: "There was not a single period during the whole of the Middle Ages," he insisted, "when these literary masterpieces were not known; in every generation we find a few people sufficiently intelligent and sensitive to be able to appreciate their work . . . the scholars of the Middle Ages knew about all the main aspects of classical civilization, but only retained what they regarded as important, what answered to their own personal needs" (1977: 168). In short, it was the medieval preoccupation with logic, not ignorance of the classical sources, which defined the special character of Scholasticism.

The distinctive feature of the Renaissance, therefore, was the decline of this preoccupation with logic, and the rise of a more refined, elegant, literary culture; and its preoccupation with classical literature was the consequence not of its "re-discovery," but rather of the need to satisfy these new, more refined tastes. The problem of explaining the Renaissance thus resolved itself into one of accounting for the rise of these new tastes; and, predictably, Durkheim argued that they were the consequence of "profound changes in the organization of European societies" (1977: 169). The primary economic causes were the growth of population, the rise of towns, the discovery of new trade routes and, most importantly, the rise of a *bourgeoisie* with new ambitions, expectations, and aspirations; and the most significant political cause was the rise of the European nation states, with their shattering of the moral and intellectual unity of

Christianity, and the ascetic ideal that it represented. While people continued to profess respect for the fundamental doctrines of the Church, therefore, each of these new groups had "its own special mode of thought and feeling," its particular "temperament" whose emphasis subverted more traditional beliefs. Soon these groups proclaimed their right of schism and free inquiry in the Reformation, "the natural result of the movement towards individualism and differentiation which was taking place at that time amongst the homogeneous mass of Europe" (1977: 171).

As these economic and political causes altered the social organization of western Europe, they literally created a demand for a new kind of human being, and hence for a new kind of education: "instruction designed to produce a good bachelor of arts initiated into all the secrets of syllogism and of argument," Durkheim noted, "would be quite unsuited to the enterprise of producing an elegant and fluent nobleman who was capable of holding his own in a *salon* and who possessed all the social graces" (1977: 172, 200–5). The Renaissance criticism of medieval education was thus epitomized in words like *barbarus, stoliditas, rusticitas.* The Scholastic teacher was not simply wrong; he was quite literally a barbarian, ignorant of all the benefits of civilization. If the primary contribution of the Middle Ages to education had been its form of social organization, therefore, the primary contribution of the Renaissance was to be its educational ideal, one by which the French would live until at least the mid-19th century.[7] Moreover, while earlier changes in educational thought had resulted from the gradual, unreflective development of grammatical and then logical formalism, the Renaissance would break with this unconscious tradition altogether, introducing an efflorescence of genuinely theoretical educational literature (1977: 179).

For Durkheim, the two major currents of theoretical opinion in the Renaissance were represented by Rabelais (c. 1494–c. 1553) and Erasmus (1466–1536). The dominant idea of all Rabelais' works was a horror of any obstacle to the free generation of human activity: "Everything which hampers, everything which restricts the desires, the needs, the passions of man," Durkheim summarized, "is an evil. His ideal is a society where nature, liberated from all restraint, can

---

[7] Educational "realism," of course, emerged well before the mid-19th century; but Durkheim insisted that the Renaissance ideal also endured long after Comenius, so that the "new kind of academic system" he sought to establish still struggled against it in the late 19th century.

develop in complete freedom" (1977: 181). The preconception underlying this idea was that nature, including those needs typically
regarded as vulgar and base, is good simply because it is natural; and
the view of man underlying this preconception was one of unlimited,
unrealized potential. Above all else, the realization of this "true life"
required knowledge; and this requirement in turn yielded a theory of
education – one which emphasized not selected branches of knowledge, but knowledge in its entirety. Like his contemporaries,
Rabelais gave highest priority to the study of ancient languages and
literature; but for Rabelais, this study was not to make the student a
literary sophisticate, but to provide concrete knowledge of facts, of
"what the ancients thought and said about nature and about
themselves, about things and about their lives" (1977: 186). The book
remained preeminent, for Rabelais' focus was still on what the
ancients *said* about "things" rather than things *themselves*; and this
confusion of books and things would become the characteristic
feature of Renaissance science. Moreover, the Renaissance would
continue to pursue knowledge as an end in itself, without any
thought to its pragmatic value. But "what a transformation,"
Durkheim exclaimed, "what a revolution has taken place!":

> Something quite different is being sought for in the book: beyond the book,
> behind it, one can just see emerging, however timidly and uncertainly, the
> Thing . . . Here at last there appears for the first time the idea of a new
> kind of curriculum whose object will be not to train the mind in formal
> intellectual acrobatics, but rather to nourish it, to enrich it, to give it some
> substance. (1977: 187)

With Rabelais and the Renaissance, therefore, we see for the first
time the idea that would epitomize Durkheim's view of science,
education, and social realism – the preeminence of *things* over *ideas*,
of the newer over the older rationalism, of induction over deduction,
of experiment over logic.

At first glance, Erasmus seems to have been imbued with the same
thirst for knowledge, and to have imposed the same polymathic
demands upon the Renaissance teacher; but in Erasmus, Durkheim
discovered, this breadth of knowledge was required, not that it might
be transmitted to the students, but rather that they might be relieved
of it. Students were required to know only the best classical authors
– Lucian, Demosthenes, Herodotus, Aristophanes, Homer, Eur-
ipides, Terence, Plautus, Virgil, Horace, Cicero, Caesar, and Sallust
– a list which, in Durkheim's opinion, was not terribly long. But this

merely reflected Erasmus' conception of the purpose of education, which was the pursuit of knowledge, not as an end in itself, but as a tool for the development of the *orationis facultas* – the art of speaking or writing. The only way to teach students to write in a pure, elegant style was to immerse them in the great literary works of antiquity; and this in turn explained Erasmus' preoccupation with the study of Greek and Latin, as well as his brief, discriminating list of authors who wrote in those languages (1977: 193–6). About to be delivered from educational formalism by Rabelais, Durkheim observed, we are re-subjected to a new, literary formalism by Erasmus.

Durkheim's contempt for this educational ideal – with its academic exercises, competitions, and prizes, its appeal to the child's sense of honor and taste for praise – was increased by his sense that it still survived in the secondary schools of the Third Republic (1977: 196). The resulting indictment was simultaneously social and moral. Socially, the Renaissance preoccupation with elegance and style clearly reflected the needs and interests of a leisured class – or those who, like the rising *bourgeois* of the Second Empire, aspired to it – and a concomitant ignorance of and indifference to that larger mass of people whose material, moral, and intellectual conditions would have been improved by a very different kind of education. "In order to struggle effectively in the world of persons and the world of things," Durkheim explained, "more substantial weapons are needed than those glittering decorations with which the humanist educationalists were concerned to adorn the mind to the exclusion of anything else." In fact, for this "world of persons and things," the Scholastic emphasis on dialectic and debate had provided far superior weapons (1977: 206–7).

Morally, the educational ideal of the Renaissance provided an occasion for Durkheim's oft-repeated, puritanical insistence that aesthetic values breed immorality. "Any culture which is exclusively or essentially aesthetic," he argued, "contains within itself a germ of immorality, or at least of inferior morality." The basis for this claim seems to have been that deep respect for the morality of simple, unrefined peoples, and concomitant suspicion of the ethics of literate, *bourgeois* society, which Durkheim shared with Rousseau, and which appears quite powerfully in his treatment of anomic suicide (see chapter 5, pp. 268–90). Art, by definition, is preoccupied with the unreal and the imaginary, while morality concerns itself with action and reality. Here again, therefore, Durkheim affirmed the preeminence of *things*. But above all – and here again the debt to Rousseau and Kant is palpable – Durkheim felt that the Renaissance attempt to revive the ethics of antiquity had passed over the single, most important consequence of the intervening centuries – the Christian idea of *duty*.

In fact, for all his admiration of Aristotle, Durkheim's assessment of pagan ethics, particularly in light of the austere, Protestant morality he inherited from Kant, was always rather negative. The Greeks and Romans had "a very vague and flimsy notion of [duty]," and regarded morality as "a seductive ideal which is inherently attractive and which spontaneously gives direction to the will of anyone who has managed to see it clearly." All pagan ethics, Durkheim objected, "even the most sublime, even those of the Stoics, were derived from the eudaemonic ethics which they were never able to shake off" (1977: 209). In sharp contrast, the Christian idea – seemingly paraphrased from Kant's *Religion within the Bounds of Mere Reason* (1793) – was that "all considerations of personal happiness were banished," because they "could only serve to corrode and diminish the moral value of our actions." The Christian ethic is "to do one's duty because it is one's duty, to obey the rules because they are the rules" (Durkheim 1977: 209). The disastrous consequence of the Renaissance ideal was that the child was forced to live in both moral environments simultaneously, making him a "moral hybrid, divided against himself, torn between the present and the past and enfeebled by the conflict" (1977: 210).

Durkheim thus endorsed the Scholastic view that pagan education led to internal conflict, confusion, and the corruption of moral agency. And for similar reasons, he preferred the Rabelaisian quest for encyclopaedic knowledge to the "narrowly egotistical" pursuit of praise represented by Erasmian humanism. But above all, he admired Rabelais' elevation of things over ideas; for to understand things one must "step outside oneself and out of the internal world of images in which the pure man of letters delights" (1977: 212). This preference for "the real world" of things was not simply a theoretical whim; on the contrary, it was above all a practical, moral matter. For Durkheim repeatedly insisted that an immersion in the world of things not only provided a more accurate, complete conception of nature. More importantly, it provided man with a better sense of his place within it, and thus opposed his natural, destructive tendency to egoism: "by comparing himself with the immense universe surrounding him," Durkheim explained, "he understands that he is not the whole of it but only a small part. He no longer runs the risk of thinking of himself as the centre to which everything must be related; rather he perceives that he belongs to a system which goes infinitely beyond him and which has its centre outside him" (1977: 212–13). In short, Durkheim embraced the 17th-century view of science later reconstructed and anatomized by Robert Merton, the view that the practice of science ("dealings with things") was an essentially moral and even redemptive activity; and it was for these practical, moral benefits that he encouraged its introduction in French secondary education.

Durkheim's admiration for Rabelais should not be exaggerated. If he admired Rabelais' recognition of the preeminence of things – or at least what books *said* about things – he simultaneously deplored his ignorance of the practical value of their study. Approached as an end in itself, as knowledge for its own sake, Durkheim insisted, science was diverted from its true purpose, which was the amelioration of the human condition; and this left it vulnerable to an evil still more repugnant than Erasmian humanism – the skepticism of Michel de Montaigne (1533–92). With his practical mind and common sense, Montaigne in fact disdained the literary education of the humanists no less than Durkheim; but Montaigne considered a scientific education equally useless. Like Rabelais, he failed to see any ameliorative role science might play; and with his view of the mind as a "natural" entity, independent of the knowledge it held, he denied any formative role to scientific education as well. For Montaigne, in short, the only worthwhile education was a practical education – i.e., one acquired from life itself rather than teachers and schools. Here, Durkheim observed, Montaigne had identified the greatest vice of Renaissance educational theory. For its most serious question, raised and then begged by both Rabelais and Erasmus, was how these ideas, conceived on behalf of a would-be aristocracy and extolling purely aesthetic values, would fare when confronted with the harsh world of real things. "Such is the serious practical problem," Durkheim observed, "which the sixteenth century had to resolve, and upon whose resolution the intellectual and moral future of our country was to depend" (1977: 225–6). This resolution was the significant contribution of the Society of Jesus.

Durkheim's assessment of the place of the Jesuits in the history of educational thought was both complex and – considering

Durkheim's role in the laicizing policies of the Third Republic – shockingly appreciative. It began with three observations. First – and here the Jesuits combined two elements which their medieval antecedents had considered irreconcilable – they belonged to a religious order while simultaneously retaining the characteristics of the secular priesthood. That is, although subject to a severe communal discipline, they remained "in the world." Second, seeing that to guide their age they would have to assimilate its spirit, the Jesuits combined the strictest personal orthodoxy with an indulgence toward the ideas and tastes of their opponents. And third, recognizing that the most illustrious minds of the day had become converted to humanism, and that the people would thus be subject to an entirely pagan form of learning, the Jesuits saw that to preach, to hear confession, and to catechize was no longer enough; on the contrary, "the really important instrument in the struggle for mastery of the human soul was the education of the young. Thus," Durkheim summarized, "they resolved to seize hold of it" (1977: 233–4).

This should not be mistaken as the grudging admiration of a fair-minded laicizer for his worthy adversaries. On the contrary, the tone of the passages is unmistakably one of admiration *tout court*. From the first weeks of his course, Durkheim had been telling a story – the story of a gradual process of secularization whereby French education, emerging from the shadows of Church and monastery, had become progressively freed of ecclesiastical controls. But education had also lost sight of its goal of producing "whole men," the "morally cohesive environment" essential to this purpose, and the unity of reason and faith found among the Scholastics. French education was also increasingly literary, aesthetic, and totally unconcerned with the needs of real people, tendencies which culminated with Erasmus' emphasis on style and the skepticism of Montaigne. With the Jesuits, however, the centre of academic life was once again transported into the hands of a religious order. Running directly counter, not simply to Renaissance theories, but to the entire trend of educational thought, the remarkable thing was not that the Jesuits were opposed. Rather, it was that they succeeded.

How, then, did they succeed? Not because the education they offered was free, Durkheim insisted, and not because the subjects they taught were different from those taught by the university. Yet the education offered by the Jesuits differed from that available at the university in two significant respects, and in both, it looked more to the future than to the past. First, while the university teachers felt that they had re-discovered Christian morality in pagan civilization, the Jesuits had a clear sense of the distance which separated antiquity from the 16th century, "the one thoroughly impregnated with the eudaemonistic ethic, the other steeped in the contrary principle; the one regarding happiness as another aspect of virtue, however this might be conceived, the other sanctifying and glorifying suffering" (1977: 255). Acknowledging this distance, the Jesuit interpretation of Greco-Roman antiquity deliberately excluded everything specifically Greek or Roman, substituting an idealized, ahistorical civilization in which individuals were reduced to symbols of Christian virtues and vices – Achilles representing courage, Ulysses wily prudence, Numa the archetype of piety, Caesar the man of ambition, and so on. These general, unspecific "types" could then be used to exemplify the precepts of Christian morality, a project advanced by the almost complete absence of historical science in the Jesuit colleges.

Second, and more important, the disciplinary structure of Jesuit education departed significantly from its university counterpart by introducing two new principles. The first was that "there could be no good education without contact which was at once continuous and personal between the pupil and the educator" (1977: 258–9). This served a double purpose: first, by subjecting the student to constant scrutiny, it reduced the possibility of misconduct or spiritual backsliding; and second, it rendered Jesuit education more personal, and therefore better suited to the personality of the individual student. At first glance, this principle resembles that "academic organicism" which Durkheim had so admired in the education of the Middle Ages: "The child's environment followed him wherever he went," he noted approvingly, "all around him he heard the same ideas and the same sentiments being expressed with the same authority. He could never lose sight of them. He knew of no others." But it soon becomes clear that Durkheim considered Jesuit discipline far superior to that of the Scholastics, not because it was more "organic," but because it acknowledged that "education is essentially an individual matter" (1977: 259–60).

A similar acceptance of individualism marked the second principle of Jesuit discipline – the view that learning could be advanced through competition for prizes. Here again Durkheim emphasized the break with medieval tradition. In the Middle Ages, competition had been almost unknown, examinations largely a formality, and rewards or prizes nonexistent. The Jesuit introduction of competitive examinations and prizes, combined with the careful, relentless supervision to which students were subjected, thus conspired to introduce a new spirit of willful, individualistic achievement: "Everything," Durkheim summarized, "was inducing them to exert themselves. As a result within the Jesuit colleges there was genuinely intensive activity, which was no doubt flawed by being expended on the superficial rather than on the profound, but whose existence was incontestable" (1977: 261–2).

Not surprisingly, Durkheim considered this egoistic academic organization blatantly immoral, a vulgar appeal to the egotistical sentiments of the individual. But the explanation for this efflorescence of individualism was not to be found within Jesuit educational thought, nor even within the Renaissance education generally. For, as always, Durkheim considered these principles and theories as mere reflections of more fundamental changes in the "moral constitution of society," changes which, in the 16th and 17th centuries, had led to the emergence of the individual personality as a major force in Western history. The increased personal contact between student and instructor in Jesuit education thus responded to the needs of an increasingly heterogeneous student body; and the stimulus of competition and reward recognized that, "in proportion as each individual has his own particular moral life, he must be moved by considerations which are specifically appropriate to him" (1977: 264). In short, the moral organization of the school had always to reflect that of civil society, and as consciousness became more individualized, education had to follow suit.

Nevertheless, Durkheim considered Renaissance education a powerful but negative influence on the French character. Arguing against the view that humanist education had inhibited the flowering of the French language, he insisted that the study of ancient languages had produced several of the most distinctive traits of the national intellect – e.g., its taste for generalized and impersonal types (epitomized in the classical French drama of the 17th century), its tendency to abstraction and simplification, and its resulting, constitutional optimism: "When one is thoroughly imbued with the belief that things are simple or reducible to simple components," Durkheim explained, "one also believes that everything is clear or can be translated into clear terms. Thus reason is sheltered from bouts of despair, and refuses to concede that reality contains anything which is irreducibly obscure and unintelligible and over which, consequently, it can have no dominion" (1977: 276).

Durkheim's estimate of this sheltered, optimistic reason was extremely critical. This "mathematical mentality," this spirit of "extreme over-simplification," he grumbled, encourages us "to deny all reality to anything which is too complex to be contained within the meagre categories of our understanding" (1977: 275). And this lamentable feature of the national intellect reached its apogee just one century later, in the work of Descartes. In Cartesian philosophy, Durkheim complained, we see "that universal mathematics, the systematic elaboration of the French urge for simplification." For Descartes there is "nothing real about physical bodies apart from uniform, homogeneous, geometrical extension"; and in the individuality of things, he sees "mere appearances, tricks of light and shade, lacking in consistency and in reality, just as he makes the whole of consciousness consist in abstract and impersonal thought alone" (1977: 275). Through Descartes, the same mentality passed into the 18th century, resulting in the abstract individualism and disregard for historical context that epitomized the Enlightenment. This state of mind, Durkheim complained, grounded on "the illusion that the complex is a mere appearance," inflicted upon the French "a kind of intellectual blindness with regard to one whole area of reality" (1977: 276).

Despite these criticisms of Renaissance thought and its Cartesian consequences, Durkheim believed that the "philosophy of clear ideas" would (and should) remain the basis of the French mentality. To do so, however, it would have to be reformed: "Reason must acquire sufficient strength to retain its confidence in itself while at the same time being aware that things are complex and that their complexity is real" (1977: 276). These reforms – this "new rationalism" in which *things*, not books or style, were preeminent – had begun by the end of the Enlightenment. And it had begun in Germany.

THE PREEMINENCE OF THINGS

From Carolingian grammar, through Scholastic logic, and down to the literary style of Renaissance, Durkheim's constant theme in

L'Evolution pédagogique en France was the persistence of what he called "educational formalism" – the study of man rather than nature: "Things were not intrinsically interesting," he complained, "they were not the object of a special study carried out for its own sake, but were only dealt with in connection with the human beliefs to which they had given rise. What people wanted to know about was not how the real world actually is but rather what human beings had said about it" (1977: 279). Durkheim was particularly concerned that his audience understand that this preoccupation was an utterly contingent product of specific social and historical circumstances. The pre-Socratics, for example, had no such predilection, concentrating almost exclusively on the physical universe rather than its human inhabitants; and this was because the ancient Greeks considered nature itself to be sacred – a belief reflected in the ritualistic aspect of pagan religion (1977: 281–2).

With Christianity, however, this sacred quality passed from nature to the human soul – itself an emanation of the divine – while ritual practice gave way to spiritual contemplation. Christianity thus encouraged the individual to look within himself, to examine and reflect upon his conscience. For Durkheim, as for Fustel, therefore, Christianity marked the bifurcation of the world into sacred and profane – into thought, consciousness, morality, and religion, on the one hand, and mindless, amoral, nonreligious matter on the other. The primitive unity of nature – conceived as both sacred *and* profane – was lost. And since, by such a view, the supreme goal of education could only be the perfection of the human soul, the study of the profane world, of matter, of *things*, fell into disrepute.

How was this Christian resistance to education concerning the things of this world to be overcome? Thus posed, Durkheim's problem was not unlike that set by Max Weber in *The Protestant Ethic and the Spirit of Capitalism* – i.e., of transcending that "economic traditionalism" which left agricultural workers indifferent to the principles of rational profit making. For Durkheim, as for Weber, resistance could be overcome only by showing that temporal, secular, and profane things had some higher value; and for Durkheim, as for Weber, this was the special contribution of the Protestant Reformation. Protestantism, Durkheim insisted, "had a feeling for secular society and its temporal interests which Catholicism neither possessed nor could possess." Luther himself was "fundamentally tepid" toward humanism, and in the Protestant countries of Germany, the Renaissance preeminence of style "never exercised the same influence and the same authority as it did with us. From the end of the sixteenth century its influence and prestige were declining" (1977: 285–6). With the Lutheran Reformation, therefore, "the ground was prepared for the emergence of a new educational theory which, by contrast with humanism, would seek in the world of things, in the world of reality, the tools of intellectual culture" (1977: 286).

This new educational theory was called *realism*, and while sometimes traced to the attacks on classical learning found in the works of Rabelais and Montaigne, the origins of the movement are more commonly found in *De Tradendis Disciplinis* (1531), a work of the Spanish humanist Juan Luis Vives (1492–1540) which recognized the limitations of Aristotelian logic and metaphysics, recommended state support for education, urged the study of nature as well as books, supported education for all classes and both sexes, and praised the inductive over the deductive method (Monroe 1900: 16–24). Similar emphases on induction, on the direct, close, and personal contact with nature, and on state-supported education are of course to be found in the works of Francis Bacon (1561–1626), where they were conjoined with that Puritan context indirectly acknowledged by Durkheim and later explored by Robert Merton. In fact, Durkheim repeatedly evinced an admiration for Baconian inductivism which, in a French rationalist, might be considered unusual.[8] But Durkheim emphasized not simply the Protestant, but the *German* Protestant origins of educational realism; and though not German himself, the most important influence on the development of German realism was the Moravian educational theorist Jan Amos Komensky, or Comenius (1592–1670).

Comenius was born in Nivnitz, Moravia on March 28, 1592. Both of his parents were influential members of the Moravian Brethren, the religious organization that descended directly from the Bohemian reformer and martyr, John Huss (c. 1372–1415). Orphaned at 12, his early schooling was deficient, and he entered the Latin school at Prerau only at the relatively advanced age of 16. Precisely because he was older than his classmates, however, he quickly discerned that their lack of progress was due less to their own limitations than to

---

[8] See, for example, those sections of *Les Règles de la méthode sociologique* devoted to the observation of social facts and constitution of social types (1982: 60–72, 108–18), as well as Monroe 1900: 24–7; and Jones 1986: 62–5, 68–9.

those of the methods by which they were taught. Discouraged by Utraquist hostility from attending the university of Prague, Comenius studied Protestant theology at the German universities of Herborn and Heidelberg, returning to Fulneck, Moravia shortly before the outbreak of the Thirty Years' War (1618–48). When the Catholic Hapsburgs invaded Bohemia and defeated the Protestant forces, Comenius became a permanent exile. Finding refuge with a Moravian prince in Poland, he rapidly produced three major works in the history of educational thought – the *Janua Linguarum* (1631), the *Great Didactic* (1632), and the *School of Infancy* (1633) – simultaneously applying these theories to practices in the local *gymnasium*. Both the writings and the reforms quickly granted Comenius an international reputation, and in the summer of 1641 he came to England at the special invitation of Parliament.

The source of the Parliamentary invitation was the extreme dissatisfaction of the newly ascendant Puritans with the state of English higher education; and this in turn was inspired by the second book of Bacon's *De Augmentis Scientiarum* (1623), which complained that the English universities had failed to keep abreast of the advances of experimental science, that they should be concerned less with books than with things, and that a greater cooperation with the universities of continental Europe was a means to this end. The invitation to Comenius was a first step in addressing these failures, and his leadership in the reform movement was actively sought. But mid-17th-century England was hardly the time or the place for educational reform. Led by John Hampden, John Pym, and Oliver Cromwell, the Long Parliament was already using the Scottish rebellion to press its demands against the King, and within a year the English Civil War had begun. Seeing no reasonable prospect for the translation of his theories into practice, Comenius accepted an earlier call to Sweden, where a similar reform movement, albeit at the primary and secondary level, was already in progress. He left England in June, 1642.

These events are worth reporting because they illustrate the close connection between Protestantism and educational reform generally, and between Comenius and Francis Bacon, in particular. For among all the abundant and frequently contradictory sources that guided Comenius' educational theories, the thinker he most admired was Bacon, and the method by which he hoped to teach "all things to all men" was thoroughly inductive and encyclopaedic. Scientific education, for example, should consist not simply in learning the names of things, but in the actual observation of things themselves. Similarly, the study of language should dismiss the formal rules of grammar, to be conjoined instead with the study of the objects to which linguistic terms refer. In fact, this method should be applied to all subjects of instruction, at the earliest stages of life, publicly rather than privately, and to all classes and both sexes.[9]

Admittedly, such realism did not immediately come to dominate the educational practices of western Europe. As "schoolmaster of the Reformation," Philipp Melanchthon (1497–1560) had quickly re-established the humanist style of education; and while individual reformers like Francke, Rousseau, Basedow, Pestalozzi, Fröbel, and Herbart drew heavily from Comenius' ideas, the 17th and 18th centuries were largely indifferent to education as the study of things rather than books and ideas (Ulich 1968: 194–5). "The revival of Comenian ideas," one of his biographers thus argued, "really dates from the beginning of the present century, when Germany, crushed and dismembered, looked to her schools as the surest means of regaining fallen glory; so that the battle of Jena may be given as the date of this awakened interest in the reforms of the Moravian educator" (Monroe 1900: 169). The culmination of this revival – itself the model for the reform of French education under the Third Republic[10] – was the establishment of the Comenius Pedagogical Library (Comenius-Stiftung) in Leipzig in 1871.

It is tempting to speculate that Durkheim might have visited the Comenius-Stiftung – whose collection was particularly rich in works on German education – during his stay in Leipzig in 1885 and 1886. But for the notion that Durkheim admired Comenius, and was strongly influenced by his ideas, no speculation is necessary. What was important to Comenius, Durkheim observed, was "to be familiar with things. One must completely overturn the methods which had hitherto been employed in the schools and which substituted texts for things." Education, in short, must be scientific, for "only the sciences can enable us to get to know the world." And

---

[9] Monroe 1900: 84–103. On Comenius' educational theories and their relationship to Bacon's, see Ulich 1968: 188–99.

[10] In *La Réforme intellectuelle et morale* (1872), Ernest Renan observed that the victory of Germany in the Franco-Prussian War "was the victory of science. After Jena, the university of Berlin was the center of the regeneration of Germany. If we wish to rise from our disasters, let us imitate the conduct of Prussia" (1872: 55).

in addition education must be encyclopaedic, not in the sense of giving the child an exhaustive knowledge of all the sciences, but rather of giving him a "schematic" knowledge of their fundamental principles. For the child of the future was destined to live in the world, and thus could afford to be ignorant of nothing essential to it. "It was impossible to know in advance what kind of things [the child] would have to deal with," Durkheim observed, and thus it was essential to Comenius "that none of them should catch him unprepared" (1977: 287).

It is impossible to exaggerate the extent to which, for Durkheim, these were distinctively German developments. "Everywhere in the Germanic societies," he noted with approval, "the best minds felt the need to break away from the methods of the Renaissance, no less than with those of Scholasticism, and to educate children in the school of things." Leibniz himself became the champion of this new conviction, even claiming that "a taste for the real world is one of the distinctive features of German culture." This in turn led to the establishment of the *Realschulen*, the earliest secondary schools in which literary instruction was replaced by instruction in "things" and the sciences which deal with these things.[11] Among the French, only Montaigne was repulsed by bookish education, accorded no prestige to texts, and demanded that children be placed in direct contact with things; and, as we have seen, Montaigne's opposition to traditional education derived neither from his "scientific spirit" nor from his "taste for the experimental method," but from his skepticism. "How indeed," Durkheim thus asked rhetorically, "can we fail to be aware of the abyss which yawns between a sceptic such as Montaigne, for whom all science is an empty artifice . . . and such thinkers as Comenius and Leibniz, who had such a lofty conception of scientific education" (1977: 289). It is worth noting that Durkheim felt Montaigne stood out among his French contemporaries only because of his "practical cast of mind," which Durkheim attributed

---

[11] Durkheim's use of the term "realist" to describe the educational theories of Comenius was directly derived from these secondary schools, or *Realschulen*. Durkheim specifically rejected the term "scientific" on the ground that a Cartesian theory of education might equally be considered scientific. Instead, he argued, "it is better to define the educational theory which was born with Comenius by using the word which served to designate the first schools in which it became institutionalized in Germany, and to call it Realist educational theory. This designation clearly marks the contrast which exists between it and that of the Humanists; they each gravitate towards quite different poles: one towards man in the abstract, the other towards the real world, towards things" (1977: 288–9, 291).

to his Jewish origins. But under no circumstances was he in the same class with those German thinkers, and particularly Comenius and Leibniz, who were the legitimate heirs of the "Baconian reformation" in scientific philosophy.

At what late date, therefore, did the French become aware of what the Germans had discovered? When did "educational realism" – the concerted effort to study "things" as well as ideas – begin to slip across the Rhine? Durkheim's answer to these questions recalls a central theme of *Les Formes élémentaires*, specifically, the notion that religious symbols are the means whereby primitive societies become conscious of themselves, and that these means become less necessary as individuals become aware that society itself is a sufficient object of veneration. In France, Durkheim thus argued, educational realism became possible only to the extent that the French became capable of thinking of themselves entirely outside that earlier framework of religious symbolism, in so far as *French society itself* "was coming to be held by individuals, in its own right and in its wholly secular form, in sufficient esteem for its needs and interests – even the purely temporal ones – to appear as pre-eminently respectable and sacred" (1977: 290). In other words, educational realism entered France only in the middle of the 18th century, gained strength as the Revolution approached, and enjoyed its earliest institutional expression in the short-lived "Central Schools" introduced by the Convention on 7 Ventôse, Year III (February 25, 1795).[12]

Durkheim seems to have conceived this argument as an extension (not criticism or rejection) of the views presented in Hippolyte-Adolphe Taine's *Origines de la France contemporaine* (1876–93), which treated the Revolution as an extrapolation of the Cartesian spirit from the world of mathematics and physics to that of politics and morality. Durkheim agreed with Taine that Cartesianism was the legacy inherited by the Third Republic no less than the Enlightenment, adding that "it is a legacy which we must cultivate and not allow to decay." But Durkheim's originality lay in his insistence that there was also a second, more Germanic legacy: "What is characteristic of [this second legacy]," he observed, "is the feeling for reality, the feeling for things, for the place which they occupy in our intellectual and moral life, for everything they are capable of teaching us" (1977: 293). It was this second, more experimental

---

[12] On the central schools, see Lefebvre, 1964: 290–1.

condition of mind – quite different from the Cartesian mentality – which had produced the great scientific advances of the 17th and 18th centuries, and yet was virtually unrepresented in the "largely Cartesian educational system" which existed before the Revolution. To resolve this contradiction between popular realism and institutional Cartesianism, the Convention created a national system of secondary education consisting of a "Central School" in each department. The system was decentralized in the sense that the Central Schools were financed and their teachers appointed by the departments; but their curriculum was set by central decree, and included French, history, natural history, mathematics, physics, chemistry, law, drawing, and modern languages (1977: 297).

Durkheim's discussion of the Central Schools is extremely revealing. First, abandoning the system begun in the late 15th century, the Schools had established an entirely new organization in which each discipline was taught in a separate course (some of them lasting several years) by the same teacher. This provided continuity from one year to the next within the same course, while the unity of the cohort was dissolved in a plurality of parallel courses. Individual students could thus pursue as few or as many courses as they wished; and depending on their own preferences or those of their families, they might have a unified, integrated education, or a more specialized preparation for a professional career. As an admirer of the simultaneously intellectual and moral education imposed by the medieval universities, Durkheim objected to the degree of "educational individualism" this organization implied: "A society in which education has become an important factor in social and moral life," he explained, "can no more abandon the educational system than it can the moral system itself to the absolutely arbitrary choice of individuals" (1977: 300–1). But he also recognized that the increasing diversity of social functions, vocations, and aptitudes demanded a corresponding diversity in education; and thus he admired the Convention for attempting to reconcile the idea introduced by Bacon and Comenius – i.e., "that science is a unity, that its different parts are interdependent and inseparable from one another, forming an organic whole, and that consequently education should be organized in such a way that it respects and even creates awareness of this unity" – with the contradictory idea that "the important thing was to equip the child to acquit himself usefully in the social function which it would one day fall to him to fulfil"

(1977: 295). We see, then, how intimately the central theme of *De la division du travail social* (1893) – the need to reconcile the demands of increasing specialization and a complex division of labor with those of ethics and citizenship – was related to Durkheim's educational thought.

Not surprisingly, a second reason for Durkheim's interest in the Central Schools was their emphasis on natural science. During the first two "cycles," comprising four years of study, the attention of the pupils was primarily directed "towards the outside, towards the external world, towards the nature of things" – i.e., in a "complete reversal of the traditional system" (1977: 297–8). And no less impressive was the fact that these four years were followed by two more devoted to the study of the newly established social and moral sciences. Durkheim was adamant in his insistence that these new sciences were accessible to 16–18-year-old minds, and that the place assigned them in the Central Schools was "in accordance with their nature" (1977: 304). Finally, Durkheim approved of the "spirit" in which they were taught: "people strove to teach about man and matters human in the same spirit and using the same methods as with things material, that is to say, scientifically" (1977: 298).

But despite its virtues, the education offered by the Central Schools had grave organizational flaws – e.g., an enormous gap between them and the primary schools, the lack of coordination between the courses of study, and the difficulty of finding teachers for the new scientific subjects. This education was also an instrument of the Convention, itself enough to discredit it in the eyes of the Consulate; and finally, it was utterly discordant with the educational views of the ascendant Bonaparte. On 11 Floréal, Year X (1801), it was abolished through a law which, according to Durkheim, "at the same time obliterated all the educational theory of the Revolution." The Central Schools were replaced by *lycées* and smaller secondary schools, preparatory for the *lycées*, called *collèges*. The organization, subject matter, and teaching methods of secondary education became once more what they had been under the *ancien régime*. Latin again predominated, and science survived only through the service it provided to the government and the military. "It was a return to the old system," Durkheim observed. "Everything was to start again" (1977: 305). The Central Schools were an expression of radically new theoretical principles for which real, existing institutions were inadequate. With their failure, these principles would slowly, painfully be rediscovered in the far less innovative century which followed.

The record of 19th century educational reform was thus one of extraordinary instability. From 1802 to 1870, Durkheim recalled 74 promulgations, decrees, and/or circulars that had modified French education, yielding 15 significantly different sets of curricula. Scientific education in particular suffered from a "curious alliance" between humanism and the Church, in which the tools of literary education were adapted to the needs of orthodoxy, while liberals assumed the defense of a more scientific education.[13] The alliance itself was explained as the result of the historical association between the Revolution and science – epitomized in the short-lived Central Schools – as well as the more general association of science with "the profane" (1977: 310). These associations made, the Church sided with the literary tradition of Renaissance humanism, and the resulting conflict with liberalism and science left education subject to the inconstant winds of political fortune, from the Consulate and the First Empire to the very eve of Durkheim's lectures in 1904.

Durkheim's goal was to resolve this antinomy through a secondary education which was neither vocational (its purpose was not to prepare students for a particular skill or profession) nor purely literary (it should still prepare students to benefit from such career training later in life). Durkheim's intentions here are perhaps best approximated by saying that he felt secondary education should be *theoretical* – i.e., it should cultivate "the reflective faculties," teaching students how "to think, to judge and to reason" (1977: 314–15). Ironically, this emphasis on reflection, judgment and reasoning (in the apparent absence of any specific subject-matter) gave Durkheim's pedagogical theories an initially "formalist" aspect reminiscent of the Scholastics and humanists. Was secondary education thus to fashion the mind, in a general kind of way, or was it to furnish and nourish it? But Durkheim's point was precisely that such alternatives, framed in this dichotomous manner, distort the nature

[13] Here Durkheim took issue with Alfred Fouillée (1838–1912) who, together with Jean-Marie Guyau (1854–88), led the defense for a more traditional, humanist approach to French secondary education in opposition to the realism of Durkheim. Objecting in particular to Fouillée's assertion that "classical studies have always had the honour to be suspect under despotisms," Durkheim insisted that, while he "would not dream of claiming that cultivation of the humanities implies and necessarily imposes a particular political attitude," the "association of the Humanist spirit with the spirit of traditionalism does indeed seem to be incontestable" (1977: 309).

of reflection and reasoning itself. The mind, he insisted, "is not an empty vessel which can be directly moulded in the same way as one moulds a glass, which one subsequently fills up. The mind is made for thinking about things, and it is by making it think about things that one fashions it. Right thinking is a matter of thinking aright about things" (1977: 318).

The right way of thinking also varies according to the nature of the things thought about. Echoing Boutroux's criticism of Descartes, for example, Durkheim argued that we don't reflect upon mathematical things in the same way that we reflect on physical objects, for there are "diverse forms of reflectiveness which are a function of the objects to which it is applied" (1977: 318). In addition, thinking varies according to the *substantiality* of such things. In the Middle Ages and Renaissance, for example, reflection was applied to a subject-matter which was "infinitely tenuous and transparent in texture; the knowledge which it comprised constituted a very small body of information; it was even, in a sense, composed of abstractions, of intellectual concepts, rather than objectively given realities existing outside the mind." In realist education, by contrast, thought would be applied "to solid, consistent and resilient objects, to objects from which we have much to learn, and which the mind is forced to reckon with, according to which it must fashion itself" (1977: 318).

What, then, were these "solid, consistent and resilient" objects to which thought should be applied? Such objects, Durkheim observed, were comprised in two large categories – the one of *physical nature*, the other of *persons and consciousness* – and both occupy an important place in secondary education. Durkheim's discussion of the first category reveals his belief in the moral value of scientific education, as well as its roots in Christian idealism. We have already seen how Durkheim praised the medieval notion that the principal aim of education is *not* to give the child "pieces of knowledge," but rather to produce "some deep and internal state of mind" (1977: 30). The same spirit led Durkheim to reject any utilitarian explanation for or justification of scientific education. If the rapid growth of science in the 17th and 18th centuries could be *explained* by the needs of an increasingly commercial and industrial society, for example, then only engineers, industrialists and businessmen would require a scientific education. But Durkheim insisted that *some* scientific education is essential for magistrates, lawyers, historians, men of letters, or statesmen as well, for without it one is inevitably regarded as being intellectually incomplete. Similarly, if a scientific education were to be *justified* only on the ground of its utility, it would be an inferior kind of education; for "teaching is educational only in as far as . . . it has the capacity of exerting a moral influence on the way we are and the way we think; in other words, in as far as it effects a transformation in our ideas, our beliefs and our feelings" (1977: 336).

This observation was a part of Durkheim's broader conviction – so powerfully developed in *Les Formes élémentaires* – that Christian doctrine comprised not so much false propositions as profound truths encoded in symbols. Transposed into the realm of educational policy, this conviction yielded an insistence that modern education, rightfully and necessarily secular, must still acknowledge the real moral and spiritual needs of its constituents. The existence of cosmologies in even the most idealist religions, for example, reflects a recognition of man's place in nature, and his dependence upon it. That secular education which would replace its Christian antecedent, therefore, must also teach man his place within the order of nature.

The example of religious cosmologies, incidentally, was not chosen haphazardly, for as a student of Boutroux, Durkheim was always deeply concerned with the philosophical questions of freedom, necessity, and determinism. "Depending on how we envisage the world," he felt, "we develop quite different conceptions of the part we have to play in it, and consequently of what we ourselves truly are. The world will appear radically different depending on whether it is conceived of as being governed by the arbitrary whim of fate (as in ancient times) or by a benevolent personal Providence, or at the other extreme by laws of necessity which we can do nothing to alter." Durkheim considered this question far too important to be left to philosophy. The truth about natural necessity must be taught, not by philosophers, in their general, abstract way, but rather by scientists, and "in a particular sort of way, just as humanity itself gradually came to understand it in the course of its history, by observing the clustering of phenomena according to necessary connections deriving from the nature of things" (1977: 338).

The study of nature, in short, was the first step to a deeper knowledge of ourselves. Durkheim thus seems to have shared the humanist view that all education – including scientific education –

was essentially anthropocentric. But for Durkheim, the crucial premise underlying this view was the conviction that man was himself a part of nature. The human domain, he argued, was simply "the natural domain . . . subject to the same essential laws as the other realms of nature." And if human reality was thus a reality like any other, then there could exist "no special privileged procedures for understanding [its laws], no mysterious avenues which allow us to dispense with the tortuous and toilsome roads which physicists, chemists and biologists are forced to follow in their investigations." Here Durkheim's social realism came into direct conflict with his Cartesian culture, for here "privileged procedures" and "mysterious avenues" referred unmistakably to the traditional methods of French rationalism – introspection and deduction – which were now to be dismissed. Instead, Durkheim insisted, we must observe human reality "in the same way as we observe things in the external world, that is to say from the outside; we must experiment and make use of induction or, if experimentation in the strict sense is in practice impossible, we must find a way of setting up objective comparisons which can fulfil the same logical functions" (1977: 342).

Durkheim's call for educational realism was thus a call for a "new rationalism" in French thought. The "old" rationalism of Descartes had set itself the admirable task of molding human reason; but this had been the reason of the 17th and 18th centuries, of mathematicians who "could only see things in simplified and idealised form, who reduced man to clear thinking and the world to its geometrical forms." In some sense, of course, the French must always remain Cartesian rationalists – i.e., "men who are concerned with clarity of thought" – for this is "the essential attribute of our race; it is our national quality, and the qualities of our language and our style are only a result of it." But the French rationalists of the future would have to acknowledge that things, "whether human or physical, are irreducibly complex," that "simple conceptual combinations" could no longer be mistaken for reality itself, and that the "infinite richness" of nature, including human nature, would have to be more carefully observed (1977: 348).

The study of the second category of "solid, consistent and resilient" objects – i.e., *persons* and *consciousness* – had of course been a distinctive feature (albeit from a special point of view) of Renaissance humanism. But for two reasons Durkheim felt that the humanist approach to the study of man no longer met the needs of the modern world. The first was the Renaissance preoccupation with classical – and especially Roman – civilization. As we have seen, from the very first of these lectures, Durkheim had emphasized that education requires a culture; and the only culture available to the early Christians was, paradoxically, that of pagan antiquity. Moreover, since Christianity evolved within the context of the Roman Empire, and since Latin was inevitably the language of the Church, the Christians naturally viewed Rome as a society created by Providence, in which "for the first time man had succeeded in achieving self-awareness, a knowledge of his true nature, and consequently of the principle on which true morality and true religion are grounded" (1977: 322). The resulting postulate of Christian humanism was that Latin literature provided the best source of knowledge about human nature, a postulate which, according to Durkheim, was still the foundation of the defense of a classical education.

In opposing this postulate of Latin preeminence, Durkheim again revealed the extent of his debt to the German romantics – particularly Herder and von Humboldt – and their rejection of the Enlightenment's preoccupation with Roman antiquity. "Latin civilisation," Durkheim flatly asserted, "is in no way entitled to a position of pre-eminence." Roman innovations in law and political organization notwithstanding, Greek genius is reflected in art, poetry, history, philosophy, and science. "If there ever has been a society where human beings succeeded in realising to the full their essential nature," Durkheim observed, "it is far more plausible to locate that society in Athens rather than Rome" (1977: 324). It would be a mistake, however, simply to class Durkheim with the German rather than the French humanists – i.e., as one who preferred the Greek to the Roman model of human nature and civilization. For Durkheim's attack was on humanism itself; and this brings us to the second, and more decisive, of Durkheim's reasons for opposing Renaissance and Enlightenment theories of education.

Such theories, Durkheim observed, are based on the premise that human nature is "universally and eternally the same," that its essence "does not vary from one age to another," that man "has had this particular nature ever since he came into being, and it is only his lack of self-awareness which has prevented his true nature from expressing itself freely" (1977: 321, 324). Implicit within the Roman legal system (the idea of a system of laws valid for all humanity), this same premise could be found in the Christian idea of original sin (an essential human nature corrupted by a contingent historical event), the Renaissance study of classical literature (the means to rediscover the essential traits of human nature), and the Enlightenment criticism of the artificialities of modern civilization (distortions and corruptions of a more natural, sublime human character). And this premise granted, there could be but one kind of education – the confrontation of the child with this pure, original, unified, and uncorrupted human nature.

There was no idea to which Durkheim was more opposed. "This assumption," he insisted, "constitutes the most flagrant contradiction of everything we know from the study of history. Far from being immutable, humanity is in fact involved in an interminable process of evolution, disintegration and reconstruction; far from being a unity, it is in fact infinite in its variety, with regard to both time and place." Moreover, Durkheim here referred not simply to variations in the "external forms of life" – e.g., language, clothing, ritual, etc. – but, more deeply, to "the fundamental substance of their way of conceiving the world and conducting themselves in it."[14] For Durkheim, this insistence comprised both moral and epistemological components. The first reflects Durkheim's ethical relativism: "The view that there is one single moral system valid for all men at all times," he argued, "is no longer tenable. History teaches us that there are as many different moral systems as there are types of society" (1977: 325). The Renaissance conception of "man" itself, despite its generalized and abstracted character, was the "idiosyncratic and transitory" product of "very special circumstances" (a peculiar confluence of Greek, Roman, and Christian elements) in the history of European civilization; and in the same way, the "cult of the individual" was a peculiar, spontaneous emanation of modernity which, transposed into the Graeco-Roman world, would have introduced principles leading to the very destruction of those societies. Like Fustel, therefore, Durkheim again

---

[14] The plausibility of the humanist conception of a permanent, essential human nature was itself the product of particular historical conditions – i.e., the Renaissance synthesis of Christian, Roman, and Greek ideals. "This explains why there is something abstract and relatively universal about [the ideal man of the Renaissance]," Durkheim observed, "for he is the product of a kind of spontaneous generalisation. Yet for all its generality, this ideal is still idiosyncratic and transitory, expressing the very special circumstances in which European civilisation developed" (1977: 324).

stressed the chasm which separated the ideas and institutions of antiquity from those that succeeded the Revolution; but where, for Fustel, this insistence embodied an affection for the institutions of the *ancien régime* and an Enlightenment conception of intellectual progress, for Durkheim – as we shall see in chapter 4 (esp. pp. 185–209) – it reflected the influence of German romanticism and experimental science, and a resulting effort to discredit the ideal of a classical education.

Quite aside from this ethical relativism, Durkheim's educational theories also embodied that epistemological relativism more fully and famously expressed in "De quelques formes primitives de la classification" (1903) and *Les Formes élémentaires de la vie religieuse* (1912). Like those works, *L'Evolution pédagogique* takes the "principle of non-contradiction" – the notion that, by definition, self-contradictory propositions are false – as paradigmatic. More than any other, Durkheim observed, this principle seems to us inseparable from logical thought itself. Yet there are symbolic systems which, in the course of history, have played a role at least as great as that of modern science, but in which this principle is violated with impunity. Here Durkheim was referring particularly to the symbolic systems of religion, or religious myths, but he was perfectly willing to extend the same argument to include "different systems of logic" which are "equally grounded in the nature of reality, that is, in the nature of different societies" (1977: 326; 1915: 25–33, 53–7). If it was thus "natural" for 17th- and 18th-century rationalists to conceive of man in an abstract, generalized fashion, Durkheim regarded this conception as inadequate in the light of the empirical studies of history and society of the 19th century. What was needed, therefore, was not so much a new approach to the study of man, for this had already been provided by the German historians and social scientists; rather, what the French needed was a new conception of human nature itself – i.e., one which acknowledged its "irreducibly diverse" variations and their social causes.

Durkheim's relativism here was a direct extension of his political commitments. For while he admitted that human nature "cannot become just anything at all," he also argued that the plasticity of human nature is far greater than popular opinion suggests. If the present moral order seems to us the only one possible, it is simply because we are so accustomed to living within its constraints. History, by contrast, "showing that this moral order came into being at a particular time under particular circumstances . . . justifies us in believing that the day may eventually come when it will give way to a different moral order based on different ethical principles." Inversely, of course, history also encourages caution in the face of utopian, revolutionary enthusiasms, teaching us that "man does not change arbitrarily" or "at will on hearing the voices of inspired prophets." Change takes place "only in response to the demands of necessity," as the consequence of "the whole network of diverse causal relationships which determine the situation of man" (1977: 329–30). In sum, ethical and historical relativism – underwritten, as we shall see, by German realism, historicism, and social science – was among the more powerful resources Durkheim brought to his arguments for political and educational reform.[15]

The lectures comprising *L'Evolution pédagogique* were lectures on the *history* of educational thought; and their central theme was that this history – by revealing the diversity and relativity of educational ideals – subverts the humanist and Enlightenment conception of an abstract, unified human nature. A society's ideal conception of man, which its educational system then strives to reproduce, is always the contingent product of changing forms of social organization. Pedagogic ideals thus express, not the proclivities of human nature, but the needs of particular societies; and education is the means by which societies continuously reproduce the conditions of their own existence. What, then, were the needs of Durkheim's *own* society? What educational ideal would provide their most adequate expression? What conception of man was the contingent product of those forms of social organization characteristic of the Third Republic? These, of course, are *sociological* – not historical – questions; and in 1898–9, Durkheim had offered a lecture-course on moral education at the university of Bordeaux, where he attempted to answer them.[16] In 1902–3, this became the first of the courses on education he

---

[15] An additional resource may have been Durkheim's growing interest in the new "psychology of the unconscious." Quite aside from Wundt – to be discussed in chapter 4 (see pp. 209–30) – Pierre Janet had been a classmate of Durkheim's at the Ecole Normale, and Théodule Ribot had collaborated with Durkheim on the *Revue philosophique*. "Within us," Durkheim observed, there live "other men than those with whom we are familiar," which reveal "the existence of an unconscious psychic life beyond that of consciousness: a life which science alone is gradually managing to uncover, thanks to its special methods of investigation" (1977: 330).

[16] Lukes (1972: 110) notes that the course was first offered in 1889; but the version of the lectures contained in the 1961 translation by Everett K. Wilson and Herman Schnurer has recently been dated to 1898–9 (see Besnard 1993: 127; Miller 1996: 111).

offered at the Sorbonne, to be repeated in 1906–7 and 1911–12; and though the transcript of the lectures is incomplete,[17] its publication as *L'Education morale* (1925) provides us with some of the clearest insights into Durkheim's social realism.

DISCIPLINE, ATTACHMENT, AND AUTONOMY

To understand *L'Education morale*, it is important to have a grasp of two of Durkheim's fundamental ideas. The first – extremely important in his later studies of comparative religion – is his notion of "the duality of human nature" (1913a; 1914; Jones and Vogt). In each of us, Durkheim argued, there are two beings: the first comprises all the mental states (e.g., desires, interests, inclinations, etc.) which apply to us as individuals; the second includes those ideas, sentiments, and practices (e.g., moral, religious, political, occupational, etc.) which express the groups of which we are a part. In one sense, this idea represents a kind of sociological interpretation of the traditional Kantian antinomies. But one must also take seriously Steven Lukes' remark about how closely Durkheim here resembles Freud. Like Freud, for example, Durkheim saw nothing in the congenital nature of human beings which might make them adhere to moral rules, worship divinities, or obey political leaders. On the contrary, at birth, the individual child was a selfish, asocial, egoistic being; and to this being, as rapidly as possible, another must be added by the educational institutions of a society. "Education is not limited to developing the individual organism in the direction indicated by nature," Durkheim insisted, or "to eliciting the hidden potentialities which need only be manifested. It creates in man a new man, and this man is made up of all the best in us, of all that gives value and dignity to life" (1956: 124–5). As Durkheim's work matured, he increasingly saw this imposition of society upon the individual as one wrought with conflict. The requirements of society, he observed,

---

[17] The original lecture-course of 1902–3 comprised twenty lectures. The first, on the relations between pedagogy and sociology, was published in the *Revue de métaphysique et de morale* in 1903, and was reprinted in *Education et sociologie* in 1922. The second, on the methods of pedagogy, is not extant. The remaining eighteen lectures were published in 1925 as *L'Education morale*. Steven Lukes reports a conversation with the late Georges Davy, during which Davy indicated that the text of *L'Education morale* is a combination of the texts of various courses of different dates. Lukes adds his belief that Henri Durkheim possessed lecture-notes taken at an early delivery of the course, but that he was unable to make use of these. Lukes' discussion, like my own, is thus based on the published texts just mentioned (1972: 110 n. 7; and Fauconnet 1961: v–vi).

"are quite different from those of our nature as individuals," and thus society could not maintain itself "without our being required to make perpetual and costly sacrifices." In short, we must "do violence to certain of our strongest inclinations."[18]

Durkheim's second idea was that these "new men" of the Third Republic – who were to be secular, rational, and in direct contact with *things* – could not be produced simply by removing all supernatural elements from their education. On the contrary, Durkheim constantly criticized his fellow republicans and radicals for thinking of secularization as a purely negative operation (1961: 7–8). Religion and morality, Durkheim observed, had been inextricably related throughout human history, a connection so deep and long-standing that some moral ideas had become virtually indistinguishable from their religious connotations: "[I]f, in rationalizing morality, one confines himself to withdraw[ing] from moral discipline everything that is religious without replacing it, one almost inevitably runs the danger of withdrawing at the same time all elements that are properly moral. Under the name of rational morality, we would be left only with an impoverished and colorless morality" (1961: 8–9).

In short, Durkheim explained, it is not enough just to remove or eliminate the supernatural; on the contrary, a "profound transformation" is necessary, which means replacing it with something concrete and real: "We must seek, in the very heart of religious conceptions, those moral realities that are, as it were, lost and dissimulated in it. We must disengage them, find out what they consist of, determine their proper nature, and express them in rational language. In a word, we must discover the rational substitutes for those religious notions that for a long time have served as the vehicle for the most essential ideas" (1961: 9). In his later work, Durkheim was thus preoccupied with the idea of *taboo* – the veritable exemplar of the "sacredness" of moral rules – which he had first discovered in Fustel's *La Cité antique*, then rediscovered in the more detailed ethnographic studies epitomized in Frazer's *The Golden Bough*. The rules of morality, like those objects considered *taboo* by primitive peoples, were things "set aside," granted a special dignity, removed from common scrutiny, not subject to free discussion or criticism. And this similarity between the rules of morality and those

---

[18] Durkheim 1960a: 338–9. As Lukes notes, there is no evidence that Durkheim had any knowledge of Freud's work; but as a student of the new experimental psychology, he had long been drinking from the same well (1972: 433–4).

of taboo were still more obvious when these rules were violated; for in both cases, violations were accompanied by a kind of indignation and outrage not provoked by mere transgressions of practical wisdom or professional technique.

How, then, was this special feature of morality – i.e., its sacred, categorical, obligatory quality – to be explained? So long as religion and morality had been inextricably related, Durkheim reminded his audience, this question could be answered easily. The sacred, categorical, obligatory quality of moral rules was regarded as the direct emanation of the divinity, and no further explanation was required. But such an explanation was palpably inconsistent with Durkheim's "rationalist postulate" – i.e., that nothing in the natural world is beyond explanation by human reason. This was the problem which Kant had left the modern world, one which Kant himself found inexplicable outside of some sort of religious context (MacIntyre 1981: 53–4). It was also Durkheim's problem and, so far as Durkheim was concerned, the fundamental problem of the Third Republic: "[I]f we methodically reject the notion of the sacred without systematically replacing it by another," he observed, "the quasi-religious character of morality is without foundation, (since we are rejecting the traditional conception that provided that founda-tion without providing another). One is, then, almost inevitably inclined to deny morality" (1961: 10).

Moreover, it is abundantly clear that Durkheim did not conceive of this as a merely theoretical or philosophical problem. On the contrary, it was eminently practical, for in so far as this sacred quality of moral rules lacked any *explanation*, it also lacked any *justification*; and in the absence of justification, it would be impossible to make the children of the Third Republic – the "new men" of the future – experience its reality at all. It is here, therefore, in the first pages of *L'Education morale*, that the discussion of the Jesuits found in *L'Evolution pédagogique* becomes transparent. Feeling that he was speaking in the name of a higher reality, Durkheim now observed, the schoolmaster "elevated himself, invested himself with an extra energy. If we do not succeed in preserving this sense of self and mission for him – while providing, meanwhile, a different foundation for it – we risk having nothing more than a moral education without prestige and without life" (1961: 11). Durkheim, of course, was convinced that there *was* a "different foundation" for it in "the nature of things" – and one thus perfectly consonant with his rationalist postulate. And (*pace* Kant) precisely because a new, secular, moral order was impossible without a rational explanation (and thus justification) for the categorical aspect of moral rules, the discovery of this "foundation in the nature of things" was the first task of those who would secularize education. Science, including social science, thus took on a morally imperative character of its own.

As we have seen, Durkheim was clearly an ethical relativist, convinced that both the form and content of moral injunctions should change in response to the new social conditions facing the Third Republic; but he was also an ethical traditionalist, in so far as he insisted that morality should retain each of the "basic elements" that had typified it since the Middle Ages, hidden beneath the "guise" of religion. How were such elements to be discovered? The answer of the traditional rationalist, Durkheim observed, had three parts. The first was the premise of the self-sufficient moral agent, that "each of us carries within himself all the elements of morality." The second was the method of introspection, that "we have only to look inside ourselves with a little care to discover the meaning of morality. So the moralist engages in introspective inquiry and, from amongst the ideas that he has more or less clearly in mind, seizes upon this one or that as seeming to represent the central notions of morality" (1961: 21–2). And third, this idea (e.g., utility, perfection, human dignity, etc.) firmly in hand, the traditional rationalist logically deduced rules or principles applicable to specific circumstances, which serve as the guides for moral behavior.

Durkheim was extremely critical of the traditional rationalism in all three areas. The Kantian notion of the self-sufficient moral agent, for example, was contradicted by the ultimately social nature of all moral categories; but this was less Durkheim's premise than his conclusion, and it bore commensurately less weight at this early point in the lectures. Of the introspective method, Durkheim simply observed that it was "arbitrary" and "subjective," yielding only those ideas which the moralist himself had personally contrived: "We cannot base practice on such subjective hypotheses as these," he insisted, "We cannot regulate the education that we owe our children on the basis of such purely academic conceptions" (1961: 22–3). Durkheim's major objections to the more traditional rationalism were thus directed primarily at its reliance on deduction, its concomitant and apparently complete disregard for empirical evidence, and its unwillingness to extend the study of legal and economic facts to their ethical counterparts – in short, its reluctance to study moral facts as *things*: "[O]ne can inquire what morality ought to be," he observed, "only if one has first determined the complex of things that goes under this rubric, what its nature is, what ends it serves. Let us begin, then, by looking at morality as a fact, and let us see what we are actually able to understand by it" (1961: 23).

What does this empirical examination of moral facts reveal? Initially, Durkheim observed, all moral behavior seems to conform to preestablished *rules*. In this sense, we can say that morality consists of "a system of rules of action that predetermine conduct. They state how one must act in given situations; and to behave properly is to obey conscientiously" (1961: 24). But where traditional rationalists, both Kantian and utilitarian, had insisted that these rules were derived from some more general principle, Durkheim insisted that they were the products of quite specific social circumstances. Like his discussion of the educational theories of the Renaissance and Enlightenment, therefore, Durkheim's treatment of the derivation of moral rules bore a strongly romantic, anti-intellectualist cast. Neither the categorical imperative nor the law of utility had or could yield a single moral rule; on the contrary, these rules constituted the reality from which such philosophical principles were later abstracted: "[I]n fact and in practice," Durkheim insisted, "it is not according to theoretical insights or general formulae that we guide our conduct, but according to specific rules applying uniquely to the special situation that they govern. In all significant life situations, we do not refer back to the so-called general principle or morality to discover how it applies in a particular case and thus learn what we should do. Instead there are clear-cut and specific ways of acting required of us."[19]

Thus far, Durkheim's argument placed a strong emphasis on constancy and regularity, on the function of morality in eliminating the arbitrary element in human behavior: "Morality is basically a constant thing," he insisted, "and so long as we are not considering an excessively long time span, it remains ever the same. A moral act ought to be the same tomorrow as today, whatever the personal predispositions of the actor" (1961: 27). The traditional rationalism,

---

[19] Durkheim 1961: 26. The argument here depended heavily on examples drawn from the comparative study of primitive societies (e.g., the rules of chastity and incest).

he seemed to suggest, with its insistence on philosophic principles, reflective decision, and rational agency, should yield to a quite different rationalism, one which acknowledged the unconscious, unreflective influences on moral behavior. In short, Durkheim wished to forge a close relation between custom and morality.

This powerfully suggestive association, so opposed to the more traditional rationalism of the 17th and 18th centuries, was one of Durkheim's more distinctive contributions to French thought. But it was almost never put forward without a caveat reminiscent of Kant. For the regularity and constancy of custom, like that of habit, is experienced as the expression of an inclination or a preference. A moral rule, by contrast, is experienced as something external, an order originating outside ourselves, regardless of any personal preference: "There is in it," Durkheim insisted, "something that resists us, is beyond us. We do not determine its existence or its nature. It is independent of what we are. Rather than expressing us, it dominates us" (1961: 28). In addition to the notion of *regularity*, therefore, the conception of rules involves the idea of *authority*. And it is because of this authority, not because of the inclination born of habit or custom, that we do what we ought to do. Moral behavior thus comprises both constancy and command; and these are joined together in the idea of *discipline*, the first element of morality. "Discipline in effect regularizes conduct," Durkheim observed. "It implies repetitive behavior under determinate conditions. But discipline does not emerge without authority – a regulating authority. Therefore . . . the fundamental element of morality is the spirit of discipline" (1961: 30–1).

The notion that discipline was an element of morality, of course, was hardly original with Durkheim. On the contrary, it already held a special place in the arguments of both Kantians and utilitarians, where it identified and then directed the behavior required by either the categorical imperative or the principle of the greatest good for the greatest number. The distinctive feature of Durkheim's argument, therefore, was his insistence that discipline was good *intrinsically*, that it derived its *raison d'être* neither from the particular behavior in question nor from the consistency of the maxim guiding it with some abstract principle, but quite literally from itself. It is *good* that man is disciplined, Durkheim argued, regardless of the specific acts which such discipline constrains him to perform, because discipline is *natural* to human beings.

It is important to understand the specific features of Durkheim's argument here, for it expressed his most characteristic views of human nature and freedom, as well as his social realism. From 18th-century classical economists to Bentham to "major socialist theoreticians," the tendency had been to regard moral and legal constraints as "doing violence to human nature," and thus as justifiable only on the ground that the behavior it secured was useful or even essential to human welfare. But Durkheim's point – unmistakably drawn from Rousseau – was precisely that these constraints imply no interference with the normal workings of human nature whatsoever. On the contrary, discipline is necessary because it is demanded by nature itself; and the inability to restrict one's needs and desires within certain limits is unnatural and pathological. As we shall see in chapter 5 (see pp. 291–301), Durkheim's argument here was identical to the one presented in *Le Suicide* (1897), where he insisted that happiness is possible only given the acceptance of limits upon one's aspirations, and where anomie results from the absence of such constraint. As in *Le Suicide*, for example, Durkheim appealed to physical and biological analogues to underscore the "natural" aspect of constraint (1961: 40–1; 1951: 247). The moral and spiritual life, he acknowledged, transcends the physical and organic sphere, and thus enjoys no material limitations to its expansion (1961: 41; 1951: 247–8); but both physically (as a part of the universe) and morally (as a part of society), man is a particular, limited being, a part of the larger whole.

The constraints imposed upon human beings were thus less violations of nature than the means whereby human nature realized itself. If we regard discipline as good, Durkheim thus observed, "it is not that we regard the work of nature with a rebellious eye, or that we see here a diabolical scheme that must be foiled; but that man's nature cannot be itself except as it is disciplined. If we deem it essential that natural inclinations be held within certain bounds, it is not because that nature seems to us bad, or because we would deny the right to gratification; on the contrary, it is because otherwise such natural inclinations could have no hope of the satisfaction they merit" (1961: 50–1). This position owes a great deal to Rousseau, in that constraints imposed upon one's desires increase rather than decrease one's freedom; but it is also unmistakably hostile to liberal individualism, in that constraints are imposed, not by reason or nature, but by society. But as Durkheim would argue in *Les Formes élémentaires*, reason is the product of social forces, and society is itself a part of nature.

Like his discussion of anomie, Durkheim's remarks on educational discipline also had an unmistakable contemporary referent – i.e., the "malady of infiniteness" felt by the *bourgeoisie* of the Third Republic. Moral discipline having lost its ascendancy over the individual will, Durkheim viewed his contemporaries as beset by unlimited aspirations which, inevitably unfulfilled, in turn gave rise to the pessimism and anguish so poignantly described in Goethe's *Faust* (Durkheim 1961: 43). But precisely because he saw moral discipline not as ruthlessly suppressing a recalcitrant human nature, but rather as the means by which that nature fulfilled itself, Durkheim cannot be cast as simply a sentimental conservative longing for the imagined moral certainties of the past. For human nature, like its physical counterpart, has a history; and as that nature changes through time, becoming "stronger and more vigorous," so also must that moral discipline through which it is expressed.

Durkheim thus complained of the arrogance of those static systems of thought which "would prohibit us from going beyond the points reached by our fathers, or would wish us to return there. The normal boundary line," he insisted, "is in a state of continual becoming, and any doctrine which, under the authority of absolute principles, would undertake to fix it immutably, once and for all, must sooner or later run up against the force of the changing nature of things" (1961: 51–2). Moreover, as he had already argued in *De la division du travail social*, this "continual becoming" was not limited simply to the constant expansion of the range of morally respectable behavior. It comprised changes in the forces constraining that behavior as well. Habit, custom, and tradition might be sufficient for relatively simple societies; but with the growth of commerce, industry, and a complex division of labor, reason, reflection, and social criticism must come to the fore. A belief in the spirit of discipline – the first element of morality – need not imply a blind or slavish submission. But it did involve authority, and the question of how such authority could be maintained in a manner consistent with the "new rationalism" lay at the very heart of Durkheim's social realism.

This preliminary focus of *L'Education morale* on discipline – on the formal aspect of moral rules – was decidedly rationalist, still echoing the concerns of Rousseau, Kant, and their 18th-century predecessors. But the lingering atmosphere of rationalism quickly faded as Durkheim turned to the content of the moral life. Ignoring Kant's insistence that experience had nothing to teach us about ethics, Durkheim's approach was determinedly inductive, searching out those acts to which the adjective "moral" is in fact attached, and then classifying them according to their common characteristics. The word "moral" is incorrectly predicated of acts in the pursuit of personal goals, for example, simply because "there never has existed any people among whom an egoistic act – that is to say, behavior directed solely to the interest of the person performing it – has been considered moral" (1961: 58). So the behavior prescribed by the rules of morality must always be that in pursuit of impersonal ends. Durkheim's point was not simply that "moral" acts must be those which look to the interest of others – even many others. On the contrary, Durkheim agreed with Spencer that the morality which elevated the interests of others above those of the self could never be universalized (and thus could never be a "morality"), for no one could then accept the self-denial of others, renunciation having become impossible. Philanthropy, in short, is a reciprocal activity in which some must play the role of beneficiaries. Morality, by contrast, must by definition be common and accessible to all, and addressed to a living, sentient being outside the self. The only empirically observable entity fitting this description is that which individuals create through their association – i.e., society. Like Hume, therefore, Durkheim rejected the benefits enjoyed either by the self or by others as the criterion for the determination of distinctively moral acts. Moral acts are rather those which are "publicly" useful, addressed to society as a whole, not to its individual members; and the moral life begins where the individual becomes attached to a social group.[20]

In this way, Durkheim smoothly folded a major part of the traditional morality of the Church – the good works done by one individual for another, or many others – beneath the "higher" morality of the Republic. There are no genuinely moral ends besides collective ends, and charitable acts "of person to person" thus have no intrinsic moral value. Is society wrong, therefore, in placing a value on such personal acts? Certainly not. But the value thus

---

[20] Hume, of course, referred not to acts, but to character traits; but the argument is still quite similar. See Hume 1957: 40–58.

attached to charity is derived indirectly. Here Durkheim presents two arguments which are not always distinguishable: first, the tendency to perform charitable acts "prepare[s] and incline[s]" one to seek genuinely moral ends; and second, since – by Durkheim's conception of the duality of human nature (see above) – society is reflected in each individual, it is impossible to serve the former without simultaneously serving the latter as well. "Charity," Durkheim concluded, "has moral value only as a symptom of a moral state with which it is associated; because it points to a moral propensity to sacrifice, to go beyond one's self, to go beyond the circle of self-interest, it clears the way for a true morality" (1961: 83). Here again Durkheim blends utilitarian arguments with those of Rousseau and Kant. The individual rendered helpless against the growing tide of social evils, the only truly effective remedy lies in the social organization of welfare. And while this more collective approach denies the individual the pleasure of observing the consequences of his charitable act, social welfare acquires a higher moral status precisely because it is so general and impersonal.

The "attachment to social groups" thus became the second element of any truly "moral" education. And just as the first – the spirit of discipline – had introduced an apparent, almost Platonic opposition between human desires and self-discipline (resolved through Durkheim's appeal to the "natural" and "intrinsic" qualities of constraint), the second now seemed to imply a similar renunciation, the submersion of the individual personality in that of the group. This second renunciation received the same treatment as the first. The first two elements of moral education thus recapitulated the distinction between "regulation" and "integration" explored in *Le Suicide*.[21] Acknowledging that the individual and society were "different beings, with different natures," Durkheim went on to insist that "far from there being some inexpressible kind of antagonism between the two, far from its being the case that the individual can identify himself with society only at the risk of renouncing his own nature either wholly or in part, the fact is that he is not truly himself, he does not fully realize his own nature, except on the condition that he is involved in society" (1961: 67–8). The formal element of discipline was thus counterbalanced by the

---

[21] Philippe Besnard has recently dated the lectures on moral education to 1898–9 – i.e., shortly after the publication of *Le Suicide* (1897) – adding that they share the same conceptual scheme (1993: 127; Miller 1996: 111).

content of the moral consciousness – the ideas, feelings, habits, and inclinations which constitute the "most important part of ourselves." But these, like the spirit of discipline, have their origin in society, creating the "strongest and most intimate connection" between the individual and the social order.

To what groups, therefore, ought one to be attached? One's family? One's country? Or humanity itself? And in what degree? In this period of increasing hostility between France and Germany, what was the appropriately "moral" posture for a French citizen? Durkheim's answer introduced and articulated what might be called "centripetal patriotism." Family, country, and humanity represented different, mutually complementary stages in the social and moral evolution of France. In the present, each had its proper function, engaging the individual in a different way, and answering a different moral need. But there was no need to choose between them; indeed, a man could be "morally complete" only when simultaneously governed by all three. Yet these three groups could not be of equal moral value, for Durkheim had a clear sense of the declining role of the family relative to the State. Because the family was closer to the individual, it provided less impersonal – and thus less morally elevated – goals. In addition, societies constantly evolved toward more centralized, public activities which drew the individual out of the domestic circle, and involved him in more generalized activities.

The real question – crucial to Durkheim's social realism – was whether the State should in turn be subordinated to humanity. "There could not be a graver issue," Durkheim observed, "since the orientation of moral activity will be altogether different and moral education understood in almost contrary fashion, depending on the group to which priority is accorded" (1961: 75). Of course, the same arguments that cast the family in a role subordinate to the State – e.g., the impersonality of the State's moral goals, their removal from temporal, spatial, and ethnic contingencies, the generally more public trend of social evolution, etc. – might easily be invoked on behalf of humanity. But here again we must recall that Durkheim's constant preoccupation with the idea of society as both a necessary and a sufficient moral entity was justified by its *concrete objectivity* – its preeminence as a *thing*. For only when understood in this way could society become an adequate, secular substitute for the traditional Church. "Humanity," by contrast, was a mere *abstraction*, a word used to describe the sum of states, nations, and tribes, but possessing no consciousness, individuality, or social organization of its own. As such, it could never be a sufficient object of our moral conduct.

How was the resulting paradox – i.e., the apparent contradiction between the concrete objectivity of society and the impersonality of genuinely moral goals – to be resolved? Durkheim's answer was that we should pursue these goals, however ideal and impersonal, through the most concrete, well-defined group of which we are members – i.e., the modern nation-state. In practice, this meant that the state should not expand militarily, politically, or economically to the detriment of its neighbors, and should rather focus on the material and moral well-being of its own citizens. This internal, "centripetal" patriotism – so completely at odds with the early, colonialist policies of the Third Republic – need not submerge the peculiar national characters of the societies in question. The French genius for "clear and distinct ideas" might thus collaborate with the German taste for the complexities of real experience to achieve the higher ends of humanity itself.[22] Given Durkheim's conviction that only a concrete group could be the object of genuinely moral commitments, however, such collaboration became the only means to the realization of higher moral goals. And it was the function of the school – the public, state-supported, secular school – to create and maintain the individual's attachment to such groups.

Durkheim's treatment of these two elements of morality was thoroughly and determinedly realist; and it was social realism that resolved an apparent contradiction between them. Everyone distinguishes these two elements in morality – i.e., the word more typically used to describe the first, *formal* element was "duty," while the *content* of moral acts was treated by moralists under the concept of the "good." But there was also a tension and even opposition between them, in so far as Kantians and rationalists habitually deduced the good from the imperative nature of moral commands, while

---

[22] The reference to France and Germany is implicit here: "as a result of whatever it is beyond or outside of particular societies that inclines them to the same ideal," Durkheim observed, "it by no means follows that their differing individualities must vanish, losing themselves in one another. For this suprasocietal ideal is too rich in its variegated elements to be expressed and realized in its totality through the character of any one such state. There must be a kind of division of labor between the two, which is and will continue to be their reason for existence" (1961: 78).

utilitarians and empiricists frequently derived the sense of duty of the desirability of the consequences of morally obligatory acts. With his typical, scholastic enthusiasm for the resolution of antinomies, it is not surprising to hear Durkheim insist that his conception of society as the sole, necessary and sufficient object of moral conduct contained a means – indeed, the only means – that would resolve this apparent contradiction. Very briefly, "duty" and the "good" were simply two, equally appropriate ways of speaking of *the same concrete reality* – i.e., society. "There are certainly few if any men," Durkheim insisted, "who are able to do their duty for the sole reason that it is their duty and without having at least some vague sense that the prescribed act is in some respect good – in a word, without being disposed to it by the same natural inclination of their feelings." Conversely, although society "may be within us and although we merge partially with it, when we act morally the collective ends we pursue are so far beyond us that in order to succeed to their heights – to go beyond ourselves to this extent – an effort is generally required of which we would be incapable were it not for the idea of duty, the feeling that we ought so to act, that we are obliged to do so, which re-enforces and sustains our commitment to the group" (1961: 99). So there is no genuinely moral act which is not guided by "duty" and the "good."

This antinomy resolved, however, Durkheim recognized that these constituted distinguishable "types" of morality – e.g., the disposition for discipline predominating among some individuals, and an expansive affection characterizing others. And what is true of individuals is equally true of societies, an observation that Durkheim probably drew from Saint-Simon's distinction between "critical" and "organic" periods, but which also evokes Weber's distinction between the authority of "priests" and that of "prophets." When a society achieves a stage of stability and equilibrium, Durkheim suggested, a preference for rule and order is predominant; but in periods of rapid social change, this spirit of discipline is less pronounced, and the need for some ideal, for an object of sacrifice and devotion, comes to the fore.

The important point here – and one consistently ignored where "externality" and "constraint" are depicted as the essential features of social facts – is that Durkheim clearly saw his own century as a period of the latter type, one in which the spirit of discipline had declined naturally and dramatically, and in which a more affective, emotional morality was both appropriate and, in any case, required. It was this recognition, of course, which dictated his prescriptions for the moral education of the children of the Third Republic. Above all else, Durkheim emphasized, "the capacity for giving, for devoting one's self, should be stimulated and nourished. It is necessary to involve individuals in the pursuit of great collective ends to which they can devote themselves; to train them to cherish a social ideal, for the realization of which they may some day work" (1961: 102). Quite aside from its admittedly important role in social regulation, it was this integrative function that religion had performed admirably over the centuries. God was not simply an authority to whom we had obligations. In addition, God was an *ideal* to which we aspired, whose image we attempted to realize in our own lives. Recognizing this, Durkheim insisted, we need only substitute an empirically observable reality – society – for God, and the nature and authority of moral rules is entirely de-mystified.

It is a principle of the modern mind, Durkheim continued, that no "predetermined mode of thought" should be "arbitrarily imposed on us"; on the contrary, both logic and ethics dictate that "our reason should accept as true only that which it itself has spontaneously recognized as such" (1961: 107–8). This more recent principle – the *autonomy of the individual* – could emerge only in the context of a more rational, secular society; but it was no less fundamental an axiom in the moral education of the child, despite its apparent disharmony with the more traditional elements of morality, and particularly with the spirit of discipline. There are few passages in Durkheim's writings where he more directly and selfconsciously confronted Kant: "[N]o one has felt more strongly . . . the imperative quality of the moral law," Durkheim observed, "[yet Kant] refuses to acknowledge that the will can be completely moral when it is not autonomous, when it defers passively to a law of which it is not the maker" (1961: 108–9). Kant's solution to this paradox depended on his own conception of the duality of human nature. Briefly, Kant insisted that autonomy is the product of the will which – were it not subordinated to the senses and were it instead constituted of pure impersonal reason – would incline us naturally to duty. But the will is not so constituted, and thus we require a law of reason (the categorical imperative) by which to guide our will and restrain our senses. Pure reason, therefore, is itself autonomous. Our moral obligations are the consequence of the law imposed by this reason, in conjunction with the will, on the inferior aspects of our nature.

As we have seen, Durkheim's conception of human nature was no less dualistic; but Kant's transcendental idealism, Durkheim complained, left the obligatory character of moral rules unexplained. Reason itself being autonomous, Kant's formulation endowed the moral law with authority only in its conflict with the passions. But Durkheim insisted that the moral law is invested with an authority that imposes deference even upon the reason. "We do not only feel that it dominates our senses," he argued, "but our whole nature, even our rational nature" (1961: 109–10). Important in its own right, the argument further indicates how completely Durkheim considered his theory of knowledge – one of his most enduring contributions to modern sociology – as subordinate to and derived from his theory of morality. "Our whole nature has the need to be limited, contained, restricted," Durkheim argued, "our reason as well as our senses. For our reason is not a transcendent faculty; it is implicated in society and consequently conforms to the laws of society" (1961: 110). If the autonomy which Kant would grant us is logically possible, Durkheim thus concluded, "[it] has not and never will have anything to do with reality." Human nature comprising both the reason and the senses, we will constantly be at war with ourselves, and heteronomy "will always be the rule in fact if not by right."

Instead of a *logical* autonomy, therefore, Durkheim demanded an *effective, progressive* autonomy – something assured only by science. In so far as we understand the laws of things – i.e., why things are the way they are – we need no longer conform to these laws out of external, physical constraint, because we are incapable of doing otherwise; on the contrary, we now conform *voluntarily*, because it is good to do so, and because we have no more rational alternative. "Such conformity does not amount to passive resignation," Durkheim insisted, "but to enlightened allegiance. Conforming to the order of things because one is sure that it is everything it ought to be is not submitting to a constraint. It is freely desiring this order, assenting through an understanding of the cause" (1961: 115). But this "science" which yields an understanding of these laws is not the product of individual, Cartesian reason, any more than individual, Cartesian reason created the laws which science understands; rather, science is the collective activity dreamed of by Bacon, in which one aspect of nature (society) progressively comprehends another (the physical world).[23] This same, collective activity also extended to understanding of the laws of society. By investigating the degree to which the moral order is founded in the nature of things (i.e., the nature of society), we learn the extent to which it is as it ought to be, to which it is "normal" rather than "pathological." And in so far as it is normal, we "freely" (i.e., knowledgeably and consciously) conform to this moral order. "To act morally," Durkheim repeated, "it is not enough – above all, it is no longer enough – to respect discipline and to be committed to a group. Beyond this . . . we must have knowledge, as clear and complete an awareness as possible of the reasons for our conduct" (1961: 120).

This third element of morality played an important role in Durkheim's political and professional interests. With morality defined in this way, for example, it was clear that moral education could no longer be entrusted to the Church. For the Church taught morality by preaching and indoctrination, insisting that the de-mystification of the origin of moral rules was not only sacrilegious, but undermined morality itself. But if, as Durkheim would have it, autonomy assumed a position parallel to duties and ideals in the definition of moral facts, morality had to be taught by explaining the reasons for things, the causes underlying the particular duties of individuals and groups, and the specific ideals which emerged at certain stages of social evolution. The original element in Durkheim's argument is not his insistence that this could be done, but rather his insistence that it could be done *without diminishing the dignity and authority of moral rules*; on the contrary, as an element of morality itself, the rational comprehension of the reasons for moral rules and ideals became a *condition of virtuous conduct itself*. And this rational comprehension was the function, not of the Church, but of the school, and, more particularly, of the nascent but rapidly growing discipline of sociology.

THE DEVELOPMENT OF MORALITY IN THE CHILD

Consistent with his ethical relativism and advocacy of reform, Durkheim felt that these three elements of morality – the spirit of discipline, the attachment to social groups, and the autonomy of the

---

[23] This notion again sheds light on Durkheim's notion of the social origins of the categories of human reason, indicating the extent to which his theory of knowledge was subservient to his theory of morality. See Durkheim and Mauss 1963; Durkheim 1915: 21–33.

individual – exist in the child only as the most general predispositions. This is not to say that the child is a *tabula rasa*. Despite the
"inconstancy" of ideas and feelings which the child shares with
primitive peoples, for example, his tendency toward habit predis-
poses him to that behavioral regularity essential to the moral life.
Similarly, the child's vulnerability to suggestion encourages the
external imposition of discipline and control.[24] But these, Durkheim
insisted, are mere tendencies, inclinations which might be "crystallized" in one direction or another depending upon subsequent
education. This education begins, of course, in the family; but
precisely because the modern family is small, intimate, and supports
constant interpersonal contact, Durkheim observed, it is unable to
inspire any sense of the abstract, impersonal, and immutable
character of moral rules. So it is in the school – the public school of
the Third Republic – that the child must acquire the Kantian sense
of the moral law, learning "to do his duty because it is his duty"
(1961: 147).

For Durkheim, therefore, the discipline of the school was far more
than simply a necessary condition for learning. On the contrary, it
was learning itself, a part of the moral education of the child, and
the intermediary between the affective morality of the family and
the more rigorous ethic of civil society. "It is by respecting the school
rules," Durkheim insisted, "that the child learns to respect rules in
general, that he develops the habit of self-control and restraint
simply because he should control and restrain himself. It is a first
initiation into the austerity of duty. Serious life" – the phrase
Durkheim later used to characterize the *religious* life – "has now
begun" (1961: 149). Since it is through the teacher that these rules
are revealed to the child, such individuals must themselves be
decisive and self-disciplined; but above all, they must have a priest-
like belief in the greatness of their task – a comparison that deserves
a lengthy quotation:

It is the priest's lofty conception of his mission that gives him the authority
that so readily colors his language and bearing. For he speaks in the name
of a God, who he feels in himself and to whom he feels himself much closer

---

[24] Like Freud, therefore, Durkheim viewed children through the same lens that he viewed
primitive peoples. The habits of the child, for example, were analogous to the customs of
savages. Durkheim's discussion of the child's "natural suggestibility" was based upon his
reading of the early psychological studies of Jean-Marie Guyau, Alfred Binet, and Victor
Henry. Durkheim 1961: 131–2, 136–7, 139–42.

than the laymen in the crowds he addresses. So, the lay teacher can and should have something of this same feeling. He also is an instrument of a great moral reality which surpasses him and with which he communicates more directly than does the child, since it is through his intermediation that the child communicates with it. Just as the priest is the interpreter of God, [the lay teacher] is the interpreter of the great moral ideas of his time and country. Whatever is linked with these ideas, whatever the significance and authority attributed to them, necessarily spreads to him and everything coming from him since he expresses these things and embodies them in the eyes of children. (1961: 155)

A noteworthy feature of this discussion is that Durkheim had described both the nature of school discipline and the authority of the teacher without mentioning the idea of punishment or reward. This deliberate oversight is particularly interesting in light of Durkheim's criticism, in *L'Evolution pédagogique*, of the Jesuits' intro-duction of rewards and prizes into education, which resulted in a "blatantly immoral" emphasis on individualism and competition (1961: 261–2). "Sanctions," Durkheim here again asserted, "do not have the preponderant role sometimes assigned to them in the development of the spirit of discipline" (1961: 157). As he had been in *De la division du travail social*, however, Durkheim was convinced that there could be no rule without a corresponding sanction, and that the latter must thus in some way assist in the functioning of the former (1984: 28–9).

What, then, is the proper role of sanctions – especially punitive sanctions – in the discipline of the school? The "preventive" theory, Durkheim observed, depends upon the mental association formed between the idea of an anticipated action and that of the suffering expected to follow from it, so that the fear of the latter prevents the performance of the former. But punishment, Durkheim objected, "acts from the outside and on externals," and "cannot touch the moral life at its source"; even if effective as a constraint on disruptive impulses, it could never be a "moralizing instrument" (1961: 161). In short, what Durkheim wanted was less the student's obedience than the fulfillment of his duty, something he felt could never be assured of by punishment conceived and implemented as a deterrent. This raised the alternative, "expiatory" theory, which suggested that the role of punishment is atonement, nullifying the offense and its consequences, and restoring things to their previous state of equi-librium. The difficulty with this theory, as Durkheim acknowledged, was that it made punishment simply another form of retaliation, repaying suffering with further suffering, evil with evil – a principle "no longer acceptable to the contemporary moral conscience."[25] But what renders punishment efficacious, Durkheim insisted, is not the suffering that accompanies it; rather, it is the respect for the authority of moral rules which it restores. Moral rules, in short, are *sacred things*, endowed with intangible qualities of prestige, force, and energy; and the violation of such rules with impunity renders them vulgar and profane, resulting in the "demoralization" of the collective conscience. For Durkheim, therefore, the function of punishment was indeed expiation; but the instrument of this expiation was less suffering than the restoration of the faith in sacred things.

The expiatory function of *punition sans souffrance* thus affirmed, Durkheim turned to the more practical question of how this punishment should be applied in the school. The question raised serious difficulties for Durkheim, for as an educational realist, he was committed to the notion that children should learn under the influence and discipline of "natural things." Indeed, other writers similarly committed had already questioned whether any "artificial" discipline should be introduced in the school at all. In *Emile*, of course, Rousseau had argued that, at least until the age of twelve, punishment should simply allow misconduct to bring on its own natural consequences (1979: 77–163). Spencer, arguing on more utilitarian grounds, had extended the same theory to the child's later, moral education. An action whose consequences were beneficial and pleasurable was "good," Spencer insisted, while one whose consequences were maleficent and painful was "bad"; and since bad actions would thus quite naturally produce painful consequences for the child, and the memory of those consequences would surely prevent the recurrence of such actions, the goal of moral education could be reduced to eliminating all artificial factors which might prevent the child from experiencing the natural consequences of his conduct (1961: 169–70). And Durkheim was also aware of the school for peasants established by Tolstoy at Yosnaya Polyana in 1859, which was predicated on the assumption that the natural condition for learning was freedom, and that the only pedagogical method was first-hand experience. Inspired by *Emile*, Tolstoy had insisted that children be allowed to come and go as they pleased, following the

---

[25] Durkheim (1961: 165) attributes this objection to the expiatory theory to Jean-Marie Guyau.

"natural bent" of their curiosity, and that no constraints, formulas, dogmas, or "civilized" values be imposed upon them.

Durkheim was attracted to each of these examples of education under the influence of "natural things." But the realism of Rousseau's theory extended only to the physical education of the child, after which the artificial intervention of the teacher became necessary (1961: 168–9). Spencer's focus on the consequences of actions seemed a better long-term foundation for the moral life than a respect for authorities whose influence might later be avoided, while punishment derived from "the nature of things," following "naturally and necessarily" from actions, possessed precisely that quality of impersonality that Durkheim considered essential to the moral law. But there was no immediately apparent connection between a phenomenon and its cause, Durkheim objected, so that the child – like the primitive – was unlikely consistently to attribute present sufferings to the appropriate transgressions of the past; and this difficulty was exacerbated in advanced industrial societies, where the temporal and spatial "distance" between acts and their negative consequences was far greater than in their primitive counterparts.[26] Most important, Spencer's theory ignored the purpose of school discipline itself, which was less to establish associations between specific acts and their consequences than to inculcate the habit of self-discipline for later life. It was the habit of self-discipline, not specific actions, whose consequences were beneficent; and the injurious consequences of misdeeds were not limited to the specific consequences of acts, but extended to the subversion of the rules they violated and denied. Since these consequences would become evident only long after the child left the school, it was necessary for the teacher to intervene at an early stage, linking sanctions to rules in a manner that artificially anticipated those of later life (1961: 173, 179). And Tolstoy's theory was simply "contrary to everything we know of history." People learn not from the love of knowledge, but because their societies impose the duty or obligation of learning upon them. "What man has done only through a sense of duty from

---

[26] It is this condition of advanced societies, of course, which requires sociology itself: "Made to regulate social relationships in societies as complex as ours, morality itself is very complex. Behavior condemned by morality is repudiated because of its diverse repercussions that reach throughout the whole extent of the social structure – repercussion that cannot be seen with the naked eye but that science alone discovers step by step, thanks to its special methods and funded knowledge" (1961: 173).

the beginning of history," Durkheim concluded, "the child can do only through a sense of duty as he enters into life" (1961: 181).

Nonetheless, Durkheim considered the underlying principle of these three theories – that punishment should be the natural consequence of the act, not something artificially imposed upon it – incontestable. The original element in Durkheim's theory was his realist insistence that *society was itself a part of nature*, that the disapproval and reproach provoked by antisocial behavior was thus education "under the influence of natural things," and that rules and laws did no more than codify, organize, and systematize these spontaneous societal reactions. Punishment, therefore, was only the means to an end, that of giving the child "the most vivid impression possible of the feeling evoked by his behavior," of "reaffirming the obligation at the moment when it is violated, in order to strengthen the sense of duty, both for the guilty party and for those witnessing the offense – those whom the offense tends to demoralize" (1961: 182). For this purpose, corporal punishment – a product of the medieval school – was unnecessary. In the public school of the Third Republic, therefore, corporal punishment was to be absolutely forbidden, a posture consistent with the "religious" respect for the person found in more advanced societies. In short, the "natural" reproach of society was sufficient to instill the first element of morality – the spirit of discipline – in the child.

Durkheim insisted that the second element of morality – the attachment to social groups – was no more "innate" than the first, and this in turn led him to a discussion of the distinction between "egoistic" and "altruistic" tendencies.[27] In ordinary usage, he suggested, the distinction is found between those tendencies whose goal is the pleasure of the agent (egoism) and those whose goal is the pleasure of some other person (altruism), an antithesis so sharp as to make it inconceivable that both had the same origin. Thus we discover the source of egoism in the "natural constitution of man," that selfish human nature epitomized in the child and the savage, while the origin of altruism is found in the artificial, relatively belated influences of culture and civilization. This distinction between egoism and altruism acknowledged, and their separate

---

[27] As already indicated, the distinction between the first two "elements" of moral education (the spirit of discipline and the attachment to social groups) mirrors the discussion, in *Le Suicide*, between "regulation" and "integration."

causes admitted, the function of moral education could only be to introduce and develop those altruistic dispositions initially lacking in the child.

Adamantly and simultaneously, Durkheim resisted the distinction, the separation of causes, and the function of education this distinction and separation implied. The goal of altruistic tendencies, for example, is not always some other person(s), but may extend to abstract ideals (e.g., the scholar's disinterested pursuit of knowledge) whose value is disproportionate to any utilitarian consequences their realization might secure. There are also disinterested, utterly unselfish tendencies (e.g., the feuds between kin groups) whose object is to give pain rather than pleasure to others. And there are selfish, compulsive dispositions (e.g., those of alcoholics, kleptomaniacs, and anorexics) whose goal can hardly be described as the pursuit of pleasure. Man does not seek pleasure, Nietzsche once observed, only the Englishman does that. In an only slightly less anti-utilitarian mood, Durkheim insisted that any distinction between egoistic and altruistic tendencies derived from differences in the *kinds of pleasures* they pursued was simply incoherent.

How, then, are we to distinguish between egoistic and altruistic actions? Durkheim's answer was that we should focus on the *kinds of objects* to which we are attached. At times, for example, these objects are simply aspects of ourselves (e.g., our bodies, our health, our reputations), in which case the attachment for them might reasonably be called "centripetal" or egoistic – i.e., directed toward the self. At other times, our tendencies are "centrifugal" or altruistic – i.e., directed toward objects outside of us (e.g., family, friends, occupational groups, country, morality), which have an existence independent of our own. But neither tendency, Durkheim insisted, is more or less "natural" than the other, nor does altruism (as the utilitarians claimed) derive from a more enlightened egoism. On the contrary, our attachment for things external presupposes their representations within us. The "selfish human nature" epitomized in children and savages – and here again the presence of Rousseau is palpable – is simply the consequence of their weaker, less expansive field of consciousness, for both egoism and altruism have deep roots in our nature.

This alternative distinction in turn yielded a strategy for stimulating the altruistic sentiments so crucial to the Third Republic. For us to be attached to a social group, Durkheim had suggested, means to have the representation of that group firmly within us, so that it "is a part of our consciousness," and "cannot disappear without creating a painful void." The creation of this attachment was essentially a matter of conditioning – i.e., it was essential to repeat this representation to the child again and again, to link it with other ideas of a similar nature, and to embellish it with enough color, force, and life to stimulate action. As always, Durkheim was adamant in his insistence that moral education was not a matter of theory, reason or speculation; rather, it was a matter of action, will, and emotion:

[B]y broadening gradually the consciousness of the child so as to infuse it with the idea of the social groups to which he belongs and will belong, by linking, through repetition, these ideas intimately with the greatest possible number of other ideas and feelings, so that the former are constantly called to mind and come to occupy such an important place in the child's mind that he will resist any diminution or weakening of them; by communicating them with such warmth and sincerity that their emotive power becomes an active force; by developing that power of action through exercise – such is the general method we must follow to commit the child to the collective goals that he must pursue. (1961: 229–30)

The twin vehicles of this method of moral conditioning were to be the school environment itself and the content of its teachings. Discussing the first, Durkheim articulated his vision of the public school as an intermediary between the family and the state. More extensive than the family and based upon a fortuitous gathering of subjects by age rather than ties of blood, the school remained sufficiently small to allow intimate personal relationships to crystallize. Indeed, it was only through such associations that societies larger than the family had ever become possible. As such, the school was a "precious instrument," the natural successor to those *sociétés intermédiaires* – the province, commune, and guild – whose authority had been destroyed by the centralizing policies of the monarchy and then the Revolution. The lack of such associations in France, Durkheim argued, constituted a "serious crisis," contrasting sharply with the student life he had observed during his travels of 1885–6. "In Germany," he observed,

everything is done in a group. People sing together. They take walks together. They play together. They philosophize together, or talk about science and literature. All kinds of associations, corresponding to every kind of human activity, function in parallel ways; thus, the young man is constantly involved in group life. He engages in serious occupations in a group, and he relaxes in a group.[28]

In France, by contrast, the principle was that of the isolated individual, resistant to the group and hostile to its obligations and restrictions. Durkheim acknowledged a more recent renaissance of intermediate associations in French life – e.g., commercial and industrial organizations, scientific societies, student groups, even movements toward the administrative decentralization of the towns and provinces. For the most part, however, he treated these as "legal artifacts," external arrangements revealing a need, but not yet corresponding to deeply held feelings. "The central fact," he insisted, "is that [these intermediate associations] cannot become living realities unless they are willed, desired, demanded by grass-roots sentiment – in other words, unless the spirit of association comes alive, not only in a few educated circles, but in the deep mass of the population" (1961: 238).

To instill this "spirit of association" – so palpable among German university students of the 1880s – was the special function of the public school of the Third Republic: "[A]t this decisive time," Durkheim said, referring to the child's first steps beyond the home,

[i]f the child . . . is carried along in the current of social life, the chances are strong that he will remain oriented in this way throughout his life. If he develops the habit of expressing his interests and activities in various groups, he will keep the habit in his post-school life; and then the action of the lawmaker will really be fruitful, for it will emerge from soil that education will have prepared. This is what accounts for the tremendous social significance of the school today. (1961: 239)

The teacher must thus "lie in wait for everything" – e.g., a common emotion which grips the class upon reading a touching piece of literature, a shared moral judgment passed upon some historical character, etc. – that might lead the class "to sense their unity in a common enterprise." Such events occurring, the teacher must crystallize the resulting sentiments in the more durable, symbolic form of easily remembered precepts, maxims, and proverbs. The collective life of the class should be emphasized by sanctions that reward and punish the group rather than the individual, and the record of past awards made palpable to provide the class a sense of

---

[28] Durkheim 1961: 234. The passage is virtually identical, both in tone and content, to several in Durkheim's "La Philosophie dans les universités allemandes" (1887a). See chapter 4, pp. 178–85.

history, of enduring through time (1961: 239–48). By such devices, the shallow individualism of the child could be overcome, and his attachment to the group strengthened.

Quite aside from the moral environment of the classroom, however, there was the content of its teachings, a topic that allowed Durkheim to expand the critique of Cartesian rationalism begun in *L'Evolution pédagogique*. "[W]e understand things," Durkheim began, referring specifically to the French intellect, "in proportion as they are simple," while the complex "can be conceptualized only in a murky and confused way." From this followed the quite natural tendency to deny any reality to complex things, to view their apparent complexity as the product of our intellectual limitations, and to reduce them to their simpler elements. This tendency was epitomized in Descartes, for whom the secondary qualities of matter – e.g., form, color, sound, etc. – were illusory, while mathematical extension constituted reality itself. Cartesianism, Durkheim then explained, "is deeply rooted in our national thinking; it has become one of the characteristic traits of the French mind, at least until recent times." Every Frenchman is "to some degree a conscious or unconscious Cartesian. The need to distinguish and clarify, which characterizes our national temper, inclines us to turn away from anything too complex to be easily and clearly conceptualized; and that which we are inclined not to see and not to look at is something we are naturally inclined to deny" (1961: 253–4). The French language itself is "analytical," well suited to reduction, simplicity, and abstraction, but inadequate when faced with the depth and complexity of a Faust or a Hamlet.

This was not the prolegomena to a general critique of rationalism, for Durkheim consistently defended the central postulate of a rationalist education – i.e., that nothing in the nature of things was irreducibly irrational. But for Durkheim, there were things in nature that were *rational* and also irreducibly *complex*. One element of this belief – as we will see in chapter 3 (see pp. 153–60) – lay in Boutroux's notion of discontinuous levels of being, each displaying an element not present in its predecessor, and thus irreducible to it. For Boutroux, this anti-reductionist view provided a solution for the classic French problem of freedom versus determinism, the evolution of consciousness introducing the new, irreducible level of mind. For Durkheim, it provided an infrastructure for a realist interpretation of society. If complex wholes were reducible to their constituent parts, then only the individual was real, and society was a mere mental construct; and a mental construct, Durkheim was quick to observe, can never be the object of our moral allegiance. "It would be absurd," he insisted, "to sacrifice the real, concrete, and living being that we are to a purely verbal artifact. We can only dedicate ourselves to society if we see in it a moral power more elevated than ourselves" (1961: 257).

To "shake this simplistic prejudice" and "give the child a sense of the real complexity of things" was thus the *goal* of a truly moral education. The *means* to this end was to teach the child how science is constructed; and here Durkheim clearly meant not mathematics, but the experimental sciences:

To forestall simplistic thinking, it is . . . necessary first to give the child a defense against these constructions and deductions. The child must be brought to see how science is studied; how the labor, time and trouble that study entails contrasts with such deductive improvisations . . . In short, we must convey the need for experimentation, for observation, and the necessity of getting out of ourselves and submitting to the teachings of experience. (1961: 262–3)

This was Durkheim's response to those more mystical, irrationalist thinkers who insisted on the essential amorality of science, and advocated a more aesthetic education reminiscent of the Renaissance. The study of art and literature, Durkheim insisted, "makes us live in an imaginary environment," and should thus assume only a secondary, accessory role in education. By contrast, the study of the physical and biological sciences – far from being amoral – could play a role in the formation of moral character, for their study prepared the child for an understanding of the real complexity of the natural, empirical world – including society. Scientific education – by teaching us not only *about* nature, but about our place *within* nature – could be morally edifying.

The "whole man" required by the Third Republic, therefore, was very different from the man which had satisfied the needs of earlier societies. Faced with the seductions of an increasingly materialistic world, for example, this new man must control his desires and accept limitations; but this respect for the "spirit of discipline" would come not from the ruthless suppression of nature dictated by some abstract, absolute rule, but from respect for society – itself a natural thing – so that the acceptance of its demands would be the fulfillment rather than the violation of nature. In sharp contrast to traditional societies, which depend upon habit and custom to secure obedience, and even to more recent societies, which depend on the categorical imperative or the "greatest happiness" principle, the man of the Third Republic would thus need to know *why* society makes these demands – in short, to understand the social causes underlying the moral constraints to which he submits himself. Durkheim explained the renunciation of individual interest traditionally implied by submission to the group in the same manner – i.e., since our "most important" interests have their origin in society, subjecting private to public interests can never be a violation of the self, but rather its enlightened fulfillment; and here again, "enlightenment" meant a sociologist's understanding of the source of group demands. Finally, this same sociological understanding of "why things are the way they are" provided Durkheim's answer to the problem of freedom and autonomy – i.e., in so far as we understand the laws of things, we conform to them, *not* out of external, physical constraint, but *voluntarily*, because it's the good and rational thing to do. Freedom, in short, is a product of the rational understanding of the laws of nature.

Taken together, *L'Evolution pédagogique* and *L'Education morale* help us to place Durkheim within the larger context of anticlerical educational reform described in chapter 1. We have seen, for example, that many of the anticlericals had a reluctant admiration for the system of moral influence they were proposing to destroy, combined with some vision of a secular religion for the Third Republic. Durkheim seems to have shared both the admiration and the vision, without the reluctance, praising the Christian – indeed, Jesuit – idea of education as a kind of gradual conversion which would effect the transformation of the "whole man" of the future. The eudaemonic ethics of antiquity, revived by the Renaissance, was dismissed in favor of the more austere, Christian conception of duty. This was combined with strong criticism of the Renaissance and Enlightenment ideal of literary, philosophical education, as well as an insistence that laicization must not only remove the supernatural, but replace it with the scientific study – not of *books* or of *style* – but of *things*.

The same two works provide a fairly complete picture of what I have described as Durkheim's "social realist" vocabulary. At the center of that vocabulary, of course, was the notion that social phenomena are *things* rather than *ideas*; but in his typical manner, Durkheim reinforced this initial distinction with several other dichotomous pairs, each isomorphic with the first. Social things are *concrete*, for example, while ideas are *abstract*. Social phenomena are also more *complex*, where ideas are *simple*. Society is conceived, not only as "similar to" nature, but as itself a *real, natural thing, a part of nature*, and subject to its laws, in sharp contrast to the formulations of Hobbes and Rousseau, which made society a product of art. Deductive inferences drawn logically from first principles are repeatedly rejected in favor of inductive generalizations based on careful observations and experimentation (or, where experiments are impossible – as in some of the social sciences – systematic comparisons). And this in turn reflects Durkheim's ambivalence to – and occasional, searing hostility for – Descartes, combined with his embracement of the Baconian educational reforms of Comenius. Most important, things that are concrete and complex provide "solid, consistent and resilient objects" – i.e., objects with the power to limit and constrain the anomic and egoistic forces of *bourgeois* individualism, as well as the capacity to secure the moral allegiance and veneration of future generations of French citizens. These were things that simple and abstract ideas could never do.

The course of lectures that became *L'Education morale* has recently been dated to 1898–9 – i.e., immediately after the publication of *Le Suicide* (1897) (Besnard 1993: 127). This is important, because Durkheim's treatment of the "spirit of discipline" and the "attachment to social groups" develops the same ideas found in his 1897 discussion of regulation and integration, respectively. In the earlier work, of course, insufficient or excessive regulation and/or integration provided the theoretical scaffolding on which Durkheim's explanation of variable suicide rates was grounded. But in the lectures on moral education, Durkheim gave us a clearer sense of the social and political interests and purposes that this realist conception of social facts was contrived to serve. In the earlier work, Durkheim spoke *qua* sociologist, "discovering" social *things*. In the latter work, he spoke *qua* educational reformer, pointing to the pragmatic value of this particular vocabulary – i.e., of speaking and thinking of social phenomena *as if* they were real things.

The same passages provide occasional hints of the sources on which Durkheim drew in "cobbling together" this vocabulary. But we still have no clear sense of when and where Durkheim, the philosophy *agrégé*, became "Durkheim," the social theorist and powerful exponent of social and educational realism. Was it during his studies with Fustel and Boutroux at the Ecole Normale Supérieure? Was it through his early, independent reading of writers like Renouvier? Or should we take seriously the recent suggestion that he was influenced by Arthur Schopenhauer (1788–1860)? How important was Durkheim's visit to Germany in 1885–6? As we shall see, the recent discovery of a much earlier set of lectures – given by Durkheim at the Lycée de Sens in 1883–4 – can help us to find more plausible, concrete answers to these questions.

CHAPTER 3

The perfection of personality

Until quite recently, accounts of the "early" Durkheim typically began with a discussion of his review essays of 1885. During the summer of 1995, however, a routine inventory of the papers of the French philosopher André Lalande (1867–1964), recently acquired by the Sorbonne, uncovered a detailed, meticulous set of notes covering eighty lectures (almost 600 pages in length), and bearing the inscription: "E. Durkheim – Cours de philosophie fait au Lycée de Sens en 1883–4." The content of these lectures – almost all of them given in 1883 – reveals a Durkheim so dramatically different from the one with whom we are familiar that he might reasonably be described as the "earlier" Durkheim. Most important for our purposes, this earlier Durkheim was in no sense a social realist – in fact, he seems to have possessed no sociological sensibilities whatsoever – and thus provides us with a starting point from which to answer some of the questions just raised. But first, it will be useful to understand the larger context of the philosophy class itself, and its role in the development of the French intellect.

VICTOR COUSIN AND THE *CLASSE DE PHILOSOPHIE*

The mark by which one could recognise a Frenchman, Theodore Zeldin once observed, was not his appearance or his language, but "something much deeper and much subtler: the way he used language, the way he thought, the way he argued" (1977: 205). In his *Fragments d'un journal intime* (1883–7), the literary critic Henri-Frédéric Amiel (1821–81) thus wrote:

The French always place a school of thought, a formula, convention, *a priori* arguments, abstraction, and artificiality above reality; they prefer clarity to truth, words to things, rhetoric to science . . . They understand nothing though they chop logic about everything. They are clever at distinguishing,

classifying, perorating, but they stop at the threshold of philosophy . . .
They emerge from description only to hurl themselves into precipitate
generalisations. They imagine they understand man in his entirety, whereas
they cannot break the hard shell of their personalities, and they do not
understand a single nation apart from themselves. (Zeldin 1977: 205)

As we have seen, these were among the qualities of mind that
Durkheim hoped to displace with a more concrete preoccupation
with *things*; and the institution responsible for "developing, instilling,
and defending these qualities" was the "crowning glory" of the
French secondary school system – i.e., the *classe de philosophie*. In fact,
French schools distinguished themselves from those in most of
Europe by teaching philosophy to children, and teaching it in a
special way – i.e., not as a technical discipline, but as a general
survey of the whole of life, bringing together the disparate information the child had already accumulated into a meaningful,
coherent synthesis. The *classe de philosophie* both culminated and
completed the student's secondary education, preparing him for the
baccalauréat examination so crucial to a university education and
almost every professional career. It was in the philosophy class,
therefore, that that French acquired "their characteristic abstract
and pompous vocabulary, their skill in classification and synthesis, in
solving problems by rearranging them verbally, their rationalism and
scepticism – paradoxically conformist – and their ability to argue
elegantly and apparently endlessly" (Zeldin, 1977: 217, 207).

The philosophy class had been born in the fifteenth century, when
the schools, reacting against the deficiencies of the medieval universities and their clerical preoccupation with theology, began
introducing young students to a broader subject matter. But only the
best, most prosperous schools had the resources to develop independent philosophical doctrines or methods of their own, so that
philosophy remained firmly within the medieval tradition; and in
this tradition, Zeldin agrees with Durkheim, "arguments were
cultivated for their own sake, not from an interest in truth; a
complete lack of intellectual curiosity was easily compatible with this
verbal fencing; books existed mainly as arsenals of arguments" (1977:
207–8). Zeldin emphasizes the tenacity of this tradition throughout
the subsequent history of French secondary education. In the
Renaissance, as we have seen, philosophy became less fashionable
than literature and rhetoric – an emphasis Durkheim characterized
as the preeminence of *style*; but during the Enlightenment, while the

mere *professeur de philosophie* had sunk to the status of a contemptible pedant, the *philosophe* emerged in "a new guise, as a man of the world who could discuss all subjects – a generalist rather than a specialist – who appealed to common sense and to all classes, and who was at home equally in literature, science and art" (1977: 208–9). The *philosophe*, of course, added a crucial element of rational dissent, challenging inherited ideas and institutions in the name of reason and science; but if this mild form of rebellion aptly characterized the posture of Voltaire, D'Alembert and Diderot, it hardly described their followers, who imitated their forms of argument in "studiously conformist ways." Before the Restoration, however, "philosophy" was the preoccupation of only a handful of people, taught in no more than sixty schools, only eleven of which had enough pupils to distribute prizes. The subsequent, dramatic change in the status and significance of philosophy was largely the work of Victor Cousin (1792–1867).

Born the son of a Parisian watchmaker, Cousin attended the Lycée Charlemagne and then joined the first class of the Ecole Normale Supérieure, where he studied with a disciple of Condillac, Pierre Laromiguière (1756–1837), and established a brilliant reputation.[1] He began lecturing at the Ecole Normale in 1812, and at the Sorbonne in 1815, soon dismissing Condillac's sensationalism under the influence of the idealist and voluntarist psychology of Maine de Biran (1766–1824)[2] and Pierre Paul Royer-Collard (1763–1845).[3] Cousin also studied German philosophy (Kant, Jacobi, and especially Schelling) and, from 1817 to 1820, traveled in Italy and Germany, where he met Schelling and befriended Hegel. Cousin's "eclectic" or "spiritualist" philosophy assumed that such divergent, seemingly irreconcilable systems all contained elements of philosophic truth; but within these systems – each of them narrow, rigid, and excessive in its own way – these fragments of truth were intermingled with numerous errors, from which they had to be

---

[1] Laromiguière's *Les Principes de l'intelligence* (1815–18), a lecture-course at the Sorbonne, established a compromise between Condillac's sensationalism and the spiritualist views of Rousseau's Savoyard Vicar (Stock-Morton 1988: 29).

[2] Maine de Biran had himself been a disciple of Condillac and a skeptic in religion, but later became a spiritualist and devout Catholic.

[3] Royer-Collard, a philosopher, statesman, and noted parliamentary orator, was professor of the history of philosophy at the Sorbonne from 1811. After the Restoration, with François Guizot (1787–1874), he became a leader of the *doctrinaires*. His influence declined after the Revolution of 1830, but he remained important in educational reform.

extricated according to the broader criterion of "common sense." The epistemology of Condillac, for example, was extreme in making the human mind a passive effect of external causes, leading to atheism and materialism, and denying French citizens those permanent principles essential to the moral life. The more activist, subjectivist psychology of Schelling and Maine de Biran allowed for religious commitment, but this spiritualism needed to be "balanced" with a rationalist's insistence on the concrete existence of a real external world (Boas 1967a: 247). Such eclecticism was hardly new – Durkheim would point to antecedents in the New Academy of Carneades (214–129 B.C.), in Cicero (106–43 B.C.), and in Leibniz (1646–1716) – but Cousin had given the school its "method and principles," and applied them in "a stable manner" (Durkheim 1884: 8).

Eclecticism was a philosophical extension of Cousin's equally conciliatory political views. Joining the *doctrinaires*, a small but powerful group of moderate, constitutional Royalists led by Royer-Collard and François Guizot (1787–1874), Cousin recommended a middle course – *"le juste milieu"* – between rabid monarchism and popular sovereignty, and favored a government led by the educated elite. "Just as he considered his philosophy to be the golden mean between sensationalism and idealism," Stock-Morton observes, "so he considered the Charter to be the mean between absolute monarchy and democracy."[4] In 1820, Cousin's lectures in Paris drew large crowds of liberal students; but in the reaction following the assassination of the Duc de Berry (the heir to the French throne), Cousin was dismissed. He returned to Germany, where he was imprisoned (the nature of the charges has never been clear) and then freed after six months. The *doctrinaires* did not prosper under the ultra-Royalist Charles X (r. 1824–30); but during the brief liberalization of 1827–8, Royer-Collard was able to recall Cousin to the Sorbonne, where his radical reputation – enhanced by the story of his arrest and imprisonment in Germany – again made him a favorite lecturer.

But it was under the July Monarchy (1830–48) that Cousin came

---

[4] Stock-Morton 1988: 30. *La Charte* was the constitutional charter granted on June 4, 1814 by the restored Louis XVIII at the bidding of the Allied Powers. It upheld the social and administrative order resulting from the Revolutionary and Napoleonic eras, including a constitutional monarchy, limited popular sovereignty, freedom of the press, and the recognition of Roman Catholicism as the State religion.

to dominate French secondary education. In 1830 he was appointed to the Royal Council of Public Instruction, where he controlled all teaching of philosophy. Shortly thereafter, a tour of schools in Holland and Prussia convinced him that moral instruction should be offered in the schools under the aegis of religion. In 1833, these views were embodied in the first primary education law since the Revolution, presented to the Chambers by Guizot, who was then Minister of Education.[5] But it was in secondary education – where philosophy had been under the control of theologians for at least a decade – that Cousin's contribution to secular moral education was decisive. A charter of 1830 decreed freedom of religion, expressly omitting any special position for the Church; and as the authority of the Church over moral education declined, the provision for a secular alternative became imperative. To the liberals of 1830, Cousin's disciple Paul Janet (1823–99) later observed, "the establishment of an independent philosophy curriculum was not only the consequence of the secular state; it was at the same time an instrument of propaganda for the principles of secularism." The goal was "to create a society which rested on common and fraternal principles, without excluding the diversity of opinions and beliefs" (1885: 217, 475, 281–2; Stock-Morton 1988: 31).

Cousin's eclectic philosophy – as tolerant of the variety of religious confessions as of philosophical positions or political ideologies – thus became the official philosophy of the July Monarchy, and the *classe de philosophie* became a required course in the secondary curriculum, and an essential part of the *baccalauréat* examination. The philosophy teacher, Cousin declared in 1850, "is a functionary in the service of moral order, appointed by the state to cultivate minds and souls" (Zeldin 1977: 222). Cousin had soon developed a "philosophical army," led by the *agrégés*, with "soldiers" in every *lycée*, whose training and appointment he personally supervised. During their Easter recess, Saint-Hilaire reports, most of them called on him in Paris, where they were questioned about their work, as well as their relations with the local clergy – a matter on which he placed great importance (Zeldin 1977: 222; Stock-Morton 1988: 31). Cousin developed a syllabus for the *classe de philosophie* which survived, in its essentials, for one hundred and thirty years; and his own works were

[5] The law provided for state-subsidized primary schools, but these were neither free nor obligatory, and religion was a part of the curriculum.

used as textbooks in the course at least until 1880, when they were
supplanted by those of his disciples, including Janet.[6]

Still more important, through his position at the Sorbonne, later
as director of the Ecole Normale, and finally (however briefly) as
Minister of Education, Cousin was able to professionalize the
teaching of philosophy itself, lending it prestige and thus raising it to
a position from which philosophers could declare their independence of theology (Stock-Morton 1988: 191 n. 46). Though paid by
the state, therefore, philosophy teachers were not "tame propagan-
dists preaching an orthodox doctrine: they valued their security as
civil servants, but reacted against the implication of subservience by
increasingly assuming independent attitudes" (Zeldin 1977: 222–3).
At least until 1880, of course, this was a dangerous game – despite
the fact that eclecticism taught little more than common sense and
classic texts – as philosophy was continuously under the scrutiny of
the religious and political right; and it was especially dangerous
under the Second Empire (1852–70), as some of Cousin's students
began to question spiritualist dogma. Amédée Jacques, editor of the
Cousinist journal *La Liberté de penser*, was dismissed for his admitted
atheism, as was the philosopher Etienne Vacherot, for suggesting
that reason, experience, and faith might ultimately lead to irreconcilable conclusions. Under Napoleon III, a terrified government
temporarily abolished philosophy teaching in the schools altogether,
but in 1863, when it was restored to the *baccalauréat*, it was Cousin's
syllabus that was revived.

The significance of the philosophy course, both as a prerequisite
for the *baccalauréat* and as a preparation for French citizenship,
exposed it to a variety of abuses and criticisms. As a consequence of
its unyielding hostility to materialism, for example, Marx was
admitted to the syllabus only in 1960. Although it's starting point
was psychology, it typically construed self-knowledge as the consequence of rational reflection, thus resisting any emphasis on the
emotions or the unconscious. While its eclectic approach exposed
students to a variety of classic texts, the assumption that these texts
exhausted all there was to know left it resistant to inventive and
creative minds. The manufacture of textbooks and, still worse,
model answers to examination questions became a flourishing

---

[6] Janet's *Traité élémentaire de philosophie à l'usage des classes* (1879) was probably the textbook used
by Durkheim.

industry. Finally, as rival disciplines emerged in the secondary syllabus, the traditional supremacy of the *classe de philosophie* was challenged. Gustave Monod (1844–1912), a historian and founder of the *Revue historique* in 1876 demanded that philosophy be eliminated from the secondary curriculum altogether, and the psychologist Théodule Ribot (1839–1916), though a philosopher by training, argued that philosophy was too difficult for most secondary students, boring the majority while intoxicating the rest with generalizations and formulae that they could rarely use (Zeldin 1976: 218–19).

Still, the Cousinist framework endured into the 1880s, when the philosopher Jules Lachelier (1832–1918), inspector-general in charge of philosophy, conducted the *agrégation* examination on the principle that all that could be said in philosophy had already been said, that there was nothing more to discover or invent, and that teachers should therefore simply present the known facts in a lively manner. Determined to keep them from flirting with new subjects like anthropology or social science, he twice failed Charles Andler (1866–1933), who took the *agrégation* in 1887 and 1888, largely because Lachelier disliked his "excessive bias" toward German philosophy.[7] Cousin entrenched philosophy so firmly in the schools, Zeldin concludes, "because he deliberately adapted it to the tastes of the middle classes, whom he recognised as being firmly conservative in moral attitudes; by making it the most important subject in the final examination of the *baccalauréat*, he gave it official status as the necessary hallmark of an educated man" (1977: 209–10).

It was to prepare such "educated men" that Durkheim, having passed his *agrégation* at the Ecole Normale Supérieure in 1882, began teaching philosophy at the Lycée de Puy in October. One month later, he moved to the Lycée de Sens, where the philosopher Lalande became his student in the fall of 1883. Lalande would later recall Durkheim as an unusually conscientious teacher, who set an example of "systematic order in investigations and . . . well-organized ideas." At the end of each lesson, Lalande added, "he turned to the blackboard and reconstructed its plan, composed of titles and short, ordered formulae, which made concrete for his hearers the structure, always precise and well-constructed, of what he had just expounded in a free and continuous passion" (Lukes 1972: 64).

---

[7] Zeldin 1977: 211. Andler thus sat for the German literature *agrégation* in 1889, came in first, and was able to write his book on Nietzsche under the auspices of modern languages.

Durkheim's pupils had a great admiration and affection for him, Lalande added, some of them even following him to the Lycée de Saint-Quentin where he moved, in February, 1884, to be closer to his family. Of those who did not, most – including Lalande himself – borrowed notes taken by other students during the preceding year, recopying them in their own hand to complete the full syllabus of eighty lectures (Lukes 1972: 64; Gross 1996). With the exception of a few lectures given in January and early February, 1884, therefore, all of the notes reflect beliefs held by Durkheim in 1883 – easily our earliest, most detailed and complete evidence of his philosophical commitments.[8]

THE SCIENCE OF MIND

Philosophy, Durkheim began, is "the science of states of consciousness and their conditions" (1884: 6). Since Durkheim's students were apparently as unaccustomed as we are to thinking of philosophy as a science, this definition required some elaboration. To be a "science," Durkheim explained, a system of knowledge must have a distinct object – i.e., one not confused with that of any other science (for philosophy the object is "states of consciousness"); it must submit this object to the laws of identity or of causality (as we shall see, for philosophy this meant the latter); and it must have a method whereby the object is studied (for philosophy, the experimental method) (1884: 18–19). Durkheim thus dismissed the classical notion that philosophy was a kind of Ur-knowledge from which the other sciences were derived, as well as the Comtean notion that philosophy serves only as the concluding synthesis of positive science. Instead, he insisted that philosophy is an independent science that sustains a variety of relationships with the positive sciences, including the study of laws of knowledge on which they depend, the search for the method most appropriate to each particular science, and so on. Finally, because the states of consciousness studied by philosophy include phenomena of quite different kinds, philosophy itself was subdivided into several more distinct sciences – i.e., psychology, logic, ethics, and metaphysics – which together made up the syllabus that Cousin had designed for the *classe de philosophie.*

[8] The Sens Lectures (in French) are accessible at the Durkheim web site (http://eddie.cso.uiuc.edu/Durkheim/), together with a lengthy abstract (in English). An English translation of the lectures is in progress.

From these introductory lectures, it is clear that in its general outline, Durkheim's conception of science was already well formed by 1883. As a student of Boutroux, for example, Durkheim had already embraced the view that each science has its own object and its own method – a principle he would further advance and defend in *Les Règles* (1895). Again, Durkheim had already arrived at the view that logic, ethics, and metaphysics should be grounded in empirical science (albeit in philosophy, not in sociology), and had even embraced the notions of experimental verification introduced by Claude Bernard in 1865. But it's equally clear that, in 1883, Durkheim had no answer to the question of how this conception of science and its method might be applied to the study of social phenomena. Apparently this was because the question itself had not yet occurred to him, for he had not yet conceived of social phenomena in the manner of Alfred Espinas (1844–1922) – i.e., as part of nature, to be studied *comme des choses*.

Not surprisingly, this became especially clear when Durkheim turned to the different methods that have been applied in the study of psychological phenomena, and particularly the *psycho-physical* school of E. H. Weber (1795–1878) and Gustave Fechner (1801–87). In his *Elemente der Psychophysik* (1860), Fechner had introduced a mathematical formulation that he called the "law of intensity" – i.e., that the intensity of a sensation increases as the logarithm of the stimulus (that is, by diminishing increments) – to become known as the "Weber–Fechner law," considered by some to be the beginning of quantitative experimental psychology (Boring 1950: 293; Ribot 1886: 181–8). The law is important because Durkheim would refer to it again in *De la division du travail social* (1893), in support of his argument that the human capacity for happiness is limited, and that its pursuit must thus be dismissed as a possible cause for the division of labor (1984: 181–2). But in this fifth Sens lecture, Durkheim dismissed the Weber–Fechner law categorically, on the ground that the body is not simply a passive transmitter of physical excitations to the soul, but rather modifies them significantly, according to the individual and to circumstances (1884: 37). It was to overcome this difficulty, Durkheim added, that Wilhelm Wundt (1832–1920) had established the *psycho-physiological* school, which related states of consciousness directly to *physiological* rather than merely *physical* phenomena. For Wundt, in short, the conscious life of the soul had its roots in the unconscious life of the body. But Durkheim insisted that the soul *cannot* be reduced to the body, and that conscious psychological facts must be studied *in themselves*, by means of "internal perception." Like the discussion of Weber and Fechner, this negative assessment is extremely interesting in the light of Durkheim's visit to Wundt's laboratory in Leipzig just two years later, and his subsequent praise for Wundt's willingness "to reduce the higher forms of intelligence to experience," and subject "the life of reason" to "psychological scrutiny" (1887a: 313–38, 423–40, 329 n. 16).

From these methodological observations, Durkheim turned to the "sensibility" and – most interesting for our purposes – to the inclinations. Depending on whether an object is agreeable or disagreeable to us, he observed, we tend towards it or distance ourselves from it. In the former case, we speak of an *inclination*; and there are as many different types of inclinations as there are types of objects producing these movements within us, including *egoistic* – i.e., those that have the *self* as their object – and *altruistic* – i.e., those that have *other people* as their object. Durkheim recognized that writers like Hobbes, Pascal, and Rousseau had questioned whether altruistic inclinations actually exist, insisting instead that the sole end of our inclinations is the maintenance or well-being of the self; but Durkheim insisted that "naturally" we are "made in such a way that we are concerned with ourselves and to have need of others" (1884: 58). Unfortunately for our purposes, and "content for the moment" with his appeal to human nature, Durkheim did not expand on the relationship between our egoistic and altruistic inclinations. Instead, probably following Fustel, he turned to an evolutionary treatment of the different groups or levels – e.g., the family, the city, the society, humanity itself – of altruistic inclinations. "Society is a union of families," Durkheim explained, and "humanity [is] a union of societies. It's from the love of the family that one is raised to the love of the society, and from that for society that one is raised to love of humanity" (1884: 59). And when he returned to the relationship of egoistic and altruistic tendencies in the lecture on civic morality (see Lecture n. 64), his equally unenlightening reference was to the "voice of nature."

Still, this passage in Lalande's notes is intriguing, for here Durkheim insisted – as he would later in *L'Education morale* – that the distinction between egoism and altruism should be sought, not in the distinction between tendencies whose goal is pleasure to the agent (egoism) and those whose goal is the pleasure of some other person (altruism), but in the distinction between the *kinds of objects* to which the agent is attached. For as he would later argue, the notion that egoism and altruism could be distinguished by an appeal to different kinds of *pleasures* made it inconceivable that they had the same origin, and led to the typical Enlightenment view that egoism was a part of "human nature," while altruism was the laborious, "artificial" construction of culture and civilization. By focusing instead on the kinds of *objects* to which agents become attached, Durkheim had left open the door to the possibility that the distinction between egoistic and altruistic sentiments was not one between "nature" and "art." But in 1883 Durkheim seems to have had no sense of how our attachment for things outside us presupposes the existence of their representations within us and, still more important, how such representations might be created and maintained by a society's institutions. As we shall see, the full realization of this point required a far closer reading of Rousseau than Durkheim had done by 1883.

Turning from the sensibility to the intelligence, Durkheim asked and answered a series of questions that help us to understand the sense in which he was an epistemological realist. First, against John Stuart Mill (1806–73), Durkheim insisted that our idea of "the external world" is *given* rather than *constructed*.[9] Second, against Sir William Hamilton (1788–1856) and Maine de Biran (1766–1824), Durkheim embraced the Kantian view that this idea of externality is given, not through *experience*, but *a priori* – i.e., by the very nature of the human mind (1884: 87–9). And third, he embraced the notion that the external world is "objective" – i.e., not the product of subjective mental events (1884: 91–4). These answers brought Durkheim to the crucial question for an epistemological realist: Is the external world as we perceive it? Do our sensations correspond to qualities naturally inherent in things?

Durkheim's answer to these questions depended heavily on the classic distinction between the primary and secondary qualities of matter. *Secondary* qualities include things like heat, color, taste, odor, etc., for we can conceive of bodies without these things, and in fact not all bodies have them. The only two *primary* qualities are extension and movement, for we can't conceive of a body that is not

---

[9] Durkheim 1884: 84–7. See Mill's *Examination of Sir William Hamilton's Philosophy* (1865) and "Berkeley's Life and Writings" (1871).

both extended *and* mobile, and in fact all bodies have these two qualities. So Locke's distinction at least enables us to say what the external world *is not* – i.e., since *secondary* qualities, as Durkheim put it rather awkwardly, "are only the appearances of forms of primary qualities, uniquely different through the intervention of our senses," there is no more to matter than the *primary* qualities of extension and movement (1884: 101–2). Matter, in short, is an extension susceptible of motion. Extension is also continuous, and thus must be divisible into parts. But here we confront a contradiction – i.e., these parts cannot be *finite* in number, for each of the parts is itself divisible *ad infinitum*; and the number of parts cannot be *infinite*, for the notion of an infinite number is itself contradictory.[10] So the idea of extension itself, Durkheim argued, is a deceptive appearance, a deformation suffered by things when we perceive them through the intermediary of our senses; and since motion is simply a change in extension, the same applies to other primary qualities as well.

Durkheim's solution is extremely important. If the body is not extended, it is still divisible into a *finite* number of *unextended* parts – a conclusion that conforms to the atomistic hypothesis of physics and chemistry. These unextended elements of bodies are *beings*, Durkheim observed, and thus we can understand them only by analogy with the sole being of which we have knowledge – i.e., our *selves* or *souls*. What kind of beings are we? Briefly, we are *conscious, sensible, intelligent* forces that *move* themselves. We have no reason to attribute consciousness, sensibility, or intelligence to the unextended elements of bodies; but we *can* imagine them as "similar to what our souls would be" if they *lacked* consciousness, sensibility, and intelligence – i.e., active, unconscious forces that limit and suppress the self. Just as our will acts upon our intelligence, entirely outside of extension, so these active, unconscious forces operate in the external world, placing limits and constraints on human beings.

This argument is important, not just because it reveals Durkheim as a *realist* at this early stage of his career, but because it tells us explicitly *what kind* of realist he was. If we conceive of the external world in the mechanistic manner of Descartes – i.e., as comprised of extended bodies in motion – we face the difficulties implied by the incoherence of the idea of extension. But if we imagine the external

---

[10] By its very definition, Durkheim observed, a "number" is susceptible of being indefinitely augmented or diminished; but "the infinite" is fixed, and the notion of an "infinite number" is thus meaningless (1884: 98).

world as comprised of beings *similar to ourselves*, but whose consciousness is almost entirely extinguished, in the manner of Aristotle and,
above all, Leibniz, then there is no interruption in the continuity of
nature: "From the perfect mind down to inorganic matter, everything is mind, everything is force." Dead and inert properties do not
exist, for everything in nature is animated and alive.[11] "It is only a
question," Durkheim concluded, "of the degree of consciousness"
(1884: 101).

If the senses thus provide us with knowledge of the external world,
consciousness is the faculty whereby we acquire knowledge of the
internal world. What, then, is the epistemological status of "internal
perception" – i.e., the psychological method Durkheim had recommended in response to the German psycho-physical and psycho-
physiological schools? First, just as external perception requires the
existence of an external object, so internal perception requires some
sort of "internal, psychic modification." Second, just as the "intervention of the self" is essential to external perception, so it is equally
important to knowledge of the inner world. With the exception of a
sense which serves as the intermediary between a subject and an
external object, therefore, the conditions of internal perception are
identical with those of external perception. As we have just seen,
however, Durkheim was a Leibnizian realist who believed that the
external world is comprised of bodies themselves comprised of other,
smaller bodies, *ad infinitum*. When we perceive bodies, however, we
do not consciously perceive the microscopic bodies of which they are
composed, which had led Leibniz to distinguish between *conscious*
perceptions (*apperceptions*) and *unconscious* perceptions ("little perceptions").[12] Durkheim was fully aware of this Leibnizian notion of
unconscious psychic phenomena, as well as the extended use of it by
writers like Schopenhauer and Hartmann; and by the late 1890s, as
we have seen, Durkheim himself would suggest that there live within
us "other men than those with whom we are familiar," suggesting
the existence of "an unconscious psychic life beyond that of
consciousness" (1884: 330). But in 1883, this was an idea with which

[11] In support of this view, Durkheim cited George Henry Lewes' observation, in *The Physical
Basis of Mind* (1877), that "[t]he scientific conception of inert, insensible matter . . . is
reached only through a long education which consolidates a mind capable of abstraction;
very certainly, animals and savages never attain this [kind of mind]" (p. 308). Durkheim
had apparently encountered this important passage in Alfred Espinas' *Des sociétés animales*
(1978: 413).

[12] See Leibniz, "New Essays on the Understanding", in Wiener 1951: 373–80.

Durkheim was uncomfortable. All the examples of *unconscious* psychic phenomena, he insisted, can be explained just as well by an *extremely weak* consciousness of such phenomena; and the idea of unconscious psychic phenomena is itself incoherent – i.e., What would a psychic phenomenon that "left" consciousness become? Having left consciousness, how would it return? In the psychological life, Durkheim concluded, there is nothing that is absolutely unconscious.

As we have seen, Durkheim's treatment of sensory perceptions of the external world had asked whether the idea of exteriority was given by consciousness itself, or was rather constructed or invented by the mind. His discussion of internal perception now asked the same question about the idea of the self – and arrived at a similarly realist conclusion. Here Durkheim's argument was addressed directly to Taine who, in *De l'intelligence* (2 vols., 1870), had first distinguished between "exterior sensations" (or perceptions) and "internal emotions," and then described the self as the "imaginary container" of the latter. But the self, Durkheim objected, appears to us, not as a *container*, but as a *center* – i.e., a point of convergence where all states of consciousness are centralized. Moreover, Taine's distinction presumes states of consciousness (i.e., exterior sensations) given outside the self, while in fact, every state of consciousness requires *both* a subject (one conscious of itself prior to sensation) *and* an object. The self is thus the indispensable, antecedent condition of every state of consciousness, and is thus given rather than being constructed. The difference between external and internal perception is that there is an abyss which separates the external world from us. The idea of the self, by contrast, is perceived *directly* in consciousness, and unlike the the external world, its non-existence is inconceivable. The existence of the self is demonstrated simply by the fact that we *have* the idea in the first place.

This argument – clearly derived from Condillac's *Traité des sensations* (1754) – was extremely important, for it laid the foundation for Durkheim's account of the *nature* of the self. Consciousness and reasoning, Durkheim explained, suggest that the self possesses three natural attributes: *unity* (it is indivisible and has no parts), *identity* (by contrast to the endless flux of the external world, the self remains identical to itself), and *causality* (we know that we are among causes of our actions). And this in turn led to Durkheim's notion of "personality," with all of its significant consequences for his early, teleological ethics (see below). A being possessing unity, identity, and causality, he observed, is what we call a "person"; and while all persons are to the same degree "one" and "identical," they are not all to the same degree "the causes of their own actions." In other words, each self is not a "person" to the same degree.

Thus described, perception and consciousness are the "experimental faculties," and the distinctive nature of the judgments they provide is that they are *contingent* – i.e., the mind can conceive of the contradictory judgment. The judgment: "Man is a sensible being," for example, is contingent, for we can conceive of a man who lacks sensibility. But consider another judgment: "Every phenomenon has a cause." In this case, the contradictory judgment is inconceivable; thus, we say that the proposition is *necessary* rather than contingent. Since judgments of this kind have a character just the opposite of the judgments provided by experience, there must be a faculty – the *reason* – responsible for providing them; and necessary judgments are possible only in so far as they are *a priori* – i.e., they inhere in the very nature of the mind. What derives from the nature of a being, Durkheim added, is what we call the laws of this being; thus, reason is "the totality of the laws of the mind."[13] And since the *mind* has *its* nature and laws, and the *external world* also has *its* nature and laws, things are known to the mind in so far as they are "in harmony" with the laws of the mind.

Durkheim's account of the *principles* of reason recalls his later distinction, in his writing on education, between the clarity and simplicity of ideas and the complexity of real, concrete things. In essence, he observed, the mind is *simple*, and *understands* only that which is simple. When the mind examines things that are *concrete* and *complex*, therefore, it introduces the unity, order, and simplicity that its nature requires. First, the multiplicity of things given in experience are ordered by being placed in certain *contexts* – i.e., external perceptions given by the senses are placed in *space*, and internal perceptions given by consciousness are located in *time*. Thus we arrive at the first two rational principles: *All states of consciousness are in time*; and *all phenomena given by sensation are in space*. This initial order,

---

[13] Durkheim was careful here to distinguish this specifically Kantian notion of mind from the theory of *innate ideas* – i.e., "There are no ideas completely formed, engraved in our minds prior to experience. Before experience, there is nothing there" – as well as the notion of an *impersonal reason*, first advanced by Plato, and more recently by Cousin and Bouillier (1884: 126).

however, is entirely "external," so the mind is necessarily led to conceive of phenomena as the modifications of a *being* – i.e., a reality independent of the intelligence itself – which is called *substance.* Hence another rational principle: *All phenomena are modifications of a substance.* The mind cannot conceive of one phenomenon without assuming another. This gives us still another principle: *Every phenomenon has a cause.* Finally, the mind is led to represent these *series* of phenomena as converging toward their common goal or end, resulting in the principle: *Every phenomenon or series of phenomena has an end.* These are what Kant called the five "constitutive principles of experience" – i.e., time, space, substance, causality, and finality. Once constituted, however, our knowledge itself has certain laws, which Kant called the *regulative* principle of knowledge, or the principle of *identity* and *contradiction* – i.e., *All that is, is; a thing cannot, at the same time and at the same perspective, be itself and its contrary.* Whatever exists, Durkheim thus concluded, there are two different kinds of rational principles – those governing the acquisition of knowledge, and those governing the kinds of knowledge acquired.

It was these "principles," of course, for which Durkheim sought to provide sociological explanations in "De quelques formes primitives de classification" (1903) and *Les Formes élémentaires* (1912). So it's worth noting that, in 1883, Durkheim was already aware of efforts – the "most remarkable" being that of Herbert Spencer (1820–1903) – to deny the *a priori* origin of these ideas and explain them empirically. Before experience, Durkheim paraphrased Spencer, we do not possess the idea of time; instead, we have only states of consciousness with certain relations of position between them – i.e., some in front, some behind. We generalize from these relative positions of the states of consciousness, constructing the idea of time; and from this idea, those of temporal co-existence and then space are also constructed. But if the idea of time did not *already exist*, Durkheim objected, we could not conceive of states of consciousness *before* and *after* one another. Similarly, *geometric figures* are not abstracted from generalized observations, but are rather constructed a priori, by the mind itself. For in a generalization there is nothing more than the things generalized, which are concrete and imperfect; and geometric figures have the additional characteristic of *perfection* – something that cannot be learned from experience. This is why the mathematical sciences are so clear, and we understand these objects so well – i.e., we are the ones *who have made them.*

An alternative empiricist account of reason – "best studied" in Mill's *System of Logic* (1843) and *Examination of Sir William Hamilton's Philosophy* (1865) – argued that the "necessity" of rational judgments can be explained as the consequence of *habit* and the *association of ideas*. Briefly, when two states of consciousness occur together in the same order a certain number of times, the mind tends to reproduce them in this order, with as much force as the frequency with which the experience has been repeated. When the frequency is without exceptions, the association of ideas becomes so strong that it is indissoluble, and the judgment formed is called "necessary." All phenomena are thus presented to us as forming inseparable pairs, including an antecedent (cause) and a consequent (effect). To say that all phenomena have an invariable antecedent is to say that every phenomenon has a cause. To these arguments of Mill, Durkheim made three objections. First, Mill had shown that arguments now considered to be "necessary" were at other times regarded as absurd; but "absurd," Durkheim observed, is not the same as *inconceivable*, and the characteristic feature of rational judgments is precisely that their contradiction cannot be conceived. Second, while the tendency to associate ideas that are frequently produced together is incontestable, Durkheim denied that this tendency ever approaches the *impossibility* of separating the terms uniting them. In fact, there are ideas we always unite, but which we can, if we wish, imagine apart.[14] Experience, in short, never undermines the freedom of our thought. And third, in order for us to accept the necessity of a relation of succession that we have observed several times, we must already know that they are disposed in inseparable pairs – i.e., we must already have the idea of causality. "With subjective sensations," Durkheim concluded, "we cannot construct anything objective. With phenomena, we cannot construct the idea of substance. With the contingent, we cannot construct the necessary. One can accumulate lots of contingent truths, but they don't change in nature. One cannot find in experience that which is its very condition" (1884: 151).

But if *individual* experience thus fails to account for our possession

---

[14] Durkheim recognized that Mansel had refuted Mill on precisely this point. "We can imagine," Mansel says, "the same stone sinking in water ninety-nine times, and floating on the hundredth, although experience shows us only the first phenomenon. Experience always shows us a man's head on his shoulders, and the horse's head on the horse's body. But there's no impossibility in our imagining a centaur" (1884: 149).

of rational judgments, what about the experience of *the species*? In his *First Principles* (1850), Herbert Spencer had accepted the view that rational ideas are innate in each individual, while insisting that they are a "trust" formed by the accumulated experience of the species, and transmitted through heredity. Durkheim's initial objection here was one he had also entered in opposition to associationism – i.e., "evolutionism" has a marked tendency to consider differences as only apparent, and to attempt to reduce them to a single type. But nothing, Durkheim insisted, proves that objects present this absolute unity; on the contrary, everything conspires to suggest that multiplicity and diversity are the law of things. The best method to follow, therefore, is *to look for differences and to respect them*. Second, since it is obviously impossible to find even a primitive tribe whose members lack rational principles, evolutionism is a *hypothesis* that is impossible to *verify experimentally*. Third, empiricism necessarily regards the mind, before experience, as a *tabula rasa* – i.e., *without a determinate nature of its own*. But the indeterminate does not really *exist*, Durkheim insisted, so the empiricists are reduced to arguing that the *mind* exists only at the moment when *experience* begins. Yet even empiricists like Spencer admit that, to form rational judgments, the multiplicity given in experience must be integrated in the mind. If the mind does not possess an integrative faculty, such judgments are impossible. So again, Durkheim concluded, empiricism leads us into a vicious circle.

With regard to reason, therefore, Durkheim took a strongly Kantian position in opposition to empiricists like Mill and Spencer. There are two sources of knowledge: experience and reason; and since reason cannot be derived from experience, Durkheim insisted that rational ideas and principles are innate within us. But if rational principles are thus the laws of *mind*, Durkheim observed, it remains to show that they are also the laws of *things*. Do the laws of the mind have an *objective value*? For Kant, Durkheim observed, rational principles had only a subjective value. Though not denying the existence of the external world, Kant had insisted that the sensible multiplicity that experience provides is confused and disordered. In order to know things, we must transform and denature them, imposing an artificial order that enables us to understand them.

Durkheim's response to Kant was a classic example of eclecticism. For the *empiricists*, he reminded his students, knowledge is produced exclusively by *the action of things* on the mind. For *Kant*, by contrast, knowledge is produced exclusively by *the action of the mind* on things.

Both of these theories, Durkheim then argued, are too extreme. Of the two, *empiricism* is the less logical, for it denies the mind its own, determinate nature; but if Durkheim thus agreed with Kant that the forms of the mind are definite and immutable, he also insisted that there are equally definite and concrete external objects. Knowledge must therefore be a *synthesis* of objective and subjective elements, which raises the question: What comes from things? And what comes from the mind? To answer these questions, we need an objective principle – one which is not itself constitutive of experience – and Durkheim found this in the *principle of identity and contradiction*. Applying this principle to our knowledge of the external world, Durkheim then repeated parts of the Leibnizian argument presented earlier, showing that our notions of continuity and infinity embody contradictions, that they cannot be in *things*, and that they are thus merely subjective necessities of the *mind*.

What was Durkheim's early position on free will versus determinism? This question is important, in part because later critics would consider Durkheim's social realism incompatible with freedom of the will, and also because Durkheim had been a student of Boutroux, whose *De la contingence des lois de la nature* (1874) was an important contribution to the antideterminist position. Freedom, Durkheim paraphrased Kant, is the faculty each of us has to *commence a series of actions* – i.e., for our will to be the *first term* in any series of events, without *itself* being determined by any *prior* term. That we possess such a faculty is proved *directly* by the idea that we *have* of our freedom – i.e., we could not have acquired this idea from our experience of the external world, for it is governed by an absolute determinism; and the same conclusion is reached *indirectly* by the fact that, without freedom, we cannot explain certain facts – e.g., contracts, promises, civil punishment, reward, etc. – of daily life, and also by Kant's categorical imperative – i.e., the moral law that would be impossible if human beings lacked freedom.[15]

Determinists object to this idea of freedom, of course, arguing that it is incompatible with the principle of causality. *Psychological* determinists like Leibniz and Mill, for example, argue that the idea of freedom contradicts the laws of the internal world of the mind – i.e., our actions are guided by our motives, which derive from our

---

[15] Durkheim 1884: 258. As we shall see, one of the more distinctive elements of Durkheim's treatment of ethics was his reversal of this Kantian argument – using the idea of freedom to establish the moral law.

intelligence, accidents of life, our character, habits, etc., which are determining causes; and even where we have a choice among several motives, the struggle between them is itself determined by causes of the same kind. Everything, in short, passes mechanically in our wills. Where we have several motives, Durkheim agreed, then once the decision as to which is the stronger motive is made, the action is "determined." Freedom, in short, does not lie between this *decision* and the *execution of the action*. But freedom *does* reside, Durkheim insisted, between the *conception of the end* of the action and the *choice of the strongest motive*. Indeed, it is this capacity for reflection and deliberation that distinguishes us from the lower animals.

Scientific determinists, by contrast, insist that freedom is incompatible with the laws of the external world of nature. When we think of nature under the form of *causality*, Durkheim reminded his students, it is revealed to us as an *immense series of causes and effects*; and if a person could act freely, it would interrupt and disturb this series, contradicting the principle of causality. The most vigorous effort to resolve this difficulty presented by scientific determinism, Durkheim observed, was that of Kant. The self, Kant argued, can know itself only by thinking of itself under the form of rational principles, which are the condition of all knowledge. The self must therefore apply to itself the *a priori* forms of the sensibility, and the categories of the understanding; and in doing so, the self denatures and transforms itself. The real, primitive self was not subject to these principles; but the conscious, reflective self thinks of itself under the form of time, and under the concept of space. Two selves are thus formed: the *noumenal* self, which is, but is *not known*; and the *phenomenal* self, which is *known*, but which is *not*. Kant thus resolved the antinomy of freedom versus determinism by assigning *science* and *ethics* to two different worlds: the principle of *causality* rules in the *phenomenal* world; and *freedom* reigns in the *noumenal* world.

This description of the classic Kantian distinction between the noumenal and phenomenal worlds is extremely interesting, for it would do a great deal of work in Durkheim's later treatment of the duality of human nature; but at Sens in 1883, Durkheim rejected Kant's argument on the ground that the doctrine conserves, not *real* freedom, but only *possible* freedom.[16] The actions of our lives, being

---

[16] Durkheim added that the theory is subject to a number of other, more important criticisms; but he considered this argument alone sufficient to refute it.

purely phenomenal, would be determined, while the will, impri- soned in the noumenal world, would be unable to exert its influence on phenomena. The freedom Kant offers us is thus only a virtual, sterile, metaphysical freedom. At this early stage in his thinking, therefore, Durkheim agreed with the determinists that so long as we think of things solely under the form of causality, there is no contingency, and thus no freedom. How, then, is freedom to be made consistent with the principle of causality? Briefly, Durkheim observed, if the *relation between* phenomena is determined, the *direction* in which the series of phenomena is tending is not. For the direction of the series is decided according to the principle of *finality*, and the necessity called for by this principle is *far less rigorous* than that of causality – i.e., the same end can be achieved through quite different means. The ends assigned to innumerable series of phenomena can be fulfilled in a variety of ways, and this is where freedom can be introduced into the external world.

From these lectures on *psychology* – the science that *describes* states of consciousness, Durkheim turned to *logic* – the science that *explains* the laws that the mind should follow in the pursuit of truth. As we have seen, Durkheim defined "truth" as the conformity of the *mind* and *things*, adding that "certainty" is the state of mind that knows that it possesses the truth. By what criterion, then, do we know that we are in the possession of truth? The notion that this criterion is *inherent in judgments* clearly fails, Durkheim argued, for it can't explain the *diversity of opinions* – i.e., if judgments really carried their own criterion of truth, the consequence would be universal acceptance rather than disagreement and controversy. Durkheim thus suggested that there may be diverse criteria of truth, leading to at least three different kinds of certainty: *mathematical*, i.e., resulting from mathe- matical demonstration; *physical*, i.e., the intuitive certainty provided by our observations; and *ethical*, i.e., resulting in a kind of moral certainty. The criterion of *mathematical* certainty, he then observed, is *identity*, while the criterion of *physical* certainty is the authority of *concrete facts*. What characterizes *moral* certainties, however, is that they are *not unanimously taken for truths* – i.e., they possess *no objective sign* – and they are thus deprived of the criterion permitting the mind to decide immediately whether they are true or false.

How, then, are we to account for the *certainty* of our moral judgments? Briefly, Durkheim explained, in the case of moral judgments, our *understanding* – influenced by our *will* which, in turn, is influenced by our *sensibility* (temperament, education, habits, heredity) – is led in a specific direction, seeing only the reasons on one side rather than the other, and thus affirms or denies with certainty. In short, the understanding is no longer produced by the action of the *judgment on the mind*; on the contrary, it is produced by the action of the *mind on the judgment*, making our moral judgments essentially *personal*; and precisely because our will and our sensibility are so personal, we hold to our ethical judgments with a special tenacity, for without them, we would not be who we are. As we shall see, this epistemological notion of moral judgments as personal and subjective fits well with Durkheim's later Sens lectures on ethics; but of course it could hardly be more different from his arguments – just a few years later – in favor of an empirical "science of ethics."

Since Durkheim's social realist vocabulary included methodological injunctions – e.g., treat social facts *comme des choses* – as well as theoretical observations, it's also important to pay attention to what the Sens lectures say about the scientific method. In general, Durkheim seems to have considered the emphasis on method in science as excessive, insisting that important scientific discoveries "are the result of what is *not* given by method – the strength of genius" (1884: 356–7). But if method is not *sufficient* to invention, Durkheim admitted, it is nonetheless *necessary* to testing, validating, and corroborating hypotheses in the various sciences, and he dealt with this concern in his lectures on "applied logic."

Every scientific method, Durkheim observed, must include *two parts*: first, *invention* – i.e., of theorems, the distinctive contribution of genius, seated in the imagination; and second, *demonstration* with the aid of definitions, axioms, and deduction. In the physical sciences, the important role of invention lies in the formulation of hypotheses to explain the facts that have been observed. Here Durkheim emphasized the role of *analogy* – i.e., a kind of reasoning whereby we first ascertain one fact, and then apply to it the law of another fact (one which resembles but is not identical to the first), and thus produce a new discovery. In this case of a hypothesis drawn from an analogy, Durkheim repeated, there is room for considerable creativity – the distinctive contribution of the imagination – so that in the invention of every hypothesis there is a large degree of contingency. But whether drawn from analogy or not, Durkheim emphasized, a hypothesis is always a law that has not yet been verified; and it is verifiable, Durkheim cited Claude Bernard's

Introduction à l'étude de la médecine expérimentale (1865), through experimentation and then induction (i.e., the extension of the law to every possible experience), not through the direct manipulation of phenomena.

An obvious objection to this criterion of the verification of hypothetical laws was that it necessarily excluded both meteorology and natural history from the status of sciences. But this was a consequence that Durkheim was willing to accept. "Every science which lacks experimentation also lacks law," he explained, "for the existence of a law implies a hypothesis, experimentation, induction" (1884: 370). Meteorology and natural history are thus "histories" that *ascertain* and *classify* certain facts, but are not themselves "true sciences." The classification of facts aids the memory, Durkheim added, but its primary purpose is to *rediscover the order of things* according to the *ends* assigned to them. Classification, Durkheim thus explained, is guided by the principle of *finality.*

This brought Durkheim to his lecture on method in "moral" sciences – i.e., those "concerned with the human mind," including the philosophical, social, philological, and historical sciences. Having already dealt with method in philosophy, Durkheim turned first to politics, law, and political economy – where his observations could hardly contrast more sharply with *Les Règles.* The science of society, for example, is *politics* (not sociology*),* and its purpose is not to study social facts but to ascertain the best form that human societies might take.[17] In the *Republic,* Plato had approached this problem geometrically, but more recently, Durkheim observed, history has provided the means to make politics an observational and experimental science. *Law,* by contrast, begins from the foundation of human legal systems, from which it deduces applications to the particular cases of human life, while *political economy* – once treated deductively in the manner of law – is now approached primarily through observation and experience. The *philological* sciences are similarly inductive, practicing that method that looks for analogies beneath differences, leading to *comparative* philology; and finally, the *historical* sciences rely on the criticism of *testimonial* evidence. In sum, for anyone possessing what C. W. Mills once called "the sociological imagination," the discussion of the moral sciences in the Sens lectures is a crashing bore.

---

[17] The word "sociology" does not appear anywhere in Lalande's notes.

THE SCIENCE OF ENDS

Durkheim's social realism was in some ways a sociological redescription of Kant. The treatment of ethics in the Sens lectures is almost equally Kantian, but in an entirely different – and entirely unsociological – way. To accept our moral responsibilities, Durkheim began, is to accept the fact that we are subject to a moral law. But in addition to this acceptance, there are two "psychic conditions" necessary for moral responsibility. The first is *freedom* – i.e., to be held responsible, each of us must be the sole cause of his actions – and the second is the *identity of the self* – i.e., to be held responsible for things we have done in the past, the two selves (past and present) must be one and the same. The "moral law" itself must first be *absolute* – i.e., it must command unconditionally. Second, it must be *universal* – i.e., the same in all societies and historical periods. Third, it must be *obligatory* – i.e., the moral law commands, and we are bound to obey.

The problem with earlier efforts to *define* the moral law, Durkheim complained, is that they typically fail to meet one or more of these conditions. The utilitarians,[18] for example, rest the moral law on *interest*; but, in a manner not unlike his later critique of utilitarianism, Durkheim insisted that interest is essentially *personal, variable, and subjective* – i.e., a more or less immediate pleasure that varies from one person, country, or historical period to another. By what right, for example, does Epicurus affirm that his pleasures are those of everyone? The utilitarian definition of the moral law thus fails to meet the conditions of *universality*; and since nothing is more difficult to recognize than our own, individual self-interest, a moral law based upon self-interest could hardly meet the condition of *obligation* as well. Like Kant in the *Groundwork of the Metaphysic of Morals*, therefore, Durkheim concluded that experience has nothing to teach us about the moral law.

The alternative of basing the moral law on a "natural moral sentiment" is subject to at least four objections.[19] First, the sentiment is hardly infallible, leading us into error as often as into truth, and we have no way of knowing when it's false and when not. Second, a moral law based on sentiment could hardly be obligatory, for unlike

---

[18] Durkheim's critique of utilitarianism is particularly wide-ranging, comprising Aristippus and the Cyrenaics, Epicurus, Bentham, Mill, and Spencer.

[19] Here Durkheim mentions Hutcheson, Rousseau, and Jacobi, but the focus of his critique is clearly Adam Smith's *Theory of the Moral Sentiments* (1759).

our reason, our feelings are almost irresistible. We cannot be
"commanded" to love someone, for example, and the theory of
moral sentiments is thus incompatible with the notion of obligation
already described. Third, a moral law based on the feeling of
sympathy depends heavily on the presence of at least one other
person (i.e., on *society*); but social conditions are always *contingent*,
while the moral law must be such as to be independent of particular
conditions or situations. Finally, the theory of a moral sentiment
mistakes the effect for the cause. If I instinctively like one person rather
than another, Durkheim argued, this is because the first respects the
moral law, while the second doesn't. In other words, we have
sympathy for certain people because they are good, not the reverse.

Durkheim's students were thus led almost irresistibly to Kant's
initial, more formal definition of the moral law – i.e., "Act according
to a maxim such that you can always wish that it be a universal law."
And it is here that Durkheim's lectures on ethics become especially
interesting, for he refused to accept the Kantian distinction between
"hypothetical" and "categorical" imperatives. A *hypothetical* imperative, according to Kant, is simply a command that must be obeyed if
we are to realize a given end. A *categorical* imperative, by contrast,
commands *unconditionally*, and has its end in itself. For an action to be
moral, therefore, it is not enough that it *merely conform* to the moral
law; on the contrary, the action must be done *only out of respect for* the
moral law, simply *because the law commands it* – i.e., for its own sake.
But an imperative that is truly and absolutely *categorical*, Durkheim
objected, is simply *impossible* – i.e., we always want to know *why* we
should act in a certain way, a maxim of action must always act on us
through some kind of *motive* if it is to be efficacious. In short, we need
to have an *interest* (in the largest sense) in the actions we perform.
Second, we rather clearly *do* have a reason to respect the moral law –
i.e., a reason that is implicit within the categorical imperative and
transforms it into a hypothetical imperative. Briefly, we should act in
such a way that the maxim of our actions can be elevated into a
universal law *if we truly want to be human beings*. Durkheim's third
argument – despite Kant's claim that the moral law should be purely
formal – was that the later formulations of the categorical imperative
in fact granted it this material content: "Act in such a way that you
always treat human beings – either yourself or others – as an end
and never as a means." The end of the moral law, therefore, lies not
just in *itself*, but in *respect for the human personality*. A purely formal

morality, Durkheim concluded, is not far from being an empty morality; and Kant was able to avoid this consequence only by contradicting his own system.

Durkheim thus asked the Aristotelian question – what is a human being *for*? The answer to this "functional" question about human beings, he insisted, will *be* the moral law, for that law simply commands us to advance toward the realization of our *end* or *purpose*. Durkheim's *first* formulation of the moral law was thus: "Advance toward your end." But what *is* our end? Today, Durkheim answered, each of us is essentially – albeit incompletely and imperfectly – a *person*. To advance toward our end is thus to develop, complete, and perfect our *personality*, yielding Durkheim's *second* formulation of the moral law: "Act always toward the end of developing your personality." But what is a *person*? As we have already seen, the first, most essential condition of being a person is to be free – i.e., to be the cause of one's own actions. The opposite of the person is thus the *thing* – i.e., something that has no initiative, receives its movement from outside, but does not place itself in movement. The person, by contrast, is able to remove himself from external constraints, and to draw all his action from himself. As such, the person is no longer condemned to see himself used as a *means* – either in relation to external things, or by other human beings. Hence Durkheim's *third* formulation of the moral law: "Act always in a way to treat your person as an end in itself, and never as a means."

These first three formulations of the moral law, Durkheim admitted, do not yet remove us from the self, from egoism. We are commanded to respect our own personality, but we have not yet discovered a rule to govern our relations with other human beings. But if we remember that the moral law is *universal*, Durkheim continued, we will see that not only ourselves, but all other human beings as well, should develop *their* personalities – i.e., treat their person as an end, and not as a means. To strike a blow at the personality of others is to presume that the law applies to us but not to them – something that contradicts the universality of the law. Durkheim thus arrived at the "definitive" formulation of the moral law – i.e., "Act always in a way to treat the human personality, everywhere it is encountered, as an end, and never as a means." Finally, Durkheim observed, this formulation helps us to see how the moral law, although universal, can vary from one individual to another. We all realize our personality by advancing toward our ends; but we don't all understand our ends in the same way. The universality of the law is thus expressed in diverse and sometimes contradictory forms.

The foundation of the moral law is thus *the idea of finality*, which presents a double advantage over the others described: first, the idea of finality immediately implies the action in question, without which the calculation of interest would have to intervene, and also without passion playing a role; and second, the idea of finality does not command an absurd and impossible form of moral conduct. This conception of our end necessarily implies the will to realize it; but unlike Kant's "barbarous" ethics, our conception of the moral law still allows us to aspire to *happiness*. Our end, of course, is not happiness, but rather the development of our personality; but the necessary consequence of the realization of our end will, in fact, *be* happiness. Where Kant saw a radical antinomy (presumably between duty and happiness), Durkheim saw only a harmony, which in no way compromises the dignity of the moral law.

From this neo-Kantian redescription of the moral law, the more traditional vocabulary of ethics – e.g., duty, good, virtue, right, justice, etc. – followed quite naturally. "Duty" is the obligation to respect the law – i.e., to advance our end. The "good" is simply the end itself – i.e., the development of our personality. Unlike Kant, for whom the idea of the good was a consequence of the idea of duty, Durkheim thus insisted that the good is *prior to* duty – i.e., we should do our duty because the moral law is good.

"Virtue" is the *constant practice* of duty – i.e., a disposition or habitual activity in the sense described by Aristotle; and this in turn requires the exercise of a "good will" – i.e., first, to dismiss sensible motives that interfere with our reason, and prevent us from clearly and sincerely seeing our end; and second, to apply the judgment of reason under the moral law. But, *pace* Kant, it is irrational to condemn people for their possession of those sentiments that assist virtue.

"Right" is an authority to which we occasionally find ourselves entrusted; and it is a *moral* authority in the sense that is respected independently of any *material* means. Where, then, does "right" come from? In the state of nature, Hobbes argued, the right of each man is as extensive as his own strength; but under these circumstances human life is constantly threatened. Since our most active instinct is self-preservation, we agree reciprocally to abandon a part of these *primitive* rights in order to respect each other's security, creating a new "right" based upon convention. To remove this right from the capricious wills and fantasies of individuals, a monarch is invested with absolute power, to guarantee the permanencies of the contract. In short, for Hobbes, "right" has its origin in self-interest, and rests on a convention that is guaranteed by a man armed with absolute power.

Durkheim agreed with Hobbes that an individual – whatever strength he might have – is quite fragile, and an insufficient guardian of right. With Locke, however, Durkheim wondered what good it can do to remove right from the dangers of the crowd, and place it in the hands of a single man. The will of a single person or the traditions of his family are not sufficient guarantees of right; on the contrary, there would be more security in leaving the enforcement of the contract in the hands of the community. Moreover – assuming that we agree with Hobbes that strength is the foundation of right – what *is* "right"? Cousin said that it is nothing else but the *accountability of duty* – e.g., others have the *duty* to respect my life, and I thus have the *right* to require others to respect their duty. My right would thus be based on the duty that others have in relation to me. But where does this right come from? How is it that I have the right to require others to perform their duties? Is it our function to make virtue thrive in the world? If so, my right to require that others perform their duties (e.g., charity) leads us directly to socialism – and to the destruction of individual freedom. Durkheim, by contrast, based the idea of right on *our* duties, not those of others. As we have seen, we each have duties under the moral law – i.e., to develop our personality. As a consequence, we also have the right to do everything necessary to accomplish these duties – e.g., if you threaten my person, I have the right to protect it by whatever means possible. "Man has only one right," Durkheim concluded his discussion of theoretical ethics, "that of doing everything which is necessary to accomplish his duty – i.e., to realize his end."

This *theoretical* vocabulary in turn yielded four sets of injunctions – individual, domestic, civic, and social – applied to certain *practical* conditions of human life. To know what duties we owe to ourselves, for example, we need only to apply the general formula of the moral law to the particular case of an individual removed from social relations with others. We should always strive to develop our personality, for example, to respect and perfect ourselves and not fall into dependence on things. Considering Durkheim's later interests, it is worth noting that here the moral law yields an injunction against suicide, for three reasons: first, we have other individual duties to fulfill (e.g., the development of our intelligence, sensibility, activity, etc.), which require the conservation of our bodies; second, in so far as suicide is an attempt to avoid pain, it presumes that the person is an instrument for pleasure – something contrary to the moral law; and third, suicide prevents us from performing our social duties – i.e., our duties towards others. Here, Durkheim's definition of "suicide" was as inclusive as that in *Le Suicide* (1897) – e.g., the slow death caused by asceticism, privation, and/or voluntary suffering, for example, is just as immoral as its sudden counterpart; and the "courageous and honorable" death of Cato – an example of altruistic suicide in the later work – appears here in defense of the proposition that suicide is not necessarily an act of cowardice. But on the whole, it's difficult to imagine a less sociological treatment of suicide.

Quite aside from our duty simply to preserve ourselves, however, Durkheim insisted that we have duties to our *souls* – i.e., to perfect our intelligence, our sensibility, and our will. The natural end of the *intelligence*, for example, is *truth.* This means that lying was proscribed by Durkheim no less than by Kant; but in the Sens lectures, it also means that we are required to develop our intelligence. Explicitly attacking Rousseau's notion that the progress of civilization has undermined morality, therefore, Durkheim insisted that the greater a man's intelligence, the greater his morality. For intelligence is a part of our nature, and there can be no antinomy between nature and morality; thus, we can give ourselves entirely to the arts and the sciences, without fear of contradicting the moral law. The duties we owe to our *sensibility* are analogous to those we owe to our intelligence; but our sensibility, unlike our intelligence, is comprised of sometimes contradictory passions, emotions, and inclinations, and we cannot develop all of them simultaneously. Our inclinations, therefore, must be developed *harmoniously,* some being subordinated to others; and the inclination to which all others should be subordinated is that of *human dignity.* To exercise our *will,* Durkheim concluded, is to *work*; and thus work, under all its forms, is a moral duty.

The family, Durkheim's treatment of domestic morality begins, is the only institution which does a good job of raising children, for there is a natural, instinctual love of parents for their children which, though later transformed into a more reasoned affection, can never be replaced; and the family is also the first school of disinterestedness, for it is within the family that the child, who would otherwise fall prey to egoism, learns that he must occasionally make sacrifices and devotions – things that society will later demand. Apparently recalling what he had learned from Fustel, Durkheim added that the ancient city was comprised of families, and the earliest nation-states of several cities. "Society," Durkheim continued, "is like a large organism," in which the brain commands, and the actions of smaller, "secondary centers" are subordinated to the brain. Families are such secondary centers, and without them, the actions of the brain could never be transmitted to the whole, and society would be destroyed at its base.

Durkheim's discussion of the duties of parents to their children is interesting for its opposition to the theory of education presented in Rousseau's *Emile* (1762) – a work in which Durkheim later took far more serious interest (see chapter 5, pp. 285–90). According to Rousseau, the way to educate best is to educate least. The influence of the father – already corrupted by civilization – should be minimized, and the child raised far from the towns and cities. For the child is good by nature, and should thus be left to the freedom of his natural instincts. The apparent alternative to Rousseau's theory, Durkheim observed, is to give parents an authority as absolute as possible, so that they might inculcate all their ideas and habits in their children. This alternative theory, Durkheim argued, is *immoral*, for it violates the "person" of the child which, though in an undeveloped condition, already exists. But Rousseau's theory, which grants the child much greater freedom, is *chimerical*. The child is neither good nor bad, Durkheim insisted, for these things are settled only by heredity and circumstances; and the "method of abstention," which provides the child neither with instruction nor education, leaves him without weapons when he reaches the age of struggle. So we must prepare the child, which to Durkheim meant providing the child with *habits*; and for this, we must use authority – "without excess," Durkheim cautioned, "but in order to prepare the future of the human personality in the child" (1884: 456). The parents thus have the duty of providing the child with material and moral support, but always with the goal of preparing the child to be a free human being – again, a "person" who is the cause of his own actions.

Noting that some philosophers (e.g., Hobbes, Bossuet, Rousseau, etc.) considered society "artificial" and "counter to nature," Durkheim's account of civic morality advanced the argument that society is a part of nature – a view that formed at least a part of his later, social realist vocabulary. First, altruistic sentiments – as we've already seen – are as natural as their egoistic counterparts, so that the "voice of nature" urges us to associate with one another; second, we are social animals, born into the "natural society" of the family; and third, Durkheim again appealed to Claude Bernard, who had described man as composed of millions of anatomical elements possessing their own individuality and vitality. What does this prove, Durkheim asked? Briefly, that isolation itself is unnatural, that everyone has a need for association. "The large society that unites individuals is no less natural," Durkheim insisted, "than a small society which constitutes each of these individuals. The larger society, like the smaller, is a natural organism which has its brain, its nerves, its vessels, etc., enjoying only a greater complexity" (1884: 461). The view that society is a part of nature, therefore, was a part of Durkheim's vocabulary from the start; but here "nature" referred to the psychological fact of altruistic sentiments. The quite different notion that social facts are concrete, complex things – characterized by externality and constraint, and to be studied *comme des choses* – was not yet in evidence.

Why, he asked, do men unite with each other this way? Briefly, because it is natural to them, and because they cannot be self-sufficient. The life of the modern European, Durkheim explained, is such that no individual alone can fulfill the multiple functions it demands. The process upon which we depend, therefore, is the *division of labor* – i.e., each individual, charged with a special function, fulfills it better and more quickly, and thus acquires the products necessary to his life while also exchanging the products of his labor. Lest we jump to the conclusion that we are but a short step from Durkheim's first major book, however, it's important to recognize that Durkheim's source here was Claude-Frédéric Bastiat (1801–50), whose posthumously published *Harmonie économique* argued – like Adam Smith's *Wealth of Nations* (1776) – that the division of labor was important primarily because it transformed the pursuit of private interest into public goods. It was to displace this preoccupation with the purely *economic* benefits of the division of labor, of course, that Durkheim would write *De la division du travail social* (1984: 1–7).

The suspicion that the Sens lecturer lacked any sociological sensibilities is deepened still further by his discussion of the function of legal punishment. Some philosophers, Durkheim observed, have argued that the foundation of punishment is *expiation* – i.e., the person who has violated the law must be punished in order to expiate his fault. But how does a punishment erase a fault? By what right does a government impose virtue on its citizens? Does it even have the means to do so? For to expiate a fault, Durkheim observed, we must know the intention – which alone makes the act moral or immoral – as well as the act itself. A punishment, Durkheim thus argued, can never be an expiation; and neither can it "improve" the guilty (something for which, in any case, we are not responsible). For punishment often makes people worse rather than better: "To terrify a man," Durkheim insisted, "is not to improve his heart" (1884: 463). The foundation of penality, Durkheim thus concluded, is *the right of a society* – no less than an individual person – to defend itself. In *De la division du travail social*, of course, Durkheim advanced a powerful and controversial theory of punishment in which vengeance and expiation were treated as among its major functions (1984: 46–7).

What is the function of government itself? According to the *socialist* theory – of which Durkheim found a "complete expression" in Rousseau's *Contrat social* (1762) – all citizens have abdicated their rights, individuality, and "personality" by entering society, and thus they belong to the State. Since the ends of society transcend those of the individual, the government is granted absolute sovereignty as long as it serves society's ends. The alternative is *liberal* or *individualist* theory – i.e., in which *society* is an abstraction, and the *individual* alone is a reality. Here the function of government is to protect citizens against one another, and to safeguard the individuality of each. The government exercises authority and intervenes in the lives of citizens only to obligate each individual to respect the rights and liberty of others. The *socialist* theory, Durkheim responded, is "obviously immoral" – i.e., it undermines the personality of the individual, by using it as a means to the realization of its own ends. The compensation offered by Rousseau – i.e., the renunciation of individual freedom in order to benefit from an association of which one is also a member – is insufficient; for the fact that *others* renounce *their* personality doesn't mitigate the fact that *my* renunciation (as well as theirs) is immoral from the moment it is performed. The *liberal* or *individualist* doctrine, by contrast, is not immoral; but against the notion that individual ends alone have value, Durkheim insisted that each society, like each individual, *does* have an end that is appropriate to it. "By this alone," he explained, "that we are to the west of Germany, to the north of Spain and of Italy, we have certain *appropriate interests*, which are not those of other countries. We have an end which is ours, other than that of England, Switzerland, or Italy" (1884: 465). The proper function of government is thus not simply to protect the personality of individual citizens, but also to lead each society to its proper end.

Discussions of the most general obligations of social life commonly distinguish between *positive* duties: those which *command* an action (e.g., doing good to others), and might be fulfilled in a variety of ways to various degrees; and *negative* duties: i.e., those which *forbid* an action (e.g., killing someone), and are both specific and absolute, admitting of no degrees in performance. Durkheim acknowledged that the distinction holds some justification, but he questioned the tendency to assume that negative duties were somehow *more obligatory* than their positive counterparts, and that positive acts more meritorious because they are *less obligatory.* This assumption, Durkheim argued, derives from the fact that positive duties – less important to society – have no civil sanction; but the moral law – and here again the Sens lecturer sounds more like Kant than the later Durkheim – transcends the laws of society. "All duties," Durkheim here insisted, "derive from the moral law, which confers on all of them the same character of obligation. It is absolute in itself, and by consequence, there is no distinction to make in its application" (1884: 472–3).

Durkheim's example of a "negative" duty was *justice* – i.e., not "undermining the personality" of others, including their lives, sensibility, intelligence, and activity. To respect the *sensibility* of others, for example, means to be *polite.* But what do we do when this duty conflicts with the duty of truthfulness? Objecting strongly to both Rousseau and Kant, Durkheim insisted that where the choice is inescapable, we might lie if the truth would cause great sadness to another human being. To respect the *intelligence* of others is to let them think and express their ideas – i.e., *toleration* – something required not only by the moral law, but also required for the progress of science itself. Finally, Durkheim's notion of the respect for other people's *activity* was divided into two parts. To respect activity *in itself* means to respect the *freedom* of others, to resist and oppose their subordination or enslavement; and to respect the *external conditions* of others' activity means to respect their *property* – we can develop our personality only in so far as we can exercise it on external objects.

Quite aside from the *negative* duty of justice, there is also the more *positive* duty of *charity* – i.e., to do whatever we can to support others, to care for them, and to "enlarge their personality." Just as justice demands that we respect the sensibility of others by being *polite*, for example, charity demands that we respect their sensibility through the duty of *good will*. Where justice requires that we respect others' intelligence through toleration, the more positive duty of charity requires that we work to enhance this intelligence, by teaching others what we know. And where justice insists that we respect the *activity* of others by *protecting their property*, charity demands that we enable our peers to *receive property* – i.e., through the giving of *alms*. Finally, however obligatory these more positive duties, Durkheim insisted that *charity* should never contradict *justice*. Our first duty is to do no harm to others, and our second is to aid them.

Historically, Durkheim explained, the great philosophers have followed one of two methods. The *empiricist* method – which was followed by Epicurus, Spencer, and reached its "most perfect development" with Mill – begins by observing human beings and the conditions of their happiness, progresses through induction and generalization, and then develops the moral law from these observations. But as we have already seen, the empiricist method never reaches the universality which is a determining characteristic of the moral law. It reaches only local, provisional rules, good for a certain time, and for a limited number of individuals. The *a priori* method of Kant, by contrast, starts with the abstract concept of a pure moral law and, assuming that the will can act without sensibility, asks what the law of this will should be. But Kant's method is "imaginary" – i.e., it is the rule of an ideal, hypothetical activity – not of human beings as they are. Durkheim reminded his students that his own, more eclectic method was *both* deductive *and* experimental. He had begun with a fact of experience – i.e., moral responsibility – and then deduced the conditions of moral responsibility – i.e., the moral law of developing our personality. Durkheim emphasized that, unlike Kant, he had never ignored human nature – i.e., as a being endowed with sensibility, pursuing its own, distinctive ends. Where Kant had *excluded* psychology *from* ethics and Mill had *reduced* ethics *to* psychology, Durkheim claimed to have *based* his ethics *on* psychology

– i.e., "in order to know *what man should do*, we have asked ourselves *what man is*." Psychology tells us that he is a person, he explained, and our ethics thus concludes that he should be a person. As in his later work – albeit in a very different way – Durkheim thus claimed to have done justice to both the *a priori* and the *empiricist* approach to ethics, without the disadvantages of either – i.e., moral responsibility (a fact of *experience*) was his point of departure, while finality (an *a priori* idea) regulated his ethics.

When Durkheim turned from ethics to metaphysics, the significance of his Leibnizian – by contrast with Cartesian – realism became clear. When we say there is a *soul*, for example, we mean only that, within us, related to our states of consciousness, there is "a principle distinct from the matter we perceive through the senses." In his earlier lecture on the external world, Durkheim had argued that the idea of extension is *contradictory*, that the notion of *extended* matter is thus only an *appearance*, and the substratum of this appearance must be conceived as *forces* analogous to ourselves. Durkheim now turned this argument around, suggesting that the principle that we call *matter*, when it is perceived by the *senses*, is identical to the principle we call the *mind* as perceived by the *consciousness*. This is what we mean, Durkheim insisted, when we say that the soul is "spiritual" – i.e., it is "matter" different from "sensible, extended" matter.

Durkheim thus advanced four "special proofs" of the spirituality of the soul, the first three of which demonstrate a contradiction between the nature of mind and that of matter.[20] First, Durkheim observed, the mind is *one*, while matter is *multiple and indefinitely divisible*: second, the mind is *identical*, while matter is constantly *changing*; and third, mind is endowed with *activity* and *spontaneity*, while matter is *inert*. These three arguments are analogous to those used by Descartes for the same purpose – i.e., to demonstrate the difference between mind and matter. But Durkheim emphasized that his method was not the same as Descartes' – i.e., the Cartesian arguments depended upon the notion that "two concepts which can be conceived separately belong to different species," while Durkheim's arguments were based on the principle that "two orders of phenomena presenting contradictory characteristics are not

---

[20] The fourth argument for the spirituality of the soul – often conjoined with the first three – is that the soul and the body are frequently in conflict, and that this indicates the existence of two distinct principles (1884: 497–8).

related to the same substance." Durkheim thus argued that his own, Leibnizian position escaped the most common objection made to spiritualism – i.e., that it accepts the existence of two different kinds of reality. "Our spiritualism," he emphasized, "admits, on the contrary, that the soul is *not* a reality of a separate nature, arising suddenly in the scale of beings. The mind finds itself in all degrees, only more or less rudimentary: everything lives," Durkheim concluded, "everything is animated, everything thinks" (1884: 498).

The scientific method constantly enjoins us *not to multiply* causes and/or principles, Durkheim admitted, and materialists have thus attacked spiritualism for admitting *two* realities, *two* irreducible principles, provoking an immediate presumption against it. But spiritualism only does this, Durkheim objected, because most spiritualists believe that sensible matter cannot have the property of thought. Recognizing that the essence of things escapes us, Durkheim asked rhetorically, is it conceivable that someday it will be "proved experimentally" that matter is endowed with spontaneity and thought? Durkheim's initial response to this rhetorical question was to remind his students that *his own*, Leibnizian form of spiritualism *avoids dualism altogether* – i.e., reality is always the same. But seen from the *outside*, it is *material*, while seen from the *inside*, it is *spirit*. The spiritualist hope that sensible matter would one day be shown to think is purely illusory – as Durkheim had just explained in his previous lecture, the constitutive qualities of the mind (e.g., unity, identity, etc.) don't belong to matter, and the absence of these qualities implies the absence of thought. Materialists also point to the dependence of the *psychological* on the *physiological* life; but Durkheim immediately countered by emphasizing the influence of the *moral* life on our *physical health*. The reciprocal influence of these two lives on one another is thus incontestable, Durkheim observed, and this indicates that they have the same principle; but we still have no reason to believe that this principle is material rather than spiritual. Finally, materialists insist that thought varies with the brain's volume, weight, form, quality, quantity of phosphorous, circulation of blood, etc. But these facts, Durkheim argued, are explained just as well if we consider the brain as the *condition* – and not the *cause* – of thought; and the condition, Durkheim reminded his students, is simply that without which the cause cannot produce its effect, not the cause itself. What we call "matter," Durkheim concluded, is only a collection of *appearances*, and the existing substance that *underlies and supports* these appearances cannot be reached through the senses.

The concluding Sens lectures dealt with metaphysical and moral arguments for the existence of God and divine providence. It's surprising to see Durkheim treating these issues so carefully; but he seems to have taken some theological arguments more seriously than others, and it's important to look at his reasons for doing so. Descartes' argument from the idea of perfection, for example, was rejected on the ground that it presumes that our ideas are the products of external objects – whether material or transcendent – and it thus denies our minds the active role that Durkheim's spiritualism had repeatedly insisted they possess. Similarly, while the ontological argument was flatly dismissed on Kantian grounds, Durkheim credited Leibniz with first recognizing that geometric reasoning – i.e., drawing inferences from first principles – has nothing to tell us about the existence of a perfect being. Both the cosmological argument and the more abstract version of the proof by the principle of finality were quickly dispatched; but like Kant, Durkheim seems to have had considerable respect for "physico-theological proof" (i.e., also known as the teleological argument, or the argument from design).

The teleological argument begins, Durkheim explained, with the empirical observation that nature presents us with evidence of order, plan, or design. This order is contingent, suggesting that there is a cause that has produced the world, not as a force "fatally engendering" its effect, but as an intelligence which acts freely. This in turn implies the existence of a *designer* – i.e., an intelligence coordinating things harmoniously in view of some end. To this, Durkheim added Leibniz's principle of sufficient reason. At the origin of things, according to Leibniz, there was an infinity of "logically possible worlds." Who, then, made the choice among all these possibilities? Why was one world chosen from these possibilities, and existence denied to all the others? Such a choice, Leibniz reasoned, implies the existence of an intelligence combined with a will, a supreme person – i.e., God. It was God, therefore, who chose the present world because it is the best; and without God, this choice no longer has "sufficient reason" (Wiener 1951: 93–6; Durkheim 1884: 527).

All philosophers, Durkheim observed, agree with the first step of the proof: i.e., the universe *does* reveal a certain order or harmony –

e.g., the "marvelous proportion" between organisms and their environments, as well as the extraordinary coordination of the constituent elements within the organism itself. But mechanists like Spencer, Durkheim observed, explain both as the deterministic consequence of *efficient* – rather than *final* – causes. The harmony between an organism and its environment, Spencer argues, can be explained by "adaptation" and the "instability of the homogeneous" – i.e., a homogeneous mass is inherently unstable, so that an organism must *differentiate* in order to adapt to its environment. The internal coordination of parts is explained by "segregation" – i.e., the joining together of similar things into distinct systems. Durkheim's reply to Spencer reaffirmed his earlier commitment to final causes. If an organism is placed in a hostile environment, for example, it may or may not develop the organs necessary to its adaptation. But if it does develop these adaptive organs, Durkheim argued, can this development be explained simply as a consequence of the fact that the organs were necessary? If so, isn't this proof by the principle of finality? If not, isn't this development the consequence of mere chance? Moreover, where Spencer's theory might account for the *physical* coordination of the parts of an organism (i.e., the reunion of similar elements), it cannot explain their *organic* coordination – i.e., their *systematization* or *subordination to a dominant unity*. In an organism, Durkheim reminded his students, all the parts cooperate in the whole, and this subordination is repeated in each individual organ. In short, the harmony between organisms and their environments and the coordination of the constituent elements within an organism make our appeal to final causes all the more necessary (1884: 542).

If the evidence of harmony and equilibrium in nature is thus sufficient to justify the belief in a final cause, how was this cause to be represented? The physico-theological argument, Durkheim reminded his students, conceives of the world as a work of art, and attributes its finality to the intelligence of an artist; in short, it conceives of the world anthropomorphically, as the product of a transcendent mind. But why can't finality be *immanent* – i.e., things going spontaneously to their end, as if guided by instinct rather than a transcendent mind? Versions of such an argument appear in Aristotle and also in Hegel; but it was immediately clear that here Durkheim was referring to Hartmann and Schopenhauer, whose theory of immanent finality was designed to replace transcendent finality and avoid anthropomorphism altogether. The "great failure" of their argument, according to Durkheim, was that it is *irrepresentible*. Briefly, all finality assumes the *concept* of an end; and such a concept is a *psychological* phenomenon, and is thus inconceivable without *consciousness*. Because he embraced the doctrine of unconscious psychological phenomena, Hartmann was undisturbed by this objection; but Durkheim, as we have seen, had already rejected the notion of the unconscious, and was thus led to accept a transcendent finality.

Does the physico-theological argument prove the existence of God? Kant thought not, addressing two objections to the argument, and Durkheim agreed with him on both. First, while the physico-theological argument demonstrates clearly that there is an "architect" of the universe, and that its *form* is contingent, it does *not* demonstrate that there is a "creator," and that the *material* is contingent. For this, we require the cosmological argument, which Kant had also rejected. Second, while the physico-theological argument begins with experience, it is not limited to experience alone. For if the order and harmony of the world are imperfect, we cannot conclude with the existence of a perfect cause. In fact, everything given to us in experience is more or less imperfect, and thus the physico-theological argument yields at best a cause which is "very wise" and "very powerful" in relation to ourselves – but is not a *perfect* cause.

This brought Durkheim to the moral arguments for the existence of God. The first moral proof is from *common consent* – i.e., the notion, initially advanced by Cicero, that because all men believe in God, God must exist. But as Durkheim immediately pointed out, it isn't clear that all men believe in God, and even if they did, this would provide only a presumption – not a proof – in favor of God's existence. The second moral argument, of course, was Kant's – i.e., that two elements of morality seem to presume a foundation outside of morality itself. The first element is *obligation* – i.e., the moral law must *bind* us in some way, and it can do so only if we consider it as something living – i.e., as God himself; and the second element is the *sanction* – i.e., reason cries out for the harmony of virtue and happiness, and this is possible only assuming a transcendent God who puts nature into conformity with morality. So God appears to us both as the living moral law and as the sole condition on which the harmony of happiness and virtue might be realized. From the *metaphysical* arguments, therefore, Durkheim was able to conclude that God exists as an absolute end, and also that he is the *architect* – but not necessarily *creator* – of the world; and from the *moral* arguments Durkheim was able to conclude that God is the living moral law, as well as the condition of moral sanctions.

How does God relate to the world? Writers like Descartes had insisted that the world must be perpetually connected to the source from which it takes its existence – his primary metaphysical argument for the existence of *providence*. But here, Durkheim observed, it is useful to introduce the traditional distinction between a *particular* and a *general* providence. The first, as described by Bossuet, is an effective intervention of God in the human events of the world; but this doctrine of a particular providence, Durkheim complained, both contradicts the idea of human freedom and exalts the power of God at the expense of his dignity. Providence is therefore general – i.e., it is the perfect wisdom and goodness of God, exercised at the beginning of time when it established the laws that govern the world, and continuing into the present through the maintenance of these laws and the conservation of the world.

A serious objection to this notion of a general providence, however, had been made by Pierre Bayle (1647–1706), who had revived the Manichaean doctrine of evil as a principle independent of God. Evil, Bayle had observed, may be of three kinds: *metaphysical* (the physical and intellectual imperfection of all beings, including ourselves); *moral* (the weakness of our will, which leads to sin); and *physical* (suffering, illness, and death). How can such evil, Bayle asked, be reconciled with our notion of a general providence? In his *Theodicy* (1710), Leibniz responded to Bayle that none of these evils proves anything against providence, for each is but the condition of inestimable goods, which would be impossible without them. Metaphysical evil, for example, simply shows that, as created beings, we cannot be perfect – something that belongs to the absolute alone. Far from being an independent entity, therefore, this kind of evil is only the negation – and thus a condition – of the good. Similarly, moral evil is a necessary condition of moral good, for we can do good (or evil) only if we are free to choose. Finally, physical evil is the consequence of the operations of natural laws; but these laws were not created for that reason, but because without them the world would not exist. The suffering of some individuals is thus a condition of the existence of the world. Moreover, pain and suffering are "the best school of morality," raising individuals to a kind of dignity that the perpetually happy person could never achieve. At the moment of creation, Leibniz argued, God imagined the infinity of possible universes, and chose – not the *absolutely* best – but the best *possible* world. So to judge the perfection of the creation – and thus the goodness of its author – we must resist the tendency to judge each of the parts in detail, and instead judge the totality of things that exist. Evil can be considered bad only by minds that systematically limit their analysis to a part rather than the whole; and while the whole world is not perfect, neither is it bad. It is, according the Leibniz, the best of all *possible* worlds.

If Durkheim thus agreed with Leibniz's response to Bayle's theological pessimism, his real concern was to counter the *psychological* and *moral* pessimism of Schopenhauer and Hartmann, whose works he found to be "almost popular over large parts of Europe" (1884: 564–5). This is important, because S. G. Mestrovic has recently advanced the argument that Schopenhauer was a powerful influence on Durkheim's work (1988a; 1988b). The evidence of the Sens lectures, however, suggests otherwise. Schopenhauer's pessimism, Durkheim explained to his students, makes pleasure only the negation of pain, and thus makes pain the positive, normal fact of our sensibility; and while Hartmann at least granted pleasure a positive value, he also insisted that the quantity of pleasure that one can experience in life is vastly inferior to the amount of pain we are assured. If Hartmann is right, Durkheim acknowledged, then the being that created us does not merit the name of "providence"; and in fact, Hartmann insisted that the *Unconscious* – i.e., the mysterious principle of all nature – created us only to realize its own, personal ends. But Durkheim insisted that Schopenhauer and Hartmann were wrong, for two reasons. First, the pessimists treat pleasure as an objective, impersonal phenomenon; but pleasure, Durkheim insisted, is clearly an individual matter – i.e., what is "pleasurable" for one person might not be pleasurable for the next – and thus they can hardly be submitted to quantitative measurement. Second, the pessimists assume that pain obsesses the mind for long periods, while pleasure is fleeting; but memory and hope, Durkheim argued, allow us to make pleasures endure no less than pains. Aristotle's *Ethics* tells us that happiness is an art, Durkheim concluded his last lecture – and an art can be learned.

BOUTROUX, FUSTEL, AND RENOUVIER

The Sens lectures, of course, were not intended for publication, and thus they provide few indications of the writers from whom Durkheim drew these early ideas. A good place to start looking, however, is among Durkheim's mentors at the Ecole Normale Supérieure. One of the most important of these was the neo-Kantian philosopher Emile Boutroux (1845–1921). During his studies at the Ecole Normale Supérieure from 1865 to 1868, Boutroux had come under the influence of the neo-spiritualist philosopher Jules Lachelier (1832–1918), whose *Du fondement de l'induction* (1871) had challenged the foundations of rationalism and determinism on Kantian grounds (Potts and Charlton 1974: 71). Boutroux's first major work was *De la contingence des lois de la nature*, a study of determinism in its relation to the physical and moral sciences, for which he received his doctorate in 1874 and which ultimately proved to be his *magnum opus*. After teaching at Montpellier and Nancy, in 1877 Boutroux received an appointment in philosophy at the Ecole Normale, where he remained for the next nine years – including the period from 1879 to 1882, when Durkheim was his student.

In discussing his undeniable influence on Durkheim, it is customary to focus on Boutroux's insistence on the distinctiveness and irreducibility of the various sciences; but as W. W. Miller has recently emphasized – and as the title itself implies – *De la contingence* is primarily about causality itself, and the issue of necessity versus contingency (1996: 61). "If [the laws of nature] were actually necessary," Boutroux wrote in the preface, "[they] would signify the immutability and rigidity of death. If they are contingent, they dignify life and constitute points of support or bases which enable us constantly to rise towards a higher life" (1916: vii). Boutroux's goal was thus to show that the laws of nature are contingent rather than necessary, and that they indeed make a "higher life" possible. Boutroux did not deny that the principle of causality could be stated in such a form that it would be necessarily true; but he did insist that this is not the sense in which the principle is actually used in the natural sciences. On the contrary, for the purposes of scientific practice, the more Humean, empiricist notion of "relatively invariable relations" between the phenomena is all that is required for the formulation of scientific laws. The idea of necessity is simply not required. The principle of causality is derived from experience, as "a very general and abstract expression of observed relations" (1916: 23–5). So the development of the sciences themselves suggests that the laws of nature do not express objectively necessary relations. Scientific laws are useful, but they are not definitive. "There is no equivalence," Boutroux thus insisted, "no relation of causality, pure and simple, between a man and the elements that gave him birth, between the developed being and the being in process of formation" (1916: 32).

In opposition to the rationalist conception of a single world comprised of logically deducible necessary relations, therefore, Boutroux insisted on "several worlds, forming, as it were, stages superposed on one another" (1916: 151–2). These include the world of pure necessity (i.e., of quantity without quality), the world of causes, the world of notions, the mathematical world, the physical world, the living world and, at last, the thinking world. At first, Boutroux acknowledged, each of these worlds seems to depend on those beneath it, and to receive from them its existence and its laws; but again, the examination and comparison of these forms of being, as well as the sciences that study them, show that it is impossible to connect the higher to the lower forms by any link of necessity. This means, in turn, that the universe is not made up of equal elements capable of being transformed into one another like algebraic quantities; on the contrary, each world contains something new, something more than the worlds below, so that within each world the amount of being and the degree of perfection is indeterminate (1916: 158–9). Each world, in short, is indeterminate and contingent – i.e., might *not* have existed, or might have existed *in some other form* – rather than logically or causally necessary.

Clearly, this was a view that had obvious consequences for Darwin's theory of evolution by natural selection. "The creation of man, a conscious being," Boutroux made clear, "cannot be explained simply by the operation of the physical and physiological laws. His existence and action impose on nature modifications which she herself cannot understand, and which appear as contingent, if we adopt the standpoint of the physical and physiological worlds" (1916: 127). And as this passage implies, Boutroux – a devout Roman Catholic – considered God the creator of both the existence and the essence of all beings. From the religious standpoint, therefore, the doctrine of contingency was quite literally a theory of divine providence (1916: 180).

What is the effect of this doctrine of contingency on the positive sciences? Those "static" sciences based on the principle of the conservation of being (e.g., mathematics, physics, etc.), Boutroux admitted, are reduced to an abstract value, for these have no other role than to deduce consequences from stated conditions, under the hypothesis that these conditions must be exactly determined and the quantity of being not varied. But on the "dynamic" sciences (e.g., biology, psychology, sociology, etc.), the doctrine of contingency imposes only the condition that science become genuinely empiricist rather than rationalist in orientation. Observation and experiment become "the indispensable method of the dynamic sciences," the "eternal source and rule of science, in so far as this latter would know things in truly objective fashion, i.e., in their history as well as in their nature, which, after all, is but one of their states" (1916: 165–6). So the doctrine of contingency condemns only the rationalist claim that science might dispense with experience: "we cannot have the reduction of the historic to the static sciences," Boutroux insisted. On the contrary, "the former become the truly concrete sciences, whereas the rest, in various degrees, are but abstract sciences" (1916: 167).

Descartes, of course, had simply dismissed history and the "human sciences" as being of no interest to genuine seekers after truth, for they were incapable of yielding either precise definitions or the clear rules of evidence from which irrefutable conclusions could be drawn by logical deduction.[21] By contrast, Boutroux's doctrine of contingency suddenly made history "singularly important." The history of things was no longer the logical, necessary development of their intrinsic nature. On the contrary, things might have been otherwise, or not at all, and thus the conditions of their development up to their present, contingent state became a matter of serious empirical investigation (1916: 166–7). An obvious corollary of this contingency and indeterminacy is freedom of individual thought and action. The individual, Boutroux thus insisted, "is not only the creator of his character, he can also intervene in the events of his life and change their course; every moment he can strengthen his acquired tendencies or endeavor to modify them" (1916: 172). Forty

---

[21] Descartes 1985: 113–15. "[P]roud and magnificent palaces built only on sand and mud," Descartes characterized moral philosophy, and "in so far as they borrow their principles from philosophy," he added of other sciences, "I decided that nothing solid could have been built upon such shaky foundations." See Berlin 1980b: 133–4.

years after *De la contingence*, Boutroux could thus write: "I have restored to man, *qua* man, his thoughts and feelings, his will and action, that reality and affective influence over the course of things which common sense attributes to them . . . Man is able to act on nature because nature itself is neither a brute force nor a lifeless thought, but rather a veritable being, which, even now, in its own way, tends to exist and develop, to create and transcend itself" (1916: vi–vii).

The significance of *De la contingence* to the development of Durkheim's sociology is well known. In 1907, responding to Simon Deploige's "accusation" that the distinction he had drawn between psychology and sociology had been borrowed from Wilhelm Wundt (1832–1920), Durkheim at first acknowledged that "in Wundt, there is a tendency in this direction, intermingled in other places with contrary tendencies." But Durkheim went on to insist that he had acquired the idea elsewhere:

I owe it first to my master, Boutroux, who, at the Ecole normale supérieure, repeated frequently to us that each science must, as Aristotle says, explain [its own phenomena] by "its own principles" – e.g., psychology by psychological principles, biology by biological principles. Most impressed by this idea, I applied it to sociology. I was confirmed in this method by the reading of Comte, since for him, sociology is irreducible to biology (and consequently to psychology), just as biology is irreducible to the physico-chemical sciences. When I read Wundt's *Ethik*, I had already been moving in this direction for some time. (1907: 612–13)

In *De la contingence*, of course, this idea was combined with an insistence on the contingency (by contrast with necessity) of the laws of nature, opposition to determinism and affirmation of free will, denial that the evolution of the human mind could be explained by natural selection, a preference for empiricism rather than rationalism, an anti-Cartesian emphasis on the importance of history, a teleological notion of human perfection as the goal of life – all reflected in the Sens lectures.

But if Boutroux's influence on Durkheim is not deniable, neither is it unambiguous. Durkheim's later, extremely ambitious claims for sociology, for example, went far beyond anything that Boutroux could condone. In his inaugural lecture at Bordeaux (1887), Durkheim insisted that "all natural entities from the mineral world up through man come within the province of positive science, that is to say that all that concerns them occurs according to necessary laws. This proposition no longer partakes of conjecture; it is a truth which experience has demonstrated, for these laws have been found, or at least we are discovering them little by little" (1978a: 47). The obvious, Boutrouxian objection – i.e., that the notion of necessary laws of human behavior contradicts that of free will – "can hardly interest us," Durkheim insisted, "and we can ignore it, not out of disdain, but through the application of method." One must choose: "Either one recognizes that social phenomena are accessible to scientific investigation," Durkheim insisted, "or else one admits, for no reason and contrary to all the inductions of science, that there are two worlds within the world: one in which reigns the law of causality, the other in which reign arbitrariness and contingency" (1978a: 48).

Boutroux, of course, would have resisted such a conclusion; but *De la contingence* contains no explicit discussion of "laws of social behavior." Boutroux's theory of qualitatively different, irreducible levels of being culminated with the "thinking world" of human self-consciousness – not human societies. In 1892–93, however, Boutroux gave a series of lectures at the Sorbonne, subsequently published under the title *De l'idée de loi naturelle dans la science et la philosophie contemporaines* (1895), in which the status of sociological laws was treated in much greater detail (Boutroux 1914). Where the philosophic quest to find laws that are both "universal" and "real" had failed, Boutroux began, science has succeeded by effecting a compromise between the ideal of mathematics and the reality of experience. Science has achieved this by trying to find "an appropriate positive principle for each order of realities," eventually producing laws that are both concrete and intelligible. "The sciences have thus been emancipated, one after the other," Boutroux repeated the argument of *De la contingence,* and "have been set up as autonomous, with the aid of special principles regarded as irreducible" (1914: 18–19). To truly understand the idea of natural law, therefore, we should begin with science, appealing to philosophy only for the interpretation of the result. Boutroux thus took each group of laws – e.g., logical, mathematical, mechanical, physical, chemical, biological, psychological, and sociological – "just as the sciences offer them," only then asking the important philosophical questions (1914: 19–21).

When Boutroux turned his attention to the possibility of establishing scientific laws in the realm of society and politics, his approach was again deeply historical; and again, it emphasized the role of contingency. In the teleological world of Greek antiquity, he observed, nature is the artist, and the *polis* is nature's ideal societal expression. In the 17th and 18th centuries, by contrast, Hobbes, Montesquieu, and Rousseau conceive of society as a work of art rather than a work of nature – i.e., as the artificial product of human reason. But from the 18th century on, writers like Condorcet, Comte, and Spencer have advanced the notion that society is a product of nature, not of art.[22] "What is the notion of sociological law," Boutroux asked, "which results from this historical evolution from antiquity to the present? Does this notion correspond with the nature of the things themselves?" (1914: 194).

Boutroux's answer to these questions first noted that such a conception of sociological laws eliminates a strictly human faculty, i.e., conscious, reflective, purposeful action: "To explain phenomena, it is declared, is to condition them to the law of efficient causes. If sociology, then, would be a science like the rest, it must connect facts with conditions, not with ends."[23] But even if sociology thus limits itself to efficient causes, Boutroux asked, why should it be modeled on the natural sciences? The whole point of Boutroux's historical survey of sociological thought was to show that such models are historically contingent, not logically necessary. In the 17th and 18th centuries, for example, the mathematical sciences were preeminent, and it was assumed that sociological laws should take on a mathematical form. In the 19th and 20th centuries, the natural sciences have achieved greater status, so we assume that these should now be our models. But why, Boutroux again asked, should not sociology demand particular postulates and a method of its own?

As we saw in his writings on education, Durkheim would ask himself the same question; but Boutroux's answer was quite different. First, he insisted that *sociological* laws are like *historical* laws, for, at least in theory, historians connect the present to the past by means of efficient causes. But such laws, Boutroux observed, are not *necessary* laws – i.e., "the antecedent is never considered as necessarily

[22] This historical survey is important, not just for understanding Boutroux, but also for understanding Durkheim. Boutroux "revealed to [Durkheim] the great philosophers of the past," Davy reports, "and, in his penetrating and objective fashion of reconstructing and rethinking systems, revived and presented scientifically before his pupils the history of philosophy" (Lukes 1972: 58).

[23] This elimination of the human faculty for purposeful action, Boutroux observed, is parallel to the dismissal, by experimental psychology, of the human soul (1914: 194).

compelled to entail any one consequent to the exclusion of any other. An antecedent is regarded as an influence, not as a cause strictly so-called" (1914: 196). More fundamentally, however, Boutroux joined his former colleague at the Ecole Normale, Fustel, in questioning whether historians ever discover "laws" at all. A law, Fustel had observed, "implies the reappearance of one and the same antecedent." But historical facts "are too complex and unstable intermixtures to be reproduced as they are. If they exhibit laws," Boutroux concluded, "it is in their elements, not in their concrete sequence, that we must seek them" (1914: 197).

Boutroux thus turned to a second alternative – i.e., that we try to connect social facts, not with their equally social antecedents, but with external conditions capable of being observed and measured (e.g., geographical features, density of population, amount of sustenance, etc.). An initial difficulty here, however, is the potential circularity of such explanations: "Man, the social human being, intervenes in the former class of conditions: therefore they are, to a certain extent, social facts; to demand from society an explanation of them is partly to take for granted what we purpose to explain" (1914: 197–8). But Boutroux also saw a second difficulty with the effort to derive social facts from external conditions – a difficulty he illustrated by a familiar example:

Suppose, for instance, we explain the development of the division of labor by the progress of social density, the interdependence of the members of a society. The saying of Darwin is recalled, that different beings live side by side more easily than similar beings: they inconvenience one another in a less degree and the struggle for life amongst them is not so keen. Man obtains this salutary diversity by developing division of labor, and so this division of labor shows itself as the necessary result of the struggle for life. Vital competition: a physical cause, thus explains division of labor: a social fact. (1914: 198)

The example, of course, was taken from *De la division du travail social* (1893), the doctoral thesis defended by Durkheim during the spring of the same year Boutroux's lectures were given (1984: 200–25). In fact, Durkheim's thesis had been dedicated to Boutroux; but according to Bouglé, Boutroux accepted the dedication with a grimace, and according to the Doyen's report of the defense, Boutroux's discontent was particularly addressed to Durkheim's mechanical, necessitarian mode of explanation (Lukes 1972: 296, 297–8). Concerning the "law" that the increase in the division of labor is a direct result of the increasing density and volume of population, for example, Boutroux argued that the increasing division of labor was not the only possible solution. In reply, Durkheim insisted that he "did not wish to show that [his] law was the only possible consequence, but rather that it was a necessary consequence. There are others, but they are secondary and weak" (Lukes 1972: 298). Apparently Boutroux was unhappy with this reply; and he was no happier two years later, when his lectures were published. Does the law stated by Darwin, he asked, *necessarily* apply when we are dealing with man? Is it correct to say that, in a human society, diversity of functions is *invariably* a principle of mutual tolerance? "Look at capital and labor," Boutroux insisted, "the difference that separates them does not prevent them from combating each other. It often happens that diversity of education and occupation inclines men to misunderstand and despise one another. If men are to agree," he concluded, "it is not enough that they cannot understand one another" (1914: 198–9).

But even if we accept Durkheim's argument that the division of labor is a "necessary consequence" of the Darwinian struggle, Boutroux observed, it is surely *not* "a relation of necessity" in the sense of Newtonian mechanics. In Durkheim's theory, the division of labor is "necessary" in the sense of a condition essential to the realization of a particular end – i.e., the cessation of the struggle for life. "This," Boutroux emphasized, "is by no means a mechanical and inevitable necessary"; on the contrary, the struggle for life "admits of other solutions, the simplest of which is the eating of one another. That is really the law of nature, and division of labor is instituted for the very purpose of impeding the fulfillment of this law" (1914: 199). The division of labor is "necessary," therefore, only in the sense of being *preferable* – i.e., "more in conformity with the idea of humanity, responding more completely to that sympathy with the weak which we assume to exist in man." What can this mean, Boutroux asked, except that "what we took to be a crude law of causality involves a relation of finality, and that we are assuming the intervention of the human intellect and will where we think we are bringing into action none but external and material conditions?" (1914: 199–200). In short, the Durkheim of *De la division du travail social* was no longer the Durkheim of the Sens lectures, and Boutroux knew it.

A second important influence on Durkheim at the Ecole Normale

Supérieure was the great French historian, Numa Denis Fustel de Coulanges (1830–89). Like Boutroux, Fustel himself had been a student at the Ecole Normale, where he studied with Victor Duruy (1811–94), and read the works of Descartes, Montesquieu, Michelet, Tocqueville, and Guizot. When the *coup d'état* of Louis Napoleon on December 2, 1851 led to the suppression of non-classical studies, Fustel first studied Latin and Greek, and then drifted into the history of classical antiquity. By then, Fustel had already embraced the inductive method, writing an essay in praise of Bacon that shocked his fellow students.[24] In 1853, he joined the newly established Ecole française d'Athènes, moving to the Lycée Amiens in 1855, then to the Lycée St. Louis in Paris in 1857. Called to the chair of medieval and modern history at the university of Strasbourg in 1860, Fustel's "vigorous and scholarly lectures" produced "phenomenal success" and "un enthousiasme naif" throughout the next decade (Thompson 1942: 364).

While in Greece, Fustel collected a number of manuscripts which provided the foundation for his earliest publications, including his *Mémoire sur l'île de Chios* (1856), the highly praised French thesis, *Polybe, ou la Grèce conquise* (1858), and his Latin thesis, *Quid Vestae cultus in institutis veterum privatis publicisque valuerit* (1858). But Fustel's masterpiece remains *La Cité antique*, written over a six-month period at Strasbourg in 1864, comprising lectures given the two previous years. Initially published at his own expense, the work quickly won Fustel a following at the court of Napoleon III and, by 1890, it had seen its 13th edition. On the recommendation of Duruy (the Emperor's Minister of Public Instruction), Fustel was called to Paris in February, 1870 to give history lectures at the Ecole Normale.

Fustel's declared purpose in *La Cité antique* was "to show upon what principles and by what rules Greek and Roman society was governed" (1956: 11). But at least a secondary purpose – motivated by Fustel's desire to restore respect for the *ancien régime* – was to emphasize the radical discontinuity between Greco-Roman and French civilization. French schoolchildren, he complained, learned about the Greeks and Romans from their earliest years, comparing ancient revolutions with their French counterpart, and ancient history with that of 19th-century France. Such comparisons did more

---

[24] Thompson notes that it was under similar influences that Taine – of whose "rationalist empiricism" Durkheim wrote approvingly in 1897 – received his training at the Ecole Normale a few years later (1942: 363–4).

than simply perpetuate the misunderstanding of the past, Fustel observed:

Having imperfectly observed the institutions of the ancient city, men have dreamed of reviving them among us. They have deceived themselves about the liberty of the ancients, and on this very account liberty among the moderns has been put in peril. The last eighty years have clearly shown that one of the great difficulties which impede the march of modern society is the habit which it has of always keeping Greek and Roman antiquity before its eyes. (1956: 11)

But if we study the Greeks and Romans as if they were "entirely foreign," Fustel suggested, their institutions will be revealed as "absolutely inimitable." We shall attempt to show by what rules these societies were regulated," he proposed, "and it will be freely admitted that the same rules can never govern humanity again." Fearful of that revolutionary intoxication which had identified the ancient heroes with the protagonists of the Terror, therefore, Fustel "deepened the gulf which separates our conflicts from the ancient ones and made it virtually unbridgeable."[25]

Such an emphasis on the discontinuity between past and present presupposed an explanation for the transition from one to the other; and for Fustel – as Durkheim would later complain – this explanation was provided by the progress of the human mind (1984: 178–9). In the present, Fustel argued, "[m]an has not . . . the way of thinking that he had twenty-five centuries ago; and this is why he is no longer governed as he was governed then." For Fustel, therefore, institutions provided no explanation of their associated beliefs. When we examine the institutions of the Greeks and Romans, they appear obscure, whimsical, and inexplicable; but when we examine their religious ideas, these institutional practices become quite transparent. "If, on going back to the first ages of this race," Fustel observed, "we observe the idea which it had of human existence, of life, of death, of a second life, of the divine principle, we perceive a close relation between these opinions and the ancient rules of private law; between the rites which spring from these opinions and their political institutions" (1956: 12, 13). *La Cité antique*, Fustel thus explained in his conclusion, describes the history of a belief – i.e., the

---

[25] This contrast between ancient and modern freedom, Momigliano (1982: 333) adds, had already been formulated in Benjamin Constant's *De l'esprit de Conquête* (1814); but in Fustel it led, not to a defense of modern liberalism, but to the religious ideas of ancient peoples (1956: 12).

belief in a life after death. When that belief was established, "human society was constituted. It was modified, and society underwent a series of revolutions. It disappeared, and society changed its character."[26]

Fustel's description of this history – with its account of communal sacrifices, the priority of ritual over belief, the essentially religious nature of all human association, the integrative function of religious practices, religious doctrine as the mere symbol of some deeper, underlying reality – powerfully evokes the ideas of *Les Formes élémentaires*. And when Fustel turns from the idea itself to its effect on social institutions, he adopts the vocabulary of social realism. Consistent with familial independence, for example, the belief in souls of the dead required that the dwellings and grave sites of each family be separated from those of others. Both the hearth and the burial place had to be bound to a specific location, lest the families become confounded and the worship of one's own ancestors neglected or even abandoned. Each family thus took possession of a certain plot of land, which thus became imbued with the religious sentiments of its members and eventually their moral responsibility. "Without discussion, without labor, without a shadow of hesitation," Fustel thus observed, the ancients thus "arrived, at a single step, and merely by virtue of their belief, at the conception of the right of property; this right from which all civilization springs, since by it man improves the soil, and becomes improved himself" (1956: 67). This was Fustel's answer to Locke as well as to fashionable theories of primitive communism; and like Durkheim would later, it emphasized the power of social institutions to function independently of individual wills. "Found property on the right of labor," Fustel observed, "and man may dispose of it. Found it on religion, and he can no longer do this; a tie stronger than the will of man binds the land to him" (1956: 70–1; Momigliano 1982: 333).

Law, government, and ethics followed a similar evolution. Upon its emergence, the ancient city found the law of the family already established and deeply rooted in custom and habitual observance. Far from being instituted by some ancient legislator, therefore, the law rather had its birth in the religious authority of the father, and was thus imposed upon the legislator, who adapted it to the needs of

---

[26] Fustel, 1956: 396. The contrast between these views and those of W. R. Smith (1972) and the later Durkheim (1915) could hardly be greater..

the city by degrees. Ancient law "had its birth in the family," Fustel thus observed. "It sprang up spontaneously from the ancient principles which gave it root. It flowed from the religious belief which was universally admitted in the primitive age of these peoples, which exercised its empire over their intelligence and their wills" (1956: 86). As for ethics, if Fustel resisted the notion that ancient religion *created* moral sentiments, he at least suggested that these religious beliefs were *associated with* the "natural sentiments" of morality, in such a way as to "fortify them, to give them greater authority, to assure their supremacy and their right of direction over the conduct of man" (1956: 95). For the moral sentiments were initially limited to the mutual duties and obligations of members of the same family, and only later insensibly evolved to comprise the duties of citizens, and eventually those prescribed by natural law. Fustel thus accounted for the "religious aura" of moral commands by referring his readers to their evolutionary origins in the institution of the family, whose own authority, as we have seen, was based upon the ancient religion (1956: 97–8).

In 1893, Durkheim would criticize Fustel for deriving these early forms of social organization from religious ideas; but in fact, Fustel's subsequent treatment of the evolution of legal, moral, and religious ideas placed enormous emphasis on changing forms of social organization, in a manner similar to the conclusion of the second book of *Les Formes élémentaires*. A certain number of families, Fustel suggested, joined together to form a group (the Greek *phratry* or the Latin *curia*): "Even at the moment when they united," he added, "these families conceived the idea of a divinity superior to that of the household, one who was common to all, and who watched over the entire group. They raised an altar to him, lighted a sacred fire, and founded a worship" (1956: 118). When several *phratries* or *curias* joined together, forming a tribe, another religion was formed; and when several tribes gathered to found the confederation which constituted the ancient city, still another, more comprehensive worship was established. Speaking particularly of the confederation, Fustel emphasized the role played by religion in creating a social bond among people who were otherwise quite diverse, free, and inconstant:

To bring them under the rules of a community, to institute commandments and ensure obedience, to cause passions to give way to reason, and individual right to public right, there certainly was something necessary, stronger than material force, more respectable than interest, surer than a philosophical theory, more unchangeable than a convention; something that should dwell equally in all hearts, and should be all powerful there. (1956: 132)

This passage bears a resemblance to Montesquieu's argument, in *De l'ésprit des lois*, that the Romans adopted such a religion in order to restrain their people; but Fustel resisted such comparisons, insisting that religion could not have had so artificial an origin, and also that "every religion that has come to sustain itself only from motives of public utility, has not stood long" (1956: 166). On the contrary, for Fustel, the state presupposed religion far more than religion was an instrument of the state. It was not force, Fustel observed, that created the chiefs and kings in those ancient cities: "Authority flowed from the worship of the sacred fire. Religion created the king in the city, as it had made the family chief in the house" (1956: 178). Just as Durkheim would later argue that a contract presumes, not just a divergence of individual interests, but also some underlying agreement of wills and harmonious collaboration, Fustel argued that, in ancient society, a *legal* relationship between two men required a prior *religious* relationship – i.e., "that they should worship at the same hearth and have the same sacrifices. When this religious community did not exist, it did not seem that there could be any legal relation" (Durkheim 1984: 162; Fustel 1956: 193). Citizenship itself was established entirely on religious grounds; and the stranger, by contrast, was "one who has not access to the worship, one whom the gods of the city do not protect, and who has not even the right to invoke them" (1956: 194–5; cf. Smith 1972: 121–4).

So at every level – family, *phratry* or *curia*, tribe, the confederation of the ancient city itself – the function of religion was the same: i.e., "among the ancients, what formed the bond of every society was a worship" (1956: 146). The point toward which all these observations conspired, as we have already seen, was that the ancient city enjoyed nothing even remotely comparable to what we would call "liberty." Indeed, ancient peoples "had not even the idea of it," Fustel argued. "They did not believe that there could exist any right as against the city and its gods." So Fustel's account of ancient society, as Durkheim surely recognized and appreciated, unremittingly stressed the superficiality of merely political freedom: "To have political rights, to vote, to name magistrates, to have the privilege of being archon – this was called liberty," Fustel emphasized, "but man was not the less enslaved to the state" (1956: 223). Only after the 7th century B.C., when this ancient social organization was attacked by those classes deprived of its advantages and, still later, when the triumph of Christianity introduced the separation of Church and State, did government become free of religious constraint. Henceforth, Fustel concluded, "only a part of man belonged to society," for, "in what related to his soul, he was free, and was bound only to God" (1956: 394). Private virtues thus became distinguished from their public counterparts, and the freedom of the individual – i.e., the possibility of elevating the former over the latter – became conceivable.

La Cité antique enjoyed an almost instantaneous celebrity, and has remained a classic of French historiography; and of course it was awash with linguistic resources that a later generation would almost unconsciously recognize as "Durkheimian" – e.g., the comparative method; a preoccupation with the family as the most elementary form of society; the use of evolutionary "survivals" to reconstruct beliefs and practices for which evidence was lacking; the insistence on the discontinuity between societies of different types; the dismissal of explanations that appeal to individual reason or will; the discovery of the origin of religion in a primitive form of sacrificial communion with a god; a rejection of the concern for variable religious doctrine combined with an emphasis on the stability of ritual practices; the religious origins of institutions like private property, law, and the state; and the identification of "religion" with "society" itself. Camille Jullian, who edited six volumes of Fustel's manuscripts after his death in 1889, was Durkheim's classmate at the Ecole Normale and his colleague at Bordeaux. "From his time at the Ecole Normale," Jullian would later observe, Durkheim "was profoundly affected by the influence of *The Ancient City*, and by the lectures and the example of its author. He himself has recognized this and proclaims it openly" (Lukes 1972: 60). Evans-Pritchard insisted that Fustel and Montesquieu "had a greater formative influence on Durkheim's thought than Saint-Simon and Comte" (Lukes 1972: 63 n. 93). There can be "no doubt," Momigliano agreed in 1982, "about Fustel's influence on Durkheim" (1982: 339). But as we've seen, only two of these ideas – the comparative method and the notion of the family as the evolutionary origin of society – make any appearance in the Sens lectures; and though each of these ideas would later assume an important place within Durkheim's larger, social realist vocabulary, they bore not the slightest connection with such language in 1883. If Durkheim had indeed been "profoundly affected" by *La Cité antique* – and there seems little reason to doubt that he was – Fustel's classic work seems to have provided linguistic resources for a project that Durkheim had not yet conceived.

Perhaps the most striking aspect of the Sens lectures is their enthusiasm – notably absent in Janet's textbook – for a moral vocabulary including phrases like the "principle of finality" and "perfecting of our personality." The interesting possibility here is that, by 1883, Durkheim had fallen under the spell of the neo-Kantian philosopher Charles Renouvier (1815–1903). Born at Montpellier, Renouvier studied mathematics and natural science from 1834 to 1836 at the Ecole Polytechnique, where Auguste Comte was his instructor. Upon graduation, Renouvier – whose family fortune made it unnecessary for him to work, and also subsidized the publication of his books – dabbled in Parisian intellectual and political life, falling under the influence of Saint-Simonian groups. With the abdication of Louis-Philippe in 1848, these groups hoped that the provisional government of the February Revolution would create opportunities for political and social reform; and when Hippolyte Carnot, the minister of instruction, called for a manual of civic rights and duties for use in the education of the newly enfranchised masses, Renouvier responded with his *Manuel républicain de l'homme et du citoyen* (1848). When the conservative majority of the new Constituent Assembly got wind of the *Manuel*'s radical content, they used it to force Carnot – and Renouvier as well – out of the government. The *coup d'état* of Napoleon III (December 2, 1851) marginalized Renouvier still further, and by 1866 he had settled permanently in the south of France where he wrote his *Science de la morale* (1869) and other works.

"If you wish to mature your thought," Durkheim later remarked to René Maublanc, "devote yourself to the study of a great master; take a system apart, laying bare its innermost secrets. That is what I did and my educator was Renouvier" (Lukes 1972: 54). Most of the scholarly discussion has concerned Renouvier's influence on Durkheim's sociological method and sociology of knowledge, particularly as mediated by the French neo-Kantian Octave Hamelin, Durkheim's friend and colleague at the university of Bordeaux between 1887 and 1902 (Stedman-Jones 1995; Lukes 1972: 54–8). But Georges Davy made it clear that Durkheim was inspired by Renouvier while still a student at the Ecole Normale (1879–82). "It was at this time," Davy observed, "that Durkheim began to immerse himself in the reading and reflection on Renouvier, which marked him so deeply" (Davy 1919: 8). Connecting the Sens lectures to Renouvier is tricky, because the notes are Lalande's, not Durkheim's, and Renouvier is never mentioned by name (nor, for that matter, are Boutroux or Fustel); but there are certainly enough similarities to warrant further investigation.

Like the Sens lecturer, for example, Renouvier not only rejected Kant's distinction between the noumenal and phenomenal worlds, insisting that they were one and the same, but also attacked the Kantian theory of antinomies. Appealing to the principle of non-contradiction, for example, he insisted that the idea of an infinite series of phenomena or the infinity of space implied the incoherent notion of an infinite number, and were thus disproved. In the field of ethics, Renouvier denied the distinction between categorical and hypothetical imperatives, insisting that duty, feeling, and inclination should ideally accompany one another. The moral law was then reformulated as one commanding us to realize, as fully as possible, our personality; and from this duty Renouvier derived all human rights and liberties. Virtues are those dispositions that advance the fulfillment of these ends; and justice was defined as a reciprocal respect for the efforts of others to realize their ends. Like Kant – and the Sens lecturer – Renouvier considered morality inconceivable unless freedom is an attribute of the individual human being; and as he retreated from his earlier, socialist views, Renouvier shared the Sens lecturer's disdain for any political theory that lacked respect for the individual moral agency, as well as the later Durkheim's anti-clericalism and enthusiasm for secular education (Logue 1993: 60–95; Copleston 1977: 160–7; Boas 1967b: 180–2). Durkheim's earliest publication, "Du rôle des grands hommes dans la société" (1883) – an address given to these same *lycéens* at Sens – can be read as a Renouvierist critique of Ernest Renan's *Dialogues et fragments philosophiques* (1876) (1973a: 25–6). If Renouvier's *Science de la morale* (1869) really is the model for those of the Sens lectures concerned with ethics, then Durkheim had clearly embraced a highly teleological and personalist conception of ethics while still a student at the Ecole Normale Supérieure.

In sum, the Sens lectures rather clearly *do not* reinforce what Quentin Skinner has called our "carefully contrived pleasures of recognition" (1984: 202, 197–8). On the contrary, the lectures contain a number of ideas – e.g., the surprisingly teleological, personalist conception of ethics; the embracement of the method of "internal reflection," combined with a dismissal of the very possibility of unconscious psychological phenomena; the Kantian rejection of any empirical explanation of human reason; the rejection of Kant's distinction between hypothetical and categorical imperatives; the insistence that moral judgments are essentially personal and subjective – that are not recognizably "Durkheimian" at all. There are other ideas, of course, that are more familiar – e.g., the Boutrouxian view that each science has its distinctive object and method; the notion that logic, ethics, and metaphysics could be grounded in empirical science; the Bernardian conception of experimental verification; the critique of utilitarianism; and the insistence that the distinction between egoism and altruism is to be found, not in the different kinds of pleasures we seek, but rather in the different kinds of objects to which we become attached. But even these ideas are found in new contexts, frequently accompanied by strange silences – e.g., the empirical science in which logic, ethics, and metaphysics should be grounded is philosophical *psychology*, not *sociology*; there is no indication of how experimental verification might be applied to the study of the "moral sciences"; the Smith-like preoccupation with the *material* – by contrast with the *moral* – consequences of the division of labor; the dismissal of the expiatory function of punishment; and – the distinction between egoism and altruism notwithstanding – there is no suggestion that our attachment for objects *outside* us presupposes their representations *within* us. And most surprisingly – despite his Leibnitzian, *epistemological* realism – the Sens lecturer was clearly not a *social* realist, and even seems to have lacked sociological sensibilities altogether.

Under these circumstances, it's not inappropriate to wonder if these lectures were actually given by Durkheim or, assuming they were, that they really represented his views. But there seems little reason to doubt that Durkheim was the Sens lecturer. Quite aside from the fact that he did teach philosophy at the Lycée de Sens from November, 1882 to February, 1884, and that Lalande was a student there during this period, the format and content of the notes are consistent with a description of the course given by Lalande himself in 1958 (1960: 24). The meticulous outlines that precede each lecture in the notes, for example, seem to reflect Durkheim's practice – described by Lalande in 1958 – of writing similar outlines on the blackboard at the conclusion of each class. In 1958, Lalande recalled that Durkheim had discussed Schopenhauer – a figure unknown to Lalande's fellow students – and Schopenhauer indeed appears frequently in the notes. Finally, Lalande's report that some of Durkheim's students followed him to St. Quentin in 1884 is consistent with a parenthetical remark on the first page of the notes: "La fin, qu'il n'a pas donnée parce qu'il a été nommé à St. Quentin, a été reprise sur les notes d'un élève de 1882–1883" (Gross 1996; Lalande 1960: 25).

The second question – of whether the lectures really represented Durkheim's views – should be treated more cautiously. As we have seen, the authority of Cousin's syllabus endured well into the 1880s, and the responsibility of the *lycée* professor was to prepare students for the *baccalauréat*. So there was pressure from both students and administration to avoid deviation. Most of the *lycée* professors thus patterned their lectures after one of several officially approved textbooks, and the most likely model for Durkheim's lectures would have been Paul Janet's *Traité élémentaire de philosophie à l'usage des classes* (1879). Even a preliminary comparison of Lalande's notes with Janet's textbook, however, suggests that if Durkheim outwardly conformed to the syllabus, he exercised numerous philosophical liberties as well (Gross 1996). There are extremely important arguments in the notes – e.g., the teleological ethics based upon ideas of "personality" and "finality" – that are completely absent from the textbook; and where the arguments in the textbook and the notes do coincide, the reasons given by Durkheim for accepting or rejecting these arguments frequently differ from those given by Janet.

Finally, while the extent to which they lack sociological sensibilities is somewhat surprising, the Sens lectures are not entirely inconsistent with what we've known for some time about Durkheim's early intellectual development. In 1928, Marcel Mauss recalled that, at the time of his *agrégation* (1882), Durkheim had already settled upon the relations between individualism and socialism as the theme for his doctoral dissertation; but he did not see the topic as particularly "sociological," and rather approached it in an abstract, philosophical manner. By 1883, Durkheim had refined his focus to the relations between the individual personality and social solidarity; but here again, there is no reason to think "individual personality" meant anything other than what it meant to the Sens lecturer and to Renouvier. So it was only between the first plan of the work, in 1884, and its first draft, in 1886, Lukes observes, that Durkheim decided that the problem belonged to "the new science of sociology" (1972: 66–7). And it was during the same period, of course, that Durkheim made his visit to the universities of Berlin, Marburg, and – most importantly – Leipzig.

CHAPTER 4

A l'école des choses

In three successive volumes over the period 1905–7, the Catholic philosophy journal *Revue néo-scolastique* published a series of essays collectively titled "Le Conflit de la morale et de la sociologie." These essays, published as a book in 1911, were written by the Belgian priest and neo-Thomist philosopher Simon Deploige, and they contained a sharp attack on the social realism of Durkheim and his disciples. "All these views," Deploige observed after summarizing Durkheim's sociology, "pass in France as M. Durkheim's own. But they are of German origin" (1911: 122).

Durkheim was deeply offended. Had Deploige "wanted to convince people that I have abused my compatriots," he replied on October 20, 1907, "he could hardly have expressed himself in any other way." Deploige's language seemed to imply that Durkheim had made "carefully concealed borrowings among certain German writers." "I owe much to the Germans," Durkheim admitted, but "the real influence that Germany has exercised on me is quite different from what he says" (1907: 606–7). Within four days, Deploige replied with explicit references to Durkheim's alleged indebtedness to Schaeffle, Wagner, Schmoller, Wundt, Simmel, Lazarus and Steinthal; and a second letter from Durkheim, dated November 8, contained not only a detailed refutation of Deploige's "errors," "inaccuracies," and "insinuations," but what has surely become the most famous autobiographical passage in all of Durkheim's writings – i.e., the statement that it was only in 1895, under the influence "of the works of Robertson Smith and his school," that he had first discovered "the means to approach the study of religion sociologically" (1913b: 326). Again Deploige replied; and when his essays appeared as a volume in 1911, Durkheim reviewed it savagely in *L'Année sociologique*, alluding again to "all that we owe to Robertson Smith and to the works of the ethnographers of England and America" (1913b: 326)

While Durkheim's autobiographical remarks have led to a productive focus on Durkheim's British sources, less detailed attention has been granted to the substance of Deploige's argument. In *The Structure of Social Action* (1937), for example, Talcott Parsons flatly dismissed Deploige's suggestion while insisting that Durkheim was the "spiritual heir of Comte," and Steven Lukes has added that while Durkheim "was influenced by these German writers," they simply "clarified and reinforced existing tendencies in his thought" (Parsons 1968: 307; Lukes 1972: 92). The historian William Keylor has equally emphasized the Cartesian elements in Durkheim's thought, and his resulting resistance to German influences (1975: 111–15). But in fact, the influence of German social science on Durkheim's sociological thought was both deep and complex, and must be understood within the institutional and intellectual context already introduced.

THE FRENCH ADMIRATION FOR GERMAN SCIENTIFIC EDUCATION

By the end of the First Empire, Robert Gilpin has observed, the system of scientific education that would persist in France until the end of the Second World War had been firmly established (1968: 86). First, the Revolution swept away the scientific institutions of the *ancien régime* – e.g., the Collège Royal, founded in 1530 to supplement the conservative teaching of the Sorbonne, became the Collège de France; the Jardin des Plantes Médicinales, founded in 1625 for the purpose of cultivating and studying the effects of medicinal herbs, was reconstituted as the Muséum d'Histoire Naturelle; and the Académie Royale des Sciences, founded by Jean-Baptiste Colbert in 1666 for the study of mathematics, physics, and natural history, was suppressed in 1793. The Convention and Napoleon then re-established French higher education under new institutional forms – e.g., the Conservatoire des Arts et Métiers, the Ecole Polytechnique, and the Ecole Normale Supérieure, all founded in 1794 and reconstituted under the Empire; and the Université Impériale, created in 1808 by Napoleon, which brought the previously autonomous, self-governing universities under a central, Parisian administration, simultaneously subdividing them into the five faculties of arts, science, law, theology, and medicine.

An immediate, positive consequence of this centralization was the migration of French scientific talent to the newly created institutions in Paris, resulting in a concentrated, self-conscious, scientific elite, and a period of undeniable – if ephemeral – brilliance in the history of French science. But for a variety of reasons, this centralized, elitist approach to scientific practice either failed to solve traditional problems or created new ones. In any case, the Napoleonic system proved ill-fitted to the future needs for professional scientific manpower, and France found itself admiring German models of scientific education by the second half of the 19th century. One reason for this failure was that science became increasingly technical and complex, requiring more formal training, greater specialization, and scientific professionalization. Institutions like the Académie des sciences and its Napoleonic successor, the Institut de France, which depended upon a small elite of Paris academicians, were simply inadequate to these needs. Complicating this inadequacy was the administrative fragmentation of French science, which subdivided scientific intellectual activity among three different sets of institutions – the "grands établissements scientifiques," the university *facultés*, and the *grandes écoles* (Gilpin 1968: 87). The first were research institutions which boasted great scientists (e.g., Georges Cuvier, André-Marie Ampère, Marcelin Merthelot), but placed no emphasis on teaching and thus trained few scientists. The university *facultés* taught science, but were essentially professional schools for the training of medical doctors or teachers for the *lycées*, and have only recently became centers for research. Of the *grandes écoles*, of course, the Ecole Polytechnique and the Ecole Normale Supérieure admittedly represented a new type of scientific institution – i.e., the first in which science was taught as valuable in itself rather than as auxiliary to some profession. But even the *grandes écoles* would fail to meet the demands of the new scientific age.

The abolition of the individual French university as a corporate, self-governing entity also left the administration of French higher education divided between two separate, and frequently opposed, levels – the Ministère de l'Instruction Publique and the individual professors. The Ministère had authority over the curriculum, finances, and examinations, but its primary concern was with the professional education of secondary teachers (who, in turn, were to prepare students for the State examinations) rather than with the advancement of science. Even had these priorities been reversed, the Ministère could hardly introduce piecemeal reforms without undermining the uniformity essential to the national examination system, and wholesale reforms required re-distribution of resources and thus faced political obstacles. The French professoriat, meanwhile, had inherited a "democratic" system of recruitment which diffused the power of nomination to vacant chairs among the entire *faculté* rather than granting it to departmental, disciplinary, or university-wide committees. Appropriate to a small *faculté*, the system had become anachronistic with the increasing size and specialization of higher education, resulting in highly politicized nominations and elections in which professors repeatedly passed judgment on scholars in fields unfamiliar to them (Gilpin 1968: 115–17). In short, the separate universities and academic departments had little authority beyond what they derived from above (the Ministère) or below (the professors).

By sharp contrast, "Germany" – at least until 1860 – was a cultural rather than a political expression; and the 19th-century German universities were thus creatures of the individual states, enjoying a high degree of institutional autonomy, and a long tradition of intense rivalry. Inter-institutional scientific competition guaranteed that the German universities would be responsive to the need for new courses, new chairs, new research facilities – to the new science generally (Gilpin 1968: 113–14). The University of Berlin, founded by Wilhelm von Humboldt, became the model for this transformation, re-defining the purpose of the university as the advancement of scientific knowledge, replacing the self-taught, virtuoso academic with the specialized scientific professional, and providing formal scientific training for generations of German scientists. But in the French university, the professor continued to be conceived as a State official whose duty was to transmit a cultural tradition and prepare students for the State examinations: "At the most," Gilpin summarizes, "research traditionally has been regarded as a privilege extended to professors who have conscientiously performed their primary responsibilities of teaching and examining" (1968: 96–7).

The Ecole Polytechnique, of course, had been the first institution to introduce the research laboratory into higher education, and in the early part of the century its incomparable facilities attracted eminent scientists like Gaspard Monge, Charles Fourier, and Pierre-Simon LaPlace. But in contrast to the German Technische Hochschule, where students learned the methods of science and became capable of advancing knowledge in their fields, students at the Ecole Polytechnique learned only the content of science and how to apply already existing knowledge (Gilpin 1968: 88–90). The crucial difference between French and German scientific training, Gilpin emphasizes, is that "in Germany it was not enough to know science; one had to be able to do science" (1968: 100). This subordination of research to teaching and of the needs of higher education to those of secondary education was epitomized by the Ecole Normale Supérieure, created to train the teachers required by Napoleon's Université Impériale; and it resulted in a French career pattern that routed the aspirant professor through years of teaching in the *lycée* prior to his accession to the university. In fact, most French scholars spent years teaching at the secondary level, and some remained in the *lycées* by preference throughout their lives. As the Sens lectures suggest, this pattern provided France with an excellent system of secondary education, but it also meant the loss of promising scholars who might otherwise have become practicing scientists.

Nor were there incentives to stimulate other career patterns. The relatively few *faculté* chairs were spread among general fields such as "zoology" or "physics," and no one could predict when one would become available. For those who aspired to a university chair, therefore, it was prudent to maintain as broad a competence as possible, and thus to increase the number of one's options. Nor were new chairs forthcoming. "In a period of static population and a Malthusian fear of overexpansion," Gilpin explains, "very few new chairs were created, and the conservatism of the *facultés* severely limited the number of existing chairs that were converted from older, effete fields to newer, productive ones" (1968: 99). And again, the criteria by which professors were awarded such chairs encouraged them to cultivate their erudition rather than to push boldly against existing orthodoxies. There was also the French national examination system, established in the Napoleonic law of 1808, which gave the State a monopoly in the awarding of academic degrees, and thus the power to control access to the professions. Its purpose was to assure France of a small, uniform, and highly qualified elite to administer its centralized institutions; but its effects included rigid study regulations, prescribed curricula, and the diversion of the energies of both students and professors – themselves selected through the same examination process – from the conduct of research to the task of preparation for the examinations.

Compounding these difficulties was the traditional self-image of the French professoriat. "The French idealized the professor as a man of broad culture and encyclopedic knowledge," Gilpin emphasizes, "rather than as a narrow specialist whose purpose was to make some original contribution to knowledge. He was a *savant*, steeped in an ancient and classic culture that was to be passed on via his students to the next generation" (1968: 97). This was a tradition, of course, with which Durkheim had little sympathy: "The man of parts, as he once was," he said in the introduction to *De la division du travail social*, "is for us no more than a dilettante, and we accord no moral value to dilettantism. Rather, do we perceive perfection in the competent man, one who seeks not to be complete but to be productive, one who has a well-defined job to which he devotes himself, and carries out his task, ploughing his single furrow" (1984: 4).

Such objections were increasingly common as the century advanced. Patriotic French scientists like Louis Pasteur begged the government to established research institutions, and the historian Victor Duruy, who, as Ministre de l'Instruction Publique under the Second Empire, had been horrified by the utter uselessness of the classical syllabus to French children, introduced a number of reforms, including the establishment in 1868 of the Ecole Pratique des Hautes Etudes (Zeldin 1977: 248). After 1880, the French government would establish laboratories for industrial research at Nancy, Grenoble, and the Conservatoire National des Arts et Métiers, and simultaneously expand the number of engineering schools and institutes, especially in chemistry, electricity, and other rapidly emerging science-based technologies. And by 1896, a reform law would re-group the separate *facultés* in each city or region into unified institutions. As expressed by Raymond Poincaré, Gilpin observes, the hope was "to introduce into France the autonomous university as it then existed in Germany, which would be a center for uniting teaching and research and for enabling science to contribute to French life" (1968: 93). But none of these reforms, he adds, altered the fundamental structure of French higher education generally, or of scientific education in particular.

The distinction between higher education in Germany and in France has aptly been characterized as one between the Baconian and Cartesian traditions in the history of science. In the *New Atlantis* (1624), Bacon had envisioned a day when ordinary men, appropriately trained and organized, would displace the individual genius as producers of scientific progress. This conception was largely realized in the universities and research laboratories of 19th-century Germany, with their focus on a specific scientific problem systematically explored through a highly integrated division of scientific labor. France, by contrast, adhered to the Cartesian image of the individual scientific genius, epitomized in the small, frequently ill equipped and isolated personal laboratory (the *laboratoire de chaire*) attached to professorial appointments, where the professor pursued his personal inclinations with a few poorly trained assistants (Gilpin 1968: 107).

This French anxiety over the superiority of German scientific education was only increased by the outcome of the Franco-Prussian War. In *La Réforme intellectuelle et morale* (1872), for example, Ernest Renan observed that the victory of Germany in the Franco-Prussian War was the victory of science. "After Jena," Renan insisted, "the university of Berlin was the center of the regeneration of Germany. If we wish to rise from our disasters, let us imitate the conduct of Prussia. French intelligence has been weakened; we must strengthen it. Our system of education," he concluded, "especially of higher education, has need of radical reform" (1872: 55). Renan's views were widely shared, and they were reflected in that policy of the Ministère de l'Instruction Publique already established by the historian Victor Duruy, of awarding scholarships to the brightest young French *agrégés* so that they might visit Germany to become acquainted with the latest scholarly and scientific advances. As we shall see, it was with this support that Durkheim visited the universities of Leipzig, Marburg, and Berlin in 1885–6.

DURKHEIM IN GERMANY

It was well understood that this German superiority extended to the social as well as the physical sciences. Numerous studies of German higher education and social science had already appeared in the *Revue internationale de l'enseignement*, the *Revue philosophique*, and the *Journal des économistes*; and before Durkheim's visit, Louis Liard – the devout republican, Renouvierist, and Directeur de l'Instruction Supérieure – would encourage him to pay special attention to the state of the social sciences during his stay in Germany, in the hope that they might provide a foundation for the reform of French higher education (Lukes 1972: 95). But as the career of Alfred

Espinas (1844–1922) suggests, there were changes taking place in the social sciences within France as well.

"Can even the near future of [our] country," Espinas had asked himself in the wake of the Franco-Prussian War, "be predicted with any degree of probability?" To lend itself to prediction, he answered, a society must be "an object of nature, submissive to laws like any other object, an object that could be understood scientifically. Now that requires that social facts be considered in their generality" (1901: 449). Within a year, Espinas had thus conceived the notion of studying animal societies "with the avowed intent to extract from this study some laws that were common to all societies." Such sociological studies were hardly in vogue: "Neither Schaeffle's *Bau und Leben des sozialen Körpers* nor Spencer's *Sociology*," Espinas recalled, "had yet appeared. Aside from a few friends with whom Littré had just founded an ephemeral sociological society, there were not ten people in France who were favorable toward this kind of research." Four years later, when *Les Sociétés animales* (1877) was presented as a doctoral thesis to the Faculty of Letters of the university of Paris, two spiritualist disciples of Cousin – Paul Janet (1823–99) and Emile Caro (1826–87) – both members of the examining committee, greeted it as a vulgar, sociological intrusion into their more literary, abstract, philosophical domain. Though Espinas referred to the possibilities for peaceful coexistence between sociology and ethics, Janet ultimately forced him to suppress the historical introduction to the thesis because he was unwilling to delete a reference to Auguste Comte (1901: 449).

This experience helps us to understand the warmth with which Espinas approached his subject in "Etudes sociologiques en France" (1882). "[T]o establish political doctrine firmly on the ground of realities," he explained, "one must take the side of those who admit that sociology is only the continuation and expansion of biology, that human society is a concrete, living thing, of the same order as animal societies" (1882: 566–7). Espinas praised Edmond Perrier's *Les Colonies animales* (1881) – a "magnificent study of animal morphology" – for its sociological interpretation of the formative processes of biological organisms, while complaining of the "latent finalism" and "vague religiosity" that compromised its otherwise unrelenting scientific determinism (1882: 606). Society is not simply "a sum of juxtaposed individuals," Espinas embraced Henri Marion's *La Solidarité morale* (1880), but "a new being, a true whole, individual in its turn and its way. It is a living body." Espinas simultaneously criticized Alfred Fouillée (1838–1912) for describing society as "an *abstraction*" (1882: 342–3). Sociology requires "a complete anatomical study of the diverse parts of the collective organism," Espinas agreed with the first volume of Albert Schaeffle's *Bau und Leben des sozialen Körpers* (1875) – an analysis "conceived in a whole other spirit from similar studies made among ourselves . . . whose length far surpasses the total attention that the French public grants to these kinds of studies" (1882: 351).

By August, 1883, these views had brought Espinas into conflict with Boutroux as well as Janet and Caro. Boutroux could observe that, while the philosophy journals still published articles on Plato, Descartes, Malebranche and Spinoza, these were increasingly accompanied by studies of "the speed of neural transmission, the theory of reflexes, cerebral irritability, Darwinism, space in *n* dimensions, problems of the nervous system, animal colonies, sociology, ethology, and ethnography" (1883: 865). But despite this convergence of philosophy with the positive sciences, the content of the philosophy *concours d'agrégation* – the annual competitive examination required for appointment to a teaching position in a *lycée* – had remained the same. Boutroux thus asked if the time had not come for a thorough revision of the *concours*, which would establish greater harmony between the current state of philosophy and the progress of the positive sciences. His answer – which helps us to appreciate the significance of Durkheim's later claim, in *L'Evolution pédagogique* and *L'Education morale*, that the study of science could be "morally edifying" – was entirely negative: "[W]e need not be troubled," he observed, "by the view of the divergence which exists between the *agrégation* and contemporary philosophy. This divergence lies in the nature of things. The goal of the *agrégation* is not to show that young people are *au courant* with the most recent hypotheses of science. It has its own distinct field, which is that of subjective, moral philosophy" (1883: 873).

Not surprisingly, Espinas disagreed. "In reality," he responded, "it's a question of knowing if philosophy instruction as created in France by Cousin ought to stay as it is, or even if it ought to stay at all" (1884: 586). The question raised by Boutroux, Espinas added,

is only one episode of the grand struggle that engages, at this time, in every civilized country, and on every point of curricula, two opposed systems of culture – one which sets out to develop the mind by exercising it in a vacuum, on itself, by pure gymnastics; and another which wants to join to these formal exercises a substantial diet drawn from the spectacle of things. (1884: 607)

Among the "things" thus to be observed, of course, were *consciences sociales*, the collective realities created through the fusion of individual minds that Espinas had described in *Les Sociétés animales*: "They exist for themselves, and must thus be counted among the highest of realities . . . The individual is thus the product far more than the author of society." Society, he added, "is a concrete living thing" (1978: 540, 542).

Even before his departure, Durkheim had already developed interests similar to those of Espinas and Perrier, and gone beyond them in significant ways. In his 1885 review of the first volume of of Schaeffle's *Bau und Leben des sozialen Körpers*, for example, Durkheim noted that despite the discussion of Schaeffle's work by Espinas and Fouillée, the German author remained "very little discussed" – a fact which he thought made his own review "tardy but timely." Schaeffle, Durkheim emphasized, "is clearly a realist. Society is not a simple collection of individuals, it is an entity which preceded those who comprise it at present and which will survive them, which acts more on them than they on it, which has its own life, own consciousness, own interests and destiny" (1885a: 93). But where writers like Espinas had emphasized the biological foundations of human societies, Schaeffle insisted that the relationship between organisms and societies was purely metaphorical. "[T]he members of human societies are not attached to one another by a material link," Durkheim observed, "but by ideal bonds" – a distinction that affirmed Espinas' insistence on the reality of social phenomena while simultaneously asserting the independence of sociology from biology (1885a: 94–5, 110–11). Finally, the earliest hint of Durkheim's dissatisfaction with the Cartesian vocabulary of *idées claires et simples* – so clear in *L'Evolution pédagogique* and *L'Education morale* – received expression in his review of Schaeffle's *Bau und Leben*. "[T]here are few readings more highly instructive for a Frenchman," he concluded, for it is "by the practice of such patient and laborious studies that we shall fortify our spirit, now too slender, too thin, too fond of simplicity. It is by learning to face the infinite complexity of facts that we free ourselves of those too narrow frameworks in which we tend to compartmentalize things. It is perhaps no exaggeration to say that the future worth of French sociology depends on this" (1885a: 110).

Similarly, in the first paragraph of his review of Ludwig Gumplowicz's *Grundriss der Soziologie* (1885), Durkheim suggested that the work was further evidence of the German effort to advance sociological studies in every possible direction. "How regrettable it is," he added, that "this interesting movement is so little known and so little followed in France. So it is that sociology, French in origin, becomes more and more a German science."[1] The same review complained again of the insufficient and erroneous treatment given to Schaeffle's discussion of the relationship between sociology and biology. Again, Durkheim's 1885(b) review of Fouillée's *La Propriété sociale et la démocratie* (1884) complained that Schaeffle's views on socialism had been completely misunderstood (1885b: 451–2). And still again, Durkheim's 1886 review of Schaeffle's *Die Quintessenz des Sozialismus* (1885) objected to the treatment rendered that work by the liberal economist Paul Leroy-Beaulieu (1843–1916) (1886a: 76–7).

But if Durkheim was thus interested in German social science in general – and that of the "realist" Schaeffle in particular – he was not yet the social realist of *L'Evolution pédagogique* and *L'Education morale*. This is especially evident in the review of Gumplowicz: "Societies are described to us as simple, indivisible forces," Durkheim there observed, "which drive and impel violently before them the individuals of which they are composed. But is this not to admit a social principle strongly analogous to the old vitalist principle, albeit still less scientific?" Durkheim asked rhetorically. The answer was clear: "No doubt a society is a being, a person," he observed, but "this being has nothing metaphysical about it. It is not some more or less transcendent substance." On the contrary, it is a whole composed of parts, and the problem for sociology is to "break up the whole, to enumerate these parts, to describe and classify them, and to find out how they are grouped and divided" – precisely the "great service . . . rendered to science" by the first volume of Schaeffle's *Bau und Leben*. In society, Durkheim concluded, "there are only individuals, it is individuals and individuals alone that are the factors of social life" (1885c: 632).

The immediate consequences of Durkheim's visit to Germany were two essays: "L'Enseignement de la philosophie dans les uni-

---

[1] Durkheim 1885c: 627. Ludwig Gumplowicz (1838–1909) was of course Polish; but his major works – *Philosophisches Staatsrecht* (1877), *Rechtsstaat und Sozialismus* (1881), *Verwaltungslehre mit besonderer Berücksichtigung* (1882), *Der Rassenkampf* (1883), and the *Grundriss* (1885) were all written in German.

versités allemandes," which appeared in the *Revue internationale de l'enseignement* in 1887, and "La Science positive de la morale en Allemagne," which appeared in the *Revue philosophique* the same year. The second essay contained a detailed treatment of a variety of German social scientists, and is best treated in the larger context of German romanticism; but the first dealt directly with the conditions of German higher education, particularly as they existed in the philosophy faculty at the University of Leipzig. Durkheim envied the administrative decentralization and intellectual autonomy of the German universities, but considered the resulting multiplication of overlapping, ill-attended courses a "luxury without great profits," and suggested that "a little French centralization" and division of intellectual labor would be "all to the good" (1887a: 315–18). Again, he acknowledged the flexibility of the German *privatdozent* system, particularly when compared with "the rigidity of our [French] administrative organization"; but he added that the sacrifices required of a *privatdozent* discouraged many promising scholars, and threatened to create an intellectual proletariat of those who were not. In any case, Durkheim insisted, these supernumerary instructors are required by the almost absolute separation of the German *gymnasium* and the university, and the infrequency with which one rises from the first to the second; but it is precisely in the *lycées*, he reminded his audience, that the *facultés* regenerate themselves, rendering a system of *privatdozents* inapplicable to the French case (1887a: 318–20).

As for the nature of philosophical instruction itself, Durkheim again found the Germans wanting. Though no admirer of an inflated oratorical style, for example, Durkheim found the contrary fault – i.e., "the disdain for oratorical form to the point of literally dictating their lectures" (1887a: 320) – more common. The virtual absence of philosophy in the *gymnasium*, moreover, meant that philosophical teaching in the university had to be "very elementary and very general," something Durkheim regarded as "a danger for German philosophy – that is to say, for one of the greatest, most uncontested glories of Germany" (1887a: 325–6). Once enclosed within their specialities, however, German students exhibited a total disinterest in other subjects, and in public affairs generally, a narrowing of focus Durkheim attributed to the lamentable, practical concern for fees of inscription and examinations. There were at least three aspects of philosophy teaching in the German universities, however, which

Durkheim could not help but admire. The first was the tendency he perceived to increase the philosophy requirements for future professors of secondary education. "It is truly curious," Durkheim observed, "that, at the moment where our rivals recognize the advantages of our organization on this point, we, on the contrary, have begun to doubt it, and are tempted to adopt a system which they are on the point of wanting no longer" (1887a: 426–7). Here Durkheim was apparently referring, not to the quarrel between Boutroux and Espinas over the philosophy *agrégation*, but to the efforts of the historian Gustave Monod and the psychologist Théodule Ribot to replace the teaching of philosophy in the *lycées* altogether with that of newer, rival disciplines; and here, Durkheim still seems to have sided with the spiritualist defenders of the *classe de philosophie*: "Let us piously conserve the life where we have the happiness to encounter it," he insisted, "and leave philosophy in our *lycées* since it is living there" (1887a: 439). In particular, Durkheim was critical of the efforts of Ernest Lavisse, a disciple of Duruy and an expert on German history, on behalf of the teaching of history in the *lycées*. "Lavisse has told us," Durkheim observed, "how history can and must serve the national education . . . [But for better or worse, we no longer have the spirit of tradition, and our incorrigible rationalism is only slightly accessible to historical arguments . . . It is still to the professor of philosophy," Durkheim thus concluded, "that it belongs to awake among the minds which are confided to him the idea of what a law is, and to make them understand that psychic and social phenomena are facts like any others, submitted to laws which the human will cannot disturb at its pleasure" (1887a: 439–40). As W. W. Miller has recently emphasized, for Durkheim social facts are thus "will-independent" even where they are "mind-dependent" (1996: 47).

The second thing Durkheim admired about the German philosophical environment were the various sections of the Akademische-philosophische Verein, groups of 15–20 young people who met on Thursday evenings and Sunday afternoons "to talk about philosophy, with much seriousness no doubt, but without pedantry," and remained afterward to laugh and drink in "der Gemütliche Teil der Sitzung." In spite of their academic character, Durkheim observed, these meetings gave rise to personal relationships and a "corporative spirit" well adapted to the French national character (1887a: 436). Durkheim's concerns here were not trivial. On the contrary, his admiration for the Akademische-philosophische Verein was an inseparable part of his life-long repugnance for excessive individualism, and his desire to restore the corporate spirit destroyed by the Revolution. He insisted:

In spite of the rivalry of the professors, in spite of the excessive feeling that each of them has of his own independence, in spite of the radical separation of studies, when one has penetrated into the university one feels at the heart of a whole in which all of the parts conspire, even if one cannot see clearly toward what end. A certain number of collective sentiments, bequeathed by tradition, make this enormous mass of instructors and students move by common accord.

The German student, he added, does not feel the "unhealthy need which drives us to distinguish ourselves, and consequently to isolate ourselves, from one another" – indeed, the words "distinctiveness" and "originality" are almost untranslatable into German. These tastes, aptitudes, and inclinations for the corporative life "cannot be easily transplanted into France . . . [for] each of us has too much feeling for his own personality to voluntarily abandon it. Yet it is hardly contestable," Durkheim concluded, "that what we have the most need of at this moment is the revival within us of the taste for collective life. What is this entire succession of reforms which have just resuscitated our higher education, if not a long and laborious effort of concentration?" (1887a: 436–7).

The third feature of the German philosophical environment which captured Durkheim's imagination was the seminar and laboratory of Wilhelm Wundt. To understand the nature of this attraction, however, requires a grasp of the historical development of the social sciences in Germany in the 19th century, and of their foundation in the German romantic movement.

THE POSITIVE SCIENCE OF ETHICS IN GERMANY

In the century following the Peace of Westphalia (1648), the Germans had been the least nationally minded of all European peoples. The microscopic German states of the Holy Roman Empire had no perceptible common border, and the area of German speech simply faded out as one approached Alsace, the Austrian Netherlands, Poland, Bohemia, or the upper Balkans. Priding themselves on a more cosmopolitan outlook, the upper classes became contemptuous of much that was German and, in particular, adopted French fashions, dress, etiquette, manners, ideas, and language. At Potsdam, Frederick the Great befriended Voltaire, wrote his own books in French, and even hired French tax collectors.

An initial sign of the precariousness of this cosmopolitanism was the appearance of Johann Gottfried von Herder's *Ideen zur Philosophie der Geschichte der Menschheit* (1784–91). A Protestant pastor and theologian who considered the French frivolous and affected, Herder felt that the imitation of foreign customs made people shallow and artificial. All true culture or civilization, he argued, must arise from native soil, and especially from the *Volk* or common people, which possessed its own genius or *Volksgeist*. This conception of the *Volksgeist* rebelled not only against the French, but against that entire pattern of thought which had characterized the Enlightenment, with its emphasis on reason, the identity of human nature, the universal rights of man, the timeless principles of natural law, and the classical rules of aesthetic judgment. For these Enlightenment ideas, Herder and his followers now increasingly substituted those of intuition, the diversity of human nature, the social and historical origins of particular rights and laws, and the peculiar genius represented by the art of each particular people.

This initial form of "nationalism" was largely cultural; but with the Revolution and the rise of the Napoleonic Empire, it acquired increasingly democratic and political overtones. The Revolution, by showing how a people could raise themselves to the dignity of citizenship and participate in the affairs of their country, made the Germans acutely conscious of their own politically retarded condition; and the Empire, by conquering Germany and establishing France as the greatest power in Europe, deepened their humiliation still further. Johann Gottlieb Fichte (1762–1814), an early admirer of Rousseau, the Revolution, and the Republic, reversed himself when Napoleon conquered Germany, embracing Herder's idea of the *Volksgeist* in its most passionate form. There is a primordial, immutable German spirit, Fichte insisted in his *Reden an die deutsche Nation* (1808), more noble than that of other peoples, from whom its purity must thus be protected. Germans, in short, became preoccupied with ideas of political unity and national greatness, precisely because they had neither; and this preoccupation found a ready outlet in the social sciences which grew rapidly under the aegis of its secular, autonomous universities.

Introducing his 1887 essay on "La Science positive de la morale en Allemagne," Durkheim noted that the science of ethics had not begun among moral philosophers at all, but rather "among the jurists and above all among the economists. It is in political economy," he insisted, "that the entire movement began" (1887b: 34). The seminal figure here was Adam Heinrich Müller (1779–1829), the intellectual spokesman for the reactionary forces of post-Napoleonic Prussia who epitomized both the cultural and political dimensions of the German romantic movement in the social sciences. Born in Berlin, Müller studied at Berlin and Göttingen before moving to Vienna in 1802, where he became a friend of the politician and economist Friedrich von Gentz, and captured the attention of Metternich. In Dresden (1806–9), Müller joined with the romantic dramatist Heinrich von Kleist in editing *Phöbus*, and upon returning to Vienna and joining the Austrian government service, he became associated with the emerging school of "romantic political economists," including Gentz, Karl Ludwig von Haller, Johann Joseph von Görres and Franz von Baader. All were deeply influenced by Fichte, and opposed the cold rationality, individualism, and emphasis on material values characteristic of 18th-century political economy. Deeply inspired by the more "integrated" social organization of the Middle Ages, they sought to develop a political economy based on an organic conception of society, and thus to recapture the "German spirit."

These features are particularly evident in Müller's *Die Elemente der Staatskunste* (1809), based upon lectures he had given at Dresden. Here Müller suggested that political, economic, religious, moral, and aesthetic elements be indivisibly merged in the German state, which would thus represent "the mysterious reciprocity of all the relationships of life." The economic aspect of society, Müller thus argued, could not be separated from these other elements, but rather had to be studied as but one part of an organic unity. The classical, 18th-century concept of wealth, for example, was rejected in favor of Müller's conception of "spiritual capital," including not only material objects, but also the less tangible traditions of the nation's past, its constitution, its language, the motivations and character of its people, its distinctive forms of knowledge and technology – in short, all the nonmaterial features of the society's culture (Bowen 1968: 522).

Müller's influence on his contemporaries was limited, but his ideas eventually found expression in the works of Georg Friedrich List

(1789–1846) who, visiting the United States in 1825, had been deeply impressed by the "economic nationalism" exhibited there – i.e., high tariffs established to protect nascent, domestic manufacturers from competition from British imports. The classical doctrine of free trade, List realized, was less a system of absolute economic truths than a doctrine suited to the interests of 18th-century British industry, which would reduce other countries to the role of supplying raw materials in return for British exports. This was a *Güterwelt*, List insisted, a non-existent world of abstractions in which the competition between individual economic interests, everywhere the same, would be resolved through the working out of ineluctable economic laws.

For this abstract, unreal world contrived by British political economy, List substituted the economic realities of specific societies, in which material interests were inextricably related to all other aspects of the culture, including language, literature, and history. Particularly in *Das nationale System der politischen Ökonomie* (1841), List insisted that economic laws vary from one society to another, that individual interests are always pursued in a social context conditioned by a variety of social institutions, and called for a "national economy" controlled and directed by the German state, whose policies would be based upon the empirical observation of German realities – and, at least temporarily, would include economic protectionism. List's particular version of the *Volksgeist*, Durkheim would write in 1903, "is undoubtedly an obscure, mystical idea, and the very definition of a national economy rules out the possibility of truly scientific laws, since its object is conceived as unique, thereby excluding comparisons." But List had made an important advance, Durkheim immediately added, "by introducing into economic speculation the idea that society has a real existence, and that the manifestations of its own life comprise relationships interacting with economic phenomena" (1982: 197–8). This insight was quickly taken up by the "older historical school of economics" – e.g., Bruno Hildebrand (1812–78), Wilhelm Georg Friedrich Roscher (1817–94), and Karl Knies (1821–98) – and eventually by their "younger" counterparts, the so-called "socialists of the chair" (*Kathedersozialismus*).

The primary objection of the "older" historical school to classical economics was methodological – i.e., that the appropriate subject matter of economics is not a body of inferences drawn from abstract principles of economy, but rather the empirical observation of the economic realities of past and present societies – in short, that economics is an inductive rather than a deductive science. In *Die Nationalökonomie der Gegenwart und Zukunft* (1848), for example, Hildebrand attacked the alleged universality of the principles guiding Adam Smith's *Wealth of Nations* (1776), insisting that Smith's premises simply did not apply to the peculiarities of German conditions (Kisch 1968a: 357). Similarly, in *Die politische Ökonomie vom Standpunkte der geschichtliche Method* (1853), the patriotic Knies – Hildebrand's student at Marburg – attacked the classical emphasis on individual self-interest, not simply as ahistorical and insensitive to social and cultural context, but as "subversive" of his conception of a stable social order, "an organically evolving community, which at each stage of its development requires a particular form of economic analysis" (Kisch 1968a: 423).

Finally, in a series of volumes, Roscher – whom Durkheim called "the founder of the historical school" – defended his "historico-physiological" method in contrast to the "philosophical-idealist" approach of the classical economists, insisting that the object of political economy was not to establish the best possible state of things, but to describe the actual stage at which each society's economy, in conjunction with its other institutions, had arrived in the course of its historical development (Salin 1968: 559). Durkheim summarized:

> This school has had an original influence on the evolution of political economy. . . Without ever having entirely abandoned the idea of historical research as a means of judging the value of a given political action in any given political circumstance, it has interested itself in facts remote both in space and time, attempting to study them solely with a view to understanding them. To some extent, it has introduced comparisons into economic history. (1982: 198)

But it was the "younger historical school" or "socialists of the chair" (*Kathedersozialismus*), led by Gustav Schmoller (1838–1917) and Adolf Heinrich Gotthelf Wagner (1835–1917), whose works truly captured Durkheim's imagination (1982: 198–9). Unlike its "older" predecessor, Hayek explains, this "younger" school was not simply interested in the history of unique economic institutions or distinctive historical situations; rather, they regarded historical research as providing the empirical foundation for genuine theories of society: "Through the study of historical development it hoped to arrive at the laws of development of social wholes, from which, in turn, could be deduced the historical necessities governing each phase of this development" (1968: 125).

Initially, Hayek's characterization seems ill fitted to Schmoller, Professor of Political Science at the Universities of Halle (1864–72), Strasbourg (1872–82), and Berlin (1882–1913), whose rejection of classical economic theory with its insistence that all economic laws are inductive generalizations sometimes resembled a desire to replace theory with history altogether. At the very least, Schmoller was convinced that useful economic theory can only be the result of an enormous amount of descriptive analysis of both past and present events, institutions, and social structures (Fischer 1968: 61–2). It was this view of theory which the Viennese economist Carl Menger attacked in his *Untersuchungen über die Methode der Sozialwissenschaften und der politischen Ökonomie insbesondere* (1883); and when Schmoller replied the same year in his *Jahrbuch*, the result was the *Methodenstreit* which dominated German social sciences for the next fifty years. But Schmoller's historically informed calls for conservative social reforms were not quite so innocent of theoretical presuppositions as his role in the *Methodenstreit* would suggest. In *Über einige Grundfragen des Rechts und der Volkswirtschaft* (1874–5) – a work Durkheim studied "with care and interest" (1907: 612) – Schmoller based his demand for a more equitable distribution of income on theoretical premises of undeniable romantic provenance. Quite beyond material factors, Schmoller argued, there are psychological and ethical causes which determine the nature and degree of social and economic progress; and the bond which links these material and non-material factors is not simply the state, but "something deeper: the possession in common of language, history, memories, customs, and ideas. It is a world of common emotions and ideas, a mastery of common objectives; more than this, it is a common way of life arising out of these correlated psychological elements and becoming a reality. It is a common ethos influencing all the actions of mankind and so also its political economy" (1975: 44). Durkheim described Schmoller's *Grundriss der allgemeinen Volkswirtschaftslehre* (2 vols., 1900–4) as "a whole sociology seen from the economic viewpoint" (1982: 206).

Wagner, who was Professor of Political Economy at the university of Berlin from 1870 to 1916, and who joined Schmoller in establishing the Verein für Sozialpolitik in 1872, tried to maintain a *via media* between Schmoller and Menger in the *Methodenstreit*, although his sympathies probably lay more with Menger (Meyer 1968: 430).

An "Old Prussian" by choice, Wagner's rejection of classical economics and industrial–commercial capitalism (and thus his frequent agreement with many of the German socialists) was based on arguments that were not only economic but also moral, Protestant, romantic, nationalistic, and occasionally anti-Semitic. In *Allgemeine oder theoretische Volkswirtschaftslehre* (1876), whose discussion of the concept of liberty Durkheim greatly admired, Wagner described political economy as "an organic permeation, not a mechanical parallelism, of individual characteristics. Like the nation, it is a real whole which in crises shows itself to be an organism."[2] In language that anticipated his later discussion of anomic suicide, Durkheim praised Wagner for showing that "whatever has previously been said about it, individual liberty has no absolute value in itself, but has, on the contrary, grave inconveniences which must be forestalled by limiting that liberty. In the present condition of our societies, liberty is thus morally good only if it is restrained" (1887b: 41–2).

Of these *Kathedersozialisten*, Durkheim acknowledged, much is heard in France. "But if the word is known," he added, "the thing is known far less well." Referring to the burgeoning literature on Wagner and Schmoller which had been appearing in the pages of the *Journal des économistes*, Durkheim complained that "the orthodox economists, who among us retain that powerful influence that they have lost in other European countries, have done everything possible to misrepresent the mind and character [of the 'socialists of the chair']" (1887b: 34). Clearly, Durkheim conceived his role as one of re-introducing the German *Kathedersozialisten* to a largely uncomprehending French audience, and of explaining their place in the future development of French social science. The most significant idea of the *Kathedersozialisten*, Durkheim explained, is their intimate *rapprochement* between political economy and ethics – one which "has simultaneously revitalized these two sciences." According to the opposing arguments of the Manchester school, Durkheim observed, the individual is both the original source and the ultimate goal of all economic relations, a position which reduces "society" to a metaphysical status unapproachable by science. Referring in particular to Gustave de Molinari's *L'Evolution politique et la révolution* (1884),

---

[2] This was Wagner's revision of K. H. Rau's *Lehrbuch der politischen Ökonomie* which, in later editions, would be titled *Grundlegung der politischen Ökonomie*. Durkheim referred to the work under Rau's title. See sections 149 and 151 of Wagner 1892–4, which are cited in Deploige 1911: 124 n.10.

Durkheim noted that "the most consequential" of the Manchester economists "have not hesitated to declare that national sentiments are only the survivals of prejudices destined to one day disappear. Under these conditions," Durkheim warned, preparing arguments to be directed against Spencer in *De la division du travail social*, "economic activity can have no other motive than egoism, and thereby political economy is radically separated from ethics, if indeed any moral ideal remains to humanity once all social bonds have been dissolved" (1887b: 37).

Against this mistaken and potentially destructive British conception, Durkheim observed, Wagner and Schmoller have insisted that the needs and interests of individuals are really abstractions, while those of society are real and concrete; that society is thus a "veritable being" with "its own nature and its personality"; and that the practical functions of ethics and political economy, which is to make societies possible, thus coincide: "albeit from different points of view," Durkheim observed, "both . . . seek to know how societies can live and grow" (1887b: 38). This seeking of the *Kathedersozialisten*, Durkheim added in his "Cours de science sociale" (1888), was decidedly inductive rather than deductive; indeed, it was only by inductive means that they – and, arguably, Durkheim himself – became *Sozialisten* at all. Durkheim observed approvingly:

Instead of starting with human nature and deducing science from it as the orthodox economists did, the German school attempts to observe economic facts as they present themselves in reality . . . If this school openly leans toward a certain form of socialism, it is because, when we seek to see things as they are, we observe that, in fact, in all known societies, economic phenomena transcend the individual's sphere of action, that they constitute a function which is not domestic and private but social. (1978a: 60)

In 1887 Durkheim also entertained three objections to the *Kathedersozialisten*. The first was that the differences between British and German political economy had been exaggerated, for the utilitarians, no less than the *Kathedersozialisten*, had made the collective interest of a society's members the foundation of ethical judgment. But for Durkheim, whose thinking about egoism and altruism had clearly deepened since 1883, the differences were important. For the utilitarians, he observed, collective interest "is only a form of personal interest. Altruism is only a disguised egoism, which complacently ignores its true nature; and if, in this doctrine, there is some trait common to both ethics and political economy, it is because the utilitarians reduce both to being nothing but the implementation of egoism. For the German economist, by contrast, the interests of the individual and those of society are far from constantly coinciding. Just as society is something other than the arithmetic sum of its citizens, it has in each category of functions its own ends, which infinitely transcend those of individuals and are not even of the same type. Its destinies are not ours, and yet we must work for them" (1887b: 38–9).

A second objection to the *Kathedersozialisten* was that this convergence of the realms of ethics and political economy ignored all differences between them. But Durkheim argued that the German achievement was precisely to have identified the distinction between ethics and political economy as one between form and content, and then to have described accurately their reciprocal relations:

What properly belongs to ethics, is this form of obligation that becomes attached to certain ways of acting, and marks them with its stamp. Economic phenomena can, under certain conditions, assume this form like all social facts . . . When [the] collective utility [of economic phenomena] has been clearly demonstrated, when they have received the consecration of time, they appear to consciences as obligatory, and are transformed into juridical or moral prescriptions.

The origin of law and ethics thus lies in custom – i.e., "collective habits, constant ways of acting which are found to be common to an entire society . . . [the] crystallization of human conduct." This crystallization achieved, the ethical prescriptions in turn react back on economic phenomena. Ethics, Durkheim emphasized, "is not absorbed by political economy; rather, all social functions contribute to produce that form to which economic phenomena are obliged to submit even as they contribute to making the form" (1887b: 39–41).

The third objection, raised in Menger's *Untersuchen über die Methode der Sozialwissenschaften*, was that these relations between ethics and political economy – alluded to by a variety of ingenious historical examples – remained insufficiently developed in economic theory. Thoroughly aware of the *Methodenstreit* and the issues it raised, and consistently skeptical of historical description in the absence of theoretical generalization, Durkheim was understandably sympathetic with Menger: "In order to make intelligible a perfect intimacy of political economy and ethics," he agreed, "it is not enough to show, through some examples, that economic events have a repercussion in ethics; for everything in the world is interconnected, and there is nothing astonishing in two parts of that reality reacting on one another. Rather," Durkheim concluded, "we would have to show that these two orders of facts, even while remaining distinct, are nonetheless of the same nature" (1887b: 36) – the demonstration, of course, from which *De la division du travail social* derives much of its force.

For Durkheim, therefore, the ultimate significance of the German economists was their contribution, not to economics, but to ethics. Initially, this significance derived from their insistence on an inductive method:

> Until now, for every school of ethics, for the utilitarians as for the Kantians, the problem of ethics consisted essentially in determining the general form of moral conduct, from when the content of moral conduct was then deduced. One began by establishing that the principle of ethics is the "good," or "duty," or "utility," and then drew from this axiom certain maxims which constituted "practical" or "applied" ethics. From the works that we have just summarized, [referring to Wagner and Schmoller], it results, on the contrary, that here as elsewhere the form does not pre-exist the content, but derives from and expresses this content. One cannot construct the whole of ethics in order to then impose it on things; rather, one must observe things in order to induce ethics from them.

But ultimately the significance of the *Kathedersozialisten* resulted from their attacks on the philosophy of natural law – attacks that rendered all rights and duties historically contingent, and thus inherently malleable. Until recently, Durkheim observed, "the philosophy which reigned in Germany . . . believed it possible to deduce an immutable ethic from the nature of man in general, an ethic valid for all times and all places." Precisely because they were reluctant to resign themselves to the blind, inexorable processes of natural law, and thus to forgo political and economic reforms which were palpably desirable, the German economists set themselves the task of demonstrating that economic phenomena themselves contained moral elements of considerable flexibility, and thus that all rights and duties were the products of contingent historical circumstances. To have thus combatted *Naturrecht* – the doctrine of natural law – was "one of the great services performed by the German economists" (1887b: 42–3).

Durkheim's gratitude for this service was not unleavened by scientific reservations: "From the fact that moral phenomena are more mobile than others," he observed quite critically, the German

economists "have concluded that such phenomena might be transformed voluntarily by the legislator. Because they have their origin
not in the nature of material things, but in the conscience of man,
they have seen there artificial combinations which the human will
can unmake or remake as it made them." But one of the most
important contributions of contemporary psychology, Durkheim
argued, was its demonstration that social facts were as "natural" as
any other phenomena, distinguishable from the other realms of
nature only by differences of degree. While more flexible than
material facts, the complexity of social facts rendered them no less
malleable by rational means: ". . . the majority of moral and social
institutions are the result, not of reasoning and calculation, but of
obscure causes, of subconscious sentiments, of motives unconnected
to the effects which they produce, and which they cannot, as a
consequence, explain" (1887b: 45; Miller 1996: 26). Misled by their
exaggerated confidence in legislative action, the *Kathedersozialisten*
had unwittingly returned to an inorganic, Rousseau-like conception
of society as an "artificial arrangement unrelated to the nature of
things" – an interpretation of Rousseau he would later reconsider
(see chapter 5, pp. 268–301). "At bottom," Durkheim concluded in
his reply to Deploige, "I have rather an aversion for the socialism of
the chair, which itself has no sympathy for sociology – whose
principle it denies" (1907: 613–14).

But if Durkheim thus admired the *Kathedersozialisten* for their
recognition of the ethical dimension of economic phenomena, he
also urged that "it is not with economic facts alone that [ethics] is in
relation, but with all social facts from which it derives and which
form its contents" (1887b: 49). Here in particular Durkheim referred
to "[t]hat part of ethics that is called the philosophy of law" which,
by this reasoning, had much to learn from the practical realities of
"positive" law. The initial advantage of the Germans here was that
the philosophy of law had never been reserved for philosophers
alone; on the contrary, Durkheim observed, even during the 18th-
century preoccupation with natural law, German jurists had concerned themselves with legal philosophy, and unconsciously directed
the study of law in a slightly more positive direction. As the romantic
movement gathered strength in the early 19th century, this tendency
was accentuated, producing effects in the study of law similar to
those in the study of political economy.

The central figure here was Friedrich Karl von Savigny

(1779–1861), the founder of the historical school of jurisprudence. Born in Frankfurt am Main to a wealthy, aristocratic family, Savigny taught Roman law at Marburg and Landshut before becoming professor of law and eventually rector at the newly created University of Berlin in 1810, where he remained for the next 32 years. In his pamphlet *Vom Beruf unserer Zeit für Gesetzgebung und Rechtswissenschaft* (1814), published as an argument against the popular demand for the codification of German civil law on the model of the French and Austrian legal codes, and again in his introduction to the first volume of the *Zeitschrift für geschichtliche Rechtswissenschaft* (1815), Savigny molded the ideas of Montesquieu, Burke, and Justus Möser into the foundations of the romantic, historical school of law.

Positive law, Savigny insisted, is not the product of reason, but rather of the common, collective beliefs of a particular society – in short, of its *Volksgeist*. Like its language, manners, and customs, a society's positive law thus evolves as the result of a continuous, organic process, subject to silent, anonymous, and largely irrational causes rather than any intentional, creative effort. Since positive law is thus determined by the peculiar history and nature of the society in question, legal reform must not be arbitrarily attempted through legislation alone, but only gradually introduced after detailed historical research has yielded the "organic principle" of a society's law – a task Savigny undertook in his monumental *Geschichte des römischen Rechts in Mittelalter* (7 vols., 1815–34) and *System des heutigen römischen Rechts* (8 vols., 1840–9). These historical, evolutionary, and inherently sociological arguments faced significant opposition in Germany, particularly from Hegel and his followers; but in fact, the historical school of jurisprudence dominated the study of law in German universities for the next half century.

For Durkheim, the most interesting products of this dominance were Rudolf von Ihering (1818–92) and Albert-Hermann Post (1839–95). A professor of law at Göttingen, Ihering resisted certain arguments of both Hegel and Savigny – e.g., Hegel's indifference to the role played by private interests and public utility in the determination of legal phenomena, and Savigny's parallel indifference to the conscious, purposive aspect of the struggle to protect these private and public interests. But Ihering was no less an antagonist of *Naturrecht* than Savigny. In *Der Zweck im Recht* (2 vols., 1877–83), he insisted upon constraint as the "external condition" of law, and argued that legal phenomena could not be understood without a grasp of the ends or purposes giving rise to them. This "new conception of the philosophy of law," Durkheim observed, "has made a certain clamor in Germany," but "appears to remain quite unknown in France" (1887b: 50, 58) – a situation his 1887 essay was written to correct.

"Since Socrates," Durkheim observed, "philosophers have taken on the habit of reducing reality to combinations of concepts. They think they have explained the life of the individual as much as that of society by reducing it to a system of abstract ideas which are logically connected." Proceeding in this utterly Platonic manner, philosophers grasp only the "general frameworks in which things move," not the "energy which moves these things." But to live, Durkheim insisted, adopting a more Aristotelian posture, is not simply to think, it is to act – i.e., "to affirm one's existence by an act of personal energy (*aus eigener Kraft*)." The source of such individual acts is the idea of an end, of a final cause; and the only way to explain "the facts of the interior life" is thus to reveal its goals. "[I]t is the same for social life," Durkheim then argued, "and since law is a sociological phenomenon, we must, in order to explain it, search for its end. To demonstrate a rule of law is not to prove that it is true, but that it performs some function, that it is well adjusted to the end that it must fulfill (*richtig*)" (1887b: 51) – precisely the functional theory of law advanced in *De la division du travail social*.

Durkheim thus embraced Ihering's essentially Aristotelian approach to the explanation of legal phenomena by the ends that they serve. What he rather clearly could not embrace was Ihering's conscious, purposive notion of the meaning of ends: " . . . by an end, [Ihering] seems to understand the conscious idea of a goal, or at least of one of the goals of conduct. If such is the meaning of the word," Durkheim observed, "there is a multitude of our actions from whence any idea of ends is absent. How many times we act without knowing the goal toward which we tend!" This dismissal of Ihering's "rather metaphysical" conception of conscious ends Durkheim owed, not only to Spinoza's *Ethics* (1677), which he greatly admired, but also to a precocious grasp of the significance of psychological experiments into hypnotic suggestion currently conducted in France, and thus to the emerging psychology of the unconscious – an interest that Durkheim had clearly acquired *since* his Sens lectures: "To explain how these kinds of unconscious adaptations are made," Durkheim urged, "it would be necessary to go beyond the conscience, to study the nature of that obscure and diffuse intelligence which has no small role in the direction of our lives, the mechanism of the emotions, inclinations, instincts, habits, their action on our conduct and the way in which they are modified when the circumstances require it." In societies, as in the individual, Durkheim now pursued the analogy, "changes occur which have causes and no ends at all, something analogous to Darwin's individual variations. Some can be found which are useful, but this utility was not foreseen, and was not the determining cause" (1887b: 51–2).

Of this new psychology, Ihering appeared utterly ignorant. Still, Durkheim agreed with Ihering's general proposition – i.e., that social phenomena derive from practical causes. What, then, was the practical cause of law? Briefly, according to Ihering, it was "the need to assure the conditions of the existence of society," where "conditions" were subdivided into those to which law is irrelevant, those to which law is relevant only accidentally, and those which can be realized only through law. Interestingly, Ihering's second set of conditions, which arise when natural impulse fails to guarantee the social interest, included the prevention of suicides, celibates, pauperism, strikes, and monopolies: "As the society suffers from all these evils, it protects itself from them and fights them by means of law. Albeit exceptionally," Durkheim observed, "it replaces the internal impulse which is lacking through an external, mechanical pressure" (1887b: 53). But even the first set of conditions, Ihering argued, where the interests of society are sufficiently in accord with those of individuals that laws need not intervene (there are no laws, for example, "enforcing" self-preservation or procreation), provide no legitimacy for a doctrine of natural rights. "[W]e must not think," Ihering and Durkheim agreed, "that, in this sphere where society does not ordinarily intervene, the individual exercises rights which derive from his own nature and belong to him in his own right. Law is the hand of society weighing on the individual, and there the latter ceases to make itself felt, there are rights no longer." Even property rights, Durkheim insisted, exist only at the indulgence of society, and activities once considered voluntary (e.g., military service and elementary education) were now imposed by a society on its members (1887b: 53–4).

If this was the *end* of law, what were its *means*? On this point, Durkheim observed, the Germans were indeed unanimous: "All," he noted approvingly, "make of constraint the external condition of law" (1887b: 55). The later criticism of Georges Sorel notwithstanding (Lukes 1972: 12–14), the conception of constraint Durkheim found in Ihering seems to have been relatively differentiated: "[T]here are various kinds of constraint," Durkheim observed, including that exercised by one individual on another; that exercised by an entire society under the form of manners, custom, and opinion; and that organized and concentrated in the hands of the State. "It is the last kind which assures the realization of law," he observed. "Where it is not present, there is no law, and it is all the more inconsistent as it is the less well organized" (1887b: 55). But how does this organized, concentrated form of constraint work? What renders it efficacious? What motives, in short, lead people to respect the law? "No doubt," Ihering admitted, "the most general and most powerful motive is self-interest, and it is to self-interest above all that the constraint exercised by the State is addressed." Yet, however necessary, the dictates of self-interest were clearly not sufficient: "In order for society to be possible," Ihering and Durkheim again agreed, there had to be some "disinterested sentiment" – specifically, the inclinations of love (*die Liebe*) and duty (*Pflichtgefühl*) which, transcending the sphere of law, belonged to that of pure morality (*die Sittlichkeit*). Without such a pure morality, therefore, no law could exist.

Efficacious legal statutes thus presuppose an infrastructure of common moral sentiment; and even though ethics and law thus pursue the same goal (of making society possible) by the same means (constraint), Durkheim was clearly pleased by Ihering's emphasis on the more flexible, capacious, and ultimately transcendent realm of ethics: "[T]his constraint," Durkheim agreed, "does not consist in an exterior, mechanical pressure, but rather has a more intimate, psychological character. It is not the State which exercises it, but the whole society." Repeating his earlier objection to the *Kathedersozialisten*, Durkheim insisted that the State "is too large a mechanism to regulate such complex movements of the human heart." Ihering, Durkheim concluded, "has performed a great service to ethics by definitively integrating it with the study of customs . . . an idea that Wundt has just taken up again" (1887b: 56–8).

The second representative of historical jurisprudence in whom Durkheim expressed interest was Albert-Hermann Post (1839–95). As a positivist and empiricist interested in primitive forms of law, ethics, and the family, Post had attempted to construct a system of "ethnological jurisprudence," a universal history of law culminating in deterministically conceived, evolutionary goals. In 1887 Durkheim's primary concern was with Post's *Die Grundlagen des Rechts und die Grundzüge seiner Entwickelungsgeschichte* (1884); and his judgment, which focused entirely on Post's historical method, was largely negative: ". . . the science of morals," Durkheim insisted, "must not be confused with the history of morals, from which it draws its content. To describe the evolution of an idea or of an institution is not to explain it. When we know in what order the phases that it goes through succeed one another, we still know neither what its cause nor its function are" (1887b: 282).

But just a year later, Durkheim spoke of Ihering and Post in the same breath, as juristic counterparts of Wagner and Schmoller. "Though they belonged to very different philosophical schools," Durkheim observed, Ihering and Post "both tried to induce the general principles of law from the comparison of texts on laws and customs," and thus "discovered the subject matter for a new science in law." Political economy and jurisprudence thus comprised a "double movement, economic and legal," which rendered an inestimable service to the development of sociology: "From that point on," Durkheim insisted, "sociology ceased to be a kind of universal science, general and confused, including just about everything. It was divided into a certain number of special sciences which attacked ever more determinate problems. The study of political economy had long since been established, even though it had long been languishing. The science of law, though newer, was basically but a transformation of the old philosophy of law. Sociology," Durkheim concluded, "thanks to its relationship to these two sciences, lost that erstwhile air of sudden improvisation which had sometimes cast doubt upon its future" (1888: 60–1).

The failure of French sociology also provided the context for Durkheim's growing interest in German ethnography. Comte, Durkheim acknowledged, had given sociology an object to study – Society. But in a sense, he added, "Society" does not exist; only "societies" exist, in all their varieties, types, and species. "An adversary of Lamarck," Durkheim observed, Comte "did not think it possible that the mere fact of evolution could differentiate organisms to the point of giving birth to new species. According to him, social facts are always and everywhere the same, with variations in intensity, while social development is always and everywhere the same, with variations in rate. The most savage nations and the most cultivated peoples," Comte had thus concluded, "are but different phases of a single and identical evolution, and it was the laws of this unique evolution which he sought." This explains Comte's use of the terms "society" and "humanity" as if they were synonymous, Durkheim added, as well as his exclusive focus on civilized, German–Latin peoples (1888: 52–3).

Comte had been encouraged in this perspective, Durkheim admitted, by the imperfect state of the ethnological sciences in his day; but today, Durkheim insisted, "it is manifestly impossible to maintain that there is a human evolution which is everywhere identical and that societies are all just different versions of a single and identical type" (1888: 53). Zoology had long ago renounced the linear classification, insisting instead that the genealogical descent of organized beings was "a very bushy tree whose branches, issuing haphazardly all along the trunk, shoot out capriciously in all directions. And it is the same," Durkheim insisted, "with society." Pascal's formulation notwithstanding, "humanity" could hardly be compared "to a solitary man who has lived all these past centuries and still survives. Rather, [humanity] resembles an immense family, the various branches of which, as they diverge more and more from one another, gradually detach themselves from the common source to live their own lives" (1888: 54). The comparison of various societal types, Durkheim concluded, might still yield general laws applying to all societies; but such laws would never be revealed by even the most attentive observation of a single, isolated type.

The foundations for such a comparative study of societal types, Durkheim suggested, had been laid at "the dawn of the century" by Wilhelm von Humboldt (1767–1835). Prussian statesman, humanist and linguist, older brother of the scientist and explorer Alexander von Humboldt, friend of Schiller and Goethe, and founder of the university of Berlin, Humboldt's early education had been in Greek, philosophy, natural law and classical political economy. During his university years at Frankfurt an der Oder (1787) and Göttingen (1788–9), however, Humboldt had begun to question the rationalistic presuppositions of the Enlightenment: "Like Herder," one scholar has observed, Humboldt increasingly viewed human society "as a manifold of organic forces, closer to nature than to reason, and came to believe that true knowledge of humanity depended on the cultivation not of pure analytical reason but of deep-lying intuitive faculties" – ideas that found expression in *Über das Studium des Altertums und des griechischen insbesondere* (1793), *Plan einer vergleichenden Anthropologie* (1797), and *Die Aufgabe des Geschichtschreibers* (1821). To establish the unity of the human spirit asserted in these works, Durkheim argued, scholars like J. C. Prichard (1786–1848) and Gustav Klemm (1802–67) were inevitably led to the classification and comparison of human civilizations, races, and languages (Durkheim and Fauconnet 1982: 199).

Deploige's "accusation" of 1905–7, however, referred more specifically to the German *Völkerpsychologie*, the collective product of a group of anthropologists cum psychologists led by Theodor Waitz (1821–64), Heymann Steinthal (1823–99), and Moritz Lazarus (1824–1903), whose works had been introduced to French audiences through Ribot's *La Psychologie allemande contemporaine* (1879). Waitz, the son of a clergyman and seminary director, had studied at Leipzig, published a critical edition of Aristotle's *Organon* (1844) and, in 1846, joined the philosophy faculty at the university of Marburg. Deeply indebted to Herbartian psychology, Waitz's early works sought to reconcile an empirical study of the human mind with his utterly devout religious beliefs. But it was his *Anthropologie der Naturvölker* (6 vols., 1859–72), initially conceived as the empirical foundation for a philosophy of religion, which provided much of the (admittedly rather meager) ethnographic substance of *De la division du travail social* (1893) (1984: 89–90, 97, 103, 128–9, 134, 189). The *Anthropologie der Naturvölker*, Durkheim observed in 1903, "synthesized the ethnographical and anthropological labours of a whole era" – thus completing the "early, descriptive" stage of ethnographic research (Durkheim and Fauconnet 1982: 199).

According to Ribot, the most significant contribution of Lazarus and Steinthal to the social sciences was the *Zeitschrift für Völkerpsychologie und Sprachwissenschaft*. Founded in 1859, the *Zeitschrift* had declared its intention to publish essays concerned with "the discovery of the laws of ethnic psychology," reports of "historical, ethnological, geological, and anthropological facts," and to study language "not as the philologist or the empirical linguist, but in order to discover, with the aid of physiology, the psychological laws of language" – a "noble program, well-defined," Ribot suggested in 1886, although one which remained largely unfulfilled. "In addition to ordinary psychology, which deals with individual man," Ribot explained, "there is room for another science, devoted to social man, or, more exactly, to groups of men." This is what the *Zeitschrift* intends by the phrase "ethnic" or "ethnological" psychology. But the successful realization of such a science, he immediately added, depends upon certain theoretical presuppositions; and it was these presuppositions which would appear to Deploige as the sources of much of Durkheim's sociology (1886: 60–1).

For ethnological psychology to have a "real object," Ribot observed, it must be proved that the study of the individual alone is insufficient. The essential condition of this proof is the demonstration that "society" is a whole greater than the sum of its individual parts: "If it be true," Ribot thus suggested, "that the social whole is something else than a simple addition of individuals, if the formation of groups gives birth to new relations, to new forms of development; briefly, if the whole be not an arithmetical sum of units, but a chemical combination differing from its elements, it must be admitted that *Völkerpsychologie* has a province exclusively its own. And this," Ribot then added in a most Durkheimian manner, "is the truth. The social whole differs as much from each of its parts as the laws of political economy differ from the principles of domestic economy urged by a father upon his son, by a teacher upon his ward." The individual tree, Lazarus had observed, constitutes a legitimate object of study for the botanist; but fifty thousand trees make a forest, and this forest becomes the object of another science altogether, "a science which rests without doubt on the physiology of plant life, but which has, nevertheless, an end and means of its own" (1886: 61–2). The "real object" of ethnological psychology was precisely this *Volksgeist*, this "spirit of a people" independent of its individual members.

What is the nature of this *Volksgeist*? And whence does it come? To such questions, Ribot observed, Lazarus and Steinthal "reply in a rather mystical style, that 'it is not a substance, but a subject'; that it is 'a monad that penetrates and combines individuals'; that it is an 'objective spirit.' In other words," Ribot explained, "whenever men form a group, live together, constitute a society, there arises from the consensus of individual (subjective) spirits a common (objective) spirit, 'which becomes at once the expression, the law, the organ of the subjective spirit'" (1886: 63). The elements of this common, objective spirit (including language, mythology, religion, culture, art, custom, law, etc.), as well as their development, interaction, growth and decline, constituted the work of ethnological psychology. But however "noble" and "well-defined" the program of the *Zeitschrift*, Ribot felt that Lazarus and Steinthal had not succeeded. Admittedly, they had produced a number of documents on attractive subjects (e.g., the history of religions, literary criticism, linguistics, anthropology, the history of customs, law, and politics); but their treatment seemed "as much literary as scientific," "too general for this kind of investigation," and lacking in "exact results" (1886: 64–6). The English anthropologists, by contrast, "have apprehended better the conditions of a psychology of the races. They have sketched it in monographs" – e.g., Lubbock's and McLennan's studies of the primitive family, and Tylor's *Primitive Culture* (1871) (1886: 66–7).

By 1888, Durkheim had reached largely similar conclusions. "In every society," he observed, "there exists a certain number of common ideas and sentiments. These are passed from one generation to another and simultaneously assure the unity and the continuity of collective life. Among these are popular legends, religious traditions, political beliefs, language, and so on. All these phenomena are psychological in nature, but they do not have their source in individual psychology, since they infinitely transcend the individual. They must, therefore, be the object of a special science charged with their description and the investigation of their preconditions. This science could be called social psychology. This," Durkheim added, referring explicitly to Lazarus and Steinthal, "is the Germans' *Völkerpsychologie*." The difficulty for Durkheim, as for Ribot, was that "no results have yet been produced" (1888: 63). By the time results were produced, Durkheim's estimate of their significance had been deeply colored by the comparative – and largely British – study of religion. "Armed with the theory of survivals," Durkheim wrote in 1903, Mannhardt, Tylor, Lang, W. R. Smith, Frazer, Hartland, and Wilken "annexed at a stroke for the comparative science of religions the whole body of facts relating to folklore or *Volkskunde* which the Germans had observed, recorded and compared since the beginning of the century, and which thereby took on a new significance. The agricultural customs of our countries, magical practices, ideas concerning the dead, tales and legends, all appeared to be the residue of ancient cults and beliefs. Thus the religions of the most highly cultured societies and those of the lowest tribes," he concluded, "were linked, each serving mutually to explain the other" (Durkheim and Fauconnet 1982: 200).

Political economy, jurisprudence, and ethnography: "[w]hat emerged from all these investigations," Durkheim summarized, "was the fact that social phenomena could no longer be deemed the product of fortuitous combinations, arbitrary acts of the will, or local chance circumstances. Their generality attests to their essential dependence on general causes which, everywhere that they are present, produce their effects." Beneath "what was once held to be the preponderant influence of princes, statesmen, legislators and men of genius of every kind," historians were increasingly discovering these "impersonal forces" which dominate historical processes. "[I]t is not we who think," Durkheim agreed with Post, "but the world which thinks in us." Morals, customs, even the art and literature of a society were the unconscious work of the peoples themselves; and "if peoples have their own ways of thinking and feeling," Durkheim concluded, then "this life of the intellect can become an object of scientific study, just as that of individuals" (Durkheim and Fauconnet 1982: 201).

The extent of Durkheim's debt to German sociology is more difficult to ascertain. Durkheim's early resistance to Gumplowicz's social realism has already been noted. After 1887, however, Durkheim's objections to German sociology sometimes suggested they were not realist enough. In his 1889 review of Ferdinand Tönnies' *Gemeinschaft und Gesellschaft* (1887), for example, Durkheim praised the characterizations of both *Gemeinschaft* and *Gesellschaft*, and agreed with the German author that these were indeed the two great societal types. Against Tönnies, however, Durkheim insisted that the modern, *Gesellschaft* type "is every bit as natural as that of small aggregates. It is neither less organic nor less self-contained. Aside from purely individual activities, there is in our contemporary societies a truly collective activity which is just as natural as that of the less extensive societies of former times" (1978b: 121). And in a manner consistent with his earlier praise of the *Kathedersozialisten*, Durkheim objected to Tönnies' focus on abstract concepts rather than concrete social realities: "The only way to succeed," Durkheim argued, "would have been to proceed inductively, that is, to study *Gesellschaft* through the laws and mores which are associated with it and which reveal its structure" (1978b: 121–2).

Durkheim had similar objections to the views of Georg Simmel, whose works he and Paul Fauconnet discussed in a lengthy review article entitled "Sociologie et sciences sociales" (1903). According to

Simmel, Durkheim observed, the distinction between the particular social sciences and sociology *per se* corresponds, respectively, to that between content (i.e., the various phenomena which occur between individuals in association) and the form that "contains" them (i.e., the association itself, within which these phenomena are observed). "The association," Durkheim noted in summarizing Simmel's position, "is the only expressly social thing, and sociology is the science of association *in abstracto*." Such a process of abstraction and classification, Durkheim admitted, is essential to science itself; but it must be carried out methodically, "in conformity with the nature of things" (Durkheim and Fauconnet 1982: 189–90, 191). For Durkheim, the difficulty with Simmel's classification was thus the utterly metaphorical character of terms like "form" and "content," which corresponded to nothing in nature itself; on the contrary, Durkheim argued, they simply described two aspects of social life, the one more general, the other more specific – but both equally "sociological." In fact, he insisted, there is no way to determine the degree of generality a phenomenon must have for it to be considered "sociological" at all, a problem of indeterminacy characteristic not only of Simmel's distinction but of his work as a whole: "The problems raised," Durkheim concluded, "do not relate to determinate categories of facts: they are general themes for philosophical meditation" – but not for positive science (Durkheim and Fauconnet 1903: 190–4).

Among German sociologists, therefore, the most prominent place must belong to Schaeffle. A rationalist, socialist, and ardent anti-individualist, Schaeffle rose rapidly to a professorship at the university of Tübingen and became a member of the Württemberg diet. He later occupied a chair at the university of Vienna while editing the *Zeitschrift für die gesamte Staatswissenschaft*, and by the late 1870s was among the German sociologists of greatest interest to French writers. As we have seen, Espinas discussed Schaeffle's *Bau und Leben des sozialen Körpers* (4 vols., 1875–78) in the second edition of *Les Sociétés animales* (1878), Fouillée discussed the same work again in *La Science sociale contemporaine* (1880), and in 1885, Durkheim's first published work had been a review of the first volume of *Bau und Leben* for the *Revue philosophique*.

Schaeffle argued, for example,

Human society is a living organism of a peculiar kind. The social body works through and for its active components . . . but it maintains itself above these as a continuous collective conscience with a tradition of spiritual and material properties governing these individuals . . . It is not an organism in the biological sense. In an empirical sense, it is an independent entity of a higher order . . . Society is not the sum of individuals. Its totality consists in the change of individuals and it outlasts generations of individuals and families. Social consciousness is more than the totality-content of individual consciousness. (1875: 1ff.; in Deploige, 1911: 124–5 n. 12)

"[T]his idea," Durkheim observed in his "Cours de science sociale" (1978), "without which sociology cannot exist, has always been very much alive in Germany, and was eclipsed only during the brief period when Kantian individualism held undisputed sway. The Germans have too profound a sense for the complexity of things to be easily content with so simplistic a solution. The theory which compares society with living organisms was therefore well received in Germany because it permitted the German to become more fully aware of an idea which had long been dear to them. Schaeffle," he concluded quite accurately, "accepts it without hesitation" (1978a: 59).

Like the *Kathedersozialisten*, Schaeffle was an avowed critic of liberalism, insisting that "liberty and equality must not be promoted at the expense of order, unity, and association, because in this event they would bring about weakness instead of power, suicide instead of self-preservation of the whole" (1875: 134ff.; in Deploige 1911: 140). But unlike the *Kathedersozialisten*, Schaeffle shared Durkheim's view of the insufficiency and even danger of State intervention as a remedy for liberal anarchy. The "excessive plasticity" which Wagner and Schmoller attributed to law and ethics, Durkheim observed, is denied by Schaeffle, who rather views society as "a living being which is moved from within. The legislator does not invent laws, he can only confirm them and form them with clarity. . . The legislator does not play in their formation the exorbitant role that the socialists of the chair sometimes assign him, and his importance diminishes proportionately as that of society grows." It was in this sense that Schaeffle "was the first to extract the moral consequences of the work of the political economists, without making their mistakes" (1887b: 47, 45).

So skeptical of State intervention, Schaeffle called for the restoration – albeit under a new form – of the occupational corporations of the Middle Ages: "The corporation," he insisted, "is a need of all times, of the present as well as of the future. However, it has special forms in every period of history" (1875: 757–65; in Deploige 1911:

140–1). In *Le Suicide* (1897), Durkheim too would call for a restoration of the medieval guilds, outside of (though subject to) the State, which would perform social functions (e.g., the supervision of insurance, welfare, and pensions; the settling of contractual disputes; the regulation of working conditions; etc.) as well as moral functions: "Besides the rights and duties common to all men," Durkheim explained, "there are others depending on qualities peculiar to each occupation, the number of which increases in importance as occupational activity increasingly develops and diversifies. For each of these special disciplines, an equally special organ is needed, to apply and maintain it" (1951: 380).

Though a moralist, Schaeffle insisted that both law and ethics be studied in their empirical, social context rather than artificially deduced. "Ethics," Durkheim could thus write approvingly of Schaeffle's *Bau und Leben*,

is not a system of abstract rules that man finds written in his conscience or that the moralist deduces from the back of his closet. It is a social function, or rather a system of functions, which forms and consolidates itself little by little under the pressure of collective needs. Love in general, the abstract inclination to disinterestedness, does not exist. What really exists is love in marriage and in the family, the free self-devotion of friendship, the municipal spirit, patriotism, the love of humanity; and all these sentiments are the product of history. It is these concrete facts which form the content of morality. The moralist can thus neither invent nor construct them; but he must observe them where they exist, and then seek in society their causes and conditions. (1887b: 46–7)

Finally, Schaeffle had a vision of the method and organization of sociological study quite similar to the later Durkheim. He complained of the lack of integration of the special social sciences, while simultaneously rejecting the more comprehensive, but speculative and abstract philosophies of history and society characteristic of Comte and Spencer (1875: 52; in Deploige 1911: 129 n. 25). Admitting that the observations of individual scholars must always be fragmentary, incomplete, and reflective of personalities and prejudices, he advised the use of statistics, the study of historical documents, and the collection of ethnographic data; and "to disengage the causes of phenomena," Schaeffle observed, following Mill, the sociologist should "prudently choose one of the four methods" – i.e., of concordances, differences, residues, or concomitant variations (1875: 124; in Deploige 1911: 130).

Durkheim's admiration for Schaeffle's works was hardly unqualified. He argued that Schaeffle's frequent use of biological analogues threatened to undermine the very independence which he had sought for sociology (1885a: 98–9). He complained that Schaeffle's estimate of the role of consciousness and reason in society (ironically, the basis for Schaeffle's insistence on the independence of sociology from biology) was not only exaggerated and the prerogative of an isolated elite, but would return society to the very anarchistic individualism which both Durkheim and Schaeffle abhorred (1885a: 99–100). Similarly, Durkheim found Schaeffle's definition of ethics, which restricted moral actions to those resulting from a purely spontaneous movement of the will, narrow and imprecise (1887b: 46). The latter difficulties, in particular, Durkheim attributed to the unwholesome influence of German psychology, which had traditionally encouraged a discontinuity between the realms of *Natur* and *Geist* (1887b: 48). But Durkheim felt that the influence of Descartes had been equally unhealthy for the French, and that Schaeffle's sociology was a practical, potential corrective: ". . . there are few readings more highly instructive for a Frenchman," Durkheim said of *Bau und Leben* in 1885, for "[i]t is by the practice of such patient and laborious studies that we shall fortify our spirit, now too slender, too thin, too fond of simplicity. It is by learning to face the infinite complexity of facts that we free ourselves of those too narrow frameworks in which we tend to compartmentalize things. It is perhaps no exaggeration," Durkheim concluded, "to say that the future worth of French sociology depends on this" (1885a: 97).

WUNDT AND EXPERIMENTAL PSYCHOLOGY IN GERMANY

"After Kant," Ribot observed, "metaphysic reigned in Germany for half a century, and all science of the phenomena of consciousness was forgotten or despised." Even in the reaction which followed, "men continued to treat [psychology] as an illegitimate child of metaphysic, and wrote books which were epitomes of artificial, profitless, and insoluble questions; discarded altogether a positive basis of harmony, physical flux, occasionalism, materialism, and pantheism, in all their forms. Men seriously discussed the relative merit of 'traducianism' and 'creationism.'" Yet even then, Ribot added, real scientists, "as it were by chance and through the study of details, were preparing for the birth of scientific psychology" (1886: 287).

For Ribot – as for most historians of experimental psychology – these preparatory labors began with Johann Friedrich Herbart (1776–1841), a student of Fichte, successor to Kant at Königsberg, and professor of philosophy at the university of Göttingen. In his *Lehrbuch zur Psychologie* (1815) and especially *Psychologie als Wissenschaft* (1824–5), Herbart sought to establish a basis for psychology independent of the prevailing "faculty" psychology of Christian Wolff, by showing that the laws of mental processes could be expressed in precise mathematical form. Herbart "sets out from *a priori* principles," Ribot complained, "gives little room to facts, [and] much to reasoning and mathematics"; but among Kant's numerous disciples, he added, Herbart "alone . . . can be called a psychologist" (1886: 21).

At least equally important in the pre-history of experimental psychology was Johannes Müller (1801–58), a student and then professor at Bonn until called to the chair of anatomy and physiology at Berlin in 1833. This "post of great distinction," Boring has observed, "served to mark Müller as the foremost authority on physiology of his day," and his *Handbuch der Physiologie des Menschen* (1833–40) became "the primary systematic treatise" (1950: 34). Herbart, meanwhile, had been succeeded at Göttingen by Rudolf Hermann Lotze (1817–81), whose *Medizinische Psychologie* (1852) became the first systematic work on physiological psychology. Although "employing experience," Ribot again complained, Lotze in fact "never separated psychological researches from metaphysical hypotheses, and we can say without hesitation that the 'psychology without a soul,' which has gained a goodly number of adherents in Germany. . . never had his entire allegiance" (1886: 21).

As indicated above (see p. 120), experimentation and the use of quantitative methods in psychology were greatly advanced by Ernst Heinrich Weber (1795–1878) and Gustav Theodor Fechner (1801–78), both professors at the university of Leipzig. In *De Tactu* (1834) and *Der Tastsinn und das Gemeingefühl* (1846), Weber reported the results of a series of experiments on touch, pain, pressure, and temperature, from which emerged "Weber's law" – i.e., that the smallest increment in a stimulus required to produce a difference in the sensation experienced is relative to the magnitude of the stimulus in question. Convinced that the mysteries of the relation between mind and body could be resolved by determining the precise mathematical relations between such stimuli and sensations, the more metaphysically inclined Fechner reduced Weber's law to quantitative terms. Weber's law thus became the "Weber–Fechner law," and the "psycho-physical methods" which Fechner designed for its verification – all in the interest of anti-materialism – marked the beginning of quantitative experimental psychology (Boring 1950: 293; Ribot 1886: 22, 135).

The other significant figure in German experimental psychology before Wundt was Hermann Ludwig von Helmholtz (1821–94), the physicist and physiologist, student of Müller, and author of both the *Handbuch der physiologischen Optik* (3 vols., 1856–66) and *Die Lehre von dem Tonempfindung* (1863). If Fechner had "showed that psychology could employ the scientific method of measurement," Boring observed, these two works:

showed what could be done in research and in the accumulation of facts in the two leading sense-departments [vision and hearing, respectively] . . . With a method of measurement available, with an exhibit of what could actually be done if the experimenter would but get to work, and with the general notion already explicit, it only remained for Wundt to seize the opportunity, to cry the slogan, and psychology as "an independent science" would be "founded." And that, is exactly what Wundt did. (1950: 303)

Wilhelm Wundt was born in the duchy of Baden, in Neckarau, a suburb of Mannheim. At the age of 6, his family moved to the village of Heidensheim where, after two years in the *Volkschule*, his education was undertaken by the local vicar, Friedrich Müller, a man deeply admired by both Wundt and his parents, and when Müller moved to Münzesheim, Wundt accompanied him and continued his education. At 13, Wundt entered the Gymnasium at Bruschal, moving the following year to the Heidelberg Gymnasium, where he developed the habit of intensive reading that led to his later, encyclopaedic erudition. Boring observed:

[A] sober childhood and a serious youth, unrelieved by fun and jollity, which prepared the young Wundt for the endless writing of the ponderous tomes which eventually did so much to give him his place in history. He never learned to play. He had no friends in childhood and only intellectual companions in adolescence. He failed to find parental love and affection, substituting for the more happy relationship this deep attachment for his vicar–mentor. One can see the future man being formed, the humorless, indefatigable, aggressive Wundt.

In 1851, Wundt attended the university of Tübingen, where he decided to study physiology. Wundt entertained serious doubts as to whether he was suited for the medical profession; but his father had died, his mother's means were limited, and medical training offered him (as it had offered Lotze and Helmholtz before him, and would soon offer Freud) a compromise between becoming a doctor, which would earn him a living, and becoming a scientist, for which his scholarly temperament was more clearly suited. The medical faculties of the German universities "gave a truly academic training," Boring explains, but one which might later be rendered profitable; thus "modern psychology began as physiological psychology" (1950: 317).

In 1852, Wundt moved to the university of Heidelberg, where he received a thorough practical training in medicine, simultaneously conducting research and producing his earliest publications. But the intellectual environment of Heidelberg was too practical for Wundt's scientific disposition, and in the spring of 1856, he went to Berlin to study physiology with Johannes Müller. "[T]he character of German science at Berlin," Wundt explained, is "purer in its depth and in its many-sidedness than in the university of southern Germany" (Boring 1950: 318). Besides Müller in physiology and H. G. Magnus in physics, Wundt learned much from the physiologist and philosopher of science Emil du Bois-Reymond (1818–96), who was then trying to settle a controversy on the nature of muscular contractions. "If anything remained to determine Wundt for the academic life," Boring observes, "this stimulating experience at Berlin was decisive" (Boring 1950: 318).

In the fall of 1856, Wundt returned to Heidelberg, where he took his doctorate in medicine, and then habilitated as a *Dozent* (instructor) in physiology from 1857 to 1864. Lecturing in alternate semesters on experimental physiology and medical physics, Wundt simultaneously produced three papers on physiology (1856–57), and his first book, *Die Lehre von den Muskelbewegungen* (1858). More significantly, drawing heavily on the works of Müller, Lotze, and Weber, Wundt published the first section of his *Beiträge zur Theorie der Sinneswahrnehmung* (1858), which contained a brief discussion of unconscious inference (*unbewusster Schluss*) as the mechanism of perception. At about the same time, Wundt became preoccupied with Herbart's *Psychologie als Wissenschaft* (1824–5), and began to flesh out some of his nascent epistemological notions in a series of introductory lectures on the study of natural science. Like Herbart, Wundt soon concluded that psychology must indeed be a "science"

(*Wissenschaft*). But unlike Herbart, Wundt also agreed with Fechner that, "as a science" (*als Wissenschaft*), psychology must be based upon experiment. While all psychology begins with introspection (*Selbstbeobachtung*), Wundt argued, scientific psychology ultimately depends upon two means (*Hilfsmittel*) by which the scientist proceeds inductively – i.e., experiment and "the natural history of man" (*Geschichte*, or anthropology). The completed *Beiträge* of 1862, Boring thus concludes, "has some claim to being the beginning of experimental psychology, partly because it is in content experimental psychology, partly because it presents a formal plea for experimental psychology, called by that name, and partly because, for all its shortcomings, it is Wundt's first book in experimental psychology" (1950: 320).

In 1862, Wundt began offering a course of lectures on "psychology from the standpoint of natural science," publishing them the following year as *Die Vorlesungen über die Menschen- und Thierseele* (1863). The lectures raised a number of issues which would constitute the subject-matter of experimental psychology for years to come, and in 1867, the course-title was changed to "Physiological Psychology," in preparation for "the most important book in the history of modern psychology" – the *Grundzüge der physiologischen Psychologie* (1873–4). This was Wundt's "great argument for an experimental psychology," one which, in a sense, he would never surpass. Simultaneously the "concrete result of [his] intellectual development at Heidelberg," the "symbol of his metamorphosis from physiologist to psychologist," and "the beginning of the new 'independent' science," the *Grundzüge* was "a systematic handbook in both senses of the word; it was built about a system of psychology," Boring, observes, "and it attempted systematically to cover the range of psychological fact" (1950: 322–3).

An *ausserordentlicher Professor* (associate professor) since 1864, Wundt had been the presumed successor to Helmholtz's chair of physiology; but when Helmholtz left for Berlin in 1871, Wundt was passed over for the physiologist Willy Kühne (1837–1900). In 1874, Wundt thus accepted the chair of inductive philosophy at the university of Zürich and, just one year later, was called to the chair of philosophy at Leipzig. "This change," Boring observes, "is significant. It brought Wundt formally into the field where psychology was supposed to belong, and it brought him there from physiology. Thus began that paradoxical situation . . . whereby experimental laboratories grew up as adjuncts to German chairs of philosophy" (1950:

323). Indeed, granted space in 1875 for the experimental demonstrations related to his lectures, Wundt established, in 1879, the Physiologische Institut – the world's first laboratory of experimental psychology: "a primitive affair of a few rooms, soon increased to eleven," Boring observes, "it was in this first building that experimental psychology actually got its *de jure* independence" (1950: 324). Enormously productive, the new laboratory soon required its own medium of publication, and in 1881 Wundt founded the *Philosophische Studien*, the first effective organ of experimental psychology.

Despite the numerical superiority of the Berlin philosophers, Durkheim could thus observe in 1887, "it is always Leipzig that is preferred by foreigners who come to Germany to complete their philosophical education. It is to Wundt and his teachings that this persistent vogue is due. It is this same cause," he added, "which led us to Leipzig, and kept us there longer than anywhere else" (1887b: 313–14). The university of Leipzig generally – and the Physiologische Institut in particular – thus became the focus of Durkheim's "La philosophie dans les universités allemandes" (1887), which described the problems under study – e.g., the measurement of reaction time, the estimate of durations, the measurement of sensations of sound, the feeling for musical intervals, the verification of psychological laws by the method of mean graduations, etc. – in considerable and often tedious detail. Durkheim emphasized:

We see how each of these topics is precise and restricted, [b]ut however specialized these studies may be, nothing is more capable of raising in young minds the love of scientific precision, to divest them of vague generalizations and metaphysical possibilities, and finally to make them understand how complex are psychological facts and the laws which govern them – all while showing them that, if this complexity is an obstacle, there is nothing in this to discourage the observer. (1887a: 433)

But Durkheim was at least equally emphatic on the limited extent of Wundt's influence on German scholarship. Whatever autonomy psychology had achieved from philosophy had been won on the early 18th-century ground of Christian Wolff's distinction between rational and empirical psychology, wherein the latter embraced methods like "personal observation," "ideological analysis," and an unhealthy dose of metaphysical speculation – but hardly experimentation. Lotze, in Durkheim's view, was "a metaphysician who has never seen psychology as a positive science," his "quite involuntary" contribution to experimental psychology being "grafted onto a metaphysical hypothesis"; and "it is the metaphysician in Lotze," Durkheim observed, "which Germany honors" (1887a: 331). Fechner was "no less a metaphysician than Lotze," Durkheim added, "and it is to his ontological fantasies that he owes the great authority which he enjoys in Germany. As for his psycho-physical researches, which have made his fame here in France, the Germans treat these as relatively worthless" (1887a: 331).

Wundt, by contrast, "is the first German psychologist who has pretty nearly broken all connections with metaphysics; but his compatriots have found it very difficult to forgive him for this, and his efforts remain rather isolated." There was nothing exceptional about the number of German students in Wundt's laboratory, Durkheim added, and they failed to give Wundt's lectures "the interest that they warranted" (1887a: 331) – a situation for which Durkheim offered both institutional and intellectual explanations. Institutionally, Durkheim observed, this resistance was the consequence of the organization of philosophical instruction described in "La philosophie dans les universités allemandes" (see above). "Receiving at the university only a very general education," Durkheim explained, "young philosophers would have some difficulty in then setting about these special studies. They would have to forget a good part of what they had learned, and begin again a new education" (1887a: 332). Intellectually, "everyone [in Germany] agrees with Kant," by refusing to reduce the higher forms of intelligence to experience – a refusal which removes the life of reason from any conceivable psychological scrutiny. This predisposition "makes even the most advanced Germans seem rather timid when they are compared with certain psychologists in France and in England" (1887a: 329). Germany, Durkheim insisted, "has nothing which can be compared to the great movement of psychological studies which has its center in the *Revue philosophique* and in the Société de psycho-physiologie" (1887a: 439). Durkheim even went so far as to argue that Wundt's fame "is an entirely French [and English] thing. I know some extremely cultivated Germans – academics from Leipzig," Durkheim observed, "who discovered Wundt during the course of traveling in France. It was in Paris that they learned . . . of the great position which he occupies in the scientific world" (1887a: 331).

Paradoxically inspired by this unlikely combination of German achievement and French reception, Durkheim called for a "scientific philosophy" – i.e., a method which would treat the questions of philosophy according to the procedures of the positive sciences (1887a: 333). In fact, the period during which Durkheim visited Leipzig had become Wundt's *philosophische Jahrzehnt*, comprising the completion of his *Logik* (2 vols., 1880–3), his *Ethik* (3 vols., 1886), and his *System der Philosophie* (2 vols., 1889). And not surprisingly, the particular philosophical questions to which Durkheim hoped to apply "the procedures of the positive sciences" were those of ethics. It is to Wundt's great *Ethik*, therefore, and its impact on Durkheim, that we now turn.

WUNDT'S *ETHIK* (1886)

"It has been my object in the present work," Wundt stated in the first sentence of his preface, "to investigate the problems of ethics in the light of an examination of the facts of the moral life." Without denying the earlier contributions of metaphysics, psychology, or even utilitarian ethics, therefore, Wundt declared his own commitment to establishing ethics on an empirical, anthropological foundation. "The straight road to ethics," Wundt added, "lies . . . through ethnic psychology, whose especial business it is to consider the history of custom and of ethical ideas from the psychological standpoint" (1897: vi).

The vocabulary that Wundt brought to this enterprise was German, idealist, and decidedly romantic: "We have forgotten what the romanticists believed about language and myth and history," he acknowledged, "their fanciful pictures of ancient civilization, drawn upon so slight a background of fact, have given place to the results of a more sober method. Nevertheless, it is to their efforts," he immediately added, "that we owe the impetus to a more sympathetic research into strange worlds and distant periods, such as was hardly felt at all in the century of the Enlightenment. And from this widening of the horizon came that more universal conception of mental life, which, to-day the common property of all the mental sciences, found its full expression for the first time in the philosophical idealism that came after Kant" (1897–1901: viii). Like his romantic antecedents, Wundt was convinced that the development of morality began with language, and like Durkheim, he was equally convinced that this development occurred according to concrete, objective laws, which could be discovered through inductive generalization (1897–1901: 23, 47).

But the witness of language, Wundt warned, despite its "complete objectivity," provides only the outward symbol of moral development. To understand the conditions underlying the moral development thus revealed, we must examine two other sources of evidence – i.e., *religious conceptions*, which reveal the inner motives of moral action, and the *social norms of custom and law*, which manifest its external aims. The further back we go, Wundt explained, the more religious feelings and moral sentiments coincide. Like Durkheim, however, Wundt was a secular moralist; and this argument was thus conjoined with the assertion that religious motives were not essential to the subsequent evolution of moral ideas: "[T]here is nothing in the facts," Wundt insisted, "to prove the impossibility of a complete separation of morality from its ultimate religious connections in some one of the later stages of the moral life . . . [R]eligious motives, while they are indispensable to the origin and initial development of moral ideas, are not indispensable to their continuation, or to the final culmination of their development" (1897–1901: 125–6). But if morality is thus to be "cut off from its original substrate of religious ideas," Wundt added, it must be supported by other motives; and "there is only one group of phenomena which can furnish motives at all comparable with the religious motives in moral power: the customs and usages which have their root in the social conditions of human life" (1897–1901: 126).

What is custom? Briefly, Wundt observed, a custom is a non-obligatory norm of voluntary action, developed in a national or tribal community, which depends for its obedience on neither the subjective command of morality, nor the objective compulsion of law (1897: 131). What is its origin? Even among civilized peoples of the present, Wundt answered, most customs are the survivals of primitive ceremonial acts – particularly those of sacrifice and commensality (1897–1901: 142) – whose original purpose had been forgotten, and which had subsequently been pressed into the service of new ends. Like Durkheim, therefore, Wundt insisted on the analytical distinction between cause and function, and on the religious origin, not only of morality, but of custom as well. Custom was always "at first an act of worship, and so owed its obligatory power partly to the universality of religious ceremonial, and partly to the important place that ritual holds in general estimation by reason of its supposed influence on the favour or disfavour of the gods" (1897–1901: 134). And the origin of religious worship itself –

i.e., of the act of sacrifice – lies beyond the reach of scholarly observation (1897–1901: 150–1).

What, then, is the relation of custom to morality, on the one hand, and law, on the other? Like morality, Wundt observed, custom possesses a subjective means of compulsion – i.e., the natural dislike, closely akin to the imitative impulse, of making oneself conspicuously different from one's fellows; and like law, custom also possesses an objective means of compulsion – i.e., the negative social consequences of any deviation from the normal mode of behavior in any society. This notion of an early period of "non-obligatory constraint" provided the basis for Wundt's attack on 18th-century theories of legal evolution which postulated a primal period of societal chaos later relieved by the special creation of determinate laws by powerful legislators (the "primitive Lycurgus"). In the 19th century, Wundt observed, such theories have been largely replaced by those acknowledging that "the looser bond of custom only gradually gave way to the firmer bond of law" (1897–1901: 153).

Wundt's conception of the relation of custom, law, and morality, therefore, was one of an evolutionary differentiation, wherein the latter two, initially almost indistinguishable from custom, gradually became detached, and assumed their respective roles of external and internal obligation. This evolution, Wundt suggested, was the consequence of our increasing need to distinguish between two kinds of customs – i.e., "the one containing all norms of conduct upon whose observance a high value is set – a value so high that in certain circumstances appeal is made for their maintenance to physical force – and the other covering the rules that may safely be entrusted to the gentler form of constraint afforded by the simple desire to do what others do, in order to share with them the approval of the community" (1897–1901: 152–3). And like Durkheim, Wundt saw this evolution as "progressive" in nature: "[I]t is the expression of a refinement of ideas," Wundt observed, "which paves the way for the improvement of practical morality" (1897–1901: 155–6).

In Wundt's *Ethik*, this evolutionary treatment of language, religion, custom, law, and morality was offered as an answer to the more psychologistic formulation of Ihering's *Der Zweck im Recht* (1877–83) – an answer, as we shall see, with which Durkheim agreed. In studying the development of custom, Wundt admitted, we cannot do without psychological interpretation; and such interpretations quite naturally encourage the transformation of the logical connections between ideas like "habit," "usage," and "custom" into a chronological succession: "First of all, one might think, the individual habit finds its imitators. Then some utilitarian purpose which it happens to fulfil takes possession of it. And so it gradually takes on an obligatory character, whose stringency varies directly with its extension in space and time" (1897–1901: 159). But, however psychologically plausible such a reconstruction, Wundt argued, this is a question which must always be settled by historical fact; and

there is, as a matter of fact, no single national custom of any considerable range or importance – none, i.e., that really deserves the name of custom – where there is factual proof of a development from individual habits . . . The derivation of custom from individual habit is simply a fiction, analogous to the fictions of a first property-holder, or a first law-giver, or a first language-maker, which have been set up to explain the origin of property, of the state, and of language . . . [T]he most important creations of the community - language, myth, custom, law – although influenced by the individual, can never be individually created. (1897–1901: 159–60)

Wundt's answer to Ihering's *Der Zweck im Recht*, was not, it must be emphasized, a categorical denial of the influence of "great individuals" in human history. On the contrary, like Durkheim's answer to Herbert Spencer's *Principles of Sociology*, it was an insistence that "the individual" *per se* was itself a social fact, the product of a particular, and quite advanced, stage in social evolution (Durkheim 1984: 141–6). "The first condition of personal influence," Wundt thus argued, "is a degree of social freedom that allows individual views to grow and ripen. And freedom," he added, "is wholly and absolutely an achievement of civilisation" (Wundt 1897: 162).

In order to understand the appeal that Wundt's *Ethik* held for Durkheim, we must first examine Durkheim's conception of the gradual separation of psychology and ethics from traditional philosophy, and the implications of this separation for French higher education. Ancient philosophy, Durkheim felt, had for years been undergoing a "veritable dismemberment" (1887b: 48–9). Psychology, especially in England and France, had already achieved its independence, primarily as the result of its affinity with the biological sciences generally, and physiology in particular. In Germany, with the notable exception of Wundt, this independence of psychology from philosophy had come more gradually; but the progress of ethics in Germany had been exemplary: "More and more," Durkheim observed, ethics "stops gravitating around metaphysics and vague philosophy, drawn as it is into the sphere of influence of the social sciences. It is through these social sciences that it will emancipate itself" (1887b: 49). This, of course, was the point of Durkheim's "La Science positive de la morale en Allemagne" (1887) – i.e., that the "special social sciences" in Germany could play the same role for ethics that physiology had played for psychology in France and England, thus liberating ethics from metaphysics, and allowing French scholars to examine philosophical problems in the spirit of the positive sciences.

How had the Germans, so slow to develop a genuinely scientific psychology, achieved so much more in the field of ethics? For Durkheim, again, the explanation had both an institutional and an intellectual dimension. Institutionally, "the Germans see, in ethics, a social discipline, which must above all be the object of practical instruction, which it is necessary to inculcate in the child from an early age" (1887a: 333). This early, social, practical emphasis of the German *gymnasium* explained both the German distinction (perverse from the French standpoint) between ethics and moral philosophy, and the virtual absence of both from the German universities. Relieved of both practical and philosophical responsibilities, the German professoriate was left to develop a "positive science of ethics" at least equally relieved of both utilitarian and metaphysical preoccupations. Intellectually, the French were burdened with an ethical tradition fundamentally mistaken in its premises, its method, and its conceptions of the individual, society, and morality. The *premises* of this tradition, Durkheim observed, are that "there is a law and a valid morality for all men of all times and all places," and that the prescriptions of ethics can thus have their foundation in "human nature in general" (1887a: 336). Its *method*, whether practiced by rationalist or utilitarian, is deduction: "The only difference that exists between intuitive ethics and the ethics called inductive," Durkheim argued, "is that the first takes for its principle an *a priori* truth, while the second takes for its principle a fact of experience. But for both, science consists in drawing from these premises, once posed, the consequences that they imply" (1887b: 275). And its conceptions of the individual, society, and morality maintain that the first is "an autonomous whole, who belongs entirely to himself by virtue of his absolute liberty," the second is merely "the establishment of relations between all these independent wills," and the third has "no other object but the perfecting of the individual" (1887a: 337).

To these premises, this method, and these conceptions, Durkheim
offered unmistakably German objections and alternatives. Against
the *premises*, German scholars had insisted that "this general man,
always and everywhere identical to himself, is a pure abstraction,
and has never existed in reality. The real, concrete man," Durkheim
observed, "changes with the physical and social milieu which
surrounds him, and quite naturally, morality changes with men . . .
[E]very morality carries . . . the mark of the special context where it
was born." Theoretically more accurate, this alternative premise
was also of superior practicality: "Morality no longer appears as
something abstract, inert, and dead, which is contemplated by
impersonal reason. It is a factor of the collective life" (1887a: 337).
Against the *method*, Durkheim's objection was threefold. First, it is
simply not true that "morality can be reduced to a single rule and
held within a single concept"; second, even if it were true, this truth
could be reached only inductively, not deductively; and third, even if
such a truth were reached by inductive means, no particular moral
truths could be deduced from it. For "[d]eduction can only apply
itself to very simple – i.e., very general – things," Durkheim
observed, and "moral phenomena are the most complex in the
world. The use of deduction there is thus absolutely misconceived"
(1887b: 276–7). The significant methodological contribution of the
"German School," therefore, was precisely its "protestation against
the use of deduction in the moral sciences, and [its] effort to
eventually acclimate there a truly inductive method" (1887b: 278).
And against the traditional, mechanical *conceptions of the individual,
society, and morality*, Durkheim observed, the German school offered a
more "organic" notion:

It has pointed out that this claimed autonomy [of the individual] is only
apparent; that there is no abyss between each of us and other men; that
heredity reduces us to being only the continuation of our ancestors; that
the existence of common feelings erases at every moment the alleged line of
demarcations which separates our consciousnesses and confounds them.
The individual is an integrated part of the society where he is born. That
society penetrates him in every part. To isolate himself and abstract himself
from it is to diminish himself. Such a pronounced feeling for the collective
life for its reality and its advantages, seems destined to be, up to the
present, the essential characteristic of German ethics (1887a: 337–8)

It is important to understand that these were not simply
Durkheim's intellectual preferences; rather, they were a part of his

continuing support for Jules Ferry's program of educational reform, and the vocabulary Durkheim used to praise German social science was similar to that he would later use in *L'Evolution pédagogique* and *L'Education morale*. Moral education, Durkheim insisted, "can be organized in the *lycée* only if it is already constituted at the university. A science can comfortably be the object of elementary instruction," he added, "only if it is already quite advanced" (1887a: 440). The education of most French political leaders, Durkheim complained, consists of the interpretation of legal texts, of speculation about the intentions of some legislator of the *ancien régime*; but these leaders "have no idea of the nature of law, customs, morals, religions, what is the role and the relation of the diverse functions of the social organism, and so on." This is the "national illness of our country. How can we hope to get rid of it," he asked rhetorically, "if we don't try to reach it at its very roots?" "It is urgent," he concluded, "that we import these [German] studies into France, for we indeed have even more need of them than the Germans, since we have undertaken to lead and to govern ourselves" (1887a: 440).

For Durkheim, Wundt's *Ethik* (1886) was a "synthesis of all these isolated views, of all these special studies with which we have just been concerned" (1887b: 136). Moreover, by drawing these "isolated efforts" together, the *Ethik* had simultaneously become their "philosophical expression," and had "given substance to these attempts, which until then had remained rather indecisive and unconscious of themselves and of the goal toward which they tended" (1887b: 33). In particular, Durkheim admired Wundt's methodological insistence on induction rather than deduction, on experience rather than reason: "There is no philosophical science," Durkheim cited Wundt, "where pure speculation is less fruitful than in ethics. For the complexity of the facts there is such that every system constructed by reason alone seems quite worn and impoverished when it is compared with reality . . . In ethics, as elsewhere," Wundt had thus concluded, "we must begin by observing" (1887b: 113–14).

In two closely related areas, Durkheim felt that Wundt had gone beyond his German colleagues. As we have already observed, Wundt's predecessors – particularly the *Kathedersozialisten* – granted a large role to calculation and will in the evolution of moral ideas. The implication of this concession, Durkheim suggested, is that morality and society are, at least in part, "reflective creations" of the human reason. But if reflection had constructed the social world, he added, reflection could "reconstruct" it – i.e., understand it – and thus we would be returned to a rational, deductive method. "To observe, to experiment," Durkheim thus insisted, "is to resign ourselves to remodeling our ideas on things. But such a method is necessary only if things do not always follow the laws of the understanding" (1887b: 136–7). Despite their "veritable horror for logical abstractions and deep feeling for the complexity of facts," therefore, the net effect of the German insistence on calculation and will in the evolution of moral ideas was an unwitting return to reason and dialectic.

For Wundt, Durkheim observed, the question of the nature of morality was rather one, "not of knowing what ought to be according to rigorous logic, but of what is." Here Durkheim referred directly to Ihering's explanation of customs as individual habits which, once found useful, had gradually been generalized throughout society. However rational such an explanation might appear, Durkheim said, endorsing Wundt's response, it is observation, not reason, which must decide; and observation tells us that "a social custom is never derived from a private habit." However strange it might appear, Durkheim thus observed, "customs have always been produced by other customs or, at the origin, by religious practices" (1887b: 137). This was an important idea – critical to Durkheim's later sociological thought – and it is worth noting that Durkheim had at least one more reason for believing it than had Wundt. For Wundt, the insistence on this essentially "irrationalist" posture derived from his belief in what Max Weber has called the "unintended consequences of social action" – i.e., the belief that "the motives of our actions are not in rapport with the ends that they produce" (1887b: 137). Durkheim concurred, but added a second, largely psychological argument in support – i.e., the belief that we ignore not only the ultimate consequences of our actions, but their true motives as well: "Not only does our action escape from the circle of consciousness by a kind of unforeseen ricochet," Durkheim observed, "but it was never conscious even at the origin. We act without knowing why, or the reasons that we give ourselves are not the true reasons" (1887b: 137). Durkheim, in short, had by now embraced the psychology of the unconscious.

A second, closely related issue on which Durkheim preferred Wundt to his predecessors was the question of whether the study of morality could be "scientific." Recognizing that moral phenomena vary with time and place, Durkheim observed, both the *Kathedersozia-listen* and the members of the historical school of jurisprudence had a tendency to see morality more as an art than a science: "According to them," Durkheim summarized, "it belongs to each century to see what is most appropriate to it, and to make that its morality. Above all, it is an affair of practical skill on the part of societies, of their statesmen" (1887b: 137). Wundt, in sharp contrast, argued that "if moral ideas evolve, their evolution occurs according to laws that science can determine, and makes the determination of these laws the first problem of ethics" (1887b: 137–8). It was this "positive science of ethics," of course, to which *De la division du travail social* would be Durkheim's first major contribution.

But if Wundt's *Ethik* had taken German social science two steps forward, Durkheim observed, it had also taken it one step backward. The essential function of morality, Durkheim had already agreed with Wundt's German predecessors, "was to adapt individuals to one another, and thus to assure the equilibrium and the survival of the group." In fact, Wundt also agreed that morality was "a necessary condition to the existence of societies." The true object of morality, he insisted, "was to make a man feel that he is not a whole, but the part of a whole, and how he is a small thing in view of the unlimited milieux which surround him. As society is found to be one of these milieux, and one of the most immediate," Wundt had argued, "morality has, as its consequence, to make society possible" (1887b: 138).

But for Wundt, Durkheim complained, morality performs this essential function *en passant*, "accidently and as a consequence," almost "without wishing it." Morality, Wundt argued, results from the efforts man makes to find an enduring object, one to which he can attach himself, and from which he can taste "a kind of happiness which is not passing." The first objects he encounters in this search are his family, his city, and his country. But these things have their value, Wundt insisted, not because of what they are in themselves, but because of the ideal which they imperfectly symbolize. In short, morality maintains societies (as well as the instincts and inclinations which are its condition) because societies constitute the means whereby the moral sentiment is realized; but societies are never more than transitory phases through which morality passes, "one of the forms that it successively goes through" (1887b: 138). This was probably the source of Durkheim's observation that Wundt's "imposing mass of facts" was nonetheless "animated by the breath of idealism," and particularly the idealism of Fichte: "[I]t is . . . of Fichte whom we think, since Wundt told us of this undefined and indefinable moral ideal of which exceptional minds alone succeed in achieving consciousness" (1887b: 136).

If we accept Wundt's position, Durkheim warned, one of the essential properties of morality – i.e., its obligatory force – becomes utterly inexplicable. Wundt acknowledged this property "in principle," Durkheim admitted, but he failed to identify its source, the authority in whose name its commands were uttered. For the religious believer, of course, that name was "God"; but for the agnostic Durkheim, who sought a secular substitute for God, such an explanation was clearly insufficient. For the rationalist, moral commands might be issued in the name of reason, and in recognition of the happiness which follows moral behavior; but reason, Durkheim argued, leads only the mind, not the will, and what is desirable for our own happiness is not thereby obligatory upon us.

Durkheim did not deny Wundt's fundamental, idealist premise: "It is a sure fact," he agreed, that "we need to believe that our actions do not exhaust in an instant all their consequences, that they do not hold completely within the point of time and space where they were produced, but rather that they extend their effects more or less far, in duration as in expanse. Otherwise they would be very small things" (1887b: 139). But Durkheim did deny that this was the essential factor in moral evolution, arguing, on the contrary, that society was not merely "the means whereby the moral sentiment is realized," but its very source; that society secures less ephemeral pleasures for us precisely because it is not "transitory," but rather infinitely outlasts the lifetime of any individual; that morality, in short, was a function of society rather than the reverse (1887b: 140).

DURKHEIM'S "POSITIVE SCIENCE OF ETHICS"

In 1882, the Faculty of Letters at the university of Bordeaux established a course in pedagogy, the first of its kind in France, designed to instruct schoolteachers on the practical questions of primary and secondary education. As part of its national drive for a new system of republican, secular instruction, the State began to support the course in 1884, and Espinas, who occupied a chair of philosophy at Bordeaux, assumed the responsibility for teaching it.

By 1887, he would be called to the higher administrative rank of Dean of the Faculty of Letters, and a replacement for the course on pedagogy would be needed. Fortunately, Louis Liard, also a former Bordeaux professor, just called to the still higher rank of Minister of Public Education, had someone in mind – an instructor at the Lycée de Troyes who had recently visited Berlin, Marburg, and Leipzig, returning to publish two provocative essays on German education and social science.

Durkheim was thus appointed *chargé de cours* of social science and pedagogy in the Faculty of Letters at the university of Bordeaux. Durkheim's first lecture-course on social science (1887–8), given each Saturday morning, was titled "La Solidarité sociale," and its opening lecture described "the succession of transformations through which sociology has passed since the beginning of this century" (1978a: 44). After noting the achievements and limitations of the classical political economists, Comte, Spencer, and Espinas, Durkheim went on to praise the works of Schaeffle, Wagner, Schmoller, Ihering, and Post. "We have seen [sociology's] birth with the [classical political] economists," Durkheim summarized, "its founding with Comte, its consolidation with Spencer, its orientation with Schaeffle, and its specialization with the German jurists and economists" (1978a: 61–2).

On the Saturdays that followed, Durkheim's lectures set out the argument which would become *De la division du travail social* (1893).[3] The "initial problem of sociology," he emphasized, is social solidarity; indeed, before the lecture-course could venture further, "we [have] to know what bonds unite men to one another or, in other words, what determines the formation of social aggregates" (1978d: 205). Focusing in particular on functional questions, therefore, Durkheim argued that the role of creating and maintaining social solidarity, once performed by "common ideas and sentiments," was now performed by an increasingly specialized division of labor, a fundamental, evolutionary change in the nature of morality itself. Modern economic relationships, Durkheim agreed with the German political economists, thus had unmistakable moral consequences, and these were best studied through the detailed, inductive observation of legal sanctions.

---

[3] Although no transcript of this lecture-course exists, Durkheim summarized its content at the outset of the lecture-course that followed, on the sociology of the family (1978d: 205–7).

At the outset of his second lecture-course, "La Famille: origines, types principaux" (1888–9), Durkheim could thus tell his audience that "another opening lecture" was unnecessary, for "sociology is no longer a foreign discipline to which you must be introduced" (1978d: 205). Instead, this second, "more specialized" course would deal with "one specific type" of sociability: ". . . the simplest group of all, the one whose history is most ancient" – i.e., the family (1978d: 207). But the method which Durkheim would employ in this second course was no less German in inspiration than the first. How do we discover the causes which account for the forms and relations of the modern European family? In the natural sciences, Durkheim observed, causes are discovered through experimentation; but experiments "in the strict sense" (i.e., the artificial reproduction of the events of nature), he admitted, are not possible in the social sciences. As he had in the Sens lectures, however, Durkheim appealed to Bernard's *Introduction à l'étude de la médicine expérimentale* (1865), insisting that the "essence" of experimentation is not the production of artificial phenomena, but rather the comparison of phenomena under variable conditions, enabling the scientist to distinguish "accidental" conditions from their "essential" counterparts, and to identify the latter as the causes (or effects) of the phenomena in question.

Still, Durkheim acknowledged that experimentation in the social sciences is different from that in their natural scientific counterparts. In the latter, experimentation is "direct" (i.e., the scientist artificially produces the variable conditions in the laboratory) while in the social sciences, it remains "indirect" (i.e., the variable conditions must be discovered in "nature" itself). And even indirect experimentation, Durkheim admitted, presupposes a fund of empirical knowledge (e.g., of the various types of the family, of their constituent elements, of the types of their interrelationships, of their origin, etc.) which simply did not exist. "Although great efforts to advance this problem have been made since the middle of the century," Durkheim observed, "the results obtained, while very important in other respects, are still incomplete and in some cases in dispute. We can, therefore, neither limit ourselves to those which are definitely established, nor accept without prior examination those which are still under discussion" (1978d: 210).

Under these circumstances, Durkheim observed, the only method is to proceed historically and inductively, concentrating on customs, mores, and laws – "the residue of the collective experiences of a whole series of generations" – and gathering as large a body of facts as possible (1978d: 214). Where are such facts to be found? Durkheim admitted that few of the works in which these documents are found are written in French, although he mentioned Fustel in a passing reference to studies of the Roman family, and specifically cited Giraud Teulon's *Les Origines du mariage et de la famille* (1884) and Charles Letourneau's recent *L'Evolution du mariage et de la famille* (1888). Of studies in English, Durkheim referred to Henry Sumner Maine's *Ancient Law* (1862), W. E. Hearn's *The Aryan Family* (1879), and the third part of Herbert Spencer's *Principles of Sociology* (1876) – "devoted in its entirety to this subject, but from which there is little to retain" – and the increasingly significant work of the British and American ethnographers. But by far the most significant body of works, were by German authors.

De la division du travail social was itself the product of Durkheim's lengthy immersion in these German sources. The work begins with a critique of classical political economy – i.e., of Adam Smith's exclusively economic conception of the consequences of an increasingly specialized division of labor – and proceeds to argue that the division of labor is also a law of nature and a moral rule, the "categorical imperative" of the modern European conscience (1984: 1–3). Even more than Maine's *Ancient Law* (1862), it insists that law, far from being "an artificial creation of the legislator," rather "expresses customs, and if it acts against them, it [acts] with a force that it has borrowed from them" (1984: 98–9). To understand the evolution of law, therefore, we must reconstruct the customs of antiquity by historical, inductive means, in the manner of Theodor Waitz's *Anthropologie der Naturvölker*. And in support of his deeply held and repeatedly expressed conviction that the human capacity for happiness is extremely limited, and that the desire for happiness must thus be causally insignificant, Durkheim cited the law of Weber and Fechner, and the modifications it had undergone in Wundt's laboratory, which showed that pleasure is always the mean between two extremes (1984: 180–2).

Perhaps the clearest evidence of the German provenance of the arguments of *De la division du travail social*, however, is the suppressed and frequently ignored preface to the first, 1893 edition.[4] How,

---

[4] In the preface to the second, 1902 edition, Durkheim said: "We feel justified in suppressing about thirty pages of the old introduction, which appear useless to us today" (1984: xxxi).

Durkheim asked, do we know that a particular rule is "moral"? The traditional answer, he observed, is to confront the rule with some preestablished, *a priori* formula, and to give the rule a moral value to the extent that rule and formula coincide. But to grant this answer any authority, Durkheim argued, the formula itself must be "an incontestable scientific truth"; and not only are there as many formulae as there are moralists, their diversity belying any "so-called objective value," but the formulae themselves are palpably inadequate.

Here Durkheim rehearsed his attack on both rationalist and empiricist ethics, arguing again that, albeit in different ways, both make the same mistake. "The procedure of one, as well as the other," he insisted, "is the following: they start from the concept of man, deducing the ideal from what seems to them suitable to a being who is thus defined; and having set up this ideal, they derive from it the supreme rule of conduct, the moral law" (1933: 421). Why does this method fail? First, Durkheim observed, it fails because the concept of "man" upon which it depends has no empirical basis (1933: 421–2). Second, even if this concept were "perfectly exact," the deductive inferences derived from it would remain merely conjectural; for deduction, Durkheim repeated, "does not constitute sufficient proof" (1933: 422). But most important, Durkheim argued, these "logical operations" utterly misconceive the function of ethics itself – i.e., they assume that the *raison d'être* of all ethical rules is to ensure the development and perfectibility of the individual man, when it is at least equally plausible that such rules serve social ends, to which the individual remains subservient. In the Sens lectures, of course, Durkheim had also assumed that the role of ethics is to ensure the perfectibility of the individual person; but by 1893, that goal had been replaced by the ends of society.

What are these ends? That question, Durkheim repeated, can be answered only "through the observation of moral facts; which is to say, that multitude of particular rules effectively governing conduct. It would have to be begun by establishing a science, which, after having classed the moral phenomena, would look for the conditions upon which each of these types depends, and would determine its role. This means a positive science of ethics."[5] In one sense, this is what Wundt had attempted in the first volume ("The Facts of the

---

[5] Here Durkheim referred readers to his 1887 essay by that title (1933: 422).

Moral Life") of his *Ethik* (1886). But Durkheim, as we have already seen, viewed Wundt as a Fichtean idealist, and found confirmation of this view in the second volume ("Ethical Systems"), a survey of the different systems of ethics as they have succeeded one another from antiquity to the present day.[6] Such a survey has value, Durkheim argued, only on the assumption that moral rules are "eternal verities receiving their value from themselves or from a transcendental source," that these truths are gradually revealed to man throughout history, and that their social and historical context has but the "secondary influence" of bringing such truths periodically to light, facilitating but not determining their progress (1933: 422–3).

By 1893, Durkheim was far too much of an historical and ethical relativist to entertain such an argument. History, he argued, "has shown that what was moral for one people was immoral for another, not only in fact, but in law." Indeed, had the tribe or the city-state respected individual freedom as we do, Durkheim observed, those societies could not have survived; for if such societies were to maintain themselves, "it was absolutely necessary for the individual to be less covetous of his independence." Wundt's idealism, in short, would lead us to judge as "moral" some activities which would literally subvert the societies in which they were practiced. "[M]oral rules," Durkheim concluded, "are moral only in relation to certain experimental conditions; and, consequently, the nature of moral phenomena cannot be understood if the conditions on which they are dependent are not determined" (1933: 423–4).

In sum, the failure of the French system of scientific education had roots that reached back to the Revolution and the First Empire. Well before the humiliation of the Franco-Prussian War, therefore, the recognition of this failure had led to the system of awarding scholarships to the brightest French *agrégés*, and thus to Durkheim's visit to Germany in 1885–6. Encouraged to pay special attention to the state of the social sciences in Germany, and already intimately familiar with the works of Espinas and Schaeffle, Durkheim was especially attracted to developments in political economy, jurisprudence, ethnography and (to a lesser extent) sociology that – taken

---

[6] Despite his otherwise detailed treatment of the *Ethik* in "La Science positive de la morale en Allemagne," Durkheim deliberately avoided any discussion of this second volume (1887b: 114).

together – suggested ways of thinking and speaking of social phenomena as "will-independent," and as the consequence of impersonal social and historical causes. This "positive science of ethics" was epitomized in the work of Wilhelm Wundt, whose Leipzig laboratory Durkheim visited and praised for its study of psychological phenomena in all their concrete complexity, and whose *Ethik* – indebted to the German Romantics – liberated ethics from metaphysics, and connected it empirically to custom and law.

Returning from Germany, Durkheim began to work out the arguments that became *De la division du travail social* (1893), whose dependence on these German sources is palpable on every page. But Wundt's Fichtean idealism had left Durkheim with no explanation for the distinctive, obligatory force behind moral commands. In the preface to the 1893 edition, for example, "moral facts" are defined as rules of conduct bearing necessary, predetermined, societal sanctions; but this, Durkheim admitted, is merely a "more precise and scientific" articulation of their obligatory force – a better definition perhaps, but not yet an explanation (1933: 424–5). By the second, 1902 edition, however, Durkheim was able to present a relatively complete theory of the "religio-moral" authority of the ancient and medieval occupational groups, emphasizing the origin of their authority in the celebrations, banquets, and sacrifices of ancient religious cults (1984: esp. xxxix–xliv). Several significant events had intervened, including Durkheim's lecture-course on religion in 1894–5, during which he apparently became acquainted with the works of "Robertson Smith and his school," and still later, his disagreements with James Frazer over the interpretation of Australian totemism. Among the most important of these events, however, was Durkheim's confrontation with his most formidable opponent, Gabriel Tarde, which – together with the Dreyfus Affair – led him to re-read and re-assess the resources available to him in Rousseau's *Le Contrat social* and *Emile*.

CHAPTER 5

The yoke of necessity

At this point, my argument – that Durkheim was cobbling together a social realist vocabulary to replace the problematic legacy of Cartesian rationalism – seems to face an obstacle. For while *De la division du travail social* follows logically from his German visit, Durkheim also wrote a Latin thesis, *Quid Secundatus Politicae Scientiae Instituendae Contulerit* (1892), on Montesquieu's *De l'esprit des lois* (1748). Why, one might ask, would Durkheim make Montesquieu – the "greatest exponent of the Cartesian interpretation of history" (Thompson 1942: 61–2; Peyre 1960: xiii) – the focus of this thesis? If Durkheim's goal was to replace the language of Cartesian rationalism, including its emphasis on clear and distinct ideas deduced from first principles, with this quite different vocabulary emphasizing induction carried out through the careful observation and collection of concrete *things*, why would he have been so preoccupied with the place of Montesquieu in the development of modern social science? If Durkheim's attachment for the Enlightenment was as ambivalent as *L'Evolution pédagogique* and *L'Education morale* suggest, and his early sources as German and romantic as his 1887 essays indicate, why would the Latin thesis begin with the assertion that it was Montesquieu who had "laid down the principles of the new discipline"?[1]

---

[1] Durkheim 1997: 7e. Until recently, most Durkheim scholars have had to depend on the English translation by Ralph Manheim in *Montesquieu and Rousseau: Forerunners of Sociology* (1960). But this itself is a translation, not from the original Latin, but from the French translation published by Armand Cuvillier in 1953. The Cuvillier translation itself replaces Durkheim's Latin translations of passages from Montesquieu with the original passages themselves, suppressing differences between them, adding several misprints and mistakes in the main text, and reprinting Durkheim's notes — which are full of mistakes — without correction. Manheim's English edition of Cuvillier reproduces the errors of the latter, adding some of its own, and dropping most of Durkheim's notes. For these reasons and others, I have used the most recent, 1997 translation of the original Latin text by W. W. Miller and Emma Griffiths.

AMBIVALENT CARTESIANS

To answer these questions, one must first appreciate the extremely ambiguous position Montesquieu occupied within the context of the French Enlightenment, as well as the ambivalent nature of his own commitment to Cartesian rationalism. For it was precisely this ambiguity and ambivalence that made Montesquieu the perfect subject for the Latin thesis, and the latter an ideal vehicle for Durkheim's own attempt to come to terms with his problematic Cartesian legacy.

To understand Montesquieu's thought, Isaiah Berlin once argued, we must first have some grasp of the way French rationalists viewed the world at the time Montesquieu wrote *De l'esprit des lois* (1748). As a consequence of the scientific, philosophical, and mathematical innovations that took place between the publication of Copernicus' *De Revolutionibus Orbium Coelestium* (1543) and Newton's *Philosophiae Naturalis Principia Mathematica* (1687), the world of *nature* was conceived as one governed by clear-cut laws and principles, in terms of which the movement of each particle in space appeared explicable through logical, deductive inference, while the world of *culture* and *society*

seemed uncharted and unchartable. The human science presented itself as a field for the play of blind chance and irrational forces, good and bad fortune, the whims of despots, adventurers, and popular passions, which left the way open to metaphysical and theological explanations unsupported by anything worthy of the name of evidence, conducted by methods the opposite of rational, the happy hunting-ground of bigots and charlatans and their dupes and slaves. (1980b: 133)

This view of two distinct realms – one governed by regular laws and the other left to chaos and caprice – was widely shared by rationalists and anticlericals of the 17th century. Descartes himself simply dismissed history and the "human sciences" generally as being of no interest to genuine seekers after truth, for they were incapable of yielding either precise definitions or the clear rules of evidence from which irrefutable conclusions could be drawn by logical deduction. "[P]roud and magnificent palaces built only on sand and mud," Descartes characterized moral philosophy, and "in so far as they borrow their principles from philosophy," he added of other sciences, "I decided that nothing solid could have been built upon such shaky foundations" (1985: 113–15).

It is in this context that we should understand Montesquieu's claim and conviction that he had made a "stupendous discovery" – i.e., that "for the first time in human history, he had uncovered the fundamental laws which govern the behaviour of human societies, much as natural scientists in the previous century had discovered the laws of the behaviour of inanimate matter" (Berlin 1980b: 134). "Those who assert that a blind fatality produced the various effects we behold in this world talk very absurdly," Montesquieu asserted, "for can any thing be more unreasonable than to pretend that a blind fatality could be productive of intelligent beings?" (1949: 1). Social things, like natural things, were seen to be subject neither to chance nor to fate. Human behavior was intelligible, and once its laws were understood, a science of man was possible. This, in turn, would create the foundation for the rational science of government, one that would fit means to ends in accordance with principles derived from experience and observation.

Much of this, of course, was consistent with Enlightenment optimism and its underlying faith in science and education, political reform and social progress. But throughout Montesquieu's work, there was also a more skeptical mood. Some of his opinions on specific social and political questions irritated the Encyclopedists, who became concerned about his reservations regarding the perfectibility of man and society, and thus suspicious of his commitment to their ideals. Montesquieu's 18th- and 19th-century critics ascribed this reticence to his timidity, and also to his "natural conservatism"; but a more likely explanation is his deeply felt attraction for the writings of Montaigne, a fellow-Gascon and aristocrat whose intellectual traits – e.g., an urbane skepticism, a facility for unmasking illusions, subjective empiricism, a repugnance for religious fanaticism, and a feeling for the diversity of customs and the richness of natural forms – he also shared (Hulliung 1976: 113–14). Neumann thus argues that Montesquieu always read Descartes "through the skepticism of Montaigne," and that this has been "inadequately stressed" by other scholars and commentators (1949a: xviii–xix, xxxiii).

Berlin argues that this skepticism penetrates to the very core of Montesquieu's thought and explains its internal contradictions, while simultaneously raising the stature of *De l'esprit des lois* far above the more optimistic works and radical proposals of his Enlightenment contemporaries. "By temperament," he observes, "Montesquieu is an empiricist who seeks to explain everything by naturalistic means wherever and whenever he can" (1980b: 137). This is not to say that he entirely avoided metaphysical concepts; on the contrary, *De l'esprit des lois* – as its famous opening lines testify – reeks of the language of natural law. But what Montesquieu principally stressed, Berlin insists, was the fruit of observation:

He observed curiously, minutely and insatiably, all his life. His accounts of his travels, his historical sketches, his scattered notes on a wide variety of topics, are detailed, vivid and penetrating. He was fascinated by what he saw and what he learnt, for its own sake, whether or not it offered evidence for a hypothesis or pointed a moral that he wished to emphasise. (1980b: 137)

This in turn explains certain features of Montesquieu's works. His descriptions of characters and events are neither the caricatures nor the consciously idealized exaggerations typical of 18th-century literature. Usbek and Rica of the *Lettres persanes* (1721), for example, are characterized not as superior or inferior to Parisians, but rather as utterly dissimilar, representing the sheer, irreducible *variety* of practice, habit, and custom, so that what is obvious and "normal" in one culture appears ludicrous and perverse in the other. Similarly, despite its posture as a systematic, logically constructed political treatise, *De l'esprit des lois* abounds in sudden digressions and episodic asides, ostensibly called forth as evidence in support of more general laws and hypotheses, but which rather reflect Montesquieu's fascination for the particular, the detailed, and the concrete. The resulting chaos has been acknowledged by many scholars – "initial bewilderment," Franz Neumann once observed, "is the inevitable fate of every reader of *The Spirit of the Laws*" (1949a: xxxi). Recognizing that it "would be ungenerous to disparage the devoted labours of so many scholars and commentators," Berlin asks if this is not "all so much misdirected ingenuity," for

Montesquieu is not a systematic philosopher, not a deductive thinker, not a historian, not a scientist, and one of his great merits lies in the fact that although he claims to be founding a new science in the spirit of Descartes, his practice is better than his professions, and he is, in fact, doing nothing of the kind, because he realises that the material will not allow it.

In short, if Montesquieu's "stupendous discovery" included the notion that social facts could be studied scientifically, it equally included his recognition that the attempt to impose upon these facts some preestablished, metaphysical conception was "an excessively artificial proceeding, repugnant to the nature of this particular topic," one which would "turn out, as later sociology has all too often proved to be, exceedingly sterile in results" (1980b: 138).

But if the concrete particularities of human experience were thus resistant, by their very nature, to the abstract, metaphysical concepts of French rationalism, what was Montesquieu's method? "For all that Montesquieu *speaks* of Cartesian methods," Berlin assures us, "he does *not*, fortunately for himself and posterity, *apply* them." Instead, he advances "tentative principles and hypotheses," defends them by "adducing the never wholly conclusive evidence of observation," and uses them "in the manner which the subject-matter seems to call for." Montesquieu's famous attack on Hobbes' state of nature and the social contract, his conception of societies as analogous to biological organisms, his notion of different social and psychological "types" – all were "bold and fruitful notions," Berlin admits, but ones that "rested on *aperçus* and unsystematic observations dominated by moral purpose, not on careful and exhaustive, morally neutral researches like those made by his contemporaries Buffon and Linnaeus" (1980b: 138, 40).

The heart and soul of these *aperçus* and observations (as Durkheim recognized so well) was Montesquieu's classification of societal "types" – i.e., despotism, monarchy, and republic (the latter subdivided into democracies and aristocracies) (1949: 8–18). The classification was an attempt to improve upon Aristotle's, and it owes an equal debt to the ancient, metaphysical doctrine of natural kinds. Each of these societal types thus possesses its own distinctive "principle" or "inner force" (i.e., the principle of despotism is *fear*, that of monarchy, *honor*, of democracy, *virtue*, and of aristocracy, *moderation*) which enables it to function as it does (1949: 19–28). Each principle quite naturally reflects the physical circumstances and material conditions (e.g., climate, topography, population size and density, etc.) of the society in question; but Berlin emphasizes the extent to which Montesquieu's model here is biological rather than chemical, depends upon final rather than mechanical causes, and was thus precisely the one which had been *abandoned* by the "new science" of Galileo and Newton (1980b: 140–1). This is important because Durkheim recognized it instantly, and it became the basis of his most important objection to *De l'esprit des lois*, one reflected in both the Latin thesis and *De la division du travail social*. The laws appropriate to a particular society, Montesquieu insisted, should always relate to the principle of its distinctive type: "The relation of laws to this principle," Montesquieu explained, "strengthens the several springs of government; and this principle derives thence, in its turn, a new degree of vigor" (1949: 40). Inversely, when laws ignore or contradict a society's "inner principle," the society becomes liable to decay and disaster (1949: 109–25).

The simile of intelligent legislation, as with Aristotle and also with Durkheim, was thus *medical*: "The business of legislators and administrators, judges, and of everyone concerned with social issues in any form, is to preserve, maintain, improve the health of society" (Berlin 1980b: 141). But Montesquieu was unusual among his Enlightenment contemporaries, Berlin emphasizes, in his insistence that what constitutes this societal "health" will vary from one society to another, according to its particular environment and the distinctive inner "principle" which guides its response to these conditions. While the Encyclopedists and *philosophes* struggled to find some objective criterion or abstract, universal standard in the light of which a "good" society or institution might be known, Montesquieu – like a good physician – was content to observe carefully, to recognize things for what they are, and to make recommendations accordingly (Berlin 1980b: 142–3).

This taste for what was real and concrete rather than ideal and abstract left Montesquieu open to charges of moral relativism and indifference to ultimate values, from both radicals and reactionaries. "There are many local laws in various religions," an example of Montesquieu's offense against the latter began, "and when Montezuma with so much obstinacy insisted that the religion of the Spaniards was good for their country, and his for Mexico, he did not assert an absurdity; because, in fact, legislators could never help having a regard to what nature had established before them" (1949: 42). *De l'esprit des lois* offended the Encyclopedists and *philosophes* as well, not simply through its skeptical, Montaignian mood, but also because of its opposition to any universal criterion of rationality, which – like Durkheim's argument in *Les Formes élémentaires* (1912) – subverted any effort to show that all religions were tissues of falsehood (1915: 13–15). Voltaire and Helvétius were no less frustrated by Montesquieu's sense – deeply felt by Durkheim – of the sheer complexity of concrete social phenomena, which led him to resist simple, radical solutions for fear of their unpredictable consequences (Berlin 1980b: 146–7).

Finally, while no figure in the 18th century did more than

Montesquieu to draw attention to the influence of material factors on society and culture, he never embraced an aggressively determinist position. In a manner more reminiscent of Max Weber, Montesquieu suggested that the laws that govern human behavior are somehow less binding than those that govern physical matter, that some material causes simply render certain social consequences "more probable" (not inevitable), and that these causes can, to a significant degree, be counteracted by deliberate human action. And the goal of such action was not some utopian state, but rather the preservation of an unstable equilibrium in which each law or force was checked by another, producing an "elaborate mosaic" of countervailing powers. This, of course, became Montesquieu's most famous and influential idea – i.e., the notion of a constitutional "separation of powers" – inspired by his travels in England (1729–31) despite the fact that such a separation existed there no more than it did in France.[2]

This brings us to the subject of liberty, which the separation of powers was designed to protect. "It is true that in democracies the people seem to act as they please," Montesquieu acknowledged in book XI, "but political liberty does not consist in an unlimited freedom. In governments, that is, in societies directed by laws, liberty can consist only in the power of doing what we ought to will, and in not being constrained to do what we ought not to will." Liberty, in short, is "a right of doing whatever the laws permit" (1949: 150). But if liberty is thus the freedom to act unless such an act is prohibited by law, Neumann is quite right to suggest that "the character of the restraining laws must necessarily move into the center of his theory" (1949a: l). What underlies these laws and renders them legitimate, especially in so far as they are taken as setting the parameters of human liberty? What are we to make of the possibility of an unjust law which, by this conception, we have no right to violate?

Montesquieu's answers to these and other questions about liberty and justice indicate how deeply he was still indebted to the ancient and medieval tradition of natural law. "Before laws were made," Montesquieu insisted in book I, "there were relations of possible justice. To say there is nothing just or unjust but what is commanded

---

[2] Here, Neumann suggests, Montesquieu's rationalism got the better of his empiricism (1949a: li--ix).

or forbidden by positive law, is the same as saying that before the describing of a circle all the radii were not equal" (1949: 2). In a completely rational society, therefore, unjust laws would not exist, for all laws would conform to natural law. But "the intelligent world," Montesquieu added, "is far from being so well governed as the physical." No human society is capable of fully realizing this natural standard of absolute justice. Montesquieu's discussions of the various types of government are thus attempts to find approximations of natural law, with particular attention to those conditions – climatic, topographic, demographic, social, and psychological – which render these approximations incomplete and unsatisfactory. For Montesquieu, civil society itself thus became an agent of history, and the proper focus of sociological study (Neumann 1949a: xxxix–xl).

The tension – if not downright contradiction – between these two themes in *De l'esprit des lois* has been a focus of Montesquieu's critics at least since Hume's *Enquiry Concerning the Principles of Morals* (1751) (1975: 196–7, 197 n. 1). On the one hand, Montesquieu invoked the rationalist doctrine that positive law must always be measured against the standard of some transcendent set of metaphysical principles. On the other, with stunning originality, he introduced the more empiricist doctrine that laws are the evolving expression of the largely unconscious moral habits, beliefs, and attitudes of particular societies at particular times and places, which themselves reflect the specific material conditions in which they emerged. The first represented the Roman and Napoleonic tradition of codified law, committed to the application of general principles whose validity was regarded as timeless and universal. The second – as we've seen in chapter 4 (pp. 185–209) – reflected a more conservative, pragmatic tradition, epitomized in German jurisprudence, in which law was the organic expression of the deepest traditions of a nation, culture, or community, not to be deflected by arbitrary and artificial reforms (Berlin 1980b: 156).

The same ambivalence can be seen in Montesquieu's use of important words like *reason* and *nature*. In his more rationalist moods, for example, Montesquieu uses "reason" in the manner of Descartes, i.e., to refer to the intuitive perception of general laws; but in other, more empiricist moods, it seems to refer to a more pragmatic grasp of what a particular society needs in order to adapt to specific conditions and circumstances. Similarly, in the Cartesian context, "nature" takes revenge on those who legislate in ignorance of or indifference to natural law; but in other contexts, nature is simply the way things are, the material causes of particular institutions adapted to them, and thus the proper subject of sociological investigation. In all of Montesquieu's writings, Berlin thus emphasizes, there is "a kind of continuous dialectic . . . between absolute values which seem to correspond to the permanent interests of men as such, and those which depend upon time and place in a concrete situation" (1980b: 157).

Montesquieu's ambivalence here was no less obvious to Durkheim than it had been to Hume. On the contrary, it made *De l'esprit des lois* the perfect forge in which Durkheim would shape the tools he would use in *De la division du travail social* and later works. For, as we've seen above (pp. 77–8), Durkheim, like Montesquieu, was troubled by the legacy of Cartesian metaphysics and, again like Montesquieu, sought to temper its emphasis on "clear and distinct ideas" with a language more responsive to the concrete complexity of *things*. The Latin thesis is thus an extended exploration of the relative merits of rationalism and empiricism, of realism and nominalism, and (indirectly) of the relative contributions of their French and German progenitors. Alluding to "the leading modern writers" from Britain and Germany, for example, Durkheim denied that social science is "foreign to our ways and to the French temperament," adding that among the writers of the French Enlightenment, Montesquieu "stands far above them all," for no one before him "had seen so clearly the conditions necessary for establishing this science."[3] The first of these conditions – already evident in the Sens lectures – is a specific subject matter different from the other sciences: "No discipline merits the name of science," Durkheim observed, "that does not have a definite, limited subject matter to investigate." Second, this field must be comprised, not simply of ideas, nor even of our ideas of things, but of things themselves. "Science is con-

[3] Durkheim, 1997c: 7e, 9e. Miller (1997b: 3) notes that the Latin thesis never mentions a *scientia socialis*, almost always referring instead to *scientia politica* and its study of *res politicae*, while admitting that the Latin thesis itself – not to mention *De la division du travail social* – is clearly concerned with social science, social facts, and social things. The earlier translations of Alengry (1937) and Cuvillier (1953) adopted the latter usages, while Miller's more literal and conventional translation retains the terms *political* science and *political* things. All agree, however, that Durkheim's intended reference was to the "social" – e.g., including religion and morality – rather than the merely "political," and though I prefer the Miller/Griffiths translation and will follow it below, I will also speak of "social" science and "social" things.

cerned with things," Durkheim insisted. "Without a given to describe and explain, it exists in a void and it cannot set itself any goal beyond this description and explanation" (1997: 11e).

Social science is thus the scientific study of social things (*choses sociales*) – e.g., laws, customs, religions, suicide rates, the division of labor, etc. – which, like the other things in nature, have their own peculiar characteristics. But until quite recently, Durkheim insisted, no philosopher had viewed the things studied by social science in this way. Durkheim acknowledged that Aristotle – whose *Ethics* and *Politics* he had taught at the university of Bordeaux – was more an "empiricist" than was Plato; but Aristotle's real concern was less with the discovery of the laws of social life than with the determination of the best form of society. Aristotle's *Ethics* thus begins with the argument that happiness is the purpose of life, and that the goal of society should be to provide the context through which this end might reasonably be achieved – i.e., through the practice of the virtues. But this, Durkheim observed, is not a goal that societies actually pursue; rather, it is the way societies should be organized if they are to assist their members in the realization of their specific *telos*; and when Aristotle eventually did turn to historical facts, it was only to show how his original principles might be adapted to various situations. And, like Aristotle, later writers down to Montesquieu had continued to think that social phenomena were dependent on human will, and thus they "did not regard them as really things, just like other things in nature, which have their own characteristics and which therefore require sciences able to describe and explain them."[4]

While Durkheim thus disparaged Montesquieu's predecessors for practicing "not a science but an art," he was clearly *not* suggesting that their formulations were in any sense irrational. On the contrary, their preferences for one form of the state over another were typically conjoined with rational demonstrations and even "proofs" – e.g., that a particular preference was more "consonant with human nature" than its counterparts – a style of argument Durkheim characterized as a kind of "science within art" (see Boutroux 1914: 188–94, esp. 190–1). But in what amounts to a sweeping indictment of one of the favorite arguments of Enlightenment social and

---

[4] Durkheim 1997: 11e. This was an indictment, of course, that could easily have been extended to include the Sens lecturer.

political thought, Durkheim insisted that the deduction of such preferences from the abstract principles of human nature is psychology rather than social science, indeed, that such arguments rarely contain anything that is "social" at all. Interestingly, this argument – i.e., that at least until the 18th century, society was viewed as a work of art rather than of nature – was developed at length in Boutroux's *De l'idée de loi naturelle dans la science et la philosophie contemporaines* (1892). Unlike Durkheim, however, Boutroux saw Montesquieu as a more typical representative of Enlightenment rationalism, with a Cartesian, mathematical conception of society. In any case, for Durkheim, "true" science asserts its complete independence from art, divorces itself from immediate questions of utility, and applies itself to the description and classification of concrete *things*. For Durkheim, therefore, social facts are "will-independent" even where they are "mind-dependent," and they are resistant to change at will collectively rather than merely individually (Miller 1997a: 101; 1996: 47).

Where rationalists habitually began with axiomatic principles from which formal propositions were then deduced, therefore, Durkheim insisted that social science begin with the description of the things with which it deals. Here, "description" meant to characterize or define the things under investigation according to the features held in common with other things – in short, description presupposes classification. Only if the infinite variety of nature can be foreshortened and reduced to specific types, therefore, can social science proceed. Here again, Durkheim's debt was to Aristotle's *Politics*, with its classification of the types of the state; but Aristotle – unlike Montesquieu – had classified societies only according to their forms of government, thus ignoring religion, the family, economic life, etc. So again, Durkheim saw Montesquieu as breaking with a tradition of classification that went back to the ancient Greeks (1997: 16e–17e).

This observation brought Durkheim to a question similar to one discussed a decade earlier in the Sens lectures. Is classification, he asked, a wholly inductive procedure, "socially constructed" by social scientists themselves? Or are these societal types somehow "given" by nature itself, and only later apprehended by the human mind? This is a complicated question, and one to which Durkheim's answers were not always consistent; but at least one generalization seems justified. When Durkheim spoke of the way in which human subjects (particularly primitive subjects) "organize" their social world, he was almost determinedly constructivist, speaking an *empiricist* language that eventually resulted in his seminal contributions to the sociology of knowledge and science (Durkheim and Mauss 1963; Durkheim 1915). But when Durkheim spoke of the way in which social scientists (*qua* social scientists) understand and explain the social world, he spoke a more *rationalist* language of the order inherent in nature itself, which it is the job of social science to discover and comprehend.

This was certainly the case when, in the Latin thesis, Durkheim turned to the problem of *explanation* (i.e., the arranging of our ideas in a definite order), the next step after description in his social scientific method. For this "definite order," Durkheim argued, "involves the existence of such an order in things themselves – that is, the existence of unbroken chains, made up of parts which are so interlinked that every effect always follows necessarily from the same cause and cannot arise from others" (1997: 17e). In short, this requirement presupposes that social things are governed by laws, to the extent that without its being satisfied, no social science is possible. Among Durkheim's conditions, therefore, laws are as essential to explanation as classification is to description. In fact, Durkheim never tired of insisting that human societies are a part of nature; and since laws govern all other parts of nature, it seemed clear to him – as to Montesquieu – that they govern human societies as well.

This insistence that social phenomena are governed by laws inevitably raised another question discussed in the Sens lectures – i.e., if social phenomena are bound by laws of cause and effect, what becomes of free will? The view that the idea of law is thus in conflict with that of free will, Durkheim observed, has been one of the major obstacles to the emergence of social science. The view that it is conscious motives that underlie our actions, that it is the individual wills and personalities of "kings, legislators, and prophets" that drive history forward, that it is the most visible causes of social phenomena that provide their appropriate explanation – this view, Durkheim argued, contradicts the very idea of a social science. First, the idea of natural societal "types" – i.e., of classes of things inherent within societies (themselves a part of nature) – presupposes the idea of causes which, "at work in different times and places, always and everywhere produce the same effects" (1997: 20e). Second, so long as it is assumed that "kings, legislators, and prophets" can direct social life according to their individual wills, then social science has no object; for the subject matter of social science can consist only of "things" that have a stable nature of their own, and are capable of resisting human will.

But if this "scientifically knowable" subject matter is a necessary condition for social science, Durkheim added, it is hardly sufficient to that purpose. In addition, Durkheim argued, we need a *method* which is both appropriate to the things studied, and consistent with the more general conditions of science. Here Durkheim seems to have had the psychological experiments he had observed in Wundt's laboratory – "specialized," "restricted," "precise," and "complex" (1887a: 433) – as his model. But if Durkheim thus considered controlled experimentation the virtual model of the scientific method, he also shared Comte's conclusion that experiments were impossible in the study of human societies (1997: 21e). Some other method was thus required – one that met the austere criteria of science (i.e., description and classification, interpretation and laws), but one also consistent with the nature of the subject matter under investigation (i.e., real, concrete, diverse, complex, etc.).

This had been the special contribution of Montesquieu. To Durkheim, the purpose of *De l'esprit des lois* was clear – Montesquieu's goal was to "investigate their nature," to "seek their origins and find their causes, both in the physical domain and in that of the mind."[5] But what particularly impressed Durkheim were those elements of Montesquieu's thought – e.g., book I, chapter 3, "Of the Principles of the Three Kinds of Government" – that set him apart from his Enlightenment contemporaries, and more closely resembled the 19th-century German concern for historical context and ethical relativity.[6] Where earlier philosophers were convinced that "a single form of state and a single legal and moral doctrine fitted in with all men's nature," for example, Montesquieu understood that "rules of life differ according to the conditions of life." Recognizing the diversity of societal types, Montesquieu considered all equally

---

[5] Durkheim 1997: 22e. From the French edition, it is clear that here Durkheim was relying on Montesquieu's *Défense de l'esprit des lois et eclaircissements* (1750), a reply to his critics written shortly after the appearance of *De l'esprit des lois* itself. See the translator's note in Durkheim 1953: 43 n. 1–2.

[6] Montesquieu, of course, had been a powerful influence on German jurisprudence (see 1949: 19–28, and chapter 4, pp. 195–202).

"normal," and refused to "lay down rules valid for all peoples." And while Montesquieu clearly realized the advantages of one type of institution over another, these judgments were always rendered "in terms of norms which he derived from things themselves and which accordingly correspond with the diversity of things" (Durkheim 1997: 25e).

Montesquieu's debt to the tradition of natural law notwithstanding, he was constantly ambivalent on its relation to the laws of civil society; and this ambivalence became the source of much of Durkheim's admiration for *De l'esprit des lois*. It is true, Durkheim acknowledged, that Montesquieu recognized that societies are composed of individual human beings, that such beings have a "nature" that distinguishes them from other animals, and that the nature of human societies reflects this nature of its component parts. But it was precisely here that Montesquieu and Durkheim refused to reduce the explanation of social phenomena to psychological causes. The natural instincts that lead human beings into social relationships may "open[s] the way to society," Durkheim argued, but they do not "produce its forms, nature, or laws. There is nothing about social institutions which can be explained by this approach" (1997: 26e). Montesquieu's treatment of the problem of human nature, Durkheim thus emphasized, was "brief and sketchy," for it "is not of direct concern to his project"; and for the same reason, Montesquieu sharply separated "natural laws" – meaning the nature of individual human beings – from the civil, political, and international law of human societies.

What impressed Durkheim still more, however, was that Montesquieu – having thus refused to explain civil and political law as the consequence of human nature – equally refused to explain it by reference to an original agreement, contract, or convention. For such contracts and conventions, Durkheim argued, are artificial, have no place in nature, and thus subvert the very possibility of social science. In Montesquieu, by contrast, the laws of society "are founded in things in a different way from the others, as following from the nature, not of man, but of political societies. Their causes are to be sought, not in the human mind, but in the conditions of collective life" (1997: 27e). If we want to understand the civil laws of a given nature, for example, Montesquieu insists that we must know the size of its population and the nature of the social bonds between its citizens. Montesquieu "is remarkable," Durkheim observed, "for his understanding that the nature of societies is not less fixed and stable than the nature of man, and that it is no easier to change the species of a people than of a living being" (1997: 28e).

But Durkheim still understood the extent of Montesquieu's ties to the past. Consider the question raised earlier: If natural law and civil law conflict, how are we to decide which to obey? Confronted with this dilemma, Durkheim realized, Montesquieu insisted that we follow the laws of nature (1949: 59–62). But why, Durkheim asks, should the nature of man be more sacred than the nature of society? The only way out of this impasse, Durkheim argues, is to take a still more extreme position – i.e., to insist that "all legal and moral rules, even those concerning individual life, follow from the nature of society. But on this point as on many others," Durkheim observed, "and even in initiating a new approach, Montesquieu is still attached to an older one and held back by it" (1997: 30e).

Ostensibly, Montesquieu's treatment of the problem of classification also seemed to have a small foot in the past. Comte had thus emphasized that Montesquieu's classification of societies – i.e., republics (both aristocratic and democratic), monarchies, and despotisms – was really a classification of the ways societies are governed, and that in this sense, Montesquieu had simply adopted the traditional categories of Aristotle. But unlike Comte, who had criticized Montesquieu for this reversion to the Aristotelian classification, Durkheim recognized significant differences between *De l'esprit des lois* and the *Politics*.[7] The most important of these was that Montesquieu, while *naming* the types of societies according to their forms of sovereignty, had *classified* these types according to the nature of their social institutions (1997: 40e–41e). Where Aristotle had deduced his classification from an abstract, *a priori* principle (i.e., the number of rulers), therefore, Montesquieu had introduced a more inductive, empiricist approach, comparing real societies (e.g., Rome, Athens, and Sparta) from different regions and historical periods.

This introduction of the comparative method explains why, as Momigliano put it, "the link between Montesquieu and Fustel was in everyone's mind" during the early 1890s (1982: 339). And in *De l'esprit des lois*, it yielded empirical observations concerning the

---

[7] In general, Durkheim considered Comte a poor interpreter of Montesquieu's work and its significance. In the *Cours*, he observed, Comte's evaluation of Montesquieu's thought is "a very brief judgment, that is in part mistaken, as already seen, and that above all does not seem based on attentive, careful reflection on the theory" (1997: 71e).

nature of concrete societies reminiscent of *De la division du travail social*. In book IV, chapter 5 of *De l'esprit des lois*, for example, Montesquieu had emphasized the need for the "whole power" of education in a republic, because this form of government depends upon "arduous and painful" self-renunciation. This virtue of self-renunciation, Montesquieu added, "may be defined as the love of the laws and of our country. As such love requires a constant preference of public to private interest, it is the source of all private virtues; for they are nothing more than this very preference itself. The virtues taught in monarchies, by contrast, "are less what we owe to others than to ourselves; they are not so much what draws us towards society, as what distinguishes us from our fellow-citizens" (1949: 34, 29). The most significant difference between republics and monarchies, Durkheim agreed, is that the former exhibit a kind of political virtue that "lies in love of country, and in which we attach less importance to ourselves and our own concerns than to the state," while in the latter, everything has the effect of "turning [citizens] away from common towards private interests, and all the conditions of the virtue which is the basis of a republic are absent" (1997: 35e, 38e).

More importantly, Montesquieu recognized that this significant difference in the *esprit* of these societal types could be explained as a necessary consequence of their structural features. The division of labor in a republic, for example, is of a type Durkheim would later call "mechanical": "The part of each person's consciousness which expresses society and which is the same in everyone is large and powerful, while the part to do only with ourselves and our own individual concerns is small and feeble." The division of labor in a monarchy, by contrast, "might be compared with a living being, in which each part has a different function in line with its own nature," but in which "their diversity is in fact a source of cohesion" (1997: 36e, 37e, 38e). And in *De l'esprit des lois*, Durkheim added, such differences extend to "their whole life. Morals, religion, family, marriage, education, and crime and punishment are not the same in a republic as in despotism or in monarchy." In sharp contrast to other writers of the Enlightenment, Montesquieu seems "to have been more interested in the differences between societies than in things that they all have in common" (1997: 40e).

Durkheim thus treated Montesquieu's classification of societal *types* as a major contribution to the advancement of social science.

But its significance paled by comparison with Montesquieu's application of the concept of *law* to social phenomena – a judgment that
Durkheim derived from his notion of the historical development of
the sciences generally. "In every science," Durkheim explained, "the
idea of type always appears first, since it is easier for the human
mind to conceive of it. It is enough to cast an eye on things to notice
certain similarities and differences between them." But the "definite
connexions" we call "laws," he added, "being more closely bound
up with the nature of things, lie hidden within this; it is as if a veil is
thrown over them, which first has to be taken off to be able to reach
and reveal them." How much more difficult, Durkheim then argued,
to extend the notion of law to *society* – "so changeable, so diverse and
multiform as not to seem reducible to fixed and definite laws" (1997:
72e, 73e).

To Durkheim, this extension of the idea of law to the realm of
social phenomena was Montesquieu's greatest achievement.
"Laws," Durkheim cited *De l'esprit des lois*' famous opening, "are the
necessary relations arising from the nature of things. In this sense all
beings have their laws: the Deity His laws, the material world its
laws, the intelligences superior to man their laws, the beasts their
laws, man his laws" (1949: 1). This passage epitomized the rationalist
belief in a determinate order in nature, subject to the rational
interpretation of human beings; and it was Montesquieu's great
distinction to have extended this definition from the world of nature
to that of society. Comte, of course, had argued that the chaotic mass
of empirical data that followed evinced no order whatsoever,
insisting that Montesquieu had thus betrayed his Cartesian principles. But here again Durkheim defended Montesquieu's apostasy,
arguing that he was unique among his 18th-century contemporaries
in recognizing that the laws inherent within social phenomena are
neither fixed nor immutable; rather, they vary according to the
specific conditions of the society in which they are found.

Durkheim's favorite example here was again one that found a
prominent place in *De la division du travail social* – the influence of
social volume on societal types. The republican form of government,
for example, is most appropriate to a small population confined
within a limited geographical setting – since "the conditions of life
are almost the same for all" and "the very room for diversity is
lacking in such a community," social differentiation is rudimentary
and all citizens have a sense of their meaningful participation in

public affairs. As the society grows larger, "[c]ircumstances are much more diverse, forcing individuals to go different ways and become involved in different things"; thus, it becomes "more difficult for the private citizen to have a sense of the common good," so that the republic gives way to a monarchy. And if the society grows still larger, the monarchy gives way to despotism, for "it is impossible for a large empire to survive unless its ruler has the absolute power to hold in check many peoples spread over a vast land."[8] Again, Durkheim's admiration for this argument was not unqualified. There are numerous examples of small despotisms and large democracies, for example, and the explanation itself was "uncertain and vague." Most importantly, Montesquieu viewed social volume in largely political terms – i.e., as equivalent to the number of persons *subject to the same authority* – while for Durkheim, the crucial factor was rather the number of persons *bound by the same kind of relationship*. But Durkheim still praised Montesquieu's "intellectual sharpness" in attributing such an influence to social volume: "This cause," Durkheim argued, "has the greatest influence in determining things in the political world, and indeed we believe it is more or less the source from which the main differences between societies arise" (1997: 47e).

With factors like social volume exerting such an influence on the development of social institutions, the influence of individual political leaders – and with it that of conscious, willful action generally – would seem to be diminished. But in book XIX, "Of Laws in Relation to the Principles which Form the General Spirit, the Morals, and Customs of a Nation,"[9] Montesquieu granted a substantial role to the legislators of China and Sparta in the development of their society's laws. There were of course limits to this role – e.g., Montesquieu did not believe that laws were made arbitrarily, argued that custom and religion were beyond the power of the legislators, and held that laws relating to other matters had to be compatible with custom and religion. But "the institution of these," Durkheim observed, "is still in the hands of the legislator. Indeed,

---

[8] Durkheim 1997: 46e–47e. Durkheim's examples here are largely taken from book VIII: "Of the Corruption of the Principles of the Three Governments" (Montesquieu 1949: 120–5).

[9] See particularly chapter 16, "How some Legislators have confounded the Principles which govern Mankind," and chapter 19, "How this Union of Religion, Laws, Manners, and Customs amongst the Chinese was effected" (1949: 300–1, 303–4).

there are societies in which the ruler is able to shape not just laws but also morals and religion" (1997: 50e).

To Durkheim, this emphasis on the role of political authority seemed ill fitted to the more general principle that human laws spring "from the nature of things" (Montesquieu 1949: 1). But this assertion of Montesquieu's can be interpreted in two different ways. On the one hand, it might mean that human laws follow from the nature of societies *as an effect follows from the cause which produces it.* In this case, society would be what Aristotle called the *efficient* cause of the laws in question. On the other hand, it might mean that human laws are simply instruments that *the nature of the society requires in order to fulfill itself.* In this case, society would be what Aristotle called the *final* cause of human laws. Durkheim was convinced that Montesquieu intended the second usage – indeed, that he never even entertained the first. The laws of a democracy, for example, do not result necessarily from the limited number of its citizens "like heat from fire"; on the contrary, "it is only through [these laws] that there can come about the frugalness and general equality which lie in the nature of this society" (1997: 51e). From the view that society is thus a *final* rather than an *efficient* cause, it follows that laws cannot be formed arbitrarily; for under any particular set of social conditions, only one body of laws would be appropriate. From the same view, it follows that what laws are suitable to a particular society can be determined only by those who have some insight into its peculiar nature, a consequence that grants – as does Montesquieu – a considerable role to political authority.

Much of the explanatory power of *De la division du travail social*, of course, derives precisely from Durkheim's view that social causes are efficient (not final) causes – indeed, that legal institutions follow social forces almost "like heat from fire." The same arguments are foreshadowed in the Latin thesis. Social institutions, Durkheim argued,

do not usually become established according to a plan, and laws are not devices a legislator invents because they seem in line with the nature of a society. They are most often the result of causes that produce them with something like a physical necessity. Collective life is so shaped by a people's circumstances that it must take on a particular definite form. The laws express this form. They therefore follow from the same efficient causes with the same necessity.

It is at least arguable that Durkheim's differences with Montesquieu here derive largely from Durkheim's exposure to the German social science, and particularly the historical school of jurisprudence. "Montesquieu," Durkheim argued, "would undoubtedly have realized this if he had seen that laws are not so different in nature from morals, but, on the contrary, emanate from them" (1997: 52e). However useful laws may be to a society, this refers to their functions, not their causes; and the latter lie in the collective unconscious of earlier generations, far beyond the rational will of legislators.

Quite aside from his Aristotelian predilection for final causes, Montesquieu's conception of the laws governing social phenomena had at least two other implications that troubled Durkheim. First, Montesquieu's position that civil laws do *not* follow necessarily from efficient causes introduced an element of *contingency* in the relationship between natural and positive laws, sometimes reflected in the blunders of human, and therefore entirely fallible, legislators. But the fortuitous blunders to which Montesquieu referred were, to Durkheim, simply those "diseases" of the social organism that play such an important role in book 3 of *De la division du travail social*; and disease, Durkheim extended the metaphor, no less than health, is inherent in the nature of living things (1984: 291–341). Moreover, because both health and disease are thus parts of the same determinate order, they can be compared in a manner that advances our understanding of each. In short, like Montesquieu, Durkheim employed the classical, metaphorical language of medicine; but he used it for a different purpose – i.e., to eliminate the element of contingency from positive laws, and thus to assimilate them within his own, more mechanistic philosophy of science.

Second, while Montesquieu had insisted that laws are "the necessary relations arising from the nature of things," his parallel insistence that such laws might be violated indicated that this "necessity" was not *real* but merely *logical*. The laws might "necessarily" express what is implied in the definition of a society, Durkheim observed, while the definition itself might *not* follow rationally from the nature of the society in question. In this case, the laws would tell us what is rational rather than what is real. So here again, Durkheim sided with the realism of German social science against the Cartesian rationalist. Montesquieu, Durkheim thus complained, applies the word "laws" to relations between *ideas* rather than the relations between *things*. Durkheim was perplexed, for example, by Montesquieu's suggestion that certain institutions (e.g., slavery) were incompatible with the "nature" of certain kinds of societies (e.g., republics), despite the fact that all ancient republics had slavery. By such a view, Durkheim objected, "the order to be investigated in such terms by science is not only not something which exists everywhere and at all times, but it might even turn out that it has never existed." So Durkheim clearly suspected Montesquieu of occasionally reverting to an older, rationalist and idealist conception of social science, one concerned with things "not as they are, but as they ought to be" (1997: 58e).

"As long as politics consisted in art," Durkheim continued, "political writers mainly made use of deduction. They derived, from a universal idea of man, the form of society which suited human nature and the rules which ought to be observed in common life." To Durkheim – recently exposed to the achievements of Wundt and his associates at the Physiologische Institut in Leipzig – the French adherence to this Cartesian tradition was the greatest obstacle to a scientific sociology and, indirectly, to a secular morality for the Third Republic. Durkheim acknowledged that deduction "comes to our help with ideas that steer research through the obscurity of things"; but where we are dealing with "realities" rather than with "abstract concepts," these ideas must be confirmed by observation and, still more importantly, by experiment. In fact, it is not enough just to observe nature, Durkheim argued: "it is necessary to go beyond this and interrogate it, turn it over and over and put it through every kind of test." Because social science "deals with things, only the experimental method can succeed in it" (1997: 59e).

Durkheim's model here, as we have already seen, was Wundt's experimental psychology laboratory in Leipzig; but as we have also seen, Durkheim shared Comte's view that experimentation was impossible in the study of human societies. In short, Durkheim needed a substitute for the experimental method, one more appropriate to the nature of the subject matter under investigation, but which retained the "precision," "detail," and "control" of its psychological counterpart. He found this substitute in the comparative method. The "whole point of experiment," Durkheim observed, consists simply "in varying things more or less at will," so that they provide "a rich, extensive basis for comparison." In the same way, we can "[compare] social facts of the same kind, as they occur in different societies," identifying "which of them exist together everywhere, disappear simultaneously or change at the same time and according to the same pattern." To discover the laws of nature, therefore, we need only to "establish a sufficient number of comparisons between different forms of the same thing." This enables us to distinguish the "fixed, constant connexions which express a law" from "the chance and the transient." In social science, Durkheim concluded, comparison can take the place of experiment (1997: 60e).

Montesquieu, Durkheim then argued, instinctively realized the need for this comparative method. Montesquieu's purpose in gathering data from various cultures and throughout history was precisely to compare them and derive laws from them; indeed, Durkheim added, "the entire work consists in a comparison of the laws observed by the most diverse peoples and it can be truly said that he inaugurated, with his book, the new discipline nowadays called *comparative law*" (1997: 60e). But Durkheim still found Montesquieu's social science too much in the Cartesian tradition. "I have laid down the first principles," Montesquieu had announced, for example, "and have found that the particular cases follow naturally from them; that the histories of all nations are only consequences of them; and that every particular law is connected with another law, or depends on some other of a more general extent" (1949: lxvii). Quite reasonably, Durkheim took this as a declaration that Montesquieu intended "to treat politics in an almost mathematical manner," laying down first principles "from which the particular laws of societies follow logically" (1997: 60e–61e). Far from collecting all the relevant facts and studying them objectively, Montesquieu thus "starts with a proof, by pure deduction, of what it is he has in mind" (1997: 61e). Where he claims that there is a causal relation between two facts, for example, Montesquieu rarely shows that they appear simultaneously, disappear simultaneously, or vary in the same way. Again, an entire societal type (e.g., monarchy) is sometimes endowed with a specific property (e.g., the separation of powers) that he has observed in only a single case (e.g., England). And again, he insists that certain institutions (e.g., slavery) cannot be appropriate to certain societies (e.g., Athens) because they cannot be derived from the principles of these societies (e.g., virtue) as he conceives them. "If, then, induction makes its first appearance in political science with Montesquieu," Durkheim concluded, "it has still not broken away from the opposite method and is corrupted by the connexion" (1997: 63e).

This "ambiguity in method" of *De l'esprit des lois*, Durkheim observed, had at least two causes. The first was Montesquieu's inability to break with the powerful tradition of Cartesian rationalism, according to which the "normal" institutional arrangements of any society are implicit within the underlying "nature" of that society. These arrangements could therefore be logically deduced once the nature of the society in question has been defined; and it was these logical necessities that Montesquieu called laws. The startling thing to a more skeptical, empiricist age, Durkheim hinted, was the ease with which Montesquieu felt this underlying nature could be grasped; but this was utterly consistent with Montesquieu's rationalist principles: "Just as the connexion which exists between political facts and a society's essence is rational," Durkheim explained, "so this essence – the source of the entire deduction – has the same nature, consisting in a simple notion reason can quickly get hold of." Montesquieu thus failed to grasp the extent to which, as Francis Bacon argued in the *Novum Organum*, the "subtlety of *things*" far surpasses the "subtlety of the *human mind*" (Durkheim 1997: 63e). If "a certain logic lies hidden in [social phenomena]," Durkheim admitted, "it is different from the one we use in deductive reasoning; it does not have the same simplicity; perhaps it even follows other laws." Thus, Durkheim added, "we need to find out about it from *things* themselves" (1997: 64e). The second cause was, in a sense, the inverse of the first. However rational the laws of nature, we have already seen that Montesquieu admitted the possibility – even the empirical frequency – of their being violated and corrupted by human legislators. This possibility admitted, it becomes impossible to discover the "normal" institutional arrangements of any society by inductive means. The result, Durkheim argues, is that Montesquieu always felt the typical rationalist's distrust of the powers of empirical observation and – his "instinctive recognition" of its necessity notwithstanding – of comparison as well (1997: 64e).

Proceeding deductively or inductively, however, Montesquieu had recognized a related, equally important principle of the comparative method – i.e., that all the elements of a society (e.g., religion, law, morality, the economy, etc.) form an organic whole. "Unless there is investigation into the ways in which they harmonize and are affected by one another," Durkheim argued, "the function that each has cannot be determined. Indeed, their nature will remain completely hidden. They will be seen as so many separately existing realities, when they are merely parts of a reality" (1997: 65e–66e). And the previous failure to adhere to this principle had been severely damaging not only to social science but also – if we read carefully between the lines of Durkheim's examples – to political and economic reform. Moral philosophers, for example, had dealt with questions of ethics "As if these exist on their own," and were "uninterested in the nature of wealth in the societies concerned." Inversely, political economists had dealt with the subject of wealth "not taking any notice of the body of rules that constitutes ethics" (1997: 65e). In the strict sense, Durkheim argued, social science did not exist "until it at last became clear that these particular sciences are linked together by a strict necessity and are parts of a whole"; and "in showing such interrelationships, Montesquieu looked ahead to the unity of our science, although in a vague and confused way" (1997: 66e).

Finally, any discussion of the sources of Durkheim's comparative method must pay special attention to the powerful evolutionary perspective articulated in *De la division du travail social*. When we compare different societies, Durkheim observed, we notice that "certain forms or properties" that are "clearly tied up" in some societies are "hardly developed" in others, an observation that leads us to speak of some societies as "superior," and to suggest that these grow out of their "inferior" counterparts. Here Durkheim explicitly rejected unilinear evolutionary doctrines that placed ancient societies at the bottom and modern societies at the top. This *caveat* entered, however, Durkheim endorsed the notion that "societies arise out of one another" and that "the more recent overtake and surpass those that came earlier" as one that has transformed the method of social science (1997: 67e). Montesquieu was not completely oblivious to this notion, Durkheim acknowledged, in the sense that he preferred "the republic and monarchy to despotism, monarchy to the republic, and the republic to primitive democracy." But he did not understand that these different societal types "descended from the same root," and argued instead that "each formed separately from the others" (1997: 68e). Discussing particular peoples, while Montesquieu did not deny that "their social principle can grow or be corrupted," therefore, he did believe that "this is fixed and definite from the very beginning and must remain intact throughout their entire history." The result is that Montesquieu failed to see that "the nature of societies contains opposites," the consequence of its having emerged from a past but not yet realized its future; in short, Montesquieu did not understand that process "in which society, while always keeping to its own nature, forever embarks on an ascent of something new" (1997: 68e–69e). In effect, Durkheim was arguing that Montesquieu shared one of the more salient shortcomings of the Enlightenment mentality in general – i.e., an acute lack of historical sensibilities.

This was a shortcoming that Durkheim – having taken the full measure of the German historical school of jurisprudence – did not share. Social existence, he argued, is determined by causes of two distinct types. The first consists of present circumstances, including the society's topography and population size – matters to which Montesquieu granted considerable attention. The second type concerns causes that are more historical: "Just as any child would be different with different parents," Durkheim explained, "a society varies according to the form of preceding societies." Failing to see the "succession and connectedness of societies," Durkheim observed, Montesquieu almost completely ignored causes of this second type. The result was that Montesquieu's comparative method contrasted sharply with that of Comte, who argued that "the nature of societies is totally dependent on the moment of time at which they made their appearance," and also that social science consists "in establishing the evolutionary sequence of societies." But each of these approaches, Durkheim concluded, "expresses only one side of the truth" (1997: 69e).

In sum, virtually every aspect of Durkheim's Latin thesis on Montesquieu reflects his ambivalence concerning the legacy of Cartesian metaphysics, as well as his growing attraction for the normative vocabulary of German social science. Durkheim admired Montesquieu's recognition of the real, concrete diversity of societal types, praised his refusal to deduce "rules valid for all peoples" from artificial first principles, and – anticipating *De la division du travail social* – applauded his explanation of the *esprit* of each societal type as the natural consequence of its structural features. At least equal praise was given to Montesquieu's refusal – so unusual among his Enlightenment contemporaries – to reduce explanations of civil and political law to the principles of human nature, or to some putative, original contract or covenant. Durkheim lamented the extent to which Montesquieu was still bound by the legacy of Aristotle and by the traditions of natural law, not to mention the disturbing element of contingency which leavened the causal explanations of *De l'esprit des lois*. But, recognizing that Montesquieu's "greatest achievement" – i.e., the extension of the idea of law to the realm of social phenomena – reflected an undeniable, continuing attachment to the rationalist belief in a determinate order of nature, Durkheim still emphasized how "unique" it was for an 18th-century social philosopher to insist that these laws were neither fixed nor immutable. Finally, the notion that "social volume" affects the structures of law and society, which plays so large a role in *De la division du travail social*, was found in Montesquieu's discussion of the conditions of republican government.

This ambivalence in Durkheim's treatment of *De l'esprit des lois* was more than matched by that work itself. For, as Berlin has shown, Montesquieu was a most reluctant rationalist, an uneasy ally amidst the Enlightenment's celebration of reason, reform, and social progress, and an author whose greatest achievements derived precisely from those moments when, seduced by an insatiable curiosity and a fascination for the particular, the detailed, and the concrete, he digressed and thus deserted the rationalist credo of his *milieu*. In fact, it was precisely this reluctance and uneasiness, these digressions and this eventual apostasy, that excited Durkheim's interest. For Durkheim shared this ambivalence, sensed it in his predecessor, and thus used the Latin thesis as a vehicle for the "working out" of his own conception of the relative value of rationalism and empiricism.

THE NATURE OF SOCIAL THINGS

In the development of Durkheim's social realism, the emphasis of the works we've discussed thus far – i.e., Durkheim's early reviews and essays (1885–90), the Latin thesis (1892), and *De la division du travail social* (1893) – was on the notion of society as a part of nature. Indeed, even in the more spiritualist context of the Sens lectures, Durkheim had insisted that altruistic sentiments are as "natural" as their egoistic counterparts. As long as Durkheim was thus concerned to emphasize that societies were natural entities, subject to the laws of nature, writers like Hobbes and Rousseau, with their emphasis on a "social contract" and the related implication that social institutions were works of "art," were anathema; indeed, these early essays and theses are filled with critical remarks about both *Le Contrat social* and *Emile*. Almost immediately after the publication of *De la division du travail social*, however, Durkheim seems to have increasingly focused more on the notion that society is a *particular part* of nature, that sociological explanations are irreducible to their psychological counterparts, and that social "things" have distinctive characteristics (e.g., externality and constraint). As this emphasis changed, and as Durkheim became increasingly embroiled in *L'Affaire Dreyfus*, he returned to Rousseau, where he found a rich, complex, and powerful vocabulary upon which he drew in his theory of anomic suicide. This re-reading of Rousseau will be dealt with below; but first, it is necessary to explain why Durkheim's interests and emphasis might have changed in this way. One plausible answer is that, by 1894, he was locked in a contest with Jean-Gabriel Tarde (1843–1904) – the most formidable intellectual opponent he would face in his career.

Tarde was born in Sarlat, a small town about one hundred miles from Bordeaux. Rigorously trained in Latin, Greek, history, and mathematics at the local Jesuit school, Tarde developed a strong respect for the role of the intellect in social progress, an appreciation of the manner in which a classical education bound together the leaders of France, and a preference for a hierarchical conception of society. Fascinated by mathematics, he considered entering the Ecole Polytechnique, but an eye disease forced him to limit his reading, and he eventually settled on the study of law. After passing his initial examinations at the nearby Toulouse Faculty of Law, he completed his legal studies in Paris in 1865. Between 1869 and 1894, Tarde accepted a series of regional positions in and around Sarlat, which gave him time to read the works of Hegel, Spencer, Mill, and especially Cournot, whose *L'enchainement des idées fondamentales dans les sciences et l'histoire* (1861) inspired his ideas about imitation.

By the age of thirty, Tarde had drafted a series of notes that contained many of the essentials of his later theoretical works. But Tarde's legal work also stimulated an interest in criminology; and this, in turn, led him to read the works of Lombroso, Garofalo, Ferri, and others. This "new Italian school" had enjoyed some success explaining crime as the consequence of racial and geographical causes. Against the Italians, Tarde had soon published a series of critical articles – eventually collected for his first book, *La criminalité comparée* (1886) – which emphasized the role of socialization and imitation as causes of crime, and established him as the leading spokesman for what was later called the "French school" of criminology. A frequent contributor to the *Archives d'Anthropologie Criminelle*,

Tarde became the journal's co-director in 1893; but his last major work in criminology was *La philosophie pénale* (1890), as his interests had already turned in the direction of sociology.

Throughout the 1880s, Tarde had published a series of articles in the *Revue philosophique* which Steven Lukes has characterized as "a one-man campaign against the various forms of biologism in sociology – Darwinism, organicism, transformism – that [Tarde] found in the work of such writers as Spencer, Espinas, Worms (whom he actually converted), de Greef, Gumplowicz, Novicow, Lombroso, Lilienfeld and Roberty" (1972: 302). Against these views, Tarde advanced his own, "interpsychological" theory, a form of methodological individualism based entirely on the notion of imitation. These critical essays provided the substance of *Les lois de l'imitation* (1890), which would remain Tarde's most famous sociological work; and with the publication of *Les transformations du droit* (1893), which examined various legal questions from a sociological perspective, Tarde's sociological reputation was made. Appointed as director of criminal statistics at the Ministry of Justice – where his responsibilities included providing some of the statistical data for *Le Suicide* – Tarde moved from Bordeaux to Paris, and the confrontation with Durkheim began.

The first shot was fired by Tarde in what Lukes has rightly described as a "generous and respectful" review of *De la division du travail social* (Tarde 1893: Lukes 1972: 304–5). In fact, Tarde's review dealt not only with Durkheim's doctoral thesis, but also with Novicow's *La lutte entre sociétés* (1893) and the French edition of Gumplowicz's *Der Rassenkampf* (1883), now re-titled as *La lutte des races* (1893). "This Russian, this Pole, and this Frenchman," Tarde observed, "do not seem to know or to be mutually influenced by one another. Each has carved out and followed his own mental rut, his special furrow in the immense, fallow land of the sociological field" (1893: 618). The unconscious convergence and divergence of these independent lines of thought, Tarde suggested, form "the tissue of [the] new science" – particularly in their answers to two questions: "What is the nature of the social bond that ties together the parts of the group?" and "What is the law of social transformation?"

By contrast with the second question – which concerned "the most vital and anxious preoccupations of the present day" – Tarde suggested that the first "affords only theoretical interest"; but he was also perceptibly delighted that not one of the three authors had adopted the Spencerian metaphor of the social organism. On the contrary, in Tarde's mind, each had been led to a conception of society that had broken "the umbilical cord of sociology," thus "inaugurating its autonomy" from the "biological mother." In doing so, Tarde gratefully acknowledged, all three writers now granted a predominant role to the idea of social *similitude* – and thus to his own idea of *imitation*. In Durkheim's doctoral thesis, of course, what Tarde thus described as social similitude pertained primarily to primitive societies, whose solidarity was based on the resemblance between similar social segments (e.g., the clan, tribe, etc.) and their associated, individual members. But with increasing social differentiation and the division of labor, Tarde paraphrased Durkheim, this "mechanical" solidarity is replaced by a stronger, more intimate, bond based upon the *differences* between individuals and groups. Durkheim's answer to the first question thus turned heavily on his answer to the second – i.e., the law of social transformation.

Tarde's treatment of Durkheim's theory of social evolution was indeed generous and respectful. Durkheim "shows perfectly" the inadequacy of the *a priori*, utilitarian explanation, Tarde observed, which derives the division of labor from the desire for material well-being. By contrast, Tarde added, Durkheim explains social differentiation as the consequence of "social things," and especially the increase in the volume and density of societies. More generally, the thesis contained "numerous perceptive remarks" connected to each other in "ingenious ways," revealing Durkheim's "deep moral feeling and intelligence" on "every page" (1893: 626). But if Durkheim's theory of social change was thus true, Tarde continued, it was an incomplete truth, and one that invited serious misunderstanding. First, Tarde argued, it is imprecise to say that the segmentary (mechanically solidary) type of society is exclusively primitive. In fact, all societies – primitive and modern – are "segmentary," in the sense that they are based on the similarity of their members and constituent groups. Admittedly, the segments grow larger – Tarde described contemporary Europe as a segmentary society comprised of nations rather than clans or tribes; and they also grow fewer in number, as the consequence of violent conflict, conquest, and political annexation – things that Durkheim's interpretation of the causes of the division of labor had largely ignored. "Through the multiplication of relations among individuals previously divided," Tarde insisted, "through their security and their growing productivity, the density of the group increased at the same time as its volume; and since – according to Durkheim – these are the generating causes of the division of labor, we see that [the division of labor] itself depends . . . on the hazards of war, the abuse of force, on murder and great destruction" (1893: 627). But modern societies remain "segmentary," bound together by similarities, and these similarities are themselves the consequence of imitation.

Second, even as Tarde thus insisted that Durkheim's two causes for the division of labor – the volume and density of populations – were themselves consequences of conquest and annexation, he added a third, still more fundamental cause – innovation. Countries like China and India, for example, have large, extremely dense populations without great industry or a complex division of social labor. By contrast, some European states (e.g., France) of moderate size and relatively dispersed populations have rapidly become highly organized, with complex systems of occupational specialization. Why? Tarde insisted that these European societies have simply been more innovative than their eastern counterparts. "It's always a new invention," Tarde explained, "which sustains a new branch of activity, which is the force which makes the division of labor – not just in the economic, but also in the artistic, juristic, and scientific senses of the word – advance a step further" (1893: 628). Tarde acknowledged the famous Darwinian argument – so crucial to Durkheim – to the effect that the likelihood of innovation itself increases proportionately to the struggle for existence. But again, Tarde argued, the Asiatic and African examples suggest that this law operates only to the extent that the innovations are relatively easy and obvious. Where they are difficult, the struggle for existence simply becomes doubly harsh, and the problems of the volume and density of population remain unresolved. Finally, as the examples of the locomotive and the telegraph imply, Durkheim had grossly underestimated the role played by the wholly *accidental* quality of individual genius in solving these problems, and thus in contributing to social progress. In sum, the primary *causes* of the division of labor appear to be, not the increase of population volume and density, but rather warfare and individual genius.

Similarly, Tarde argued that the most important *functions* of the division of labor cited by Durkheim – i.e., the socializing and moralizing of citizens – are achieved in some societies but not in all. "The division of labor contributes to socializing and moralizing,"

Tarde insisted, "only at those times and places where ... it is tempered with a strong dose of similar beliefs or knowledge, of cult or of art, of customs or of rights and, far from contracting the domain of this higher communism, of this sacred individualism among fellow citizens, equal and similar at the base ... tends to deepen and extend itself" (1893: 628–9). In short, Tarde considered Durkheim's evolutionary opposition between mechanical and organic solidarity, in which the latter progressively replaces the former, an illusion. Tarde applauded Durkheim's acknowledgment that the division of labor itself *presupposes* a "community of beliefs and sentiments."[10] But he deplored Durkheim's failure to recognize that the function of the division of labor itself is "to develop and strengthen, under new forms, this intellectual and moral community, by multiplying the objects of this common wealth and singularly facilitating their diffusion" (1893: 629). In some cases, organic solidarity even *precedes* its mechanical counterpart – e.g., as where two nations or economic classes, previously foreign and dissimilar to one another, begin to render each other mutual services, exchanging merchandise, needs, and ideas, weaving the kinds of relations that assimilate them to one another and form the basis of community.

Durkheim responded to Tarde in the first part of "Les Règles de la méthode sociologique" (1894),[11] at that point where he claimed to have delineated the "exact field" of sociology as embracing "one single, well defined group of phenomena." A social fact, he explained, "is identifiable through the power of external coercion which it exerts or is capable of exerting upon individuals." The presence of this power of external coercion, Durkheim continued, "is in turn recognisable because of the existence of some pre-determined sanction, or through the resistance that the [social] fact opposes to any individual action that may threaten it" (1982: 56–7). This was the classic definition of a social fact, which in *Le Suicide* would be clothed in the language of *Du contrat social*. But at this point

---

[10] Here Tarde seems to be referring to the argument of *De la division du travail social*, book 1, chapter VII, section 2 – i.e., that "everything in the contract is not contractual."

[11] A series of articles published in the *Revue philosophique*. There are small but occasional differences between the 1894 articles and the more famous 1895 volume, as there are also differences between the deplorable 1938 translation of *Les Règles* and the more conscientious 1982 translation. The differences between the texts of 1894 and 1895 have been clarified in Jean-Michel Berthelot's 1988 edition of *Les Règles*. Tarde's immediate response was to the 1894 articles rather than to the 1895 volume, but the variations are inconsequential to my argument, so I've quoted from the more widely accessible 1982 translation.

in his argument, Durkheim added a second, alternative criterion whereby social facts might be defined. Briefly, a social fact might also be identified "by ascertaining how widespread it is within the group, provided that, as noted above, one is careful to add a second essential characteristic; this is, that it exists independently of the particular forms that it may assume in the process of spreading itself within the group" (1982: 57). This alternative criterion of "generality plus objectivity," Durkheim admitted, is sometimes "more easily applied" and "easier to establish," especially in those instances – e.g., forms of economic organization like those to be treated in *Le Suicide* – where the initial criterion of "externality plus constraint" is "merely indirect" and thus "not always so clearly discernible." But Durkheim insisted that this second criterion was simply another formulation of the first one, for "if a mode of behaviour existing outside the consciousnesses of individuals becomes general, it can only do so by exerting pressure upon them" (1982: 57).

The reader familiar with *Les lois de l'imitation*, however, might reasonably have argued that such "generality plus objectivity" was the consequence of imitation; and it was apparently concerns of this kind that led Durkheim to a lengthy footnote emphasizing "how far removed this definition of the social fact is from that which serves as the basis for the ingenious system of Tarde." Our research, Durkheim began, "has nowhere led us to corroboration of the preponderant influence that Tarde attributes to imitation in the genesis of collective facts." Further, a necessary consequence of Durkheim's definition of social facts was that "imitation does not always express, indeed never expresses, what is essential and characteristic in the social fact. Doubtless every social fact is imitated," Durkheim acknowledged, "and has . . . a tendency to become generalised." But this tendency of a social fact to become generalized, he added, is because it is obligatory. "Its capacity for expansion is not the cause but the consequence of its sociological character." If social facts were the only cause of such generalized expansion, Durkheim added, "imitation" might serve to define – but never explain – social facts; but "an individual state which impacts on [social states] none the less remains individual." And Durkheim doubted that the term "imitation" could even serve thus to "designate" the kind of proliferation caused by social facts, for "[i]n such a single term very different phenomena, which need to be distinguished, are confused" (1982: 59 n. 3).

Tarde responded to Durkheim in "Les Deux Eléments de la socio-logie," a lecture presented before the First International Congress of Sociology, also in 1894. "It is natural," Tarde referred to Durkheim's earlier emphasis that social facts are a part of nature, "that a developing science lean on those already established, as for example sociology on biology." And it is no less natural, he acknowledged, referring to Durkheim's increasing emphasis that social facts are a particular part of nature – i.e., that a new science will "seek to fly on its own wings and to establish its own separate domain. Sociology has arrived at this point: it seeks to be established *by itself* and *for itself*" (1969: 112). But however natural, it was this second, separatist tendency – i.e., the view that, though a science, sociology was a science of a special kind – that Tarde considered destructive to the discipline: "Everyone is aware of the sterility of these pretensions," he insisted, "which refuse to recognize the solidarity of the various sciences, hence the profound unity of universal reality. The same vain aspirations are to be feared in sociology, and here and there I believe I can perceive symptoms of a similar error which could be disastrous" (1969: 112–13). It was to prevent this "aberration" – born of its Durkheimian pretension to "absolute autonomy" – that Tarde under-took his own effort to determine the scope and limits of sociology.

In short, "Les Deux Eléments de la sociologie" was Tarde's rejoinder to the arguments of "Les Règles de la méthode socio-logique," and it concerned itself with two questions. The first was the determination of the distinctive character of social facts – i.e., those characteristics that distinguished them from *other* kinds of facts – a question that Tarde pursued using the analogy of mechanics. The elementary fact of mechanics, Tarde insisted, is not movement *per se* – which Tarde described instead as the mere "postulate" of mechanics – but rather the *communication* or *modification* of a *specific* movement by the action of one body on another. Similarly, he argued, the elementary fact of sociology is not consciousness – the mere "postulate" of sociology – but rather the "the communication or modification of a state of consciousness by the action of one conscious being on another" (1969: 113). From this distinction, it follows that *some* things done by members of a society, and par-ticularly those things that are purely physiological or even psycho-logical – e.g., breathing, digesting, blinking one's eyelids, mechanically moving one's legs about, absent-mindedly looking at a landscape, uttering an inarticulate cry, etc. – are not social facts at all. But *other* things – e.g., speaking to someone, praying to an idol, weaving a garment, cutting down a tree, knifing an enemy, sculpting a stone, etc. – rather clearly *are* social facts.

What distinguishes this second set of actions from the first? According to Tarde, actions of the second kind are *social* actions because they are *imitative* – i.e., human beings would not do these things but for the example of other human beings, whom they have copied, voluntarily or otherwise, from birth. It is in this sense that purely *physical* actions (e.g., walking, breathing, eating) can become *social* actions (e.g., walking in a regiment, breathing like a trained singer, eating with utensils). Only human beings perform actions of this second type. What about those (undeniably social) actions which consist of a new discovery, initiative, or invention? Tarde's answer, suggestive of recent ideas in the sociology of scientific knowledge, was that such actions become "social" precisely to the extent that they quit the individual sphere, to be copied, replicated, and propagated by example, thus entering the public domain (1969: 114).

One of the more interesting claims that Tarde made for this distinction was that it *takes no account of the motivation* for the imitation. It makes no difference, Tarde insisted, whether the action is motivated by sympathy or animosity, envy or admiration, servile docility or a free and intelligent calculation. These extremely variable, subjective psychological elements could be set aside, for their underlying psychological source would still remain the same – i.e., a "certain hidden attraction" which "irresistibly pushes men to reflect each other" regardless of their other feelings or thoughts (1969: 114). The claim is important because it provided the occasion for Tarde's "astonishment" at the reproaches made against him in "Les Règles": first, because Durkheim had criticized him for emphasizing a fact (imitation) that could be grasped externally and thus without regard for its internal source; and second, because it had been *Durkheim* – i.e., the foremost advocate of the principle that sociology should be based on purely *objective*, non-psychological considerations – who had entered this reproach. But for Tarde, of course, the real issue was Durkheim's social realism.

In "Les Règles," as we have seen, Durkheim had insisted that the generality of a fact in a given population was not itself a sufficient criterion for calling it a *social* fact. For in addition – as Tarde correctly paraphrased and emphasized – each social fact "consists either of a belief, or a tendency, or a practice which is that of the *group taken collectively and which is something quite different from the forms under which it is refracted in individuals."* But how, Tarde asked, could such a social fact be "refracted" before it exists? And how could it exist outside the minds of *all* individual human beings? "The truth," Tarde epitomized the difference between his own view and that of Durkheim

is that any social thing, a word in a language, a religious rite, a trade secret, an artistic process, a legal provision, a moral maxim, is transmitted and passed not from *the social group taken collectively* to the individual, but from one individual – parent, teacher, friend, neighbor, comrade – to another individual, and in this passage from one mind to another it is refracted. (1969: 115)

It is the totality of these individual refractions – not Durkheim's scholastic, ontological illusion – that constitutes social reality at any given time.

In fact, Tarde insisted, Durkheim's argument itself presupposes the operation of these laws of imitation in precisely the manner described. This becomes clear when – in the passage from "Les Règles" that immediately follows the one just cited – Durkheim "irrefutably demonstrates" the "duality of kind" between individual and social facts by pointing to their empirical dissociation:

Indeed some of these ways of acting or thinking acquire, by dint of *repetition*, a sort of consistency which, so to speak, separates them out, isolating them from the particular events which reflect them. Thus they assume a shape, a tangible form peculiar to them and constitute a reality *sui generis* vastly distinct from the individual facts which manifest that reality. Collective custom does not exist only in a state of immanence in the successive actions which it determines, but, by a privilege without example in the biological kingdom, expresses itself once and for all in a formula *repeated by word of mouth*, transmitted by education and even enshrined in the written word. (1982: 54–5)

However unconsciously and involuntarily, Tarde emphasized, Durkheim has here acknowledged the powerfully socializing nature of imitation – i.e., an action, frequently repeated, gives rise to a collective habit; the habit in turn becomes verbally articulated; and the repetition of the verbal formula leads to further communication and thus imitation.

In sum, wherever Durkheim insisted that social facts are characterized by "generality-plus-independence" (Lukes 1972: 14–15), Tarde might embrace the notion of "generality," but found the criterion of "independence" – i.e., the idea that social facts must be dissociated from their individual manifestations – incomprehensible. But even for Durkheim, "generality-plus-independence" was rarely more than a sign by which social facts might be recognized, not an essential aspect of their nature. Far more important for Durkheim were the criteria of *externality* and *constraint* – features that Tarde found "scarcely less surprising" than that of independence. If constraint were a characteristic of social facts, for example, then there would be nothing more "social" than the relationship between a victor and the vanquished, and nothing less social than the spontaneous conversion of an entire people to a new religious faith or political ideology. Thinking of social facts as external to the individual, Tarde explained, Durkheim felt that they could "enter" the individual mind only by "imposition" and coercion, a mistaken conception that would be generalized in Durkheim's "harsh and restrictive" theory of education. Tarde, by contrast, insisted that the basis of all education is the innate sociability of the child, without which all educational discipline and coercion is pointless (1969: 119).

This brought Tarde to what he considered (quite accurately) to be the primary *desiderata* of Durkheim's social realism – i.e., the notion that a combination of individual elements can produce a reality *sui generis*, greater than the sum of its parts. Tarde recognized that this notion, far from being limited to Durkheim alone, was "very widespread among cultivated minds" (1969: 120). And he was equally aware that the appeal of this idea lay in chemical and biological analogues – e.g., the combination of lifeless chemicals yielding life, of unconscious biological cells yielding individual consciousness, etc. "After this," Tarde acknowledged, "we ought not to judge it surprising *a priori* that the social meeting of different selves should bring forth [a society], which is supposedly something super-psychological, or essentially nonpsychological, and which exists independently of all individual consciousnesses" (1969: 121).

But it is precisely here, Tarde argued, that the analogy breaks down. For in the case of chemistry and biology, we are completely ignorant of what goes on in the depths of the individual element, while in psychology and sociology, we have an increasingly intimate, empirical knowledge of the individual human minds making up the whole. Moreover, on the basis of this empirical knowledge, we are able to affirm that "without the individual element the social element is nothing, and that there is nothing, absolutely nothing, in society which does not exist piecemeal in a state of continual repetition in living individuals." To Tarde, this meant that the individual minds "contain within themselves the complete explanation and the complete existence of their composite [i.e., society]" (1969: 121, 122). Where Durkheim had insisted that "the determining cause of a social fact must be sought among antecedent social facts, and not among the states of the individual consciousness," therefore, Tarde instead embraced the emphasis on collective psychology and history that he had discovered in Comte, Mill, and Spencer (Durkheim 1982: 134; Tarde 1969: 122).

There can be little doubt that Durkheim was deeply troubled by this quarrel with Tarde. As a dilettante who dabbled in literary circles, frequented the Parisian salons, opposed socialism, and favored an intellectual aristocracy, Tarde epitomized most of the things that Durkheim loathed. In 1898, having resolved to end the exchange, Durkheim would write to Xavier Léon, urging him to publish his "Représentations individuelles et représentations collectives" as soon as possible lest Tarde think that it was a reply to his most recent attack.[12] And when Tarde was appointed to the chair in modern philosophy at the Collège de France, Durkheim would again write to Léon that he regretted, "for the sake of both sociology and philosophy, both of which have an equal interest in remaining distinct, a confusion which shows that many good minds still fail to understand what each should be."[13] In particular, Tarde had struck at the heart of Durkheim's sociological enterprise – i.e., the independent reality of social facts and their irreducibility to psychological explanations. As he responded, Durkheim apparently renewed his acquaintance with the works of Rousseau – with powerful consequences for his sociological vocabulary.

THE CONDITION OF HAPPINESS

The notion that Rousseau had a significant impact on Durkheim's thought is hardly new. Robert Derathé, for example, has insisted that Durkheim "was fully aware of having been influenced by Rousseau, who was one of his favorite authors" (1950: 338). Sheldon Wolin has argued that Durkheim's sociology is "the purest restatement of Rousseau . . . the medium, so to speak, by which Rousseau has left his

---

[12] Letter undated, cited in Lukes 1972: 303–4.
[13] Letter dated February 7, 1900, cited in Lukes 1972: 304.

mark on modern social science" (1960: 372). And most recently, Mark Cladis has encouraged us to see Durkheim's work "as his effort to advance, in theory and in practice, Rousseau's vision of a harmonious pluralistic society in the context of the industrial age" (1992: 9).

The initial difficulty facing such claims, however, is that the evidence of Durkheim's early writings runs consistently in the opposite direction. In the Sens lectures, for example, we saw that Durkheim objected to Rousseau's conceptions of the social contract, altruism, socialism, ethics, and education as well. In his early review of Schaeffle's *Bau und Leben*, Durkheim was pleased to observe that "[w]e are not dealing with man as Rousseau conceived of him . . . that abstract being, born to solitude, renouncing it only very late and by a sort of voluntary sacrifice, and then only as the issue of a well-deliberated covenant. Every man is, on the contrary, born for society and in a society." Rousseau's "savage individualism," Durkheim continued, "is not part of nature. The real man – the man who is truly a man – is an integral part of a society which he loves just as he loves himself, because he cannot withdraw from it without becoming decadent." By showing that sociology has a subject matter no less real than that of the life sciences, Schaeffle had thus dealt the "final blow" to the doctrines of Hobbes and Rousseau (Durkheim 1885a: 98). Just one year later, in his review of Schaeffle's *Die Quintessenz des Sozialismus*, Durkheim criticized "the simplistic conception of Rousseau, to which the economic school adheres doggedly, and this after a century of experiences which hardly seem to have been favorable to the theory of the *Contrat social*" (1886a: 78–9). On his return from Germany, Durkheim criticized both the Manchester economists and the *Kathedersozialisten* as "unwitting disciples of Rousseau" who "see in the social bond only a superficial *rapprochement*, determined by the meeting of interests" (1887b: 37). If we wish to understand German political ideas, Durkheim added in the companion essay, "[w]e must not judge with our French ideas . . . For the German, the State is not what it is for us – a great machine destined to compromise this multitude of unsociable beings as Rousseau imagined." Unfortunately, Durkheim concluded, we "have only half-heartedly disowned the *Contrat social*" (1887a: 337–8).

Arriving in Bordeaux, Durkheim began his inaugural lecture with an attack on that idea "which radically prevented the establishment of sociology" – i.e., the notion of society "as a human creation, a product of art and reflection" (1978a: 44). According to this view,

Durkheim added, "there is nothing in the nature of man which necessarily predestined him to collective life; he himself invented it and established it. Whether it is everyone's creation, as Rousseau argues, or that of a single man, as Hobbes thinks, it derived in its entirety from our brains and from our imaginations" (1978a: 45). Is the ideal for societies, Durkheim asked of Spencer, "the ferocious individualism which Rousseau made their point of departure? Is positive politics just the *Social Contract* all over again?" (1978a: 58). "If man is essentially a whole, an individual and egoistic being," Durkheim again objected in his 1890 review of Ferneuil's *Les Principes de 1789 et la science sociale*, "if he has no other objective than the development of his moral personality (Kant) or the satisfaction of his needs with the least possible effort (Bastiat), society appears as something against nature, as a violence wreaked upon our most fundamental propensities. Rousseau avows this, or rather proclaims it" (1973b: 39).

In *De la division du travail social* (1893), Durkheim insisted that the notion of a social contract contradicts the principle of the division of labor. "The greater the importance one ascribes to the latter," Durkheim thus emphasized, "the more completely must one abandon Rousseau's postulate" (1984: 150). For such a contract requires that all individual wills should be in agreement on the foundations of social organization; in short, the content of each individual consciousness would be identical to every other. If social solidarity arises from a social contract, Durkheim concluded, then it has no connection to the division of labor. Durkheim acknowledged Rousseau's recognition that the hypothesized state of nature prior to the contract must necessarily be amoral. "Man is only a moral being because he lives in society," Durkheim agreed, "since morality consists in solidarity with the group, and varies according to that solidarity. Cause all social life to vanish, and moral life would vanish at the same time, having no object to cling to" (1984: 331–2). But *Les Règles de la méthode sociologique* (1895) simply repeated the argument that had by now become *de rigueur*. Durkheim complained:

Neither Hobbes nor Rousseau, appear to have noticed the complete contradiction that exists in admitting that the individual is himself the creator of a machine whose essential role is to exercise domination and constraint over him. Alternatively, it may have seemed to them that, in order to get rid of this contradiction, it was sufficient to conceal it from the eyes of its victims by the skilful device of the social contract. (1982: 142)

Durkheim's more positive assessment of Rousseau thus seems to have emerged later, around 1896. By this time, as we've just seen, he had become exhausted and frustrated by his debate with Tarde; and as a Dreyfusard from a relatively early date, Durkheim had also become involved in the Ligue pour la Défense des Droits de l'Homme. In 1896, at the grave of a Bordeaux colleague, Durkheim gave an outspokenly Dreyfusard eulogy that caused something of a sensation; and he went on to organize and become secretary of the Bordeaux branch of the Ligue (Lukes 1972: 347–8). When the anti-Dreyfusard Ferdinand Brunetière defended the army and the Right against the threats of Dreyfusard "anarchy" and "individualism," Durkheim responded with "Individualism and the Intellectuals" (1898), which embraced the "moral individualism" of Kant and Rousseau – "the one which the Declaration of the Rights of Man attempted, more or less happily, to formulate and which is currently taught in our schools and has become the basis of our moral catechism" (1973c: 45). As Mark Cladis has argued quite persuasively, this embracement of "moral" individualism (by contrast with its "egoistic" counterpart) enabled Durkheim to forge a "communitarian defense of liberalism" – one that respected the dignity and rights of individuals while still preserving the moral idiom of social tradition and the commitment to the common good (1992: 1–28).

So after 1896 – whether to respond to reactionary anti-Dreyfusards like Brunetière or to social psychologists like Tarde – Durkheim committed himself to a deeper reading of Rousseau. While still at Bordeaux, he taught a lecture-course on Rousseau's *Contrat social* (1762), for which – as was his custom – he wrote out his lecture notes *in extenso*.[14] Later he redrafted these for publication, promising them to Xavier Léon, editor of the *Revue de métaphysique et de morale*. To this study of the *Contrat social* he then conjoined some notes on *Emile*, from a later course on Rousseau's educational theory he had taught twice in Paris. Though "not generally realised," Durkheim explained, the two themes are "closely linked" (1979: 162). Upon his death, the executors of Durkheim's works decided to publish both the study of the *Contrat social* and the less developed

---

[14] Probably because the course on *Le Contrat social* was given in Bordeaux, Henri Peyre (1960: xv) concluded that the lectures must have been prepared before 1901. Some of the passages of *Le Contrat social* cited by Durkheim (e.g., 1960c: 82) make it clear that he was using the 1896 edition edited by Edmond Dreyfus-Brisac.

notes on *Emile* in the *Revue de métaphysique et de morale*, where they appeared in 1918 and 1919, respectively.

"The chief objective of *The Social Contract*," Durkheim began, "[is] to find a form of association, or, as Rousseau also calls it, of *civil state*, whose laws can be superimposed upon the fundamental laws inherent in the *state of nature* without doing violence to them." Implicit within this objective, of course, was Rousseau's judgment that such a form of association had not yet been found, for men had deviated from their original, natural condition, and they had done so unnecessarily. To understand Rousseau, Durkheim thus observed, we must learn what he meant by the "state of nature," and then determine how it is that we came to depart from this original, natural condition. "Only then," Durkheim summarized his problem, "shall we be in a position to examine Rousseau's reasons for believing that this deviation was not inevitable, and his remarks as to how the two [natural and civil] states, at variance in several respects, can be reconciled" (1960c: 66).

As Rousseau made clear in the *Discours sur l'origine de l'inégalité* (1755), Durkheim observed, his "state of nature" was a *psychological*, rather than *historical*, construct – i.e., it was not a condition in which human beings actually lived before societies came into being, but rather a device to help us distinguish between those things that we owe to society, and those that we owe to our psychological nature. The distinction was important to Rousseau, Durkheim emphasized, because he shared the "traditional confusion" which conceives the "natural" as coextensive with the "individual," and everything that goes beyond the individual – i.e., society – as "artificial." Our present forms of association either *follow logically* from human nature, Rousseau observed, or they *deform* it. The critical assessment of these forms, as well as the determination of what forms should replace them, must therefore begin with an analysis of man in his natural condition. And "to arrive at this natural man," Durkheim paraphrased Rousseau, "we must put aside everything within us that is a product of social existence. Otherwise, we should find ourselves in a vicious circle, for we should be justifying society on the basis of society, that is, of the ideas and feelings society has implanted in us."[15]

---

[15] Durkheim 1960c: 68. Durkheim's reference here was to the *Discours sur l'origine de l'inégalité*: "All these philosophers, in short, constantly talking of need, greed, oppression, desires, and pride have imported into the state of nature ideas they had taken from society. They talk of savage man and they depict civilized man" (Rousseau 1994: 24).

Durkheim was impressed with the extent to which this observation of Rousseau's second *Discours* was essentially methodological, and also with how much it owed to Descartes:

Both [Descartes and Rousseau] hold that the first operation of science should be a kind of intellectual purge that will clear the mind of all mediate judgments that have not been demonstrated scientifically and lay bare the axioms from which all other propositions should be derived. Both set out to remove the rubble and uncover the solid rock on which the entire structure of knowledge should rest; in the one case theoretical knowledge, in the other practical knowledge.

It was in this sense that Durkheim denied that Rousseau's notion of the state of nature was in any sense *romantic* – e.g., that it was "a figment of sentimental reverie," or "a philosophical restoration of the ancient belief in the golden age" (1960c: 69). On the contrary, Rousseau's observation of lower animals, combined with the theory of Condillac, convinced Rousseau that even the simplest forms of abstract knowledge presuppose language, while language itself presupposes social life (1994: 33). So, as Durkheim himself would later insist in his essay on "La Détermination du fait moral" (1906), Rousseau's conception of man in the state of nature was that of a being "reduced to sensation and hardly different from an animal" (Durkheim 1974b: 55; Rousseau 1994: 34).

This dismissal of any romantic interpretation of Rousseau was important, because it allowed Durkheim to focus on what he considered the most essential aspect of Rousseau's notion of the state of nature. Precisely because Rousseau's natural man was reduced exclusively to sensations, Durkheim observed, he could desire only those things found in his immediate physical environment; and thus his desires would necessarily be purely physical and extremely simple, resulting in "a perfect balance between his needs and the resources at his disposal" (1960c: 70; Rousseau 1994: 35). Under these circumstances, Durkheim emphasized, "man is in harmony with his environment because he is a purely physical being, dependent on his physical environment and nothing else. The nature within him necessarily corresponds to the nature without" (1960c: 71).

To Durkheim, this explained Rousseau's famous rejection of the equally famous argument of Hobbes, in *Leviathan* (1651), that the state of nature was a state of war (Hobbes 1958: 107). First, in a condition where needs were exactly proportionate to the resources necessary to satisfy them, the incentive to war – i.e., unsatisfied needs – was lacking. And second, *pace* Hobbes, Rousseau was persuaded that the primitive, unreflective form of identification that led to the feeling of pity was present in animals, and therefore also in natural man (1960c: 71–2; Rousseau 1994: 45–6). Durkheim admitted that, in the *Essai sur l'origine des langues* (1781), Rousseau seemed to contradict this second argument, leading some scholars to argue that his later work moved more in the direction of Hobbes and his theory of the state of war (Rousseau 1966: 32). But Durkheim resisted this interpretation, arguing that the later passage simply referred to the reflection necessary before the natural sentiment of pity – initially limited to that small circle of individuals with whom the natural man had relations – could be extended to all mankind. At most, therefore, the *Essai* was "a clarification and partial correction of the idea developed in the second *Discours*."[16] But if Rousseau thus denied Hobbes' equivalence of the state of nature with the state of war, neither did he suggest that natural man lived in "societies" properly so-called. Instinct and sensation sufficed for all his needs, and lacking imagination, he could not conceive of any benefits society might afford. Nor did he possess language, without which social relationships would be impossible. Natural man was thus not unsocial, but asocial; and similarly, he was not immoral, but amoral. "Thanks to a very wise providence," Rousseau observed, "his potential faculties developed only with the opportunities to use them, so that they were neither superfluous nor prematurely onerous, nor belated and unavailing when they were needed. In instinct alone man had everything he needed to live in the state of nature, and in cultivated reason, he has everything he needs to live in society" (1960c: 74–5; Rousseau 1994: 44, 43).

At this point in the lecture Durkheim appended a note, reminding himself to read the entire passage to his audience: "Very important," the note said, "for it shows that [for Rousseau] social existence is not a diabolical machination but was willed providentially, and that although primitive nature did not necessarily lead to it, it nevertheless contained potentially what would make social existence possible when it became necessary" (1960c: 75). In one sense, the note emphasized again how critical Durkheim could be of romantic interpretations of the second *Discours* as a story of man's Fall, under

---

[16] Durkheim 1960c: 72–3. This scholarly quibble reveals how well Durkheim knew Rousseau's entire *oeuvre*, as well as its secondary interpretations.

the influence of a corrupt society, from some primitive state of grace; and in another sense, it indicated the peculiar attraction that Rousseau's natural man held for Durkheim – i.e., a human nature that contained "potentially" the things that would make society possible (when external conditions called for this particular kind of association), but not so constituted that it would lead, unconditionally and "necessarily," to societal life. The proper element of contingency thus established, Durkheim turned to Rousseau's explanation of those factors that gave rise to social life.

Societies can come into existence, Durkheim observed, only if man is prevented from remaining in the state of nature. Since the only environment that affects natural man is the *physical* environment, this is where we must look for the external cause. In the *Essai sur l'origine des langues*, Rousseau thus asked us to imagine a physical environment in which all human needs were always satisfied: "I cannot see," Rousseau added, "how they would ever have surrendered their primitive freedom and given up their isolated existence, so appropriate to their natural indolence" (1960c: 77; Rousseau 1966: 38). By contrast, the obstacles human beings actually encountered in nature began to stimulate their faculties. Intelligence evolved beyond instinct and sensation. New, more complex needs developed, upsetting the primitive balance between desires and resources, and people began to realize the advantage of cooperation in their efforts to satisfy these new needs.

This first extension of physical needs thus gave rise to the tendency to form groups; and groups, once formed, aroused social inclinations, the need for civility, the duty of respecting contractual obligations, and even an embryonic ethics. Having emerged from their "embryonic indolence," their minds sharpened by frequent relations, human beings developed agriculture and its derivative arts, giving rise to the first division of labor, the partitioning of land, and the recognition of private property. This possibility of new economic rewards again stimulated new desires, and these desires in turn gave rise to competition and economic inequality. Initially the consequence of differences of circumstance, these differences among people became increasingly permanent in their effects, leading to classes of rich and poor, the weak and the powerful. *Pace* Hobbes, the state of war was not the origin of society, but rather its effect. Finally, in terms Marx would later appreciate, Rousseau described "the most astute project that has ever occurred to the human mind" – i.e., faced with this state of war, the rich proposed to their fellows that they establish rules of peace and justice to which everyone would conform, and a supreme power to protect and defend all the members of the association – the origin of all laws and governments.[17]

The resulting civil state, as Durkheim had observed as early as 1886, was not itself "natural," but rather "artificial" (1886a: 78–9). But Durkheim would never again describe Rousseau's notion as "simplistic." On the contrary, however *artificial*, the society had *emerged naturally* from the state of nature. "Although the formula seems self-contradictory," Durkheim admitted, "it expresses Rousseau's thinking. Let us try to understand it" (1960c: 81). In fact, Rousseau's civil state is artificial in at least two senses. First, as we have already seen, human beings are not constituted in such a way that they are constrained to enter social life. On the contrary, each individual is self-sufficient in the state of nature. "[T]he social virtues could never have developed unaided," but instead "required the fortuitous aid of several foreign causes which might never have arisen, and without which man would have remained eternally in his primitive state" (1960c: 81; Rousseau 1994: 53). Society comes into existence because men see that their needs will be more easily satisfied through interdependence; but interdependence itself is not rooted in human nature.

Second, though *necessary*, this interdependence is not itself *sufficient* to produce social life. To this original base, Durkheim argued, itself a product of human art, must be added something else that has the same origin. Specifically, this interdependence must be "regulated and organized in a definite way." For according to Rousseau, a society is

a moral entity having specific qualities distinct from those of the individual beings which compose it, somewhat as chemical compounds have properties that they owe to none of their elements. If the aggregation resulting from these vague relationships really formed a social body, there would be a kind of common sensorium that would outlive the correspondence of all the parts. Public good and evil would not be merely the sum of individual good and evil, as in a simple aggregation, but would lie in the relation that unites them. It would be greater than that sum, and public well-being

---

[17] Durkheim 1960c: 78–9. Durkheim's account roughly corresponds to Rousseau 1994: 55–69; 1966: 31–46.

would not be the result of the happiness of individuals, but rather its source. (1896: 248–9; transl. Durkheim 1960c: 82)

So the mere fact that men "realize that they can help each other and have fallen into the habit of doing so, even when added to the feeling that they all have something in common, that they all belong to the human race," Durkheim paraphrased Rousseau, "does not form them into a new kind of corporate body with its own specific character and composition, that is, a society" (1960c: 82).

It is difficult to exaggerate the significance of this idea to Durkheim's social realism. "This remarkable passage," Durkheim emphasized to his audience, "proves that Rousseau was keenly aware of the specificity of the social order. He conceived it clearly as an order of facts generically different from purely individual facts. It is a new world superimposed on the purely psychological world." Such a conception was, to Durkheim, "far superior even to that of such recent theorists as Spencer, who think they have grounded society in nature when they have pointed out that man has a vague sympathy for his fellow men, and that it is to his interest to exchange services with them" (1960c: 83). Vague sympathies and private interests may make for intermittent contacts and superficial relationships between individuals, but they lack what Rousseau called the "connection between the parts" that "constitutes the whole." In short, Rousseau believed that society was a "live, organized body," distinct from and greater than the sum of its parts.[18]

But again, this is not to say that society is *natural*. On the contrary, for Rousseau, only *the individual* is real and natural, so society must be the product of human reason. "The difference between human art and the work of nature," Rousseau observed, "can be felt in their effects. It is all very well for the citizens to call themselves the limbs of the state; they cannot unite as real limbs unite with the body. It is impossible to prevent each one from having an individual and separate existence and attending to his own needs."[19] Even the family, which Rousseau famously described in *Le Contrat social* as "[t]he oldest of all societies, and the only natural one," is a *natural*

---

[18] Here Durkheim was referring to Rousseau's *Discours sur l'Economie politique* (1758).

[19] Durkheim 1960c: 83–4. Durkheim notes that Rousseau was unaware that there *are* natural organisms whose parts have this same individuality. The reference here is to "a fragment from *Distinction fondamentale*" (pp. 308, 310). I've been unable to identify any work written by Rousseau that possesses this title.

group only so long as the children are attached to their parents by the need for self-preservation. As soon as the child is able to look after himself, Rousseau had observed, "the natural bond is dissolved" (1968: 50). For Rousseau, in short, "every society is an artificial entity" (1960c: 84). But what particularly fascinated Durkheim in *Le Contrat social* was its intermingling of two ideas – i.e., the notion of society as the product of *reason*, and that of society as an *organism* – ideas that we normally consider not only distinct but contradictory. Moreover, in Rousseau, each idea seems to imply the other – e.g., it is *because* society is an organism that it must be a work of art, for nature contains only individuals, and society is clearly superior to the individual.

For Durkheim, the logical step was obvious – i.e., simply acknowledge that there *is* something (society) both "real" and "natural," above and outside of the individual. But "[e]very attempt to widen the circle of natural phenomena," Durkheim admitted, "requires a great effort, and the mind resorts to all kinds of subterfuges and evasions before resigning itself to so grave a change in its system of ideas." But by this time Durkheim had already come to prefer Rousseau's "subterfuges and evasions" to those of Spencer, who "regards society as a product of nature, a living thing like other living things," but "strips it of its specific character by reducing it to a mechanical juxtaposition of individuals." If nothing else, Durkheim observed, Rousseau tried to resolve the problem without abandoning either of the two principles in question – i.e., the *individualist* principle (which underlies Rousseau's theory of the state of nature as well as Spencer's theory of natural law), and the *socialist* principle which underlies Rousseau's organic conception of society (1960c: 85).

Still, for Rousseau, society is not natural thing. Does this mean that society represents the *corruption* of human nature, an evil consequence of mankind's fall and degeneration? To understand Rousseau here, Durkheim insists, we must make a distinction. Society as we find it *today* is, indeed, "a monstrosity that came into being and continues to exist only through a conjunction of accidental and regrettable circumstances" (1960c: 86). As Rousseau had shown in the second *Discours*, those *natural* inequalities which derive from differences of age, health, physical strength, mental and spiritual qualities, etc., have been replaced by *artificial* inequalities – e.g., of wealth, privilege, status, power, etc. – that are contrary to the state of nature. These artificial inequalities initially result from inheritance; but then, stimulated by social evolution, they become stable and legitimate through the establishment of property and law (Rousseau 1994: 84–5). This first violation of the law of nature then leads to a second, which Rousseau described more fully in *Le Contrat social* and *Emile*. Briefly, in the state of nature the individual is self-sufficient, depending only on the impersonal and invariable forces of the physical environment. But as society evolves this *natural* independence is replaced by an *artificial*, servile interdependence, a society comprised of masters and slaves, in which the first are still more enslaved than the second. So, for Rousseau, there are two kinds of dependence – the dependence on *things*, which is a phenomenon of *nature*, and the dependence on *other human beings*, which is a phenomenon of *society*. The dependence on *things* – i.e., necessary, stable, impersonal, etc. – is not an obstacle to freedom; for in nature, our needs are in harmony with our means. We do whatever we desire, because we desire only what is possible. But the dependence on *other human beings* – willful, unstable, avaricious, deceitful, etc. – produces the mutual corruption and depravity of master and slave (1960c: 87–8).

It is here that Durkheim confronted the passage in *Emile* that must surely have stopped him cold: "If there is any means of remedying this ill in society," Rousseau continued

it is to substitute law for man and to arm the general will with a real strength superior to the action of every particular will. If the laws of nations could, like those of nature, have an inflexibility that no human force could ever conquer, dependence on men would then become dependence on things again; in the republic all of the advantages of the natural state would be united with those of the civil state, and freedom which keeps man exempt from vices would be joined to morality which raises him to virtue. (1979: 85)

In effect, this passage opened the door to the second half of Durkheim's distinction. If the civil state *as it is now* violates the law of nature, must the same be true of *every* civil state? Are human nature and society *inherently* antithetical? Or might they – by the means suggested by Rousseau – be reconciled?

In the second *Discours*, Rousseau made it clear that the present defects of the civil state are not necessary. In fact, what distinguishes us from animals is precisely that, with the help of circumstances, we can perfect ourselves – a concern not unlike that found in the Sens lectures (1994: 33–4). In his lectures on *Le Contrat social*, Durkheim acknowledged that this perfectibility remains dormant in the natural man until it is awakened by circumstances; but still, it is there from the start, and since it exists in nature, the events that result from it cannot be regarded as contrary to nature. And as we have already seen, reason – which is to the social environment what instinct is to the physical environment – was awakened in man by Providence. So society, Durkheim repeated, "is not contrary to the providential order" (1960c: 90, 75; Rousseau 1994: 43). In short, Durkheim rejected all interpretations of Rousseau as a radical pessimist. Society *can* be organized in manner consistent with human nature, and the purpose of *Le Contrat social* was to show us how.

As we've seen, man is unable to remain in the state of nature because of external forces that are not themselves natural. To return man to his natural state, therefore, a system of *counterforces* must thus be established; and since these forces are not given in the state of nature, they must be provided by man. But men cannot create new forces; they can only unite and direct those that already exist. Human beings thus have no other means of preserving themselves than to form, by aggregation, a sum of already existing forces great enough to overcome the resistance. "These they have to bring into play by means of a single motive power," Rousseau observed, "and cause them to act in concert." In short, "once the state of nature has become impossible, a constituted society is the only environment in which man can live" (1960c: 92; Rousseau 1968: 59–60). The problem is to organize this *new* social life in such a way that no violence is done to the law of nature. But in *Emile* Rousseau made it clear that man's original condition cannot remain unchanged (1979: 39). Paradoxically, the characteristic features of the state of nature must be transformed and yet simultaneously maintained, assume a new form without ceasing to be what they are. "This they can do," Durkheim observed, "only if social man, though differing profoundly from natural man, maintains the same relation to society as natural man to physical nature" (1960c: 93).

How is this possible? Rousseau's solution, Durkheim observed, is ingenious. In modern society, as we've seen, natural equality has been replaced by an artificial inequality, and dependence on the impersonal forces of nature by the arbitrary, willful relations of master and slave. "If instead of being appropriated by individuals and personalized," Durkheim paraphrases Rousseau, the new force born of the combination of individuals into societies were impersonal and if, in consequence, it transcended all individuals, men would all be equal in regard to it, since none would be in personal command of it. Thus they would depend, not upon each other, but upon a force which by its impersonality would be identical, *mutatis mutandis*, with the forces of nature. The social environment would affect social man in the same way as the natural environment affects natural man. (1960c: 94; see Rousseau 1979: 85)

Our dependence, in short, would once again be a dependence on *things*. So it is not enough, Durkheim emphasized, that this new force should simply be *superior* to all individuals. It must also be *based on nature* – i.e., "its superiority must not be fictitious but rationally justifiable. Otherwise, it will be precarious and so will its effects. The resulting order will be unstable, lacking the invariability and necessity characteristic of the natural order. It will be unable to endure except by a combination of accidents that may cease to exist at any moment" (1960c: 94–5). So while Rousseau places society outside the realm of nature, it's not difficult to see why Durkheim considered him a powerful ally for social realism. Although Rousseau's society is the "artificial" work of human beings, it is created *rationally* out of natural *things* – i.e., in accordance with their nature, and thus without doing violence to them. In this way – and only in this way – the *social* environment becomes a new form of the *primitive* environment (1960c: 95–6).

This argument turns heavily on Rousseau's distinction between an *aggregation* and an *association*. We have already noted that Durkheim placed special emphasis on Rousseau's insistence that social life presupposes not only "interdependence," but interdependence that is "regulated and organized in a definite way" (1960c: 82). In Rousseau's critique of Grotius, the significance of this distinction becomes clear. In *De Jure Belli ac Pacis* (*On the Law of War and Peace*) (1620–5), Grotius had attempted to provide a rational justification for the right of the strongest, arguing, for example, that if an individual may alienate his freedom, a people might do the same, and that the right of war implies the right of slavery.[20] In a justifiably famous passage, Rousseau denied that this right could be justified rationally; but even if it could – and this was the more important

---

[20] Hugo Grotius (Huig de Groot) (1583–1645), Dutch jurist, philosopher and man of letters. Rousseau's treatment of Grotius is found in book I, chapter 4 of *The Social Contract* (1968: 53–8).

point for Durkheim – this would still be insufficient to establish
social life. For a *society*, Durkheim paraphrased Rousseau, "is an
organized body in which each part is dependent upon the whole,
and vice versa. There is no such interdependence in the case of a
mob subject to a chief" (1960c: 97–8; Rousseau, 1968: 58). Grotius
argued that "a people may give itself to a king." Rousseau answered
that, "before considering the act by which a people submits to a
king, we ought to scrutinize the act by which a people become *a*
people, for that act, being necessarily antecedent to the other, is the
real foundation of society" (1968: 59).

Such an act clearly implies an *association*, Durkheim emphasized,
not simply an *aggregation*. Rousseau's problem was thus to find the
particular *form* of association which would "defend and protect with
the whole common force the person and goods of each associate,
and in which each, while uniting with all, may still obey himself
alone, and remain as free as before" (1960c: 98; Rousseau 1968: 60).
This was the problem to which Rousseau's social contract – the
immersion of each individual will into a common, general will – was
the solution. And for Durkheim, the most important aspect of this
general will was that it had "the impersonal character of natural
forces," so that we are "no less free for submitting to it. Not only do
we not enslave ourselves by obeying it, but, what is more, it alone
can protect us against actual servitude, for if, to make this will
possible, we must forgo subjugating others, others must make the
same concession. Such is the nature of the equivalence and compensation that re-establish the balance of *things*" (1960c: 99; emphasis
added).

Durkheim's understanding of the advantages of this kind of self-
alienation had changed dramatically since the Sens lectures, when
he argued that the compensation proffered by Rousseau – i.e., the
rewards one derives from an association of which one is also a
member – remains "*évidemment immorale*" from the standpoint of the
individual personality (1884: 465). Durkheim still disagreed with the
author of his textbook: "If there is compensation for the alienation
of my person, it is not, as Paul Janet has said, because I receive in
exchange the personality of others." But when I alienate myself,
Durkheim now agreed with Rousseau, it is "the body politic as a
corporate body *sui generis*, and not the individuals" which receives
me; and what I receive in return is "the assurance that [I] shall be
protected by the full force of the social organism against the

individual encroachments of others" (1960c: 100). Durkheim was equally emphatic that the advantages of this exchange are not derived from the greater *material* force that results from the association of individual wills, but rather from its general, impersonal *moral* force: "The general will must be respected," Durkheim insisted, "not because it is stronger but because it is general. If there is to be justice among individuals, there must be something outside them, a being *sui generis*, which acts as arbiter and determines the law. This something is society, which owes its moral supremacy, not to its physical supremacy, but to its nature, which is superior to that of individuals" (1960c: 103).

What is this "collective will"? In one sense, Durkheim answers, it is the sum of all particular, individual wills. But it is also more than this – i.e., the "object" to which it is applied must be as "general" as the source from which it comes. In other words, the general will is the consequence of the deliberation concerning the nation itself – i.e., the "common interest" (1960c: 105; see Rousseau 1968: 72–8). What, then, is the "common interest"? Durkheim points out that the phrase is often taken to refer to the interest of the society as a whole, by contrast with the interests of particular citizens. But this, Durkheim emphasizes, is clearly *not* what Rousseau has in mind. For Rousseau believes that "anything that is useful to all is useful to each." The common interest is thus the interest of "all individuals in so far as they desire what is most appropriate, not to this or that particular person, but . . . to each citizen." Thus the common interest exists as soon as "all continually will the happiness of each one." This is a condition, Durkheim observed, that is more egoistic than altruistic, for "there is not a man who does not think of 'each' as meaning him, and consider himself in voting for all . . . This proves that equality of rights and the idea of justice which such equality creates originate in the preference each man gives to himself, and accordingly in the very nature of man" (1960c: 106; Rousseau 1968: 63). This explains why the general will is best expressed when each individual exercises his share of sovereignty separately from the others – without actual deliberations or the formation of intermediate groups – so that the differences among individuals cancel each other out, leaving the general will as the arithmetical mean of all individual wills.

Reflecting on Rousseau's theory of the general will, Durkheim was disposed to emphasize four things. First, Durkheim reminded his audience, "we discern the horror of all particularism, the unitary conception of society, that was one of the characteristics of the French Revolution" (1960c: 107–8; see, for example, Rousseau 1968: 73). Second, we also "encounter at every turn" the two, antithetical conceptions in Rousseau's social theory – i.e., the idea of society as a "mere instrument" for the use of the individual, and the notion of the individual as dependent on a social reality that "far transcends" the multitude of individuals (1960c: 108). Third, and most important, we see again that the authority of the general will lies in its moral rather than material force. "If the community must be obeyed," Durkheim emphasized, "it is not because it commands, but because it commands the common good" (1960c: 109). The common interest does not exist by virtue of laws or decrees, but rather lies outside of and transcends them; indeed, law is what it ought to be only if it expresses the common interest. Ultimately, the general will lies in the collective unconscious of society, in its habits, customs, and traditions, and in "a persistent disposition" of individuals towards its object – i.e., the common interest.[21]

Finally, referring to Rousseau's argument that the sovereignty established by the social contract must be indivisible, Durkheim noted that the unity ascribed to it could therefore not be "organic" – i.e., could not be constituted by a system of diverse, interdependent forces. Rousseau's frequent comparisons of society to "a living body," therefore, do not imply that society is a whole made up of distinct parts, working together precisely because they are distinct. On the contrary, his view is that each is "animated by a single, indivisible soul which moves all the parts in the same direction by depriving them, to the same degree, of all independent movement." This comparison, Durkheim insisted, "is based on a vitalist and substantialist conception of life and society. The animal body and the social body are both actuated by a vital force whose synergic action produces the cooperation of the parts." In sharp contrast to the argument presented by Durkheim in *De la division du travail social* (1893), Rousseau described the division of labor as "a secondary, derivative phenomenon that does not create the unity of the individual or collective organism, but rather presupposes it." Once

---

[21] Durkheim 1960c: 109–10. Here the English translation of Durkheim's text refers to *Le Contrat social*, book II, chapter 2. This is clearly a mistake. The argument is actually developed in book II, chapter 12 (1968: 98–100). See also book I, chapter 5 (1968: 58).

constituted, the sovereign generates various "organs," which are emanations of itself, entrusted with implementing the general will. In short, Durkheim concluded, "social solidarity results from the laws that attach the individuals to the group and not to each other. They are linked to each other only because they are linked to the community, that is, alienated within it. Rousseau's equalitarian individualism did not allow him to take another point of view" (1960c: 112).

Durkheim's final lecture thus stressed the "perfect continuity" between the second *Discours* and *Le Contrat social*:

The *state of nature*, as described in the former, is a kind of peaceful anarchy in which individuals, independent of each other and without ties between them, depend only upon the abstract force of nature. In the *civil* state, as viewed by Rousseau, the situation is the same, though in a different form. The individuals are unconnected with each other; there is a minimum of personal relation between them, but they are dependent upon a new force, which is superimposed on the natural forces but has the same generality and necessity, namely, the *general will*. In the state of nature, man submits voluntarily to the natural forces and spontaneously takes the direction they impose because he feels instinctively that this is to his advantage and that there is nothing better for him to do. His action coincides with his will. In the civil state, he submits just as freely to the general will because it is of his own making and because in obeying it he is obeying himself. (1960c: 135)

From Hobbes to Montesquieu to Rousseau, Durkheim summarized for his audience, "we observe an increasing effort to root the social being in nature. But therein," he added, "lies the weakness of [Rousseau's] system." Durkheim emphasized again that, for Rousseau, society is not contrary to the social order; but still, "it has so little in common with nature that one wonders how it is possible . . . So unstable is [society's] foundation in the nature of things," Durkheim concluded, "that it cannot but appear to us as a tottering structure whose delicate balance can be established and maintained only by an almost miraculous conjunction of circumstances" (1960c: 137–8).

Durkheim's lecture-course on Rousseau*'s* educational theory was given on two occasions after he settled in Paris in 1902. As noted in chapter 2 (esp. pp. 45–111), education was a life-long interest and concern of Durkheim's and, as his note to Xavier Léon indicates, he considered the themes of *Le Contrat social* and *Emile* to be "closely linked."[22] In *Le Contrat social*, for example, Rousseau's goal had been to conceive a civil state that would suit man "in general" – i.e., a plan based on the essential elements of human nature, regardless of its particular circumstances. Similarly, *Emile* "does not enquire which form of education is appropriate to a particular country or epoch," Durkheim observed, for "[t]hese are *chance conditions* which have no bearing on the fundamental nature of things and should be disregarded" (1979: 164). Neither did Rousseau ask what kind of education is most appropriate for a specific occupation: "It matters little to me," he said, "whether my pupil is intended for the army, the church or the law. Before his parents chose a calling for him nature called him to be a man. Life is the trade I would teach him."[23] Again and again, Durkheim observed, "the need is to set aside the accidental, the variable and to get at the essential, the rock upon which human reality rests" (1979: 166).

In addition to this preference for the general rather than the particular, Durkheim emphasized Rousseau's insistence on the natural goodness of the child and the adult's propensity for evil: "God makes all things good," Rousseau observed, "man meddles with them and they become evil" (1911: 5; Durkheim 1979: 166). But Rousseau is not telling us to be less meddlesome, to adopt a *laisser faire* policy with regard to the child's education. For, by nature, the child is also weak and, in particular, lacks the "harmony between desires and strength" which Rousseau had discussed in the second *Discours*. Left in his natural, independent condition, the child would develop such a harmony, learning from *things*; but this alone would not prepare the child to live in society, to become a citizen. "Good social institutions," Durkheim thus quoted Rousseau, "are those best fitted to make a man unnatural, to exchange his independence for dependence, to merge the unit in the group, so that he no longer regards himself as one, but as a part of the whole, and is only conscious of the common life" (1911: 7; Durkheim 1979: 167). In short, education must "transform" or "denature" the natural child.

How is the educator to do this? "The mere limitation of our desires is not enough," Rousseau observed, "for if [our desires] were

---

[22] Durkheim 1979: 162. Unfortunately, the text of the lecture-notes on *Emile* is not nearly so complete and polished as that on *Le Contrat social*. It is rather an outline of each of the four lectures, combined with passages taken from *Emile* itself.

[23] Rousseau 1911: 9. For convenience I have used the 1911 translation by Barbara Foxley, which is the same used in the 1979 edition of Durkheim's lectures on *Emile*.

less than our powers, part of our faculties would be idle, and we should not enjoy our whole being; neither is the mere extension of our powers enough, *for if our desires were also increased* we should only be the more miserable" (1911: 44; Durkheim 1979: 167–8). Instead, happiness is to be found in *decreasing the difference* between our desires and our powers, thus establishing a perfect equilibrium between the power and the will. Only then, Rousseau added, "when all its forces are employed, will the soul be at rest and man will find himself in his true position." This is the condition in which nature – "who does everything for the best" – has placed the child from the start: "It is only in this primitive condition," Rousseau observed, "that we find the equilibrium between desire and power, and then alone man is not unhappy" (1911: 44; Durkheim 1979: 168). So we should educate the child in accordance with his nature. In short, education is to become scientific by basing itself on the objective study of a given reality, thus providing itself with a guarantee against subjective impressions. Before Rousseau, educational theory had conveyed only feelings, aspirations, reasons masquerading as arguments. "*Nothing to study*," Durkheim emphasized, but in *Emile*, "the idea is put forward that *to be normal, education must reproduce a given model in reality.* Not a construct, since there is something to find out, Refer to the given fact, placed beyond the realm of fantasy. Incipient science," Durkheim applauded Rousseau, is "[s]trongly *a priori*. Yet, in principle, an objective standard" (1979: 170).

Studied in this way, nature teaches us that there a certain number of basic needs – e.g., the animal's need to breathe, to move about, to exercise, etc. – that can be satisfied simply by allowing these needs to develop freely. Eventually, however, nature imposes limits, and the animal confronts "the yoke of necessity, under which every finite being must bow" (Rousseau 1911: 55; Durkheim 1979: 171). Repeated, this confrontation leads to adaptation, that "harmony between needs and means, powers and desires," that is "the true strength, the true power, the condition of true happiness." Such harmony, however, assumes that the animal "should not continue to develop endlessly and that he should stop or be stopped. The idea of a limit, of an impassable limit." This kind of harmony or equilibrium is achieved naturally in animals, and everywhere throughout the natural world, which suggests that it is a part of our destiny. But among human beings, it is far more difficult to achieve, because we possess "superfluous, potential powers" and, in particular, imagination. "*The world of reality has its bounds*," Durkheim wrote in his lecture notes, "*the world of imagination is boundless*" (1979: 172; Rousseau 1911: 45). Imagination expands our bounds of possibility, Rousseau observed,

and therefore stimulates and feeds our desires by the hope of satisfying them. But the object which seemed within our grasp flies quicker than we can follow; when we think we have grasped it, it transforms itself and is again far ahead of us . . . Thus we exhaust our strength, yet never reach our goal, and the nearer we are to pleasure, the further we are from happiness. (1911: 44; Durkheim 1979: 173)

"There is no longer anything which can satisfy us," Durkheim agreed. "We can only invent. But then, whatever we do, we are limited. The world does not yield to us. Hence a feeling of pained surprise" (1979: 173).

Durkheim recognized that here he was dealing with a notion of freedom very different from the liberal, individualistic conception advanced in Mill's *On Liberty* (1859). On the contrary, as he stressed in his notes, "*we are dealing . . . with a completely different sort of freedom. Freedom which is contained, which is limited. The notion of limitation is essential to it. Strict discipline.*" And Durkheim's notes also suggest that he grasped the fundamental principle that underlay this notion of freedom: "*The basis of this idea,*" he stressed to his audience, is less a rational idea than an obscure feeling: the feeling that "[w]hat is necessary has a reason. That which has a reason cannot be bad. Even the necessity of death . . . Obscure and scarcely rational feeling of the rightness of what is necessary" (1979: 174; see Rousseau 1911: 131, 133). So nature teaches that happiness is possible only through the recognition and acceptance of what is necessary. For education, this meant that we should not command the child to obey, for a command is an expression of will and, as such, is arbitrary and contingent. In addition, a command is typically based upon opinion, which "does not express things as they are. It denatures them. It is an artificial thing." And least of all should we moralize, for "morality is discerned by reason, and the child has no reason" (1979: 175). The child "must never act from obedience," Rousseau observes, "but from necessity. The very words obey and command will be excluded from his vocabulary, still more so those of duty and obligation; but the words strength, necessity, weakness, and constraint must have a large place in it" (1911: 53; Durkheim 1979: 177).

Where, Durkheim then asks, are we to find the power to stop and restrain the child? Rousseau's answer could hardly be more clear: in *things*. Durkheim's notes emphasize here that things *"act from necessity; impersonally*. Do not obey any individual will. Thus it is *from them alone that this early education must emanate. The power of things"* (1979: 178). Early in his life, Rousseau insisted, the child should "find upon his proud neck, the heavy yoke which nature has imposed upon us, the heavy yoke of necessity, under which every finite being must bow. *Let him find this necessity in things, not in the caprices of man; let the curb be force, not authority"* (1911: 55; Durkheim 1979: 178). Authority is thus excluded only from the child's *early* education, Durkheim observes, for it will play a large part in later life; but when it does, "it will have to be modelled on the action of things, that is to say on physical necessity. Necessity [is] the prototype of obligation" (1979: 179).

At this point in his lecture, Durkheim compared Rousseau with Spencer, noting that both reject artificial punishment in favor of the child's learning through the natural consequences of his actions. But Spencer's more utilitarian position looked to self-interest as the criterion for the judgment of these consequences, and rejected all notions of constraint or discipline. In Rousseau, by contrast, an active sentiment of self-discipline and impersonal necessity was always present. Rousseau was thus more appropriately compared to Kant – on whom he was a great influence – and Rousseau's "impersonal things" with Kant's notion of the imperative, rational moral law (1979: 179). The child must thus live surrounded by *things*, Durkheim continued, and this is consistent with his nature. "Act in such a way," Durkheim quoted Rousseau, "that while he only notices external objects his ideas are confined to sensations; let him only see the physical world around him" (1911: 53; Durkheim 1979: 179). But this is not to say that the child should have no master. The teacher is to exert no *direct* action, but exercises considerable power by acting *indirectly*, behind and through things. "The limits of the possible and the impossible are alike unknown to [the child]," Rousseau explained, "so they can be extended or contracted around him at your will. Without a murmur, he is restrained, urged on, held back, by the hands of necessity alone; he is made adaptable and teachable by the mere force of things, without any chance for vice to spring up in him" (1911: 56; Durkheim 1979: 180). Let the child "always think he is master while you are really master," Rousseau adds, for "[t]here is no subjection so complete as that which preserves the forms of freedom; it is thus that the will itself is taken captive" (1911: 84; Durkheim 1979: 180).

This is what Rousseau meant, Durkheim explained to his students, when he said that early education should be entirely *negative* – i.e., it should exclude the teacher from doing anything, except indirectly – and thus it should contain no *positive* moral content, opinion, or information. "Before the age of reason," Rousseau emphasizes, "it is impossible to form any idea of moral being or social relations; so avoid, as far as may be, the use of words which express these ideas, lest the child at an early age should attach wrong ideas to him, ideas which you cannot or will not destroy when he is older" (1911: 53; Durkheim 1979: 186). This early, "negative" education by things, however, lays the foundation for later, moral education. For it is from such a negative education that the "sentiment of absolute necessity" derives. In later education, of course, this sentiment will be modified, and take on a new form; but it must first exist if it is to later be transformed. The action of things, as Durkheim made clear in an earlier draft of the lecture, "has a positive effect. It pre-forms. It constitutes the principal part of education. Why? Because man in the natural state is the basis of moral and social man, and because everything depends on the foundations. The one is modelled on the other."[24] This, Durkheim insisted, "is the source of our sense of the real" (1979: 188). Rousseau recognized, of course, that things are instructive because they are "striking," "simply and forcefully perceived," provide a means of "avoiding abstraction," are "useful and complementary," and so on. But Rousseau also understood that they are instructive for "a deeper reason" – i.e., it is "only from them that moral action can come." For the will is capricious, and leads to immorality, while moral law is "a wall of brass which stops man." The natural education of the child leads to the "feeling of necessity, of the *resistance of things*" which, superior to the will, prepare the child for later moral life. Here again we see the principle so important in both *L'Evolution pédagogique* and *L'Education morale* – i.e., that the study of science (including social science) is morally edifying (see Durkheim 1977: 213–15).

---

[24] Durkheim 1979: 185. Durkheim emphasized elsewhere in his notes: "*Social man in the image of natural man*" (1979: 182).

SOCIAL REALISM AS SECULAR THEODICY

The notes of Durkheim's lectures on both *Le Contrat social* and *Emile* thus bear eloquent testimony to the depth and extent of his interest in Rousseau's work. Recalling Durkheim's often hostile treatment of Rousseau as late as *Les Règles de la méthode sociologique* (1895), however, one is led to ask at what point Rousseau's ideas began to be assimilated into Durkheim's own theoretical works. From the notes of the lecture-course on *Le Contrat social* – given twice before Durkheim left Bordeaux for Paris in 1902 – we know that Durkheim relied heavily on the 1896 edition produced by Edmond Dreyfus-Brisac, then editor-in-chief of the *Revue international de l'enseignement*. This suggests that the first place to look is *Le Suicide* (1897), where Durkheim took up in "a concrete and specific form" those methodological problems already examined in *Les Règles*. Among these was the principle that social facts must be studied *as things* – i.e., as realities external to the individual. There is no principle for which we have received more criticism, Durkheim admitted, "but none is more fundamental" (1951: 37–8). For sociology to be possible, "it must above all have an object all its own. It must take cognizance of a reality which is not in the domain of other sciences. But if no reality exists outside of individual consciousness," he added, "it wholly lacks any material of its own. In that case, the only possible subject of observation is the mental states of the individual, since nothing else exists. That, however, is the field of psychology" (1951: 38). The attempt to provide sociology with a foundation in nature would thus founder on the bedrock of individual psychology, depriving sociology of "the only object proper to it," leaving them with "only a borrowed existence." But "from every page" of *Le Suicide*, Durkheim announced, there would emerge the contrary idea – i.e., the impression that the individual is dominated by a moral reality greater than himself: namely, collective reality" (1951: 38).

The pages from which this idea emerged most powerfully were those devoted to the discussion of anomie. In book 2, chapter 5, Durkheim turned his attention to the curious fact that suicide rates increase, not just during economic crises, but more specifically during "crises of prosperity" – e.g., situations in which real income is increasing, or people are experiencing greater economic comfort, vitality, etc. "Every disturbance of equilibrium," Durkheim observed, "even though it achieves greater comfort and a heightening of general vitality, is an impulse to voluntary death. Wherever serious readjustments take place in the social order, whether or not due to a sudden growth or to an unexpected catastrophe, men are more inclined to self-destruction . . . How can something considered generally to improve existence," Durkheim openly wondered, "serve to detach men from it?" Unmistakably, Durkheim's answer was drawn from the second *Discours* and *Emile.* "No living being," Durkheim began, "can be happy or even exist unless his needs are sufficiently proportioned to his means." In the case of animals, which – like Rousseau's natural man – depend on purely material conditions, this equilibrium between needs and means is established and maintained automatically, for the limits of animal instincts and environmental resources are "fundamental to the constitution of the existence in question." In particular, the animal lacks any powers of reflection that would lead it to imagine any ends other than those implicit in its physical nature. Most human needs, however, depend not on the body, but on the imagination; and thus "beyond the indispensable minimum which satisfies nature when instinctive, a more awakened reflection suggests better conditions, seemingly desirable ends craving fulfillment" (1951: 246–7).

Admitting these differences between human beings and lower animals, Durkheim asked, how can we determine the quantity of well-being, comfort, or luxury to be "legitimately" craved by a human being? Here Durkheim was careful to point out that there is nothing in the organic or psychological constitution of human beings that might set natural limits to these needs and desires, an assertion that he supported by pointing to their constant increase, despite more and more complete satisfaction, throughout human history, as well as their extreme variability across socio-economic classes. "It is not human nature," Durkheim thus insisted, "which can assign the variable limits necessary to our needs. They are thus unlimited so far as they depend on the individual alone. Irrespective of any external regulatory force, our capacity for feeling is in itself an insatiable and bottomless abyss" (1951: 247). And no less than Rousseau, Durkheim considered this capacity as a sign of human degeneration and a source of extreme human misery: "Unlimited desires are insatiable by definition," he observed, "and insatiability is rightly considered a sign of morbidity. Being unlimited, they constantly and infinitely surpass the means at their command; they cannot be quenched . . .

To pursue a goal which is by definition unattainable is to condemn oneself to a state of perpetual unhappiness" (1951: 247–8).

For happiness to be achieved, therefore, the passions must be constrained; and since the individual has no internal means of constraint, the passions must be restricted by some force external to the individual. Durkheim provided at least two arguments to the effect that this force could only be society. First, since it is society that has awakened our imaginations, and thus upset the natural balance between our needs and our means, it is only society – a collective, moral force – which can place limits and constraints on our desires. Second, like Rousseau in *Le Contrat social*, Durkheim emphasized the peculiar form of legitimacy that belongs to society – i.e., society is the only moral power superior to the individual, whose authority the individual accepts. Thus, society alone "has the power necessary to stipulate law and to set the point beyond which the passions must not go" (1951: 249). And where Rousseau had here pursued the analogy between "civilized" and "natural" man, Durkheim emphasized the similar analogy between the social and the physical or organic: "A regulative force," Durkheim emphasized, "must play the same role for moral needs which the organism plays for physical needs" (1951: 248).

As we have seen, Rousseau considered the general will an arbiter of class differences, one which would destroy the artificial inequalities born of social degeneration, returning human beings to a more natural, egalitarian, and meritocratic condition. Durkheim's treatment of inequality was more sociological, and also more complacent. Society already silently estimates the reward appropriate, not (*pace* Rousseau) to individual talents and characters, but to particular occupations, functions, and social services. "At every moment of history," Durkheim insisted, "there is a dim perception, in the moral consciousness of societies, of the respective value of different social services, the relative reward due to each, and the consequent degree of comfort appropriate on the average to workers in each occupation. The different functions are graded in public opinion and a certain coefficient of well-being assigned to each, according to its place in the hierarchy . . . A genuine regimen exists," Durkheim concluded, "although not always legally formulated, which fixes with relative precision the maximum degree of ease of living to which each social class may legitimately aspire" (1951: 249).

Assuming that the individual has "a wholesome moral

constitution" – i.e., respects rules and is docile to collective authority – society thus sets an end and a goal to his passions: "This relative limitation and the moderation it involves," Durkheim explained,

make men contented with their lot while stimulating them moderately to improve it; and this average contentment causes the feeling of calm, active happiness, the pleasure in existing and living which characterizes health for societies as well as individuals. Each person is then at least, generally speaking, in harmony with his condition, and desires only what he may legitimately hope for as the normal reward for his activity. (1951: 250)

But again, legitimacy is important. Societal constraints must include rules which fix the way that specific social positions are open and accessible to individuals, and the individuals themselves must regard this differential accessibility as fair and just. "When [discipline] is maintained only by custom and force," Durkheim emphasized, "peace and harmony are illusory; the spirit of unrest and discontent are latent; appetites superficially restrained are ready to revolt" (1951: 251). But in practice, Durkheim in fact considered such conditions of unrest as abnormal and pathological, occurring only during those periods when society passes through some kind of crisis. "In normal conditions," Durkheim assured his readers, "the collective order is regarded as just by the great majority of persons" (1951: 251–2). Like Rousseau, Durkheim thus viewed society as re-imposing – albeit in a new form – those constraints otherwise imposed on us by nature itself.

The relevance of this argument to anomic suicide, of course, was that Durkheim regarded his own society as passing through just such an "abnormal" or "pathological" stage, a kind of "legitimation crisis" in which society is temporarily incapable of exercising this salutary, regulative function. Social mobility "de-classifies" and "re-classifies" individuals upward and downward in the social hierarchy, disrupting the balance of needs and means to which human beings had become accustomed through habit and tradition: "So long as the social forces thus freed have not regained equilibrium," Durkheim explained, "their respective values die unknown and so all regulation is lacking for a time. The limits are unknown between the possible and the impossible, what is just and what is unjust, legitimate claims and hopes and those which are immoderate. Consequently, there is no restraint upon aspirations" (1951: 253).

This was a condition familiar to Rousseau. In the introduction to his translation of *Emile*, Allan Bloom emphasized the extent to which its author sought to warn us of "a certain low human type" – i.e., the *bourgeois* – which Rousseau himself "was the first to isolate and name" (1979a: 4–5). Who is the *bourgeois*? To describe the inner workings of his soul, Bloom responds, "he is the man who, when dealing with others, thinks only of himself, and on the other hand, in his understanding of himself, thinks only of others." Rousseau contrasts this "debased form of the species" with both the *natural man* – whole, independent, concerned only with himself – and the *citizen* – whose "very being consists in his relation to his city, who understands his good to be identical with the common good." The imagination of the *bourgeois* has expanded his needs beyond his means, rendering him both artificial and dependent on others, whom he seeks to exploit; and Christianity has convinced him that his own good should be distinguished from that of civil society, leaving him no reason to sacrifice private interest to public duty.[25] Since Rousseau, Bloom insists, the overcoming of the *bourgeois* has been regarded as almost identical with the realization of true democracy, and the achievement of "genuine personality" (1979a: 6).

Durkheim's contempt for the *bourgeois* – although framed in the vocabulary of modern social science – rivaled that of Rousseau. For in addition to the "acute" anomie produced by economic crises, Durkheim identified a more "chronic" anomie in the sphere of business and industry, born of the collapse of feudalism and the rise of unregulated capitalism. Durkheim's account of feudal institutions thus borders on nostalgia – e.g., by regulating salaries, prices, and production itself, the guilds "indirectly fixed the average level of income on which needs are partially based by the very force of circumstances"; the state "restrained the scope of economic functions by its supremacy over them and by the relatively subordinate role it assigned them"; and religion

was felt alike by workers and masters, the poor and the rich. It consoled the former and taught them contentment with their lot by informing them of the providential nature of the social order, that the share of each class was assigned by God himself, and by holding out the hope for just compensation in a world to come in return for the inequalities of this world. It governed the latter, recalling that worldly interests are not man's entire lot, that they must be subordinate to other and higher interests, and that they should therefore not be pursued without rule or measure. (1951: 254–5)

---

[25] Bloom 1979a: 5. Here, of course, Rousseau follows the critique of Christianity in Machiavelli's *Discourses* (1517).

This passage is particularly striking in its implication that, for Durkheim as for Rousseau, social realism provided a kind of secular theodicy, reconciling individuals to their lots in life, through the belief in a higher power which was itself the very standard of social justice.

The nostalgic tone of his description of feudalism notwithstanding, Durkheim was hardly calling for a return to the Middle Ages. On the contrary, his point was rather to emphasize that these traditional sources of constraint – i.e., the guilds, the state, and the church – had declined, and that nothing had come to take their place. This, of course, was the reason for the fascination with "Christian societies" discussed in chapter 2 (see pp. 46–56). The appetites excited by industrial capitalism, Durkheim argued, "have become freed of any limiting authority. By sanctifying them, so to speak, this apotheosis of well-being has placed them above all human law. Their restraint seems like a sort of sacrilege." In the sphere of business and commerce, therefore, anomie was chronic: "From top to bottom," Durkheim observed, "greed is aroused without knowing where to find ultimate foothold. Nothing can calm it, since its goal is far beyond all it can attain." So constant is this condition, Durkheim added, that society has come to view it as normal, and even to elevate it into an ethical and quasi-religious principle. "It is everlastingly repeated," he reminded his readers, "that it is man's nature to be eternally dissatisfied, constantly to advance, without relief or rest, toward an indefinite goal. The longing for infinity is daily represented as a mark of moral distinction, whereas it can only appear within unregulated consciences which elevate to a rule the lack of rule from which they suffer. The doctrine of the most ruthless and swift progress," Durkheim concluded, "has become an article of faith" (1951: 255–6).

Perhaps more than anything else he wrote, Durkheim's treatment of anomic suicide makes clear that his injunction to treat social facts *comme des choses* was a moral as well as a methodological injunction. This in turn indicates the nature and extent of his debt to Rousseau.[26] And finally, it explains why he felt so much was at stake

---

[26] In the third and final book of *De la Division du travail social*, Durkheim discussed the "anomic division of labor" as one of its three "pathological forms." But in that earlier work, "anomie" refers, not to an imbalance between needs and means, but to a more general "lack of mutual adjustment among the parts of the social organism," a notion Durkheim attributed specifically to Comte and to Espinas.

in his exchange with Tarde, to whose "Les Deux Eléments de la sociologie" he at last responded in the third, concluding book of *Le Suicide*. When "collective tendencies" or "collective passions" are spoken of, Durkheim admitted, we often assume that these are mere metaphors for a number of average individual states. But social facts are *not* mere metaphors, but rather real, natural *things*, whose description Durkheim continuously couched in the vocabulary of permanence, necessity, and impersonality. "So truly are [social facts] things *sui generis*, and not mere verbal entities," he insisted, "that they may be measured, their relative sizes compared, as is done with the intensity of electric currents or luminous foci" (1951: 310). This is why the suicide statistics cited throughout *Le Suicide* possess a stability and regularity exceeding even those of the mortality rate. And as with mortality (a product of material forces), Durkheim thus argued, "we must likewise admit that [acts of suicide] depend on forces external to individuals" (1951: 309). These forces, of course, must be *moral* rather than material; and since – aside from individual human beings – there is no type of moral existence other than society, these forces must be *social* as well.

In Durkheim's mind, this argument thoroughly discredited the theories of Tarde. For Tarde's explanation of social phenomena – i.e., that they are passed on from one individual to another through imitation – could not possibly account for the statistical stability and regularity of suicide rates. Using the same language he had adopted in his lectures on *Le Contrat social*, Durkheim argued that these rates can only be due to the *permanent* action of some *impersonal* cause which transcends all individual cases. "The terms," Durkheim insisted, "must be strictly understood. Collective tendencies have an existence of their own; they are forces as real as cosmic forces, though of another sort; they, likewise, affect the individual from without, though through other channels." Durkheim recognized that this argument offended common sense; but in this, he added, it is no different from any new scientific proposition. More importantly, it implied that "collective tendencies and thoughts are of a different nature from individual tendencies and thoughts, that the former have characteristics which the latter lack" (1951: 310, 309).

But how can this be if there are only individuals in society? Here Durkheim followed his traditional strategy, learned from Boutroux, of appealing to the analogy with chemistry and biology. As with chemical elements and biological cells, Durkheim argued, when the

consciousnesses of individual human beings are grouped and combined, "something in the world has been altered." This change then
"produces others, this novelty engenders other novelties, [and]
phenomena appear whose characteristic qualities are not found in
the elements composing them" (1951: 310–11). The only alternative
is to argue that the whole is qualitatively identical with the sum of its
parts, and that an effect is qualitatively reducible to the sum of its
causes. But this, Durkheim observed, is precisely what Tarde has
argued – a position for which Durkheim could find only two, "truly
extraordinary" reasons.

The first reason given by Tarde, as we have seen, was that "in
sociology we have through a rare privilege intimate knowledge both
of that element which is our individual consciousness and of the
compound which is the sum of consciousness in individuals." But to
Durkheim, who had visited with Wundt at Leipzig and was a friend
of Ribot and Janet, this seemed to deny all of the contemporary
psychology of the unconscious. "Today," Durkheim reminded
Tarde, "it is generally recognized that psychical life, far from being
directly cognizable, has on the contrary profound depths inaccessible
to ordinary perception, to which we attain only gradually by devious
and complicated paths like those employed by the sciences of the
external world. The nature of consciousness is therefore far from
lacking in mystery for the future" (1951: 311). In fact, the real key to
understanding this response to Tarde's first argument lies in recognizing that, for Durkheim, the distinction was not one between the
"psychological" and the "sociological," but rather one between the
"individual" and the "social." Indeed, as he would make abundantly
clear just one year later,[27] Durkheim readily acceded to the notion
that social life has a "psychic" aspect, and that it is "made up of"
representations. But these *collective* representations, Durkheim insisted, are "of quite another character" from *individual* representations. Consider the case of primitive religion, whose origins are
ordinarily – and quite wrongly – ascribed to "feelings of fear or
reverence inspired in conscious persons by mysterious and dreaded
beings." From this perspective, Durkheim observed, religion "seems
merely like the development of individual states of mind and private
feelings." But several facts – e.g., that religion is unknown to
animals, whose social life is rudimentary; that religion is never found

[27] See Durkheim 1974a.

except where the societal mode of organization exists; that religions vary with these forms of social organization; etc. – suggest strongly that *religious* forces are really *social* forces: "The power thus imposed on [our] respect and become the object of [our] adoration is society, of which the gods [are] only the hypostatic form. Religion is in a word the system of symbols by means of which society becomes conscious of itself; it is the characteristic way of thinking of collective existence" (1951: 312). Here, Durkheim thus concluded his reply to Tarde's first argument, is "a group of states of mind which would not have originated if individual states of consciousness had not combined, and which result from this union and are superadded to those which derive from individual natures." The claim of Tarde's first argument notwithstanding, no analysis of individual human minds could possibly explain the origin and development of such religious beliefs and practices; and the same argument applies to law, morals, customs, political institutions, educational practices – in short, to all forms of social life (1951: 312–13).

Tarde's second argument was that, if we subtract the individual, "nothing remains of the social." Durkheim's initial response to this was that it was a purely arbitrary assertion. "The author may of course state that in his personal opinion nothing real exists in society but what is individual," Durkheim acknowledged, "but proofs supporting this statement are lacking and discussion is therefore impossible." And there are a great many persons, Durkheim added, who conceive of society, not as something "spontaneously assumed by individual nature on expanding outward," but rather as "an antagonistic force restricting individual natures and resisted by them!" (1951: 311). But Durkheim's second, more productive and sociologically interesting response was that it simply isn't true that society is made up only of individuals. For one thing, society includes *material things* – i.e., social facts that have become materialized even to the point of becoming elements in the external world. Such "crystallized" social facts (e.g., styles of art and architecture, forms of technology, religious doctrines, legal precepts, etc.) certainly exist outside of us, precede and survive our temporal existence, have consequences for our behavior, and sometimes resist our intentional efforts. But, more importantly, these visible symbols express a far larger and more powerful realm of moral forces, at least equally external, long-lived, consequential, and resistant to individual human effort. "Nothing is more reasonable," Durkheim thus concluded, "than this proposition at which such offense has been taken; that a belief or social practice may exist independently of its individual expressions" (1951: 320).

In my introduction I emphasized that Durkheim's social realist vocabulary embodied at least two elements: on the one hand, it described society as not only "similar to" nature, but as itself a *real, natural thing, a part of nature*; on the other hand, it insisted that society is a *particular, distinctive* part of nature, a reality *sui generis*, irreducible to psychology or biology. Although not oblivious to the second element, the Latin thesis and *De la division du travail social* tended to focus on the first; and for Durkheim's purposes in these works, Rousseau – for whom society was always the product of art rather than nature – was a constant object of criticism. But as Durkheim became more involved in the Dreyfus Affair, and more frustrated by his quarrel with Tarde, he increasingly sought a language that would do justice to the distinctive nature of social facts, and particularly their obligatory character. This led him to stronger reading of Rousseau, in whose works he now discovered a language that described society as a "live, organized body," a reality distinct from and greater than the sum of its parts, capable of imposing constraints on the egoistic appetites and desires of individuals. The civil state thus recreated the state of nature – i.e., that condition in which appetite and desire were constrained by the laws of nature – albeit in a new, moral form; but this new form, though moral, was no less natural, for societies are also a part of nature. To learn the laws that govern societies is thus to learn our place in the natural world, and it was this education *à l'école des choses* that Durkheim sought to describe and institutionalize in *L'Evolution pédagogique* and *L'Education morale*. The famous injunction to study facts *comme des choses* was certainly "methodological" in some sense; but more than this, it was part of Durkheim's larger enterprise – shared with Rousseau – of imposing limitations on a population increasingly indifferent to constraints of any kind.

It might seem odd that my interpretation – which has frequently been orthogonal to accounts of Durkheim as the heir of Comte, child of the Enlightenment, and descendant of Descartes – should thus culminate with the two greatest social theorists of 18th-century France. But this oddity disappears when we recall that neither Montesquieu nor Rousseau was a typical figure of the French Enlightenment. On the contrary, *De l'esprit des lois* was an inspiration to Savigny and the German jurists, just as Fichte was an early admirer of Rousseau. In Montesquieu's extremely ambivalent Cartesianism, and Rousseau's "yoke of necessity, under which every finite being must bow," Durkheim found the linguistic resources he needed, first to explore tentatively, and then to fill out his account of the distinctive, obligatory nature of social facts. As a moral authority transcending any individual mind, society thus provided a secular theodicy for citizens of the Third Republic. In his discussion of egoism and anomie in *Le Suicide*, Durkheim's social realism received its most complete and productive expression.

Conclusion: sociology and irony

In this book, I've tried to describe the development of Durkheim's social realism less as the "discovery" of some new, hitherto unnoticed aspect of nature than as the gradual cobbling together of a vocabulary that might prove useful in speaking about it. My focus has thus been on the nature of Durkheim's interests and purposes, the writers whose language he found adaptable to them, and the works in which the re-description of these writers and the adaptation of their vocabularies was effected. As a consequence, the Durkheim who emerges from this account may seem unfamiliar and even unattractive to some sociologists. The Sens lecturer, of course, is a complete stranger; but even the Durkheim of *L'Evolution pédagogique en France* and *L'Education morale*, of the "German" essays of 1887, of the Latin thesis and the lecture-courses on *Du contrat social* and *Emile*, of Wundt rather than Comte, Comenius rather than Descartes, is someone who rarely affords us our "usual and carefully contrived pleasures of recognition." Not unreasonably, such sociologists might ask why they should bother to become acquainted with such a figure at all. My answer – anticipated in my introduction – is that the value of such acquaintance derives precisely from this *lack* of familiarity, from that fact that Durkheim was indeed quite *different* from us. In short, this book has been concerned with the "historical" (by contrast with "rational") reconstruction of Durkheim's social realism; and the rewards of historical reconstructions are to be found, not in reassurance or self-justification, but in the "self-knowledge" or "self-awareness" that follows an encounter with vocabularies other than one's own.

Richard Rorty has provided a useful account of how such self-knowledge and self-awareness might be achieved. Each of us, he suggests, carries around something he calls a "final vocabulary" – i.e., a set of words (e.g., "true," "good," "right," "beautiful," "progressive," "professional," "rigorous," etc.) we use to justify our actions, our beliefs, and our selves. These are the words we use to praise our friends, condemn our enemies, express our deepest self-doubts and our highest hopes – in short, to tell, whether prospectively or retrospectively, the stories of our lives. Such a vocabulary is "final" in the sense that, if doubt is cast upon the value of these words, we have no non-circular argumentative recourse. Whatever arguments we might present to defend the value of these words must be constructed from the words themselves. This vocabulary, therefore, is "final" in the sense that it is as far as we can go with language, and beyond it lies only resignation or the resort to force (1989c: 73).

The "ironist" is someone who has radical, continuing doubts about the final vocabulary she uses. This is because she's encountered other final vocabularies with which she's been impressed, either by meeting other people or by reading lots of books. The ironist recognizes that arguments phrased *within* her present vocabulary cannot underwrite or dissolve these doubts, for these arguments would be circular; and she also recognizes that nothing *beyond* her vocabulary – no "foundation," natural or supernatural, physical or metaphysical – can justify, verify, or certify her own way of thinking and speaking. For the ironist, therefore, there are simply multiple, final vocabularies, and there is no neutral, meta-vocabulary within which universal criteria for the choice among other vocabularies might be formulated. Rorty's ironist is thus "meta-stable" in the sense intended by Sartre – i.e., never quite able to take herself seriously, because she is always aware that the terms in which she describes herself are fragile, contingent, and thus subject to change (1989c: 73–4).

By contrast to the ironist, a "metaphysician" is someone who assumes that the presence of a word in *his* final vocabulary ensures that it actually refers to something more essential or more real. The metaphysician, in short, doesn't question the platitudes that encapsulate the use of a particular final vocabulary, and especially the platitude that says there is a single permanent reality to be found behind the many temporary appearances. This point is often made by saying that the metaphysician believes that the world is "really out there." But simply to say that the *world* is "out there" – i.e., that it is not our own creation but rather the product of other causes – is to say something that the ironist also believes. The significant difference between the ironist and the metaphysician is thus that the latter makes the additional assertion that the *truth* is "out there" – i.e., that there is a non-human language that the world wants to speak. The ironist, by contrast, is persuaded that nature doesn't speak, that only people do, and that people cannot step outside their language in order to compare their sentences with something more basic, intrinsic, essential, or foundational (1989c: 74–8). The ironist thus resists speaking of any "essential reality" – natural or social – to which her utterances might be said to correspond.

Rorty adds that this confusion – i.e., between the notion that the *world* is out there and the notion that the *truth* is out there – is exacerbated by the focus on individual sentences rather than whole vocabularies. As long as we limit our attention to sentences like "Protestants commit suicide more frequently than Catholics or Jews," or "the members of central Australian clans are forbidden to kill or eat the totemic animal except at an annual feast called the *Intichiuma*," for example, it is easy to confuse: (a) the undeniable fact that the world contains the causes of our feeling justified in holding such beliefs with (b) the quite different, and thoroughly deniable, claim that some non-linguistic state of the world makes these beliefs true by "corresponding" to them. Such confusion is less frequent, however, when we turn from individual, criterion-governed sentences *within* language games to language games *as wholes* (i.e., games which we do not choose between by reference to criteria at all). Does the world speak Aristotelian or Copernican? Does the language of Kant or that of Nietzsche more adequately correspond to reality? Does nature prefer to be described by St. Augustine or by Freud?

But this observation – i.e., that the world does not tell us what vocabulary to use – does *not* mean that the choices we make about which language games to play are arbitrary or subjective. It simply means that, when it comes to changes from one vocabulary to another, the notions of "decision," "criteria" and "choice" are no longer useful. Europeans, Rorty observes, did not "decide" to adopt the idiom of romantic poetry, or socialist politics, or Galilean mechanics; on the contrary, they just gradually lost the habit of playing some language games, and gradually acquired the habit of playing others. It was not on the basis of telescopic observations, Kuhn argues in *The Copernican Revolution*, that Europeans "decided" that the heliocentric theory was correct, or that macroscopic behavior could be explained on the basis of microscopic motion, or that prediction and control should be the goal of scientific theory; rather, after a hundred years of inconclusive debate, Europeans found themselves speaking "Galilean" rather than "Aristotelian," and took the interconnected theses of the former for granted (Rorty 1989b: 6; see Kuhn 1957).

By now, the distinction between metaphysicians and ironists should be clear. The metaphysician, for example, will see Durkheim as having made a discovery "about the world" – i.e., that social forces are natural forces, distinguished by their characteristics of externality and constraint. The ironist will see Durkheim as someone frustrated with the language that he and his contemporaries had inherited from the 17th and 18th centuries, who managed to cobble together a normative vocabulary that worked better for 19th- and 20th-century purposes; and once sociologists found out what could be done with a Durkheimian vocabulary, few were interested in doing the things that had been done with its Cartesian predecessor. The metaphysician still seeks to fulfil the pre-Kantian, Enlightenment dream of "getting the world right," of describing societies in Nature's Own Language. The ironist, by contrast, has embraced the notion shared by French revolutionaries, Hegel, the romantic poets, Nietzsche, Heidegger, Derrida, Dewey, James, Davidson, Rorty, and others, that language is solely a human creation, that anything can be transformed simply by being re-described, and that to change how we talk is to change who we are.

Having dismissed the metaphysical insistence that we discover Nature's Own Language, the ironist alone seems fully prepared to explore the apothegm that socialization goes "all the way down." So one might assume that sociologists would be predisposed to be ironists; but in fact, many sociologists object to an ironist posture on the ground that it is incompatible with the practice of social science.[1] Durkheim himself showed that you can get good results by thinking of social facts *comme des choses*, by treating societies as concrete, complex wholes, and by careful observations, comparisons, and statistical generalizations; and this Durkheimian vocabulary has thus led later social scientists to attempt to draw some epistemological moral from its success – specifically, to suggest that Durkheim's achievements exemplified or resulted from something called "the scientific method," whose exercise will lead us to the discovery of the

[1] For a more detailed response to these objections, see Jones 1998.

reality of human societies. The significance of ironist writers like Kuhn, Dewey, and Rorty, however, lies in their argument that there simply *is no* epistemological moral to be drawn from Durkheim's success, and that there is no "method" which will help us to get our propositions to "line up" with the social world – indeed, that the very notion of discovering Nature's Own Language is itself wrong-headed. If Kuhn is right, most of the practice of modern science – including social science – is simply obeying the conventions of the discipline, being open to refutation by experience, not interfering with free discussion, not letting one's hopes and fears influence conclusions unless those hopes and fears are shared by all those in the same line of work. In this sense, Rorty summarizes, the scientific method is simply "a suitable balance between respect for the opinions of one's fellows and respect for the stubbornness of sensation" (1982d: 194–5). The metaphysical insistence that irony is incompatible with the practice of the "scientific method," therefore, is reduced to the claim that irony is incompatible with a standard that does not, in fact, exist.

How, one might ask, is this relevant to the history of social theory? Recall my earlier suggestion that the confusion between the notion that the *world* is out there and the quite different notion that the *truth* is out there tends to be exacerbated when the focus is on individual sentences rather than whole vocabularies. Such confusion, I observed, is less frequent when we turn from individual, criterion-governed sentences *within* language games to language games *as wholes* (i.e., games which we do not choose between by reference to criteria at all). Where intellectual history turns its attention from individual sentences to the larger vocabularies in which sentences are formulated – e.g., in works like Kuhn's *The Copernican Revolution* or Skinner's *Foundations of Modern Political Thought* – the notion that "the world" somehow decides how it wants to be described becomes less tenable and persuasive. The reader begins to see Copernicus and Galileo, Hobbes and Descartes, Durkheim and Weber, not as people who "got the world right," but as writers casting about for a re-description, a metaphor, or a vocabulary that might tempt the rising generation to embrace it, and then see it embodied in their institutions.

Not *every* kind of history, of course, is equally conducive to irony. In my introduction, I defended a role for "rational reconstructions" of Durkheim's ideas which, for all their occasional anachronisms, at least serve to expand the circle of edifying conversational partners. In the absence of the appropriate measure of self-consciousness, however, such reconstructions often serve metaphysical rather than ironist purposes. In so far as the "ideally reasonable and educable Durkheim" is mistaken for the Real Durkheim, for example, and a particular description of his texts is confused with what Durkheim Really Meant, these "exercises in commensuration" serve only to increase the dogmatic, assertive, and self-righteous tone of modern sociological debate. How is one to know? As indicated above, the distinction between self-conscious anachronism and its metaphysical counterpart ultimately lies in the ironist's recognition that the goal of debate is not consensus, but rather the continuation and enrichment of the conversation itself.

But more genuinely "historical" reconstructions – i.e., imagined conversations between Durkheim and his contemporaries, in their own language rather than ours – have at least the potential to encourage an ironist perspective. Like Plato in the early Socratic dialogues, Durkheim was pointing to a state of conceptual incoherence in the moral vocabulary of his culture, one that he sought to replace with what he sometimes called "the new rationalism" – i.e., a vocabulary more suitable to his own interests and purposes. Unlike the rationalism of Descartes, with its emphasis on *idées claires et simples*, Durkheim's vocabulary emphasized that social phenomena were real *things*, concrete and complex, to be studied *comme des choses*. For the ironist, however, to speak of social facts in this way is simply to describe, and then re-describe, according to one's pragmatic interests and purposes. Similarly, to say that society is "essentially" anything at all is itself a survival of the metaphysical error of thinking that Nature prefers to be spoken of in one way rather than another. Since the ironist rejects the notion that true sentences are true because they in some sense "correspond" to reality, the seemingly endless debate between rationalism and empiricism – i.e., over *what kind* of reality a given sentence corresponds to – is over (Rorty 1982b: xvi). For the ironist, there is not even a standard by which we can say that Durkheim's "new" rationalism (or "rationalist empiricism") was *better* than its Cartesian antecedent. We can only say that it has come to *seem* better to subsequent generations of sociologists (Rorty 1982b: xxxvii). In any case, to them and to us, Durkheim is interesting because he recognized the limitations of a 17th-century vocabulary when confronted with the kinds of things that 20th-century people want to do.

It will be noted that Durkheim himself – utterly humorless and (his writings on education notwithstanding) obsessed with the discovery of Nature's Own Language – seems to have been incapable of such irony. In this, he resembles many of the classic writers, whose views of scientific knowledge were more similar to those of the 17th and 18th centuries than to our own. But this, together with the observation that their vocabularies are no longer ours, is *doubly* instructive – and also deeply ironic. For what we learn from the nominalist, historicist, and pragmatist way of re-describing past sociological thought is that what were once regarded as undeniable truths – scientific propositions that were "true" because they corresponded to some putative social "reality" – were in fact the merest contingencies of a particular history, biography, language, and/or social structure. And, ironically, to learn this is surely to learn a more general truth, not just about the past, but about ourselves.

References

Auspitz, K. 1982, *The Radical Bourgeoisie: the Ligue de l'enseignement and the Origins of the Third Republic 1866–1885*, Cambridge: Cambridge University Press.

Austin, J. L. 1975, *How to Do Things with Words*, Cambridge, Mass.: Harvard University Press.

Bellah, R. N. (ed.) 1973, *Emile Durkheim: on Morality and Society*, Chicago and London: University of Chicago Press.

Berlin, I. (ed.) 1980a, *Against the Current: Essays in the History of Ideas*, Harmondsworth, Middlesex: Penguin.

1980b, "Montesquieu," in Berlin (1980a), pp. 130–61.

Besnard, P. 1993, "De la datation des cours pédagogiques de Durkheim à la recherche du thème dominant de son oeuvre," in Cardi and Plantier, pp. 120–30.

Bloom, A. 1979a, "Introduction," in Bloom (1979b), pp. 3–29.

(ed.) 1979b, *Rousseau: Emile*, New York: Basic Books.

Boas, G. 1967a, "Cousin, Victor," in Edwards, pp. 246–8.

1967b, "Renouvier, Charles," in Edwards, pp. 180–2.

Boring, E. G. 1950, *A History of Experimental Psychology*, New York: Appleton-Century-Crofts.

Boutroux, E. 1883, "L'Agrégation de philosophie," *Revue internationale de l'enseignement* 6: 865–78.

1914, *Natural Law in Science and Philosophy*, London: D. Nutt.

1916, *The Contingency of the Laws of Nature*, Chicago and London: Open Court.

Bowen, H. W. 1968, "Müller, Adam Heinrich," in Sills, pp. 522–3.

Bury, J. P. T. 1985, *France, 1814–1940*, London: Methuen.

Cardi, F. and J. Plantier (eds.) 1993, *Durkheim, sociologue de l'éducation*, Paris: l'Harmattan.

Challenger, D. F. 1994, *Durkheim through the Lens of Aristotle: Durkheimian, Postmodernist, and Communitarian Responses to the Enlightenment*, Lanham, Md.: Rowman and Littlefield.

Cladis, M. S. 1992, *A Communitarian Defense of Liberalism: Emile Durkheim and Contemporary Social Theory*, Stanford: Stanford University Press.

Clark, T. N. (ed.) 1969, *Gabriel Tarde: on Communication and Social Influence*, Chicago: University of Chicago Press.

Collingwood, R. G. 1939, *An Autobiography*, Oxford: Oxford University Press.

Copleston, F. 1977, *A History of Philosophy*, vol. ix. *Maine de Biran to Sartre*. Part ii. *Bergson to Sartre*, Garden City, New York: Doubleday.

Cottingham, J., R. Stoothoff, et al. (eds.) 1985, *The Philosophical Writings of Descartes*, Cambridge: Cambridge University Press.

Curley, E. M. 1978, *Descartes Against the Skeptics*, Oxford: Basil Blackwell.

Dansette, A. 1961, *Religious History of Modern France*, vol. i: *From the Revolution to the Third Republic*, New York: Herder and Herder.

Davy, G. 1919, "Emile Durkheim: i, l'homme," *Revue de métaphysique et de morale* 26: 181–98.

Denzin, N. K. (ed.) 1998, *Cultural Studies: a Research Volume*, New York: JAI Press.

Deploige, S. 1911, *Le Conflit de la morale et de la sociologie*, Brussels: DeWit.

Derathé, R. 1950, *Jean-Jacques Rousseau et la science politique de son temps*, Paris: Presses Universitaires de France.

Descartes, R. 1985, "Discourse on the Method," in Cottingham, Stoothoff, and Murdoch, pp. 111–151.

Durkheim, E. 1883, "Du rôle des Grands Hommes dans la Société," *Cahiers internationaux de sociologie* 43: 25–32.

1884, *Cours de philosophie fait au Lycée de Sens*, Paris Bibliothèque de la Sorbonne, ms 2351.

1885a, "Schaeffle, A., *Bau und Leben des sozialen Körpers: Erster Band*," *Revue philosophique* 19: 84–101.

1885b, "Fouillée, A., *La Propriété sociale et la démocratie*," *Revue philosophique* 19: 446–53.

1885c, "Gumplowicz, Ludwig, *Grundriss der Soziologie*," *Revue philosophique* 20: 627–34.

1886a, "Les Etudes de science sociale," *Revue philosophique* 22: 61–80.

1886b, "DeGreef, Guillaume, *Introduction à la sociologie*," *Revue philosophique* 22: 658–63.

1887a, "La Philosophie dans les universités allemandes," *Revue internationale de l'enseignement* 13: 313–38, 423–40.

1887b, "La Science positive de la morale en Allemagne," *Revue philosophique* 24: 33–58, 113–42, 275–84.

1888, "Suicide et natalité: étude de statistique morale," *Revue philosophique* 26: 446–63.

1897, *Le Suicide: étude de sociologie*, Paris: Alcan.

1905, "Sur la séparation des églises et de l'état," *Libres entretiens* 1ère série: 369–71, 496–500.

1906, "Le Divorce par consentement mutuel," *Revue bleue* 5e série: 549–54.

1907, "Lettres au Directeur de la *Revue néo-scolastique*," *Revue néo-scolastique* 14: 606–7, 612–14.

1913a, "Contribution to discussion of: Le Problème religieux et la dualité de la nature humaine," *Bulletin de la Société française de philosophie* 13: 63–75, 80–7, 90–100, 108–11.

1913b, "Deploige, Simon. *Le Conflit de la morale et de la sociologie*," *Année sociologique* 12: 326–8.

1914, "Le Dualisme de la nature humaine et ses conditions sociales," *Scientia* 15: 206–21.

1915, *The Elementary Forms of the Religious Life*, New York and London: Free Press.

1933, *The Division of Labor in Society*, New York: Macmillan.

1951, *Suicide: a Study in Sociology*, Glencoe, Ill.: Free Press of Glencoe.

1953, *Montesquieu et Rousseau, précurseurs de la sociologie*, Paris: Marcel Rivière, "Petite Bibliothèque Sociologique Internationale."

1956, "Pedagogy and Sociology," in Fauconnet, pp. 113–34.

1960a, "The Dualism of Human Nature and Its Social Conditions," in Wolff, pp. 325–40.

(ed.) 1960b, *Montesquieu and Rousseau: Forerunners of Sociology*, Ann Arbor, Mich.: University of Michigan Press.

1960c, "Rousseau's Social Contract," in Durkheim 1960, pp. 65–138.

1961, *Moral Education: a Study in the Theory and Application of the Sociology of Education*, New York: Free Press of Glencoe.

1973a, "Address to the Lycéens of Sens," in Bellah, pp. 25–33.

1973b, "The Principles of 1789 and Sociology," in Bellah, pp. 34–42.

1973c, "Individualism and the Intellectuals," in Bellah, pp. 43–57.

1974a, "Individual and Collective Representations," in Durkheim (1974c), pp. 1–34.

1974b, "The Determination of Moral Facts," in Durkheim, pp. 35–62.

(ed.) 1974c, *Sociology and Philosophy*, New York: Macmillan.

1977, *The Evolution of Educational Thought: Lectures on the Formation and Development of Secondary Education in France*, London and Boston: Routledge and Kegan Paul.

1978a, "Course in Sociology: Opening Lecture," in Traugott, pp. 43–70.

1978b, "Review of Ferdinand Tönnies, *Gemeinschaft und Gesellschaft*," in Traugott, pp. 115–122.

1978c, "Review of Antonio Labriola, *Essais sur la conception matérialiste de l'histoire*," in Traugott, pp. 123–30.

1978d, "Introduction to the Sociology of the Family," in M. Traugott, pp. 205–28.

1979, "Rousseau on Educational Theory," in Pickering, pp. 162–94.

1984, *The Division of Labor in Society*, New York: Free Press.

1997, *Quid Secondatus Politicae Scientiae Instituendae Contulerit (Montesquieu's Contribution to the Rise of Social Science)*, Oxford: Durkheim Press.

Durkheim, E. and P. Fauconnet 1982, "Sociology and the Social Sciences," in Lukes, pp. 175–208.

Durkheim, E. and M. Mauss 1963, *Primitive Classification*, Chicago: University of Chicago Press.

Edwards, P. (ed.) 1967, *The Encyclopedia of Philosophy*, New York and London: Macmillan.

Espinas, A. 1882, "Les Etudes sociologiques en France," *Revue philosophique* 13, 14: 565–607, 337–67.

    1884, "L'Agrégation de philosophie," *Revue internationale de l'enseignement* 7: 585–607.

    1901, "Etre ou ne pas être, ou Du postulat de la sociologie," *Revue philosophique* 51: 449–80.

    1978, *Des sociétés animales*, New York: Arno.

Fauconnet, P. (ed.) 1956, *Education and Sociology*, Glencoe, Ill.: Free Press of Glencoe.

    1961, "Foreword," in Durkheim 1961, pp. v–vi.

Fischer, W. 1968, "Schmoller, Gustav," in Sills 1968, pp. 60–3.

Fustel de Coulanges, N. D. 1956, *The Ancient City*, Garden City, New York: Doubleday.

Gilpin, R. 1968, *France in the Age of the Scientific State*, Princeton: Princeton University Press.

Gross, Neil. 1996. "A Note on the Sociological Eye and the Discovery of a New Durkheim Text," *Journal of the History of the Behavioral Sciences* 32: 408–23.

Halbwachs, M. 1977, "Introduction to the French Edition of 1938," in Durkheim 1977, pp. xi–xv.

Hayek, F. A. v. 1968, "Menger, Carl," in Sills 1968, pp. 124–7.

Hobbes, T. 1958, *Leviathan: Parts I and II*, Indianapolis and New York: Bobbs-Merrill.

Hulliung, M. 1976, *Montesquieu and the Old Regime*, Berkeley: University of California Press.

Hume, D. 1957, *An Inquiry Concerning the Principles of Morals*, New York: Macmillan.

Janet, P. 1885, *Victor Cousin et son oeuvre*. Paris: Alcan.

Jones, R. A. 1977, "On Understanding a Sociological Classic," *American Journal of Sociology* 83, 2: 279–319.

    1986, *Emile Durkheim: an Introduction to Four Major Works*, Beverly Hills, London and New Delhi: Sage.

    1998, "Ironists and Metaphysicians: Reflections on Sociology and Its History," in Denzin 1998, pp. 97–117.

Jones, R. A. and D. A. Kibbee 1993, "Durkheim, Language and History: a Pragmatist Perspective," *Sociological Theory* 11: 152–70.

Jones, R. A. and W. P. Vogt 1984, "Durkheim's Defense of *Les Formes élémentaires de la vie religieuse*," in Kuklick and Long 1984, pp. 45–62.

Keylor, W. 1975, *Academy and Community: The Foundation of the French Historical Profession*, Cambridge, Mass.: Harvard University Press.

Kisch, H. 1968a, "Hildebrand, Bruno," in Sills 1968, pp. 356–8.

1968b, "Knies, Karl," in Sills 1968, pp. 422–4.

Kuhn, T. S. 1957, *The Copernican Revolution: Planetary Astronomy in the Development of Western Thought*, Cambridge, Mass.: Harvard University Press.

Kuklick, H. and E. Long (eds.) 1984, *Knowledge and Society: Studies in the Sociology of Culture, Past and Present*, Greenwich: JAI.

Lalande, A. 1960, "Commémoration du centenaire de la naissance d'Emile Durkheim," *Annales de l'Université de Paris* 30: 22–5.

Langlois, C. 1996, "Catholics and Seculars," in Nora 1996, pp. 109–43.

LeFebvre, G. 1964, *The French Revolution*, vol II: *From 1793–1799*, London: Routledge and Kegan Paul.

Logue, W. 1993, *Charles Renouvier: Philosopher of Liberty*, Baton Rouge and London: Louisiana State University Press.

Lukes, S. M. 1972, *Emile Durkheim: his Life and Work: a Historical and Critical Study*, New York: Harper and Row.

(ed.) 1982, *The Rules of Sociological Method and Selected Texts on Sociology and its Method*, New York: Free Press.

MacIntyre, A. 1984, *After Virtue: a Study in Moral Theory*, Notre Dame: University of Notre Dame Press.

Mauss, M. 1925, "In memoriam, l'oeuvre inédite de Durkheim et de ses collaborateurs," *Année sociologique* n.s., 1: 7–29.

Mayeur, J.-M. and M. Rebérieux 1984, *The Third Republic from its Origins to the Great War, 1871–1914*, Cambridge: Cambridge University Press.

McManners, J. 1972, *Church and State in France, 1871–1914*, London: Church Historical Society.

Mestrovic, S. G. 1988a, *Emile Durkheim and the Reformation of Sociology*, Totowa, NJ: Rowman and Littlefield.

1988b, "The Social World as Will and Idea: Schopenhauer's Influence upon Durkheim's Thought," *Sociological Review* 39: 674–705.

Meyer, G. 1968, "Wagner, Adolf," in Sills 1968, pp. 429–32.

Miller, W. W. 1996, *Durkheim, Morals and Modernity*, London: UCL Press.

1997a, "Durkheim and Montesquieu," in Miller 1997c, pp. 83–104.

1997b, "Preface," in Miller 1997c, pp. 1–5.

(ed.) 1997c, *Quid Secondatus Politicae Scientiae Instituendae Contulerit (Montesquieu's Contribution to the Rise of Social Science)*, Oxford: Durkheim Press.

Momigliano, A. 1982, *Essays in Ancient and Modern Historiography*, Middletown, Conn.: Wesleyan University Press.

Monroe, W. S. 1900, *Comenius and the Beginnings of Educational Reform*, New York: Charles Scribner's Sons.

Montesquieu 1949, *The Spirit of the Laws*, New York: Hafner.

1997, *Quid Secondatus Politicae Scientiae Instituendae Contulerit (Montesquieu's Contribution to the Rise of Social Science)*, Oxford: Durkheim Press.

Moran, J. H. and A. Gode (eds.) 1966, *On the Origin of Language*, Chicago and London: University of Chicago Press.

Neumann, F. 1949a, "Editor's Introduction," in Neumann 1949b, pp. ix–lxiv.

(ed.) 1949b, *Montesquieu: the Spirit of Laws*, New York: Hafner.

Nora, P. (ed.) 1996, *Realms of Memory*, vol. 1: *Conflicts and Divisions*, New York: Columbia University Press.

Parsons, T. 1968, *The Structure of Social Action: a Study in Social Theory with Special Reference to a Group of Recent European Writers*, vol. 1: Marshall, Pareto, Durkheim, New York: Free Press.

Peyre, H. 1960, "Foreword," in Durkheim 1960, pp. v–xvi.

Pickering, W. S. F. (ed.) 1979, *Durkheim: Essays on Morals and Education*, London and Boston: Routledge and Kegan Paul.

1984, *Durkheim's Sociology of Religion: Themes and Theories*, London, Boston, and Melbourne: Routledge and Kegan Paul.

Popkin, R. H. 1969, *The Sceptical Origins of the Modern Problem of Knowledge*, Cleveland: Press of Case Western Reserve University.

Potts, D. C. and D. G. Charlton 1974, *French Thought Since 1600*, London: Methuen.

Renan, E. 1872, *La Réforme intellectuelle et morale*, Paris: Calmann-Lévy.

1991, *The Life of Jesus*, Buffalo, New York: Prometheus.

Ribot, T. 1886, *German Psychology of Today: the Empirical School*, New York: Charles Scribners' Sons.

Rorty, R. (ed.) 1982a, *Consequences of Pragmatism (Essays: 1972–1980)*, Minneapolis: University of Minnesota Press.

1982b, "Introduction: Pragmatism and Philosophy," in Rorty 1982a, pp. xiii–xlvii.

1982c, "Pragmatism, Relativism, and Irrationalism," in Rorty 1982a, pp. 160–75.

1982d, "Method, Social Science, and Social Hope," in Rorty 1982a, pp. 191–210.

1984, "The Historiography of Philosophy: Four Genres," in Rorty 1982a, Schneewind, and Skinner 1984, pp. 49–75.

(ed.) 1989a, *Contingency, Irony, and Solidarity*, Cambridge: Cambridge University Press.

1989b, "The Contingency of Language," in Rorty 1989a, pp. 3–22.

1989c, "Private Irony and Liberal Hope," in Rorty 1982g, pp. 73–95.

Rorty, R., J. Schneewind, and Q. Skinner (eds.) 1984, *Philosophy in History: Essays on the Historiography of Philosophy*, Cambridge: Cambridge University Press.

Rousseau, J.-J. 1896, *Du contrat social*, Paris: Alcan.

Rousseau, J.-J. 1911, *Emile, or Education*, London: Dent.

Rousseau, J.-J. 1966, "Essay on the Origin of Languages," in Moran and Gode (eds.), pp. 5–74.

Rousseau, J.-J. 1968, *The Social Contract, or Principles of Political Right*, Harmondsworth, Middlesex: Penguin.

Rousseau, J.-J. 1979, *Emile, or Education*, New York: Basic Books.

Rousseau, J.-J. 1994, *Discourse on the Origin and Foundations of Inequality Among Men*, Oxford and New York: Oxford University Press.

Salin, E. 1968, "Roscher, Wilhelm," in Sills 1968, pp. 558–60.

Schaeffle, A. 1875, *Bau und Leben des sozialen Körpers*, Tubingen: Laupp.

Schmoller, G. 1875, *Über einige Grundfragen des Rechts und der Volkswirtschaft: ein offenes Sendschreiben an Herrn Professor Dr. Heinrich von Treitschke*, Jena: Mauke.

Sills, D. (ed.) 1968, *International Encyclopedia of the Social Sciences*, New York: Macmillan.

Skinner, Q. 1984, "The Idea of Negative Liberty: Philosophical and Historical Perspectives," in Rorty, Schneewind, and Skinner (1984), pp. 193–221.

1988, "A Reply to My Critics," in Tully, pp. 231–88.

Smith, W. R. 1972, *The Religion of the Semites: the Fundamental Institutions*, New York: Schocken.

Stedman-Jones, S. G. 1995, "Charles Renouvier and Emile Durkheim: *Les Règles de la méthode sociologique*," *Sociological Perspectives* 38: 27–40.

Stock-Morton, P. 1988, *Moral Education for a Secular Society: The Development of Morale Laïque in Nineteenth Century France*, Albany: State University of New York Press.

Tarde, G. 1893, "Questions sociales," *Revue philosophique* 35: 618–38.

1969, "Sociology, Social Psychology, and Sociologism," in Clark 1969, pp. 112–35.

Thompson, J. W. 1942, *A History of Historical Writing: the Eighteenth and Nineteenth Centuries*, New York: Macmillan.

Thomson, D. (ed.) 1968, *France: Empire and Republic, 1850–1940: Historical Documents*, New York: Walker.

Traugott, M. (ed.) 1978, *Emile Durkheim on Institutional Analysis*, Chicago: University of Chicago Press.

Tully, J. (ed.) 1988, *Meaning and Context: Quentin Skinner and his Critics*, Princeton, NJ: Princeton University Press.

Ulich, R. 1968, *A History of Educational Thought*, New York: American Book.

Wagner, A. 1892–4, *Grundlegung der politischen Ökonomie*, Leipzig: Winter.

Wiener, P. P. (ed.) 1951, *Leibniz: Selections*, New York: Charles Scribner's Sons.

Wolff, K. H. (ed.) 1960, *Emile Durkheim (1858–1917): a Collection of Essays, with Translations and a Bibliography*, Columbus, Ohio: Ohio State University Press.

Wolin, S. S. 1960, *Politics and Vision: Continuity and Innovation in Western Political Thought*, Boston: Little Brown.

Wundt, W. 1897–1901, *Ethics: an Investigation of the Facts and Laws of the Moral Life*, London: Swan Sonnenschein.

Zeldin, T. 1977, *France, 1848–1945*, vol. II: *Intellect, Taste and Anxiety*, Oxford: Clarendon.

Zola, E. 1972, *The Debacle*, Harmondsworth, Middlesex: Penguin.

Index

IDEAS IN CONTEXT

Edited by QUENTIN SKINNER (*General Editor*)
LORRAINE DASTON, WOLF LEPENIES, J. B. SCHNEEWIND
AND JAMES TULLY

Titles marked with an asterisk are also available in paperback

Printed in the United Kingdom
by Lightning Source UK Ltd.
108984UKS00001B/283-291

9 780521 022101